Good Luck at your new school. Best Wishes from Highfields Sixth Formers.

THE BUILDINGS OF ENGLAND

JOINT EDITORS: NIKOLAUS PEVSNER
AND JUDY NAIRN

STAFFORDSHIRE

NIKOLAUS PEVSNER

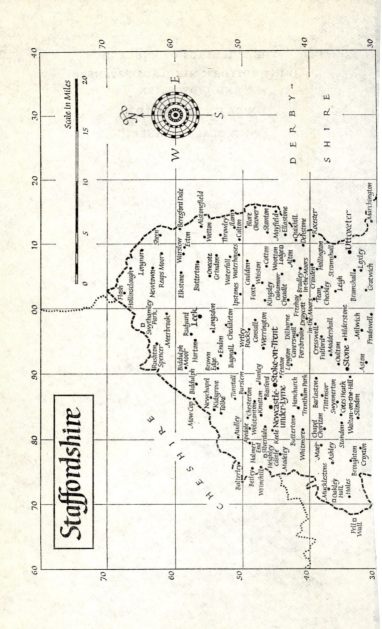

*The publication of this volume has been made
possible by a grant from*
THE LEVERHULME TRUST
to cover all the necessary research work

THE BUILDINGS OF ENGLAND

Staffordshire

NIKOLAUS PEVSNER

★

PENGUIN BOOKS

Penguin Books Ltd, Harmondsworth, Middlesex, England
Penguin Books Inc., 7110 Ambassador Road, Baltimore, Maryland 21207, U.S.A.
Penguin Books Australia Ltd, Ringwood, Victoria, Australia
Penguin Books Canada Ltd, 41 Steelcase Road West, Markham, Ontario, Canada
Penguin Books (N.Z.) Ltd, 182–190 Wairau Road, Auckland 10, New Zealand

First published 1974
Reprinted 1975

ISBN 0 14 071046 9

Copyright © Nikolaus Pevsner, 1974

Made and printed in Great Britain
by William Clowes & Sons, Limited, London, Beccles and Colchester
Photogravure plates by D. H. Greaves Ltd, Scarborough
Set in Monotype Plantin

This book is sold subject to the condition
that it shall not, by way of trade or otherwise,
be lent, resold, hired out, or otherwise circulated
without the publisher's prior consent in any form of
binding or cover other than that in which it is
published and without a similar condition
including this condition being imposed
on the subsequent purchaser

TO THE MEMORY OF
LOLA
AND
ALLEN

WHO HELPED AS LONG AS
THEY LIVED AND TO
WHOM VOLUMES ONE
AND THREE WERE
DEDICATED IN
1951

'We are in need of a means of quick orientation. I therefore move the production of a handbook which according to its name should have little bulk, be easily transported, be according to its inner organization as clearly arranged as possible and as comfortable to use on the desk as on a journey.'

GEORG DEHIO: Memorandum to start what was to become his *Handbuch der deutschen Kunstdenkmäler* (Tag für Denkmalpflege, 1906).

CONTENTS

FOREWORD 11

SOME WORDS ON COMPLETION OF
THE BUILDINGS OF ENGLAND 14

INTRODUCTION BY NIKOLAUS PEVSNER 19

BUILDING MATERIALS BY
ALEC CLIFTON-TAYLOR 44

THE ROMAN OCCUPATION BY
MALCOLM TODD 47

STAFFORDSHIRE 51

GLOSSARY 333

INDEX OF PLATES 357

INDEX OF ARTISTS 361

INDEX OF PLACES 371

Map References

*

The numbers printed in italic type in the margin against the place names in the gazetteer of the book indicate the position of the place in question on the index map (pages 2-3), which is divided into sections by the 10-kilometre reference lines of the National Grid. The reference given here omits the two initial letters (formerly numbers) which in a full grid reference refer to the 100-kilometre squares into which the country is divided. The first two numbers indicate the *western* boundary, and the last two the *southern* boundary, of the 10-kilometre square in which the place in question is situated. For example Walsall (reference 0090) will be found in the 10-kilometre square bounded by grid lines 00 and 10 on the *west* and 90 and 00 on the *south*; Stone (reference 9030) in the square bounded by grid lines 90 and 00 on the *west* and 30 and 40 on the *south*.

The map contains all those places, whether towns, villages, or isolated buildings, which are the subject of separate entries in the text.

FOREWORD

STAFFORDSHIRE, *the last volume of* The Buildings of England, *was prepared with meticulous care by Edward Hubbard, the third volume prepared by him. He also, in the same meticulous way, did the day-to-day preparing of routes through the county, taking in his stride such obstacles as the Black Country and the Potteries, and he finally drove me seven days a week eight hours a day. How many days and hours Miss Sutherland took to type the results of preparation, driving, and seeing I shudder to think; for my writing, always bad, seems to be steadily deteriorating. I am as grateful to her as to my secretaries, first Judith Tabner, then Nicky Cooney, then Judith Tabner again, who helped in the preparatory work, wrote all the letters, and kept a complicated apparatus in order. While on the journey Mr and Mrs G. W. R. Lines gave us generous hospitality at Wolverhampton and the Vice-Chancellor and Bursars at Keele.*

*My thanks also go out to those who helped unfailingly over many years: to the Ministry of Housing and Local Government, now Department of the Environment (*DOE*), whose lists of buildings of architectural and historic interest, which they put generously at my disposal, are brief but complete, to Mr M. W. Greenslade, the editor of the Victoria County History of Staffordshire (*VCH*), who allowed Mr Hubbard access to unpublished material, to the National Monuments Record (*NMR*) whose coverage of Staffordshire, by co-operation with the County Planning and Development Department, is wonderfully ample,* to the Goodhart-Rendel Index (*GR*) at the Royal Institute of British Architects, to Mr Peter Ferriday (*PF*) who placed his index of Victorian church restorations on loan in my office, to the County Planning and Development Department (*CPDD*) and especially Mr J. H. Barratt and Mr Robert Sherlock who first went to considerable trouble on my behalf and looked particularly carefully into entries referring to industrial archaeology and then read the complete galley proofs, to Mr F. B. Stitt, County Archivist, to Dr D. B. Robinson, Assistant County Archivist, who also read my whole typescript and commented on it, to Alec Clifton-Taylor who wrote the pages on building materials, to Derek Simpson who provided the entries on prehistory,‡ to Malcolm*

---

* About 75 boxes, i.e. probably between 7,500 and 10,000 photographs.
‡ No special introduction to prehistory was needed.

Todd who dealt with Roman antiquities, to Canon Clarke who put his list of faculties of 1833–82 – nearly 400 of them – at my disposal, to Mr Denis Evinson for contributions on Catholic church matters, to Dr Phoebe Stanton who supplied me with data on Pugin, and to Mr Paul Joyce who contributed data on Street. I also have to thank most warmly Dr Andor Gomme, Mr D. M. Palliser for Keele University and a dozen other amendments, Dr Paul Robinson, Mr K. D. Miller the Chief Librarian at Stoke-on-Trent, Mr H. Appleyard the City Librarian at Lichfield, Miss Jane Isaac of the Lichfield Record Office, and Miss Edith Jerram the Branch Librarian at Leek. My thanks also to Mr Paul White who did the drawings of Lichfield Cathedral and Oakley Hall, to Miss Sheila Gibson who drew the plan of Keele University, and to Miss Rosemary Cook who did the rubbing of the brass of Sir Edward Grey at Kinver. Many incumbents obliged me generously by answering questions and reading proofs (especially valuable were the comments of the Rev. A. J. Poole of Ingestre), and owners of houses not only gave me access liberally, but also put their knowledge of their houses at my disposal. I owe it to them to state here that an account of a house in my gazetteer does not mean that it is open to the public.

The principles on which the following gazetteer is founded are the same as in the forty-five volumes of The Buildings of England *which precede it. I have myself seen everything that I describe. Where this is not the case, the information obtained by other means is placed in brackets. Information ought to be as complete as the space of the volume permits for churches prior to c.1830 and all town houses, manor houses, and country houses of more than purely local interest. However, there are deplorable gaps. For instance, I have found it hard to decide what timber-framed houses to include. There must be a number of special interest by age or plan of which I was not aware, and in the cases of others I might have been guided too much by prettiness. Other gaps are a fault not only of this volume, but of the whole series, and to them I shall draw attention in a Farewell Foreword to the series which follows this foreword on p. 14.*

As in the preceding volumes, I have tried to be complete on furnishings in churches, but have not included movable furnishings in houses. The rule in the case of churches does not apply to bells, chests, hatchments, royal arms, altar tables, and plain fonts. Small Anglo-Saxon and Anglo-Danish fragments could only be included where they were of special interest, and coffin lids with foliated crosses also only in such cases. Brasses of post-Reformation date are

FOREWORD

mentioned occasionally, church plate of after 1830 only rarely. Village crosses are omitted where only a plain base or stump of the shaft survives. As for churches and chapels after 1830, I had to make a selection, and this is dictated by architectural value or by significance otherwise in the light of architectural history. But few, I trust, will be found totally missing. This is more than I could say about Nonconformist chapels and secular buildings of the C19 and C20.

Finally, as in all previous volumes, it is necessary to end the foreword to this with an appeal to all users to draw my attention to errors and omissions.

★

In the 1975 reprint, the opportunity has been taken to make about a dozen limited corrections.

Some Words on Completion of
The Buildings of England

VOLUME ONE of *The Buildings of England* was dedicated to my wife, volume three to Allen Lane. These two accompanied my daunting enterprise, my wife by driving me, preparing routes from day to day, and later by visiting most buildings with me – her eyes were sharper than mine – Allen Lane by going on believing in the enterprise in spite of substantial losses. Sir Allen Lane died in 1970, shortly before my journey through this last county, my wife had died in 1963, and after her death others had to do for me on my voyages what she had done. Their names are recorded in the volumes of the last seven or eight years. Allen Lane's confidence faltered only once, after the twelfth volume, and he suggested urgently that some charitable backing ought to be obtained for the continuation of the series. I tried this and that, and after a while Sir Miles Clifford, then Secretary of the Leverhulme Trust, offered help. That help has been generously extended by him and his successor, Lord Murray of Fairhaven, to all the volumes since. Welcome backing also came from Messrs Guinness & Sons, thanks largely to Mr W. E. Phillips, and from ABC Television, thanks to Eric Fletcher, now Lord Fletcher.

Help of another kind came from literally hundreds of friends of the series. They answered questions, they did searches, they pointed out errors and omissions. Among these pride of place must be given to the librarians of public libraries, and so I dedicated one volume to them. But could one not argue that the greatest help were those who took whole volumes, half volumes, parts of volumes off my shoulders? Some *Buildings of England* fans have paid me the compliment of expressing regret that I ever took others into partnership. I still think they are wrong, though I admit that the young, with one or two exceptions, tend to write too much. Maybe they long to put in everything they know and can say, maybe a sense of proportion grows slowly. But the volumes benefit from details; also I was glad to see a generation of architectural historians entering the field who have enough all-round knowledge to deal with such books as these. And finally, I wanted to have the series completed in my lifetime.

SOME WORDS ON COMPLETION

Here then are the names of those in these categories: David Verey who did all Gloucestershire in two volumes, John Newman who did all Kent in two volumes, John Newman again who did more than half Dorset, Ian Nairn who did half Surrey and half Sussex, Jennifer Sherwood who did half Oxfordshire, John Harris who did less than half Lincolnshire, Sandra Wedgwood who did Birmingham, David Lloyd who did parts of Hampshire, and Edward Hubbard who did some parts of South Lancashire and Cheshire.

I have often been asked how the volumes of *The Buildings of England* come about. Their genesis is the same every time. An assistant first spends a year or eighteen months full-time on reading and extracting the literature on one county. The first assistants were German refugee art historians, Mrs Schilling, Miss Schapire, Miss Bondi. I could not think of others competent by training to do the job. Then the Courtauld Institute of Art began to produce the right type, and ever since nearly all the assistants have come from that source. Nearly all are mentioned in their respective volumes. Armed with files of extracts written by one assistant, her or his county is then travelled by me, and what I see is described.

The early volumes are slimmer than the later and were moreover printed in larger type. The reason for this is plain enough. I knew less, and the assistants knew less. The most valuable sources were not tapped, because we were in ignorance of them: the lists of the Ministry of Housing and Local Government (initially Ministry of Town and Country Planning, now Department of the Environment) and the cross-reference index of the Society of Antiquaries. The difference is painfully noticeable, though what is, I hope, less noticeable is that now, when I start on a county, I know too much, thanks to all the information my assistants are offered – lists of jazzy cinemas of the twenties, lists of vernacular cottages arranged by plan types, lists of early industrial premises.

So this may be the place to look back over the more than twenty years of *The Buildings of England* and the changes I have observed, not only in the competence of preparation but also in the buildings themselves, the way I visit them, and the people connected with them. Two facts, both of practical importance, stand out. Fifteen years ago, one could still plan a day so as to end in a suitable place, drive to a suitably modest hotel, and book in for the night. That has become impossible – hotels and pubs are nearly always full up. One has to make plans for nights ahead, which limits one's freedom of movement, or one has to look for hospitality – a training college, a prep school, or whatever else. Is it that there are more tourists around? Undoubtedly, but it seems in fact rather the commercial travellers, the reps, who have multiplied. Can social investigators explain?

The other practical change is more easily explained. Fifteen years ago nearly all churches of the Church of England were open all day. Now in whole areas they are kept closed, chiefly urban areas and villages close to towns. The reason is growing vandalism and nothing else. Incumbents may regret, but insurers insist. Few porches tell you how the key can be obtained. The time wasted on hunting may be more than the time needed for viewing the church. If this development goes on, it means that the work I have done could in future no longer be done in the same time.

And here let me touch on one illogicality of *The Buildings of England* which has resulted in a serious fault of the volumes. Nonconformist churches and chapels, being locked except for services, are severely under-represented. The same is true for even less valid reasons of schools. At first I did not take enough trouble to search for them in towns and look at them in villages. Yet they may be among the most worth-while buildings in a place. And, by the way, after faults of exclusion, one of inclusion: church plate. I have been told more than once that it contradicts the principles of *The Buildings of England* to include a whole type of objects which I never look at myself. And – so my Victorian friends add – if church plate at all, why not Victorian church plate? That omission is more easily explained, even if not justified. Many existing plate surveys leave out Victorian and after, and also a selection would have to be made, and that would involve autopsy.

Which brings me to another development during the years of *The Buildings of England*. I have always – or rather for about forty years – been interested in Victorian architecture, but my readers, the users of my volumes, have only caught up with that in the last five years or so. The growth of the Victorian Society and the ever-increasing acknowledgment of Victorian buildings in the statutory lists of the Department of the Environment prove that. So whereas *The Buildings of England* in the early years contained only a very limited selection of e.g. Victorian churches, now nearly all of them are at least mentioned. Mr Nicholas Taylor estimates that in the second edition of the volume which among *aficionados* goes by the name 'London except...' there will have to be about a hundred more Victorian churches. He may well be right.

So here is a difference between early volumes and volumes now, due to a change of taste in architecture of the past. There are others, and very important ones, which are due to a recent change of taste in architecture. The style of the C20 has been slow in striking roots in England. Even in 1950 there were still so few buildings in a style quite widely used e.g. in Germany already by 1930 that I tried to include all the specimens known to me. In the fifties the numbers grew, especially in the field of schools, and selections had to be made. To me, belonging to the Bauhaus generation, that growth was desirable and seemed reasonable, and there did not appear a reason why it should not go on for several more decades. Instead, much to my surprise, a radical change set in, heralded in England by Lubetkin's Zoo buildings of before the Second World War, and made internationally viable by the late Le Corbusier of Ronchamp and La Tourette. Denys Lasdun and James Stirling are the protagonists in England. Their buildings are discussed in recent volumes, but the historian in these evaluations changes into the critic. Users will have to accept that; they will have to take the rough with the smooth, just as I have to take the rough of Brutalism of the sixties with the smooth of the International Style of the thirties.

But it is not only the appearance of buildings which has changed in the course of my *Buildings of England* years, it is also the appearance of the towns and the countryside – the towns by high blocks of flats, often unneeded and nearly always unwanted by those who have to move into them, and by speculative centre renewal, i.e. usually shopping precincts without interference by car traffic. Some of these precincts are architecturally good, some of them are bad, most of them are indifferent. In the country the principal changes are the murder of local train routes and the abandonment of tracks and the appearance of the motorways. One got used to them quickly, and it seems odd already now that only twelve years ago I sacrificed one of my one hundred illustrations to so rich a county as Northamptonshire for the purpose of showing the M1.

I have in the title to this valedictory foreword referred to the completion of the series. But the series is not complete. It is only the first round which has run its course. At the end of the normal foreword to every volume I have asked users to point out to me errors and omissions. This they have done faithfully, with the mortifying result that I know by now to the full how many mistakes I have made and an unsuspecting publisher has published. The next round will be revised second editions. The publisher is ready for them, an excellent reviser is busy. The more of these improved volumes I shall still see the happier I shall be. Don't be deceived, gentle reader, the first editions are only *ballons d'essai*; it is the second editions which count.

INTRODUCTION

WHEN people try to visualize Staffordshire – and few people do – it is the Black Country and the Five Towns that come up before their mental eye. But Staffordshire is a large county – the twentieth of England in area, if the Ridings of Yorkshire are counted separately, the seventh in population – and there is much more to it, for one thing a whole considerable chunk of the Peak District, green or brownish hills, rocky outcrops here and there, and the arbitrary-looking criss-cross of rough stone walling between this field and that. And there is also much pleasant rolling country, and there are the steep wooded banks of the Churnet by Alton. Of the great forests on the other hand very little remains, really only Cannock Chase, and that sadly reduced not only in size but also in forest character. Some forest character survives in the Bagot country near Blithfield, little in the Anglesey country of Beaudesert, and nothing by Needwood. As for the Black Country, the unbiased traveller will find it less black than he had expected; as for the Five (or to be correct Six) Towns, they could not be, urbanly speaking, much worse. But the worst are the overgrown, dingy mining villages south of Cannock Chase. Administratively, by the way, the Black Country is now five County Boroughs of which one, Warley, is in Worcestershire. The others are Wolverhampton, Dudley, Walsall, and West Bromwich, and these four together would make the Black Country, if it were all one town, with its over 650,000 inhabitants the fifth largest town in England. The Six Towns of the Potteries, with the confusing overall name Stoke-on-Trent, are the fourteenth in England.* The most attractive towns of Staffordshire on the other hand are Lichfield, the cathedral town, and Stafford, the county town.

Lichfield became the see in ANGLO-SAXON times, or, to be precise, in the late C7. Stafford has one of the two only documents of Anglo-Saxon architecture. The other is no more than a blocked doorway at Ilam of characteristic Saxon proportions. What can be seen at Stafford is more interesting: the plan in terms of excavated foundations of the church of St Bertelin, just

---

* 265,000 inhabitants plus 76,000 at Newcastle-under-Lyme.

a nave and a narrow chancel. An Anglo-Saxon plan type may also survive in the crossing of Tamworth. Here the length of the sides of the crossing is more than the width of nave, transepts, and chancel so that the corners of the crossing stick out into the aisles. In preserved Saxon form this can be seen e.g. at Stow in Lincolnshire. More rewarding to the eye are the surviving parts of CROSSES, the most famous ones of them rightly those of Wolverhampton, Leek, and Ilam. Wolverhampton and also the cross head at Rolleston in its peculiar shape are C9 and Mercian. The Wolverhampton Cross still stands up 14 ft; it is round and has a very marked entasis. The ornament is decidedly baroque; the arsenal of motifs does not include figures but rather wild acanthus foliage. The other remains of Anglo-Saxon art in the county are all or nearly all of the C11. The applied ornament is mostly interlace and fret, but at Checkley, at the foot, there are also elementary figures. The shafts are round with a band close to the lower end of the decorated part. The zone of decoration incidentally ends not with a straight horizontal but with lobes. There is a close affinity with the crosses of Cumberland, e.g. Beckermet St Bridget. Ilam and Leek have already been mentioned. Other pieces are at Eccleshall, Bushbury (Wolverhampton), and Chebsey.

When one moves from the Saxon to the NORMAN age, the situation does not change much. What is most interesting is again decoration, FONTS taking the place of the crosses. There are more Norman fonts in the county than could even be admitted to the gazetteer, though most of them are plain. The most remarkable decorated fonts are those of Stafford, Bushbury (Wolverhampton), and Ilam. At Stafford the short stem has lions symbolizing evil. The inscription proves that this is their meaning. As for ARCHITECTURAL DECORATION, one looks in Staffordshire as everywhere to doorways and chancel arches. The W front of Tutbury is the most lavish. The beakhead motif, most widely used in Yorkshire, is much in evidence, besides of course such ubiquitous motifs as zigzag. Also at Tutbury – this is by the way – the very first use of alabaster in Britain has been registered. Other ornamental doorways or chancel arches are at Longdon and on the S side of Tutbury. There are two decorated tympana: one at Ipstones, with two affronted dragons, and another at Kingswinford with St Michael and the Dragon.*

---

* Another – with a scene – was discovered at Caverswall in 1962 but did not remain exposed.

Of more strictly architectural interest are the preserved elevation at Tutbury with arcades and gallery, the elevation of the S transept at Gnosall with a triforium, and that of St Chad at Stafford with its sturdy round piers. In Lichfield Cathedral the existence of an apse and ambulatory of *c*.1130 is known from excavations.

As for other plans and elevations, one would tend to look to the MONASTIC HOUSES in the county in the first place. Most of these were indeed founded in the Norman period, but what survives or has so far been ascertained is Transitional or E.E. The houses in question are as follows. Benedictine monks: Burton-on-Trent (founded in 1004), Lapley (alien cell; founded perhaps in 1061), Tutbury (probably 1080), Blithbury (*c*.1140, later nuns), Canwell (*c*.1140), Dudley (Cluniac; *c*.1160), Sandwell (*c*.1190). Benedictine nuns: Tamworth (before 1000), Stone (before 1086, later Augustinian canons), Blithbury (*see* above), Farewell (*c*.1140), Brewood (*c*.1140). Augustinian canons: Calwich (*c*.1130), Stone (*see* above; *c*.1135), Rocester (*c*.1145), Ranton (*c*.1150), Trentham (*c*.1150), Baswich (i.e. St Thomas, Stafford) (*c*.1174). Cistercian monks: Radmore (*c*.1140; moved to Stoneleigh 1154), Cotton (1176; moved to Croxden 1179), Dieulacres (Leek) (1214), Hulton (Stoke) (1219). Franciscan friars: Lichfield (*c*.1237), Stafford (by 1274). Dominican friars: Newcastle (by 1277). Austin friars: Stafford (1344). Most of these houses were small; not one was large.

What survives (apart from Tutbury already referred to) is this: at Trentham, re-used, the Transitional round piers, at Dudley early C13 and early C14 parts of the church, at Croxden – by far the most interesting of the monastic remains – the C13 *chevet*, i.e. an E end with ambulatory and radiating chapels, large fragments with beautifully elongated lancets of S transept and W façade, and extensive remains of domestic parts, at Dieulacres two piers *in situ* and many loose fragments, at Stone a rib-vaulted undercroft and also loose fragments, at Burton some domestic parts, at the Lichfield Greyfriars one building of uncertain function adjoining the cloister, and at Ranton the C15 W tower.

The elongated lancets of Croxden are North Country in character. So is Lichfield Cathedral. Nowhere else in Staffordshire can the development of the EARLY ENGLISH style be studied and enjoyed so fully. It is true that what remains most firmly in one's memory, the three spires – unique among English cathedrals – are early C14, but the rest is almost entirely of the late

C12 and the C13. For the moment we must leave the C14 E end out of consideration. The rest was a programme in five stages: choir (the present W bays) with some echoes still of Norman c.1190 etc.; transepts c.1230–40 with lancets; chapter house as an elongated octagon and with tierceron ribs c.1240 etc.; nave with geometrical tracery inspired by Westminster Abbey c.1260–80; W front with a freer assembly of Late Geometrical elements c.1280–after 1300. While the cathedral is by far the most complete record of the C13, there are now (as against the C12) a number of almost complete smaller churches and complete parts of churches. Worth naming here are the churches of Eccleshall and Coppenhall, the nave and aisle arcades of St Mary, Stafford, the chancels of Pattingham and – later, with the charming motif of rosettes in the tracery intersections – Checkley, the W portal of St Chad at Lichfield, the excellent, broad W tower of Weston, and the octagonal W tower (octagonal from the ground) of Dilhorne. To this must be added the substructure of the former shrine of St Bertelin at Ilam with its large pierced quatrefoils and two pieces of SCULPTURE out of their original context: a small wooden figure of a saint seated (Pillaton Hall, late C13) and a magnificent seated Christ, more than 7 ft high, of about 1260–80 (Swynnerton) worthy a place in any cathedral or abbey church.

The transition in Lichfield Cathedral from E.E. to DECORATED is imperceptible. The crossing tower is of c.1300 etc., the E end with its polygonally-ended Lady Chapel of c.1310 etc. Mostly or largely Dec are Norbury with wide nave and long chancel, Audley, Bradley, Clifton Campville, Okeover, and Wychnor. At Leek the rose window with a tracery skeleton of six radii is typical of Dec inventiveness. At Wolverhampton the crossing and S transept are Dec. Most impressive as a whole is Tamworth, as the church was re-built after a fire of 1345. So Dec went on unchecked well into the second half of the C14.

PERPENDICULAR is in fact comparatively weak in the county. The most noteworthy church, because built completely at one go, is Barton-under-Needwood datable to c.1533. Major Perp pieces are the crossing tower of St Mary at Stafford and the crossing tower and N transept of St Peter at Wolverhampton.

During the rulership of the Dec and Perp styles CHURCH FURNISHINGS became more frequent and more varied, and more of them also are preserved – of FONTS e.g. so many that they cannot be even summarized here. Most of them show little resourcefulness. Among wooden SCREENS only one is Dec, that at Clifton Campville with colonnettes instead of muntins and still elementary geometrical tracery. Perp screens are frequent. They all have one-light divisions and are not specially remarkable. The most extensive set of BENCH ENDS is at Blithfield. STALLS with MISERICORDS are at Clifton Campville as early as the early C14, and of the C15 at Eccleshall, Walsall (18), Colton, Enville, Penkridge, and as late as the mid C16 at Farewell. One stone PULPIT deserves attention, that at Wolverhampton. PLATE of the C14 is rare, as everywhere in England (a silver-gilt chalice at Hamstall Ridware, a coffin chalice at Bushbury (Wolverhampton), and a German chalice and a German processional cross at Leek), and of the C15 and early C16 only a little less rare (patens at Butterton, Weston, Waterfall, and, dated 1521, Milwich, and a silver-gilt Portuguese dish at Caverswall). STAINED GLASS has more to offer, though mostly of late date. C14 figures are only at Leigh, Okeover, and Trysull, but large-scale early C16 Flemish and Rhenish glass survives in Lichfield Cathedral (from Herckenrode), and at Biddulph. Here the forms of the Italian Renaissance begin to come in marginally; but then the glass is not English.

As for the change in motifs from Gothic to Renaissance, one has in Staffordshire to watch FUNERARY MONUMENTS and secular architecture. In both fields the change is late. However, as nothing of them has so far been reported, we must go back by more than three centuries. This is necessary principally for one beautiful monument, that of a bishop of c.1240 in Lichfield Cathedral, a monument of Purbeck marble and of the same type as other Purbeck bishops in other cathedrals. Late C13 to early C14 are numerous knights with crossed legs and some ladies. Later medieval are the relatively few BRASSES (Audley † 1385, Norbury late C14, Blore late C15, Kinver † 1528, Madeley † 1528, Okeover † 1538) and the effigies of ALABASTER, a material germane to Derbyshire, Nottinghamshire, and Staffordshire. Alabaster carvers were working at Burton-on-Trent from at least the 1480s. Indeed so many alabaster slabs with incised figures of the C15 and mainly C16 exist and so many of them are fragmentary or defaced that the gazetteer does not aim at completeness. Of alabaster effigies in the round it is enough to draw attention here to Sir John de Hanbury † 1303, the earliest of all alabasters, to Elford † 1391, and then Tamworth † 1512, Leigh c.1520, Elford † 1525, Patshull † 1532, Stowe-by-Chartley † 1537, and Clifton Campville † 1545 (of outstanding quality). All these effigies go with tomb-chests decorated with figurines of children, small but mostly adult, or of angels with shields. At

Clifton Campville there are endearing little friars instead. The figurines stand against blank Perp panels or under little canopies or arches separated by twisted colonnettes or rude balusters. Pure Renaissance ornament appears first in the tomb of Bishop Sherburne † 1536 at Rolleston and Sir Walter Devereux † 1537 at Stowe-by-Chartley.

In SECULAR ARCHITECTURE the change from Gothic to Renaissance is no earlier, but it is more marked. However, as nothing has so far been said about secular architecture at all, we must again for a moment go back, though not very far, since even in CASTLES Norman is confined to walling which tells little (e.g. Dudley), the excavated plan of the chapel in the inner bailey of Tutbury, and the irregularly shaped shell keep of Tamworth, later filled in with all kinds of structures. Of Alton Castle only one wall of a tower assigned to the late C12 survives, of Heighley Castle only overgrown fragments assigned to the C13. The most interesting century for castles in Staffordshire is the C14, and the most interesting type that of a solid oblong with four corner towers, i.e. without an inner courtyard. This type, familiar from Langley in Northumberland and Nunney in Somerset, is represented by the early C14 so-called keep of Dudley Castle and the mid C14 Stafford Castle. Enclosures with inner courtyards and angle towers are at Caverswall (licence to crenellate 1275), Eccleshall (two of probably four towers late C13 or early C14), and Chartley (two of five towers; early C13). Of the fortified close of Lichfield Cathedral two towers of different shape remain (C14). The royal castle of Newcastle has disappeared; Tutbury Castle is mostly C14 to C15. In addition, Dudley Castle has substantial C14 parts, Pillaton Hall has its gatehouse and the chapel of 1488, Beaudesert part of the great hall with tall transomed four-light windows, and Throwley Hall is the ruin of what seems a Henry VIII mansion. There must also have been plenty of timber-framed houses of before the Reformation, but the more spectacular-looking ones are later. The most remarkable are the West Bromwich Manor House with its early C14 hall complete with roof and canopy of honour, and Littywood near Bradley with a hall of c.1400. Oak House, West Bromwich, is attributed to the C16. Finally, C15 and also secular, but not a private house, is St John's Hospital at Lichfield.

At Dudley Castle the C14 hall was replaced about 1550 by a composition which heralds the Renaissance. The hall is on first-floor level and has a terrace in front. L. and r. are wings projecting as far as the terrace and connected by a colonnade which separates the terrace from the bailey. The terrace rests on vaults. Apart from the columns some of the windows have Renaissance details too, and they link Dudley with Lacock in Wiltshire. So we are on the threshold of the ELIZABETHAN STYLE. How is this, which includes the first ten or fifteen years of James I, represented in Staffordshire? The first answer is: copiously after 1600, sparsely before. Sparsely, that is, in quantity, but thanks to the fabulous gatehouse of the demolished Tixall, not in quality. This gatehouse, which belongs to the 1570s, may well claim to be the grandest in England. Otherwise, what is there chiefly Elizabethan? Not the great hall of Dudley, to which at Longleat work by the Frenchman Allen Maynard belongs, because, as we have seen, it is of c.1553, but the porch of Gerards Bromley Hall (in the woods of Batchacre) which is all that is left of that mansion. The porch seems contemporary with Tixall. A little later (1588 or 1589) is the imposing ruin of Biddulph Old Hall. The rest is Jacobean or – without a change of style – even later. This survival of Elizabethan motifs till well beyond the death of James I is particularly noticeable in church PULPITS. They keep their Elizabethan stubby blank arches and their other decoration not only till Wednesbury (1611) and Kinver (1625) but till Alstonefield (1637) and Alrewas (1639).

Other CHURCH FURNISHINGS of these years need no reference here. There is an interesting, if unrewarding group of FONTS with very elementary motifs, but they are of the 1660s (Wolverhampton St Peter 1660, King's Bromley 1664, Penkridge 1668, Lichfield St Michael 1669, Sandon 1669, also probably Ashley, Pattingham, and Seighford), and there are many pieces of PLATE. Here again more of them are late than early. This is a fact of special interest in so far as in most counties, as an immediate effect of the Elizabethan Settlement, a glut of plate appeared. In Staffordshire we have 1553 once (and that, according to Oman, is of c.1570), 1562 once, 1569 once, and 1571 twice, besides of course undated pieces which may be as early.

No new CHURCHES were built between the Reformation and 1600, and what was built between 1600 and the 1660s remained entirely within Perp traditions. The following are to be named: Checkley (early C17), Maer (1610 and 1614), Betley (c.1600–40), Ilam S chapel 1618, Broughton (1630–4), Colwich W tower (1640), and the cathedral restoration of the sixties.

Betley is a TIMBER-FRAMING job; so is Rushton Spencer. For houses, small or medium-sized, timber-framing remained acceptable right into the middle of the C17. Whereas up to 1550 and probably later the framing was frankly structural, in the second half of the century decorative motifs began to appear: cusped lozenges or cusped pointed quatrefoils, balusters and the like. High House at Stafford is dated 1555, Hall o' Wood at Balterley 1557. But is their decoration indeed so early? Later dates are Betley *c.*1621 and 1622, Broughton Hall, the old part, 1637, Madeley Old Hall 1647, and even a house of 1664 at Edingale. To these must be added the undated Woodroffe's at Marchington Woodlands.

More enterprising are the stone and brick houses of 1600 to 1650. Pride of place is due to Wootton Lodge and Ingestre. Wootton Lodge is the earlier of the two and may in fact have been designed before 1600. Its nearest relatives are Heath Old Hall in the West Riding begun before 1584, Barlborough in Derbyshire of 1584, and Gawthorpe in Lancashire of 1600–5. Wootton Lodge is the most grandiose of these, high, compact, and hard with its unrelenting grid of mullions and transoms. Here, as also at Ingestre, it is the façade alone that matters. The façade of Ingestre spreads out symmetrically with windows of many mullions and two transoms, projecting angle pieces with canted bay windows and shaped gables, and a cupola over the centre.

Maer Hall has shaped gables too and a two-tier frontispiece with columns. The façade is again symmetrical, and Caverswall is as fully symmetrical too. At Hamstall Hall the gatehouse and a curious loggia remain; Willoughbridge Lodge on a hill at Mucklestone looks keep-like and remains in many ways a mystery. Windy Gates, Meerbrook of 1634 has a porch and windows in a characteristic Yorkshire vernacular, at Tutbury Castle a short range of 1631–5 has crazy rustication and is, in mood at least, reminiscent of Bolsover in Derbyshire, at Whitmore the wooden interior fitments of the stables, probably of *c.*1620–30, are wonderfully well preserved. The houses of course often have such fitments as panelling and chimneypieces. It is sufficient to mention Tamworth Castle. The elements are familiar: panels with blank arches and strapwork, tapering pilasters, columns, caryatids and atlantes, statuettes in niches, and so on. All these recur in the most sumptuous pieces of display of the period: the FUNERARY MONUMENTS. There are plenty of these, thanks to the easily available workshops of the alabasterers. The quality is usually not high. The Burton-on-Trent alabasterers were poor craftsmen. We know of a *Richard Parker* active in the forties, *Richard Royley* and his son *Gabriel Royley* active probably from the sixties to the nineties, *Joseph Hollemans* active from the nineties into the C17, and *Garrat Hollemans* active in the 1630s. There is only one Staffordshire monument documented for any of these – Garrat Hollemans's Sir Thomas Skrymsher at Forton. Monuments remain of the medieval type, with recumbent effigies on tomb-chests with shields or more often figurines of mourners – mostly the children of the couple commemorated. No break to before the Reformation is noticeable. Examples are Draycott-in-the-Moors † 1554, Penkridge † 1558, Enville † 1559, Checkley † 1560, Brewood † 1560, Yoxall † 1565, Stafford St Mary † 1568, Wolstanton † 1571, Penkridge † 1574, Wolverhampton St Peter † 1575 and † 1585, Seighford † 1593, and so into the C17 with Betley † 1610, Keele † 1613, Brewood † 1613, Wednesbury † 1618, Hanbury † 1624, Forton † 1633, and even Draycott-in-the-Moors † 1662. Sir Charles Egerton at Hanbury is semi-reclining; all the others are recumbent. Newcomers are kneeling figures, sometimes two facing one another (Betley † 1610, Brewood † 1610, Bradley † 1633), sometimes only the wife or wives kneeling, and sometimes children. A new fashion also is the use of a decorated back panel, maybe with columns and strapwork. Thus e.g. Wolstanton † 1571 has a back panel with columns and a segmental arch, and Eccleshall † 1609 an arched back panel with two kneeling wives, Sandon of 1601 columns and a top structure, Ilam † 1626 figurines against the back panel, and Colwich † 1646 two standing children against the back wall holding skulls. Other monuments in the same category are Codsall † 1630, Rolleston † 1638, Hanbury † 1662. Free-standing monuments with canopies are rare. The most ambitious are at Ashley († 1592 and † 1608) with two effigies, four columns, obelisks, a ribbed vault, large kneeling children at head and foot and smaller children on the ground, and at Blore (dates of death 1601, 1616, 1640) with screens of columns at head and foot of the effigies and kneeling daughters at the heads. At Penkridge is a monument († 1610 and † 1629) with two tiers of recumbent effigies, and the age of Inigo Jones and van Dyck is seen in *Le Sueur*'s bronze statue of Admiral Sir George Leveson in Wolverhampton parish church standing upright. This is of c.1634. A type characteristic of the second quarter of the century is busts in oval recesses. Three of them, probably of 1657–8, are at Hanbury. The most wholly classical early monument is that to George Cradock † 1643 at Caverswall which has an urn on a pedestal and no effigy at all.

The CLASSICAL STYLE OF THE SEVENTEENTH CENTURY thus begins in Staffordshire in the monuments. In buildings it appears later. For CHURCHES the *locus classicus* is of course Ingestre, which can with full confidence be ascribed to *Wren*. It is dated 1676, and in it one breathes an air of harmony and calm not attained by any church in the county for well over a century after. The most classical w tower, after that of Ingestre, is at Abbots Bromley and dates from 1688. In HOUSES the picture is more complex. There is first in rural contexts a long survival of Elizabethan motifs, notably mullioned windows. The porch of Heywood Grange near Dilhorne of 1672 even has a window with arched lights. There are incidentally ovals too, and ovals horizontally and also vertically placed are indeed nationally a sign of the seventies (see also Banks Farmhouse Rocester and Whitmore Hall). Mullioned or mullioned and transomed windows of Elizabethan and Jacobean type appear at a house at Kinver in 1690, Stone House at Denstone in 1712, the Old Grammar School at Leek in 1723, and even Bank House at Calton in 1743. Here, however, the doorway has a classical pediment, and a cottage at Penkridge dated 1740 is wholly Georgian. Cross windows took the place of mullioned windows before sash windows were introduced, and such can be seen at Dudley Castle in a small range of the late C17 and at Whitehough, Ipstones, in 1719.

So much for the conservatives. The progressives built in what the layman calls the Wren style, which is really the style of Jones, of Pratt, and of May before Wren. But there is that transitional phenomenon which Sir John Summerson has baptized Artisan Mannerism. Its weird pilasters cut in half vertically, its scrolls and volutes are much in evidence inside Blithfield, Whitmore Hall, and Tamworth Castle.

For woodwork of the Wren type one can go to Ingestre church probably by *Wren* himself, 1676, and to Calton church for the luscious communion rail. For metalwork there is nothing in the whole of England more ornate than the door furniture of Little Wyrley Hall. For houses themselves the operative dates are Weston Park of 1671, brick, three-storeyed, of eleven bays, the angle pairs of bays with big segmental pediments, stately but not ornate, and on a lesser scale the Headmaster's House of the Lichfield Grammar School of 1682, the Bishop's Palace at Lichfield of 1687–8, the Bishop's Palace at Eccleshave of *c.*1695, Wrottesley Hall of 1696, the Lichfield Deanery of *c.*1700, and so into the C18.

Into the EIGHTEENTH CENTURY. Staffordshire is a county in which the C18 has left its mark everywhere. Nearly three dozen churches were built or rebuilt, and at least as many country houses. As for the towns, if their character is not Victorian, it is Georgian. Industry set out on its momentous march. How is one to present all this material? First of all a chronological list of the CHURCHES, leaving out all those replaced later by Victorian buildings and also a number of mere towers: Weston-under-Lizard 1700–1, designed by *Lady Wilbraham*, Burslem (Stoke-on-Trent) St John 1717 (chancel 1788), Burton-on-Trent 1719–26 by the *Smiths* of Tettenhall, large, with big Tuscan columns inside, Dudley St Edmund 1722–4, Forton 1723, also with a Tuscan arcade, Gayton w tower 1732, Norton-in-the-Moors (Stoke) 1737–8 by *Richard Trubshaw*,* Baswich (Stafford) 1740, Marchington 1742 by *Richard Trubshaw*, Shareshill c.1742 with an arched screen between nave and chancel, Patshull completed 1743 by *Gibbs*, but not up to the standard of his major churches, Farewell 1745, Bradley-in-the-Moors 1750, gratifyingly unaltered, Wednesfield 1751, largely re-built in 1903, Stone 1753–8 by *William Robinson*, with pointed windows, but wholly Georgian, Onecote 1753–5, the excellent St John Wolverhampton 1758–76 by *William Baker* or *Roger Eykyn*, the tower of Norbury 1759 perhaps by *Baker*, Himley 1764, Brierley Hill 1765, Wigginton 1772, and with ever-quickening pace: Longnor 1780, Cauldon 1781–4, the tiny Ilkstone 1786–8, Hanley (Stoke) St John 1788–90, Milwich and Waterfall both 1792, Longton (Stoke) St John 1792–5, Marston and Talke both 1794, Tipton 1795–7 by *J. Keyte* and the sweet Cotton 1795 with canted transepts, and so on to *Tatham*'s magnificent but somewhat sinister Mausoleum at Trentham of 1807–8 inspired by Piranesi and the work of the young *pensionnaires* of the French Academy in Rome, to *Goodwin*'s Bilston parish church of 1825–6, to St George Wolverhampton by *James Morgan* of 1828–30, to *Ireland*'s two beautiful Catholic churches with their coffered tunnel-vaults: St Peter and St Paul Wolverhampton and St Mary Walsall, both of 1825–7.

Looking back at this long list of Georgian churches it will be noticed how many of them are in the TOWNS, i.e. the centres or future centres of industry: Burton, Burslem, Dudley, Stone, Wolverhampton St John, Hanley, Longton, Bilston, Wolverhampton St George. And it must be remembered that the examples here do not include churches since demolished for C19 replacements.

* The *Trubshaws* were the local architects, five generations of them: *Richard* 1689–1745, *Charles* 1715–72, *James Sen.* 1746–1808, *James Jun.* 1777–1853, *Thomas* 1802–42.

PUBLIC BUILDINGS on the other hand were still few in the C18, and fewer still have survived: the town hall at Tamworth of 1701, the Guildhall of shortly after 1713 at Newcastle-under-Lyme, placed as guildhalls ought to be, the fragmentarily preserved Workhouse at Cheadle of 1775 – the bulk of workhouses were built only from 1830 onwards (Stone 1792–3 and 1838–9, Stoke 1832, Stafford 1837–8, Leek 1838, Tunstall (Stoke) 1838–9, Walsall 1838–42) – the Gaol at Stafford of 1793 etc., the beautiful Stafford Shire Hall of 1795–9 by *John Harvey* in the Wyatt style – beautiful inside as well as outside – St George's Hospital at Stafford of 1814–18, the George Hotel at Lichfield with its remarkable ballroom, forming part of the plan of the hotel from the start, and, to end with, the Grecian Market Hall at Hanley (Stoke) of 1831.

As regards Georgian TOWN HOUSES there are too many even to attempt a selection. It must suffice to indicate lines of development: simplifying boldly one can state that stair rails with twisted balusters start in, and usually belong to, the late C17 (e.g. the dated communion rails at Chebsey of 1682 and Cheadle of 1687). The slimmer they are, the later will be their date (Giffard House Wolverhampton 1728). Quoin stones of equal length belong to the early C18, giant angle pilasters (Donegal House, Lichfield) and segment-headed windows are Early Georgian. After that come the strictly Palladian motifs; e.g. window pediments alternatingly triangular and segmental, or doorway pediments on Tuscan columns and with triglyph friezes, follow and last long. Rendering, though introduced earlier, is typical of the Regency and after and characterizes Grecian designs (Queen Street, Wolverhampton, 1813–35). The towns in which most Georgian houses remain are Lichfield and Stafford. The most ambitious of all is Chetwynd House at Stafford of about 1700–10, more a country house in type than a town house.

So to GEORGIAN COUNTRY HOUSES. There are not many major ones in the county. Of the early C18 Hales Hall near Cheadle of 1712 is a stylish example, with the typical quoin stones of equal length, the typical open curly pediments, and the typical volutes at the foot of the mid-window. Next the type of house which one connects with the *Smiths* of Warwick and which is best represented in Shropshire. The characteristic motifs are giant angle pilasters and attics above the main entablature. The source is such houses as Buckingham House in London of 1703–5 and Wren's Marlborough House of 1709–10 and his chapter house of St Paul's of 1712–14. The houses of the type in Staffordshire are Oakley Hall of 1710, Chillington Hall of 1724, and Swynnerton Hall of 1725–9. Swinfen Hall is of the same type, though it was designed by *Benjamin Wyatt*, James's father, as late as 1755. Equally conservative is Okeover of 1745 etc. yet following the late C17 traditions. Only the angle block and the stables are up-to-date and must be of *c*.1760. The glory of Okeover is the GATES and FENCES by *Bakewell* and also by *Benjamin Yates*.* Of the leading architects *Gibbs* is represented by Patshull, a house with a splendid axial approach and two splendid axially placed principal rooms, *Sir Robert Taylor* – an attribution, but a convincing one – by Barlaston Hall. The interiors of Patshull raise some problems, the interiors of Barlaston are ignominiously decaying at the time of writing. The best STUCCO work of the century is at Chillington (*c*.1724), Okeover (*c*.1730–40), the Molineux Hotel, Wolverhampton (*c*.1740–50), and Shugborough (*c*. 1748 and 1794).

An attractive late C18 to early C19 group is Lloyd House Wombourne, Brocton Hall, and Rowley Hall Stafford, the latter of *c*.1817. They have a central bow with detached columns around it, as if a portico had been bent. The grandest portico in Staffordshire by far is that which *Samuel Wyatt* in 1794 set in front of the house of 1693 at Shugborough. Finally *Soane* – early Soane at Chillington (1786–9) with a giant portico and a fine saloon, and late Soane at Pell Wall (now in Shropshire; 1822–8), at his weirdest in the lodge, but weird enough also at Butterton Grange near Newcastle which looks like the work of an enterprising architect of 1905–10 trying to get out of Georgian fetters. This is of 1816–17.

By then Neo-Gothic had become a serious competitor to Neo-Classical. But to get ready for the Neo-Gothic we must first cast a glance over the buildings in the grounds of the country houses, and first for a moment STABLES AND COACH HOUSES. There is, as everyone knows, a Georgian standard of these, with a central entrance, usually with a pediment over, and always with a cupola over. Okeover has already been mentioned. Others of the type are Enville, Forton, and Weston Park. Like the houses they end up Gothic – see Tixall, a monumental semicircle, Alton Towers, Ilam, and Blithfield. But as against the houses, BUILDINGS IN PARKS explore Gothic possibilities much earlier. For this kind of buildings Staffordshire may well be the richest county in

* In this context the iron communion rail at Weston-under-Lizard (early C18) deserves a reference.

England. Such massed assemblies as at Alton Towers, as late as c.1815 etc., i.e. behind the times, and as at Shugborough would be rare anywhere. But at Shugborough in the first place Athenian *Stuart* made use of his Athenian exploration, and so there is of c.1760 the Doric temple – Greek Doric for the first time in Europe, except for Hagley. Shugborough also has as the crowning structure of the park the Triumphal Arch on the treeless brow of a hill, copied from the Arch of Hadrian in Athens, and the copied Tower of the Winds, and the copied Choragic Monument of Lysicrates – the latter very prominent also at Alton Towers – besides the Shepherd's Monument, the Chinese House, and others.

Alton Towers has the Gothic Prospect Tower, a Pagoda, the Harper's thatched house, two conservatories with fantastic glass domes, and divers other structures. Enville has a Pagoda too, and a Gothic Summer House, and a Hermit's House. Prospect towers occur also at Aqualate near Forton and at Hilton Park, and a feigned ruined church tower as an eye-catcher at Mucklestone. Of eye-catchers there are two more: a farm at Chillington Hall, probably of the 1770s, and Somerford Grange, probably of c.1750, judging from the similarity with the delightful little Speedwell Castle at Brewood. In this category is also the ruin on Mow Cop which was erected as early as 1754, and – much later – the Italianate top of the tower of Trentham Park (*see* below), re-erected in Sandon Park. Sandon Park also has a cavernous memorial to Perceval, the murdered prime minister. Chillington has among others a Gothic and two classical temples, Weston Park a Temple of Diana, a Roman bridge, and a cottage with wooden veranda, Ingestre a Kentian pavilion, probably of c.1750 or before, and a rotunda, re-erected at Tixall, Heath House, Tean, a temple, Okeover a temple (of 1747–8, and an equally classical Necessary House), and the former Calwich Abbey, Ellastone, a large, delightful late C18 temple by the water, wrongly connected with Handel. Even as late as c.1850 Biddulph Grange received in its interesting and intricate garden an Egyptian temple portal and the so-called Great Wall of China.

To these must be added the divers MONUMENTS or memorials, usually obelisks (Weston Park, Tixall, Dudley – the latter to a Wedgwood) or columns (Sandon Park 1806, Trentham 1836).

For monuments, however, one would expect to have to go into the churches, but CHURCH MONUMENTS of the age we are considering at present are relatively minor in Staffordshire, at least up to 1810–20. Nothing has been said about them in this Introduction from after 1660. Typical of the third third of the C17 are florid cartouches often surprisingly subtly carved, typical of the Early Georgian decades tablets with columns and a pediment and no figures at all. They also can be of great beauty. The most interesting monuments of between 1660 and 1680 are the tablet † 1670 at Rugeley with the corpse in a winding sheet as if it were a hammock, and the Ferrers Monument at Tamworth of c.1680 with two kneeling figures in Baroque attitudes. The monument was commissioned from *Grinling Gibbons* but carried out probably by *Quellin*. The earliest monument in the grand C18 manner is Sir Richard Astley's at Patshull showing him standing and his two wives seated. He died in 1687. Nothing follows in this vein. Of the most famous sculptors Roubiliac is not represented at all, *Rysbrack* in a minor way, *Thomas Scheemakers* with the characteristic Lady Mary Wortley Montagu † 1789 in Lichfield Cathedral. *Flaxman* also shows up only in a minor way (at Upper Penn Wolverhampton and at Stoke-on-Trent parish church) and only *Wilton* with something outstanding, the Leak and Mary Okeover at Okeover († 1765 and † 1764). What is, however, a speciality of Staffordshire is the massed displays of family monuments in certain churches not built for them; the Chetwynds at Ingestre, the Kinnersleys at Ashley, the Leveson Gowers at Trentham. Most of these monuments belong to the C19, and for C19 sculptors Staffordshire is indeed a bonanza. The first of them is *Chantrey* (1781–1841) with the universally famous Robinson Children of 1814 in Lichfield Cathedral, the kneeling Countess of St Vincent of 1818 at Caverswall, the kneeling Bishop Ryder of 1841 in the cathedral, the Eusebius Horton of 1823 at Croxall, and the free-standing group, lit dramatically from above, in the Watts Russell Chapel at Ilam of 1831. *Peter Hollins* of Birmingham (1800–86) is represented just as well (Wednesbury 1828, Wednesbury 1832, Hanbury † 1839, Lichfield Cathedral 1846, Longdon † 1854, Wednesbury † 1860, Ashley † 1865) and *Matthew Noble* (1818–76) by three highly theatrical groups of over-life-size figures at Ashley (1859), Colwich (1862), and Biddulph (1872). Of the Victorian sculptors *Behnes* appears in the county with a remarkable series too.

But though in monuments and outdoor memorials we have now reached the VICTORIAN AGE, we have not yet in churches and in houses. As for ecclesiastical architecture, the most characteristic group of the second quarter of the century is the COMMISSIONERS' CHURCHES. It will be remembered that the Act of 1818 made one million pounds available for providing churches where they were most needed, and that a second half-million act followed in 1825. Staffordshire with the industrial growth in the Black Country and the Five Towns belonged to the counties most in need, and so according to Dr Port thirty-eight churches were wholly or partly financed. Only one – Christ Church, West Bromwich – came out of the first grant. It cost £17,431 and the grant was £17,273. The architect was *Goodwin*; the style is Perp, the tracery of the three-light windows cast iron. Under the second grant between *c.*10 per cent and *c.*80 per cent of costs was paid, mostly only 10 per cent or 20 per cent. All except two of the thirty-eight buildings are Gothic: only one was classical (St George Wolverhampton of 1828–30), and one Norman (Holy Trinity Hanley (Stoke) of 1848–9). Norman was a fashion, mainly of the forties, in the whole of England. In Staffordshire the first case is Moreton by *Thomas Trubshaw*: 1837–8. Five followed in the forties (St John Tunstall (Stoke) 1840–1, the façade of Pipe Ridware 1840, Butterton near Newcastle 1844, St John Brierley Hill 1844–5, Brown Edge 1844), two in a Victorian context in the sixties (Biddulph Moor 1863 and the remarkably forceful Chasetown by *E. Adams* 1865).*

The Victorian context is very different from the Commissioners' in Gothic terms as well. The characteristics of Commissioners' Gothic are easily recognized, also in churches of the Commissioners' decade but not paid for by them:‡ lean proportions, long narrow pointed windows, lancets or pairs of lancets or of two lights in Late Geometrical, Dec (reticulated), or Perp, with shallow buttresses between, and a short chancel. Architects are, apart from Goodwin, the *Trubshaws*, *Bedford*, *Lee*, *Oates*, *J. P. Pritchett*, and *Vulliamy*. A few have plaster rib-vaults (Dudley St Thomas 1815–18, the Walsall parish church 1820–1, Newcastle-under-Lyme St George 1828, Sedgley 1826–9, and the Catholic church at Sedgley 1823), fewer still possess specially noteworthy features. These are Dudley St James and St John, both 1840, with big round piers with shaft-rings, rather like Clutton's designs of the sixties, Rugeley new church of 1822–3 by *Underwood* with a remarkably competent handling of the Perp style, and the spectacular and romantic Watts Russell Memorial Chapel at Ilam of 1831. CATHOLIC CHURCHES fit in, so far as they are Gothic. Sedgley of 1823 is large and like an Anglican

---

* As interesting as Chasetown is the Methodist chapel at Stafford, a brick basilica of vague Early Christian or Italian Romanesque affinity. It is by *Hayley & Son* and dates from 1863–4.

‡ Such as e.g. the Uttoxeter nave of 1828.

parish church, and Holy Trinity, Newcastle-under-Lyme, 1833–4 by the Rev. *James Egan*, is a crazy effort in blue brick. But the finest Catholic churches are Late Georgian Classical. They are the churches of Wolverhampton and Walsall, both of 1825–7, both with coffered tunnel-vaults, and both by *Ireland*.* About NONCONFORMIST CHURCHES nothing prior to the mid thirties is worth recording on architectural grounds. What the Unitarians built at Newcastle in 1717 and the Quakers at Leek in 1697, at Uttoxeter a little later, and at Stafford in 1730 interests for age and not for style. The first more ambitious chapel is the Grecian one with an upper colonnade at Burslem (1836–7).

What would correspond in HOUSES to the Commissioners' churches is rarer. The classical houses, including Grecian ones, have already been discussed, and Gothic ones are not frequent. They, like the churches, are Gothic in intention rather than in the accuracy of features and their combination. But whereas the Commissioners' churches tend to be meagre and lacking in imagination, the Gothic houses are rich in motifs and often fanciful. Specially famous in later Georgian days was apparently Great Barr Hall, now part of a large hospital. This is of 1777 etc. The most fanciful in a town context is Speedwell Castle at Brewood of *c.*1750–60. More serious is Armitage Park, now Hawkesyard Priory, of 1760 etc. These are earlier than the Commissioners' churches, but the majority of the mansions are of the Commissioners' date: Alton Towers of *c.*1810–52, vast, picturesque, and now largely in ruins, Ilam Hall of 1821–6, now largely demolished, the house which goes with the Memorial Chapel in the church, Blithfield, provided about 1820 with battlements and other Gothic accoutrements, the stables of Tixall laid out on a semicircular plan, Wetley Abbey on a cruciform plan, and Cliffe Park Hall near Rudyard in the Peak. To these one must add the fantastic additions to Aqualate Hall near Forton done by *Nash* in 1808 and totally destroyed, and, also by *Nash*, of 1808–10, a large part of Ingestre which is, to fit the famous façade, in an imitation-Jacobean style. This deserves special stress; for Jacobean became an accepted option for historicists only twenty years later and flourished yet a little later than that. Of Neo-Jacobean, the best example in the county is the Station and the Station Hotel at Stoke-on-Trent, designed by *H. A. Hunt* and built in 1847–8. This formed the headquarters of the North Staffordshire Rail-

---

* He also did the fine Gothic chapel for Tixall, re-erected at Haywood. This is of 1828.

way (opened 1848) with further stations by Hunt, e.g. Stone. Alton and Sandon are also presumably his. Little survives of *John Livock*'s Jacobean work of *c.*1848 for the Trent Valley Railway, though his castellated tunnel entrance and classical bridge etc. at Shugborough remain. The RAILWAYS saw the Victorian Age in, but the CANALS had preceded them. The Stockton–Darlington line dates from 1825, the Manchester–Liverpool line from 1830, the first railways in Staffordshire were part of the Great Junction of 1837* and the Birmingham–Derby of 1839. But the earliest CANAL date is that of the Bridgewater Canal started by *Brindley* (who is buried at Newchapel) in 1759. Thereafter canals began to cut through Staffordshire in 1765 (Acts for the Staffordshire and Worcestershire and for the Trent and Mersey), 1768 (Acts for the Birmingham and Coventry), 1775 (Act for the Gresley), 1776 (Caldon, Dudley), 1788 (start on the future Shropshire Union), and so on. One cannot separate the canals and the railways from the INDUSTRIAL DEVELOPMENT of Staffordshire. Its first telling tokens are connected with pottery in the Five Towns and with textiles in areas near Macclesfield in Cheshire and near Derby. Etruria would have had to take first place had not nearly all been destroyed recently of what still stood by the canal which Josiah Wedgwood had sponsored. Only his house, Etruria Hall of 1768–9, remains. Thomas Whieldon's The Grove, Stoke-on-Trent, of the mid and late C18 also survives. So do Josiah Spode II's The Mount, Stoke-on-Trent, of 1803 and Hawkesyard Priory at Armitage of 1760 etc. and 1839, at which latter date the house was owned by Josiah Spode III's widow. Of the industrial premises a rapidly decreasing number of kilns is in existence with their characteristic bottle or cone shapes, and a number of large and less large brick ranges, mostly with an archway in the middle, a Venetian window over, and over that a tripartite lunette window and a pediment (Wade's Burslem, 1814; Mason's Hanley, *c.*1815, twenty-five bays long; Boundary Works, Longton, 1819, etc.). The corresponding incunabula of the silk and cotton industry are the first weavers' cottages at Leek and then the big mills of Richard Arkwright at Rocester (twenty-four bays long; *c.*1782), Cross Heath Mill outside Newcastle (seventeen bays; 1797), and the mills of the Philipses at Cheadle and Tean (1820s). For somewhat later industrial architecture one should go to Burton-on-

---

* The Birmingham–Newton-le-Willows link connected London–Birmingham with Manchester–Liverpool.

Trent and look at what remains of the older brewery buildings. The earliest dates are of the fifties and sixties.*

Another reflection of the industrial growth of the county is the need for PUBLIC BUILDINGS and particularly TOWN HALLS. The Grecian Market of 1831 at Hanley (Stoke) has already been mentioned. A second followed in the *palazzo* style in 1849. Workhouses have also already been mentioned. They turned Jacobean in the thirties under the hands of *Scott & Moffatt* (Lichfield 1841). Stoke Town Hall is by *Henry Ward*. It is classical of nineteen bays with a six-column giant portico and was begun in 1834 but completed only in the 1850s. Classical also are the Longton Town Hall (thirteen bays) of 1863 and the two Burslem town halls, the old of 1852–7 by *G. T. Robinson* compact and again with giant columns, the new with the same dominant motif by *Russell & Cooper*, 1911 – a case of 'still' in the eighteen-fifties, 'again' in the nineteen-tens. The Gothic style for whose use in secular buildings Scott had pleaded in his *Remarks on Secular and Domestic Architecture* duly (and impressively) appeared in the Wedgwood Institute at Burslem by *R. Edgar* and *J. L. Kipling* in 1863–9 and later in West Bromwich Town Hall by *Alexander & Henman* in 1874–5, the Borough Hall at Stafford by *Henry Ward* in 1875–7, the Fenton Town Hall of 1888–9, and the Burton-on-Trent Town Hall of 1894. Italianate is marginal in public buildings (the gaily enterprising Market Fountain of 1867 at Dudley and perhaps the Tunstall Town Hall of 1883–5 by *A. R. Wood*). The French pavilion roof becomes a fashion when one expects it, with the Hanley Town Hall and the Wolverhampton Town Hall, both of 1869. And so into the Late Victorian and Edwardian Baroque, with *H. T. Hare*'s brilliant County Buildings of 1893–5 at Stafford and *James S. Gibson*'s Walsall Town Hall and Council House of 1902–5.

As a postscript to these public buildings two Gothic SCHOOLS, both of exceptional interest: Denstone College of 1868 etc. by *Slater & Carpenter* and later *Carpenter & Ingelow*, one of the Woodard Schools, and with its H-shaped plan the most coherent and complete of any of them, and the small school at Wolstanton which is of 1871 and by *James Brooks* and consequently highly original. As original incidentally, as a postscript to the postscript, is the row of Gothic shops by *William White* at Audley. They are informal in composition, sparing with motifs,

---

* I am grateful to the County Planning and Development Department for pages 88 to 91 which deal with Burton breweries.

and in the illustration in *The Builder* must have impressed Philip Webb.

In HOUSES the stylistic accents are differently placed. Gothic is absent. Instead there is first a kind of Early to Mid Tudor, as in Hatherton Hall as early as 1817 and Heath House, Tean (by *Johnson* of Lichfield) of 1836, then generally Italianate in Little Aston Hall by *Edward J. Payne* of 1857–9, then the Italian villa style at its most splendid in *Barry*'s Trentham Park of 1833 etc. of which so distressingly little survives, and then much Jacobean, accurate, free, or mixed. The principal instances are Sandon Park of 1852 by *Burn*, Keele Hall of 1856–61 by *Salvin*, Hoar Cross Hall of 1862–71 by *Henry Clutton*, and finally what *John Birch* did at Ingestre, especially the interiors of the house and the swagger stables of after 1882.* Yet later is Wightwick Manor near Wolverhampton by *Ould* (1887 and 1893) with its splashing of black and white. However, a substantial part of the effect of the house is the interiors by *Kempe*.

But *Kempe*, as we all know, was primarily a designer of STAINED GLASS, and there is so much of his glass in the churches of Staffordshire that not all of it is listed in the gazetteer and much is not precisely dated. He also did glass at Wightwick Manor.‡ In quite a number of churches Kempe glass can be seen side by side with *Morris* glass, and, Morris glass being the finest between 1860 and 1900 anywhere in Europe, one can predict the outcome of critical comparisons. Early Morris glass of exquisite beauty is at Cheddleton, where the church was restored by *George Gilbert Scott Jun.* in 1863–4. Morris also designed the High Cross in the churchyard and his firm did the painted wings of a Flemish altarpiece. Also of 1864 by the way is the splendid glass at Swynnerton designed by *J. D. Sedding* and executed by *Powell*'s. This is clearly influenced by what Burne-Jones had done for the same firm before he went over to Morris's firm. First-class Morris glass of the seventies is at Leigh, Madeley, and Tamworth, of the 1890s at Brown Edge, Endon, and Kingsley. Rocester has glass by *William de Morgan* (c.1870), which is a rarity, Caverswall by *Selwyn Image* (1907), Alrewas and

---

* A nice synopsis of trends during the third third of the C19 is offered by the buildings put up at Leek by *W. Sugden* and his son *W. L. Sugden*. They pretty well monopolized architecture in the town in which their office was, from mills and villas to the Nicholson Institute which combined school of art, museum, and library.

‡ Otherwise the most rewarding domestic glass is at Dunstall Hall, where however the great lark is the brilliantly skilful wood carvings by *Edward Griffiths* of 1898.

Tamworth by *Henry Holiday* of 1877 and the eighties respectively. In Brereton church *Heywood Sumner* in 1897 painted a frieze.

But the bulk of noteworthy C19 work is of course VICTORIAN CHURCHES. We have until now only got as far as the Commissioners' style. Few buildings before 1840 showed a greater understanding of what Gothic architecture really means. *Underwood*'s Rugeley parish church has been mentioned as a rare example. All that changed with *Pugin*. In his publications, especially the *Contrasts* of 1835, he demanded that building should be truly Gothic, and in his buildings from 1840 presented the formal apparatus needed to achieve that aim. Gothic was to him Middle or Second Pointed, i.e. the style current in England from Westminster Abbey to just before the ogee became popular. Nowhere can one study and understand Pugin better than in Staffordshire – not only his forms and features but his mind, and not only his churches but his secular architecture as well. That his churches and his patrons were Catholic needs no saying. The chief patron was the sixteenth Earl of Shrewsbury. Pugin's series started with the church at Uttoxeter, largely altered. In secular building the start was made with Alton Towers, begun about 1810, as we have seen, and taken over by Pugin when most of the exterior was complete. But the interior of the large chapel must be by him and the Banqueting Hall certainly is. The Banqueting Hall is now shamefully in ruins. But it still shows traces of that abundance of decoration of which Pugin always dreamt. Only one church allowed him to give an adequate indication of how he wanted church interiors to look: Cheadle of 1841–6. How he would have admired and envied Hoar Cross! Pugin's other Staffordshire churches (Brewood, Dudley, the chapel of St Anne at Stone) are not up to much. It is in the domestic field that he showed himself a master – a master of informal compositions. Such compositions illustrate what he preached in his writings, namely that plan must come before elevation and that elevation must never impose a plan. The buildings to be examined are Alton Castle of 1847 etc., the large school and the priest's house at Cheadle, and, conventual, the Hospital of St John at Alton, of 1840 etc., the Convent of St Joseph at Cheadle, and Cotton College of 1846 etc. Alton Castle, the Hospital, and Cotton College all three have chapels the size of churches.

Pugin's son, *E. W. Pugin*, completed what his father had left unfinished when he died at the age of forty. The convent at

Oulton built by *E. W.* in 1854 when he was a mere nineteen is indeed still in the style of his father. Soon after he developed his own style – fanciful façades and oddly blunt interiors. His wholly abstract capitals like none in the Gothic centuries can always be recognized (St Austin Stafford 1861–2, St Patrick Wolverhampton 1866–7, St Mary Brierley Hill 1872–3). The other principal Catholic architect active in Staffordshire was *Charles Hansom* (convent at Stoke 1857 etc., Immaculate Conception, Stone 1852–4*).

The step from Commissioners' Gothic to a fully comprehended and accurately reproduced Gothic was made by *George Gilbert Scott* at the same moment as by Pugin, though Scott liberally recognized his indebtedness to Pugin. Scott did much in the county, both as an architect and as a restorer. Freehay is the earliest of his churches: 1840 and with lancets exclusively, but not in any way like the Commissioners' lancet churches all the same. St Mary Stafford is his earliest restoring job. He began in 1841. His sweeping restoration of Lichfield Cathedral is much later (1857 etc.). His Holy Trinity Hanley is the first of the major Staffordshire churches fully acceptable to the young men of the Anglo-Catholic Cambridge Camden Society who joined Pugin in the fight against the Commissioners' Gothic‡ and for the Middle Pointed, for accuracy of reproduction and for architectural and ritual dignity. Holy Trinity was given by Herbert Minton, and over the next decades one must watch donors; for the prosperous industrialists often spent money on a grand scale for new churches. The paramount examples are the churches in and around Burton-on-Trent given by Michael Thomas Bass and his son Michael Arthur, the first Lord Burton. Later Scott churches are the parish church of Newcastle-under-Lyme (1873–6) and the Resurrection at Longton (1853) which looks like anybody but Scott. Designed by him also is the outstanding iron

---

* E parts by *G. Blount*, 1861–3.

‡ The Cambridge Camden Society's *Handbook of English Ecclesiology* published in 1847 speaks of the 'frightful style' of the Gothic of the Commissioners. To corroborate this Mr Robinson communicated to me three passages from *The Ecclesiologist* (IV (1845), 283, VI (1847), 150, and IX (1849), 197): 'The modern "Gothick" buildings of this neighbourhood make one regret that their architects have wandered beyond their proper province of Anglican paganism. It is a consolation, however, to know that Mr Carpenter is gaining a name here.' Apropos St Mark, Pensnett: 'designed too much for effect, it labours under needless profuseness of ornament, and irregular multiplicity of parts.' And apropos St Mark Wolverhampton: 'one of the poorest designs we have seen for a long time. The style is the First Pointed – as conceived of about the year 1820.'

INTRODUCTION

choir screen of Lichfield Cathedral, made in 1859–63 by *Skidmore* of Coventry.

As for other Victorian architects, the choice of names and of examples is difficult. Bishop Lonsdale between 1843 and 1867 consecrated 156 churches, and there are almost uncountable Nonconformist chapels of the same years.* The architects must be divided into men of local and of national reputation. To the former belong *James Trubshaw Jun.* and *Thomas Trubshaw* (the 'roguish' church of Salt 1841–2 and the even more roguish Knightley 1840–1‡), and, first in partnership, it seems, with James, *Thomas Johnson*, the architect of Heath House, Tean. Johnson, although born as early as 1794, turned Camdenian almost at once and on a substantial scale – St Michael Lichfield 1842–3, Great Wyrley 1845–6, Leigh complete by 1846. Local also is *Joseph Potter Jun.*, whose Stonnall chancel of 1843 is long, i.e. Camdenian, also.

High Victorian rather than Early Victorian would be the verdict too on *J. M. Derick*'s Pensnett of 1846–9, but then Derick was Pusey's architect at St Saviour Leeds. He was not a local man, nor was – to stay with the little-known names for a moment more – *A. D. Gough*, who designed the fussy and expensive Marchington Woodlands in 1858–60.

To move to the famous names, the large, somewhat frigid chapel of Trentham Park is a rare Gothic design by *Barry*, the architect of the mansion (1844). Influenced by the medieval priory on the spot, he re-used its piers, but allowed the E.E. and the Perp as well – a very interesting case for its date. Then, one generation younger – Barry was born in 1795, Pearson in 1817, Butterfield in 1819 – *Pearson*'s St Paul Walsall (1891–3) and *Butterfield*'s completion of the church of Sheen (1851–2) with tunnel-vaulted chancel and vestry and a thoroughly Butterfieldian parsonage. Another five to ten years younger than Butterfield were Street, Brooks, and Bodley of London and Douglas of Chester – great names. Street and Brooks are manly, robust, and serious, Bodley started from Street's bluntness but soon refined

---

* The Nonconformists first turned a monumental Italianate in order not to look Anglican (Bethesda Chapel, Hanley, Stoke, 1859) and then gave in and asked for designs indistinguishable from those of the established church (Congregational Leek 1863, Wolverhampton 1863–6).

‡ *Egan*'s Catholic church at Newcastle of 1833–4 already mentioned (p. 35) looks roguish too, but the reason here is probably blissful ignorance rather than deliberate perversity. Finally in the category of rogue architecture, as Goodhart-Rendel used the term, is *G. T. Robinson*'s St Luke Wolverhampton of 1860–1. He did other, less aggressive churches as well.

his style, changed its Gothic inspiration from Second to Third Pointed, i.e. from the late C13 to the C15 and early C16, and thereby founded – or co-founded – the Late Victorian ecclesiastical style. *Street* is splendidly represented in Staffordshire, with Hollington of 1859–61, rather wilful in some features, with Denstone of 1860–2, masculine but unforced, original but quiet, with Little Aston of 1873–4, Blymhill, and the alterations and additions to Brewood and the Leek parish church.* *Brooks* (apart from the school and parsonage additions at Wolstanton) or his son did St Mary and St Chad at Longton (Stoke) in 1898, plain and powerful, brick inside and no tower. *Douglas*'s Hopwas of 1881 is small but ingenious, of brick and timber-framing.

The *Bodley* of Staffordshire is entirely a matter of the LATE VICTORIAN. One might even say that the style begins with Hoar Cross of 1872–6, large, Perp, sensitively detailed, lavishly, perhaps over-lavishly decorated. It is a *chef d'œuvre*, it is a *tour de force*, but it has nothing of the masculine, wholly architectural power of Bodley's exactly contemporary Pendlebury. The chancel of Rangemore of 1895 has the same qualities, though not the same surfeit of them. St Chad Burton-on-Trent is as late as 1903–10 – Bodley died in 1907 – and again recognizable by the same motifs and character. The tower is a masterpiece and on the way out of historicism. It is here that *Temple Moore*, of the next generation, could find stimulus – see his excellent Canwell of 1911.

But this is anticipating. What represents the final stage beyond Bodley is *Norman Shaw*'s All Saints Leek of 1885–7, Perp, but strikingly original, in its squat proportions and certain details. His Meerbrook (1870 and 1873) is less rewarding. His pupil *Gerald Horsley*'s church at Longsdon of 1903–5 with a beautiful crossing tower is patently Shaw school, All Saints Hanley, Stoke (1910–13) is of less interest.

With the two last-named and with Bodley's St Chad and Temple Moore we are in the TWENTIETH CENTURY. In ecclesiastical architecture St Martin Ettingshall, Wolverhampton represents the – not very convinced – Modern of the thirties (by *Lavender & Twentyman*, 1938–9), St Michael Tettenhall, Wolverhampton a way of leading from Lethaby's Brockhampton, Herefordshire, direct to G. G. Pace (*Bernard Miller*, after 1950). In domestic architecture *T. Sandy*'s Shawms of 1905 at Stafford is a house in the Voysey style, original in essentials but not yet

---

* *Street* usually designed his own CHURCH FURNISHINGS – stone pulpits, very low stone screens, and wrought-iron screens and grilles.

INTRODUCTION 43

out of sympathy with the past. The case of *Edgar Wood* is quite different. His Upmeads, Stafford, of 1908 is pioneer work and worthy of any book dealing with the pioneers of the C20 style internationally. As for that style itself, the contribution of Staffordshire is limited. From the thirties the Dudley Zoo of 1936–7 by *Tecton*, i.e. *B. Lubetkin* and his partners, and the pithead baths of 1935 at Madeley by *W. A. Woodland* is all that needs a mention here, and from after the Second World War two churches by *J. Madin* (West Bromwich) and *Desmond Williams* (Wolverhampton), the recent buildings for Keele University by *Bridgewater, Shepheard & Epstein*, by *Stillman & Eastwick Field*, and by *G. G. Pace*, and some scholastic buildings by *Richard Sheppard, Robson & Partners* (Walsall, West Bromwich, Wednesbury). The Teachers' Training College at Walsall of 1961–4 in particular is outstanding.

FURTHER READING

There is no comprehensive old county history such as so many other counties have. So one is in the first place confined to Sampson Erdeswick: *Survey of Staffordshire*, 1593–1603 (first published 1717); to Robert Plot: *The Natural History of Staffordshire*, 1686, and Stebbing Shaw: *The History and Antiquities of Staffordshire*, 1798–1801 (an intended standard history but incomplete); to W. West's *Picturesque Views in Staffordshire and Shropshire* of 1830 and W. White's *History, Gazetteer and Directory of Staffordshire* of 1851 (second ed.). The *Victoria County History* (VCH) is of the highest value of course, but so far only three topographical volumes have appeared (1958–63), one of these dealing with Stoke-on-Trent and Newcastle-under-Lyme exclusively, and three general volumes, one of which (1970) contains an account of the monastic houses. An excellent brief history of the county is M. W. Greenslade and D. G. Stuart: *A History of Staffordshire* (1965), an excellent summary of buildings is *The County of Stafford ... Illustrated Map* (5th ed. 1966). Excellent also is Robert Sherlock's *Industrial Archaeology of Staffordshire*, only just published. In addition there are the Buckler drawings of the William Salt Library at Stafford and the Moore drawings of 1857–60 in the Lichfield Cathedral Library. Furthermore there are of course the standard books such as Colvin's and Gunnis's dictionaries of architects and sculptors respectively, the volumes of *Country Life* for country houses, C. Hadfield for canals, H. M. and J. Taylor for Anglo-Saxon architecture, E. W. Tristram for wall paintings, G. L. Remnant for misericords, Aymer Vallance for screens, M. Wood for medieval houses, A. Gardner for alabaster tombs, Mill Stephenson for brasses, etc. Other summaries of the buildings of Staffordshire are the *Little Guide* by C. Masefield (1910) and the *Memorials of Old Staffordshire* edited by W. Beresford (1909). To these must be added the *Collections for a History of Staffordshire* of the Staffordshire Record Society and the local and regional journals, i.e. the *Transactions of the North Staffordshire Field Club*, now *North Staffordshire Journal of Field Studies*, the *Transactions of the Birmingham Archaeological Society*, the *Transactions of the Old Stafford Society*, and the *Transactions of the South Staffordshire Arch. & Hist. Society*. For Lichfield Cathedral Robert Willis, 1861, is still the best. Among numerous local and parish histories there is e.g. for Wolverhampton J. S. Roper, 1957.

BUILDING MATERIALS
BY ALEC CLIFTON-TAYLOR

In its building materials, as in other ways, Staffordshire has a good deal in common with the adjacent county of Cheshire. In both, until about the end of the C17, most of the churches and a few major houses were of sandstone; some Elizabethan and Stuart domestic buildings were of brick, but before 1700 most of these were half-timbered. From the early years of the C18 the usual material, in Staffordshire as in Cheshire, was brick.

Limestone makes only a minor contribution to the corpus of Staffordshire buildings. There is a small area of Silurian limestone from the Wenlock series near Walsall, used at Rushall; but otherwise there is only the Carboniferous limestone of the Pennine fringe, on which there are no towns but only a few grey stone farms. The miles of dry-stone walls which are such a feature of the Peak District of Derbyshire are also characteristic of the adjacent parts of Staffordshire: some are limestone but the majority gritstone.

The sandstones in the NE of the county are mainly Millstone Grit, and as building stones these are both pleasing in appearance and durable; but this too is a fairly sparsely populated area. Reddish-brown, and occasionally purplish, sandstones from the Upper Carboniferous Keele Beds occur to the W of the coalfield district around Stoke-on-Trent, and were used as the main walling stone for the Victorian rebuilding of Keele Hall. Superficially they bear a strong resemblance to the Triassic sandstones which are much the most common in Staffordshire. These come partly from the Bunter but mainly from the Keuper beds. Some are buff-coloured, or occasionally a warm grey, but pinkish and brownish shades predominate; and although in towns these are stones which sometimes blacken and weather badly, in the countryside they can be very attractive, glowing warmly among the preponderant greenery, as at Caverswall Castle. The Hollington workings near Uttoxeter are still very active – both the 'white' quarry just to the W of the church and the 'red' one at Great Gate, about a mile to the N, which supplied the bulk of the facing stone for Coventry Cathedral. This even-textured sandstone is so soft in its 'green' state that large blocks can be cut out like cheese; but happily like many other sedimentary rocks its surface hardens a good deal after exposure. Moreover, owing to its relatively high silica content this is one of the most smoke-resistant of our Triassic sandstones.

Another good Keuper sandstone was formerly quarried at Stanton, near the Dove valley: this is probably the stone to be seen at what is externally the county's most fascinating house, Wootton Lodge. Stafford itself had a conveniently close source of supply at Tixall. From 1772, when the Staffordshire and Worcestershire Canal was opened, until the principal quarry was worked out about eighty years later, this grey-buff Keuper sandstone played a notable part in the building history of central Staffordshire. No example of Tixall stone is more prominently sited than Stafford Castle.

The heavy sandstone flags of the Millstone Grit that serve to dignify many Cheshire roofs are not much in evidence here. But Staffordshire has a much less familiar material: alabaster. In the C15 this was quarried at Tettenhall, but the principal district for alabaster workings, not all in Staffordshire, has always been the vale of the Trent and of its tributary the Dove. Fauld mine, between Tutbury and Hanbury, still operates. Although widely employed for monumental effigies and other carvings at various periods, this 'dressy' substance has very seldom been used in England architecturally, owing to its softness and by no means negligible solubility.

Half-timbered buildings do not survive in Staffordshire in anything like the numbers still to be found in Cheshire, but groups of them occur in places as widely distributed as Betley in the north-west and Alrewas in the south-east, to which may be added Abbots Bromley. There are also two partly wooden churches, Betley and Rushton Spencer, and two others, Whitmore and Harlaston, with half-timbered bell-turrets. A few of the houses, such as Haselour Hall, Broughton Hall and the High House at Stafford, are of considerable size: nearly all date from the C16 or C17, and are in the exuberant style characteristic of the west and north-west, with many gables and an abundance of jetties, and usually very black-and-white. There are still a fair number of cruck cottages in the county, but thatch is no longer common. Stucco, on the evidence of White's Directory of 1851, was at one time particularly associated with Walsall.

For bricks and tiles Staffordshire has some excellent clays, and several small brickfields were certainly in operation here during the reign of Elizabeth I. The requirement might be for only a single building, as at Weston Park under Charles II: this is a large red brick house with sandstone dressings, and both the brickmaking and the stone-quarrying took place on the estate. It was not, however, until the Georgian period that local brickmaking really came into its own; the number of Staffordshire churches, and especially towers, which were built or refaced in brick during the C18 is surprising. Particularly in towns, the bricks always prove more durable than the stone.

From the end of the C18 the network of new canals helped a great deal in developing the county's brick and tile industry, while a little later the construction of railways created an almost unlimited demand for 'Staffordshire blues'. These were made not, like the others, either from the Triassic marls or from the glacial clays but from the much tougher mudstones and shales of the Coal Measures, abundantly available in the Black Country and in the Potteries: Etruria Mudstones are specially well known in this connection. If hardly beautiful, these immensely strong, hard, durable bricks are at least greatly to be preferred to the hot, dense reds of the bricks made from the shales of the Coal Measures at such places as Accrington and Ruabon; and to engineers they have long proved a great boon. Occasionally these blue-grey bricks were also employed quite effectively for non-engineering purposes, and similarly coloured tiles are not unknown.

Near Stone some of the brickwork is dark brown with a hint of purple. But the large majority of Staffordshire bricks and roofing tiles are some shade of red. The latter are usually plain; pantiles are not characteristic of this part of England. The Potteries, especially in the Victorian period, also produced huge quantities of encaustic floor and wall tiles, often more practical than pleasing. Nor can the bricks be compared aesthetically with the best products of the south and east; and in the industrial towns their dirt-encrusted surfaces never woo us as stone under a mantle of soot occasionally can. Even in cleaner places, it must be said that pink sandstone dressings are not so effective a foil for red brickwork as white or grey limestone. So in Staffordshire it is sometimes the modest brick houses without stone dressings, generally Georgian, that turn out to be the most satisfying.

THE ROMAN OCCUPATION

BY MALCOLM TODD

The greater part of Staffordshire lay within the tribal territory of the Cornovii, a people with no written history. All we know of them from ancient sources is that Wroxeter (Viroconium) in Shropshire was their *caput*, and the legionary fortress at Chester (Deva) lay on their territory. The name of not a single Cornovian ruler is known, and we have no knowledge of whether they opposed the Roman advance in the mid C I A.D., or whether they were quickly reconciled to subjection to new masters as a safeguard against the raiding of their upland neighbours to N and W. One part of the county at least was probably claimed by another tribe. The NE uplands belonged to the Brigantes, the hillmen of the Pennines.

The Roman army swept into this part of midland England about or shortly after A.D. 47, in the governorship of Ostorius Scapula. Before 47, the first governor of the province, Aulus Plautius, had established a frontier zone running diagonally across the island, linking the broad vales of Trent and Severn. The area of Staffordshire was thus not immediately incorporated in the new province of Britannia. But it lay between two regions in which a staunch spirit of native resistance was alive. Between 47 and 59, therefore, Roman campaigning forces had begun to move forward up the Severn valley and possibly into the Cheshire plain. Their objectives were the hill country of North Wales and the rich lands of Anglesey, which they invaded in 59.

The most striking visible relic of the period of invasion and military occupation is unquestionably Watling Street, which enters the county at Wilnecote in the E and crosses the western border near Weston-under-Lizard. Along the line of this road lie the major known forts which are associated with the earliest phases in the garrisoning of the area. None of these has yet been extensively excavated, and thus their detailed history cannot be reconstructed. The information provided by air photographs, however, suggests that the history of several forts was complicated, the same sites being occupied by a succession of military works of different sizes. The sites which appear to have been occupied as early as the years about A.D. 50 include a large fort at Wall (Letocetum), which has been suggested as the base fortress of the Fourteenth Legion Gemina before it was moved forward to Wroxeter. Another large military work, not yet examined, which probably belongs to the earliest campaigns is a fortress of about 26 acres in size at Kinvaston Hall Farm, near Penkridge. Both Wall and Penkridge (Pennocrucium) boast later military sites, most probably garrison posts held by auxiliary regiments. In the extreme S of the county, a sequence of two forts is known at Greensforge, near Kinver, and a mile to the NW lies a marching camp of about 35 acres.

Roman garrisons are likely to have been retained at these sites until the period 70–75. Thereafter, units were required to the W and to the N, in Wales and the North. Two military sites of the Flavian period are known to the N of Watling Street, both of them on the road from Little Chester to Chester. The one is at Rocester, the other at Chesterton, N of Newcastle-under-Lyme.

The essential complement of garrison posts was a system of roads. The early significance of Watling Street has been touched on already. Other routes developed in importance during the occupation by the army. From Little Chester and the East Derbyshire hills, Ryknield Street ran SW along the Trent valley to a junction with Watling Street near Wall and thence onward towards the lower Severn valley. Leaving Watling Street near Pennocrucium, another road, the Longford, ran NW to Whitchurch and on to Chester. To the S, Pennocrucium was linked with Ryknield Street by a branch which met the latter road in the city of Birmingham. Traversing northern Staffordshire, a road ran from Little Chester to Rocester and thence by way of Draycott-in-the-Moors and Longton to Chesterton, and on into the Cheshire plain. There are as yet no clear links between this route and the Longford or Watling Street.

No major Roman urban settlement lay in Staffordshire. In Roman terms, much of the central and southern parts of the county must have belonged to the territory of the *civita*

Cornoviorum, centred on Wroxeter. There were, however, several sizeable roadside settlements, notably along Watling Street, which served as *foci* for the surrounding rural population and, in some cases, perhaps as official posting stations. The settlements of Pennocrucium and Letocetum owed their early development to the extra-mural associates of the military garrisons, especially traders and sutlers, achieving an independent existence before those garrisons were withdrawn. These were straggling settlements of humble buildings, innocent of any formal planning. The buildings themselves have not yet been fully examined. At Letocetum there existed a substantial bath-house attached to domestic quarters. This is likely to have been one of the official installations of a posting station or *mansio*.

Staffordshire offered no great mineral wealth to the Romans, and consequently there is no sign of large-scale industrial working in the county during this period. A pottery kiln and workshop dating from the reign of Nero, found at Trent Vale S of Stoke-on-Trent, was almost certainly established for the military market, and probably under military supervision, during the early years of occupation. The Romano-British population of the area, then, as a general rule drew their livelihood from the land. Agricultural settlements of the Roman period have not yet been recorded in great numbers nor studied in adequate detail. In certain areas, humble peasant settlements appear to have been relatively numerous, notably on the alluvium of the rivers Trent and Tame in the E of the county. The evidence of air photography suggests the existence of many small farms and homesteads of the Iron Age and Roman period on the valley gravels between Burton-on-Trent and Lichfield, and between Alrewas and Rugeley. In other areas too there are indications that occupation of the Roman period may not be as sparse as it appears at present on maps of Roman Britain. The character of the valley settlements, however, can at the moment be assessed only by analogy with other parts of southern Britain. Larger and more prosperous farms, the familiar Roman villas, are a rare phenomenon in Staffordshire. Only two have so far been recorded, at Hales (Tyrley) and at Engleton on the outskirts of Pennocrucium. Both of these are modest representatives of the villa. In other parts of Cornovian territory villas are likewise very sparse, the most plausible explanation being that the wealthier landowners of this region preferred to set up their principal residences within the walled city of Wroxeter, rather than expose their property to the risk of raiding from the hills of North and Central Wales.

In the uplands of NE Staffordshire, the settlements were presumably akin to those of Derbyshire and the Yorkshire hills; that is, small groups of circular stone huts surrounded occasionally by dry-stone walls to keep out marauders. An extensive village settlement seems to have existed at Wetton, and many traces of terraced fields or strip-lynchets, some of which at least may date from the Roman period, are visible about the confluences of the Hamps and Manifold with the Dove. Another important series of lynchets can be seen in the Manifold valley N of Throwley Cottage, about Throwley Hall and Castern Hall, and in the grounds of Okeover Hall. In this same region, a number of limestone caves were inhabited in the Romano-British period, for instance, near Wetton, the Elder Bush Cave, Thor's Cave, and Thor's Fissure Cave, and near Grindon, Seven Ways Cave, Ossums Cave, and Ossums Eyrie Cave. The same phenomenon is observable in the limestone districts of Derbyshire.

The last phase of Roman administration is crepuscular. A defended enclosure astride Watling Street at Letocetum belongs to the C4 and probably reflects Roman anxiety over the security of the communication routes. Staffordshire in the C5 and C6 has no history. The only clearly discernible link between Roman Britain and Saxon England within the borders of the county is the transfer of part of the name Letocetum to the nearby town of Lichfield.

STAFFORDSHIRE

*

ABBEY HULTON see STOKE-ON TRENT, p. 266

ABBOTS BROMLEY

ST NICHOLAS. The stately W tower is of after the fall of the preceding one which took place in 1688. Quoins, W doorway with pilasters and arch, top balustrade, and urns. The N arch is of *c*.1300, see the continuous mouldings of the doorway and the window with plain intersected tracery, and see also the arcade of hexagonal piers. The S arcade is contemporary, but the S wall and indeed the rest of the church is by *Street* – early Street (*c*.1852–5). A handsome feature is the emphasis on the S chapel by groups of lancets. – FONT. Of *c*.1700, gadrooned. – REREDOS, STALLS, low SCREEN, and more by *Street*. – CHANDELIERS. Of *c*.1820; probably made in Birmingham (cf. Caverswall). – STAINED GLASS. E window by *Burlison & Grylls*. – PLATE. Silver-gilt Set of 1702 by *John Bodington*, London. – MONUMENT. Brass demi-figure of John Draycote † 1463, priest. A 14 in. figure. – CURIOSA. Reindeer horns made up into antlers and used for the Horn Dance, whose ceremonial and other equipment make a very ancient origin possible. – The LYCHGATE with its demonstratively elementary construction is by *Butterfield*.

SCHOOL OF ST MARY AND ST ANN. A Woodard School, established in 1874. Of the original building by *Carpenter & Ingelow* only a section remains between a five-bay Georgian house and a neo-Georgian range. Original however also the CHAPEL of 1875–81. This building, like the school buildings, is of brick. It has long two-light windows with plate tracery, a polygonal apse, and a low W baptistery.

Abbots Bromley has a number of worthwhile houses. The following qualify. In the MARKET PLACE is the BUTTER CROSS, hexagonal, of big timbers, and probably C17. Also CROFTS HOUSE, of five bays and two storeys with a straight door hood on brackets, and the GOAT'S HEAD HOTEL, timber-framed and possibly late C16. To the W runs BAGOT

STREET. Here, side by side, the almshouses and the best timber-framed house. The BAGOT ALMSHOUSES were built in 1705. Originally it was a symmetrical brick range of five bays and two low storeys with a centre with open curly pediment. Then an addition was made. The timber-framed house is CHURCH HOUSE. It has two gables, far from identical, and such decorative motifs as cusped pointed quatrefoils, and cusped wavy diagonals.

ACTON TRUSSELL

ST JAMES. A small church which tends to confuse.* Late C13 W tower with top and recessed spire of 1562. Nave and chancel in one. They are Dec, but over-restored (by *Street*, 1869–70). – STAINED GLASS. (Original pieces in the vestry and the E window.) – Some by *Clayton & Bell*. – MONUMENTS. Richard Neville † 1728. Good architectural tablet. – Samuel Wright † 1849. By *J. Whitehead & Co.* of Westminster. Standing angel with a garlanded cross.

MOAT HOUSE. Partly timber-framed, partly C18 brick.

OLD SCHOOL HOUSE. Good timber-framing, also with some C18 brick. Both houses are a little N of the church.

ADBASTON

ST MICHAEL. Basically a Norman church. Two chancel windows are preserved and e.g. the enormous blocks of masonry of the N aisle W wall. Norman, or rather Transitional, also, though re-used, the round arches of the N arcade. One respond of the chancel arch has small nailhead. All this points to two phases, the chancel windows C12, the rest early C13. The piers are Late Perp, as are the aisle windows. C15 Perp the tall E window. The long, straight-headed S windows are likely to be Dec. Perp W tower with a quatrefoil frieze below the battlements and eight pinnacles. Good timber S porch of 1894. – PLATE. Elizabethan Chalice and Paten. – MONUMENT. Incised slab, date of death 1441.

ALDERSHAWE see WALL

---

* The Rev. W. A. Appleby tells me that foundations traced indicate that the church was once larger.

ALDRIDGE

ST MARY. C14 W tower. The church mostly of 1852–3 by *Salvin*, Dec in style. The s aisle is of 1841, but must have been gone over.* – PULPIT. Jacobean, with blank arches and stiffly ornamented panels. – BREAD CUPBOARD. With the usual balusters; dated 1694. – STAINED GLASS. In the s aisle one window by *Powell*, 1865 (Christ and St Peter). – PLATE. Chalice by *R.D.*, 1674; Paten by *Richard Green*, London, 1709. – MONUMENTS. Defaced effigy of a Priest, early C14. – Knight, early C14, cross-legged. – Mrs Leigh † 1711. Oval wreath against drapery.

MOOT HOUSE, sw of the church. Stuccoed. Three bays, the end ones with a Venetian, a tripartite, and a lunette window and a pediment.

ALREWAS

ALL SAINTS. Two Norman doorways, both re-set. The N doorway is earlier than the w doorway, the latter hardly likely before 1200. Fine E.E. chancel with lancet windows and buttresses still shallow but with one set-off. Single SEDILIA and PISCINA. Small straight-headed N low-side window. The nave is impressive by its tall arcades. However, the piers of the s arcade (the N arcade is of 1891) were originally lower. The heightening took place probably in the C16, when aisle and chancel received upper windows. The w tower is C14. Good roofs. – FONT. Perp, octagonal, with four heads on the base. – PULPIT. 1639, with the usual blank arches and other motifs. – COMMUNION RAIL, now N aisle w. Jacobean. – REREDOS. By *Basil Champneys*, 1892. – BENCH ENDS. Two, traceried. – PAINTING. Chancel N. Badly preserved C15 representation (bishop and acolyte). – STAINED GLASS. E, excellent, not Morris but *Holiday*, 1877 – at his most Morrisish. – N aisle E *Kempe*. – PLATE. Paten by *I.S.*, 1647. – MONUMENT. Tablet of 1707 by *Thomas White* of Worcester.

Many timber-framed cottages in the village.

N of the church a COTTON MILL, originally built before 1793 for Dickins & Finloe. The present buildings are mid C19. Brick.

CHETWYND BRIDGE, 1½ m. SE. 1824 by the County Surveyor,

---

* Mrs Allibone tells me that the French Flamboyant tracery is exceptional in Salvin's *œuvre*.

Joseph Potter. Cast iron, three arches. Made by the Coalbrookdale Company. Similar to the High Bridge at Mavesyn Ridware (*see* p. 204).

ORGREAVE HALL, 1½ m. NW. A smallish L-shaped house, built probably in 1668, was considerably enlarged during the next sixty years or so and now has two contrasting fronts to N and S. The S front looks somewhat the earlier: it has two-storey wings, projecting a long way forward, with hipped gables, joined by an open arcade which seems to be Victorian but may incorporate something original. The N front is in an enjoyably naive local version of Baroque, evidently by a builder who did not quite understand what Archer and Smith were doing. It is of three storeys, with a parapet which sweeps down in convex quadrants far too close to the end windows (which are of course dummies) – a comically obvious piece of façade-mongering. The 'quoins' must be a Victorian addition to the fun, and are in fact no more than thin slices of concrete stuck on to the bricks. The splendid doorcase with fluted Corinthian pilasters and swan's-neck pediment is really of much finer quality than the rest and looks as if it came from somewhere else. E of the house are early C18 stables.*

ALSTONEFIELD

ST PETER. The church has a plain Norman S doorway and a more decorated Norman chancel arch. One order of colonnettes with scallop capitals. In the S aisle is one lancet, in the chancel are two more and two Dec windows. The aisle lancet may be early C13, the chancel lancets early C14. The S aisle also has Dec windows, but they are straight-headed. Perp arcades between the wide nave and the aisles; Perp clerestory; Perp W tower with nice doorway. Late Perp N aisle windows. – FONT. Given by Mr Brindley of *Farmer & Brindley* in 1875. It is a copy of the font in Ashbourne church (CPDD). – Much enjoyable Jacobean WOODWORK. The two-decker PULPIT is dated 1637. Of about the same time the COTTON PEW (painted grey-green in the early C19 and again recently), the BOX PEWS dated 1637 and 1639, the LECTERN (re-used parts?), the S aisle W SCREEN with its long balusters. The COMMUNION RAIL on the other hand is likely to be later C17. – STAINED GLASS. In the N aisle ancient bits. – The E window by *Burlison & Grylls*. – SCULPTURE. Small Anglo-

---

* I owe this entry to Dr Andor Gomme.

Saxon fragments of interlace in the following places: porch w, inside tower, N aisle w, N aisle N. – PLATE. Dish by *Hester Bateman*, 1787; Chalice, 1789. – MONUMENT. In the churchyard Sarah Bill of 1833 and others † 1848 and 1852. Young woman kneeling by a broken column. The whole under a canopy with a concave-sided top.

ALSTONEFIELD HALL. Dated 1587. Irregular, with mullioned windows.

The village has uncommonly many attractive stone houses, with mullioned windows, with windows in flat rusticated surrounds, and with windows in unmoulded surrounds.

STANSHOPE HALL, 1 m. SW. C17 stone house with projecting gabled wings. The windows were sashed later. Round the corner a five-bay brick front, its doorway with a Gibbs surround.

ALTON

ST PETER. The church has a Norman N arcade cut into by the C14 W tower. Six bays, round piers, square abaci, round double-chamfered arches. The arcade is ruthlessly renewed; the s arcade looks all early C19. The exterior with windows pointed on the N, with Y-tracery on the s, confirms that. In fact the building was all but re-built in 1830. Chancel and s chapel of 1884–5 by *J. R. Naylor*. – FONT. Octagonal, Perp, re-cut. With a variety of tracery motifs and two shields. – PAINTING. On the nave N wall traces of the story of the Three Quick and the Three Dead; late C14. Partly covered by later texts.

The best house is the OLD COFFEE TAVERN. Three bays, stuccoed. The middle bay has a pedimented doorway, an arched window over, and above that a large, blank, vertically placed oval. A little higher up the LOCK-UP of 1819, circular, with a stone dome.

That is all there is of Alton, if one arrives from the s. As one arrived by train along the Churnet valley (one can no longer), the picture was different. Descending, and glancing from the pretty Italianate villa-like, or rather lodge-like, STATION up the wooded bank one sees high up on the s side a fairy castle perched on the precipitous rock, and on the N a large Gothic lodge promising an estate of importance, though no promise would equal the fulfilment of Alton Towers. Alton Towers with its gardens and Alton Castle with the Hospital of St John that forms one composition with it are the creations of the fifteenth and sixteenth Earls of Shrewsbury. The fifteenth earl had succeeded in 1787 and died in 1827. The sixteenth earl was thirty-six then and died only twenty-five years later, in 1852, and that was the end of a building activity on the scale of King Ludwig II of Bavaria. But whereas Ludwig glorified royalty, the sixteenth earl's intention was to give form to the highest dreams of Catholic Romanticism.

ALTON TOWERS. Alton Towers and gardens are now open to the public for recreation and amusement. The Talbots are departed, and the house, except for one bazaar area and the former chapel, is unused and indeed in large parts in ruin. It was built between about 1810 and 1852. Illustrations of 1820 (in Neale's *Seats*) and 1830 (West) show how much was ready by then. The architects the earls employed are known, but not what precisely they did: *James Wyatt* (who died in 1813), *Robert Abraham*, *Thomas Allison*, *Thomas Fradgley*, *William Hollins*, *Thomas Hopper*, *J. B. Papworth* (documented for a bridge), and finally *Pugin*. He, according to Mrs Stanton, appeared on the scene in 1837 – aged twenty-five. Even what he did is to a certain extent controversial.

The building is of about 460 by 250 ft with walls, towers and turrets, battlements and pinnacles – eminently picturesque, externally quite incongruous, looking like the result of growth and being very probably the result of growth. The scale is beyond that of any of the castellated fantasies of other noblemen, but not of the fantasy of one commoner: Beckford's short-lived Fonthill Abbey begun in 1796. Is there a meaning in the fact that Alton Towers was first called Alton Abbey – or is that name just a means of conjuring up the Catholic Middle Ages? But whereas to the outside all seems arbitrary, the plan shows a clearly marked axial system: the main entrance (now to the bazaar) is in the SE corner. It leads into the longest axis – Armoury–Octagon (this with large Perp windows and formerly a middle pier like those of English chapter houses and a plaster vault*), Talbot Gallery, the whole 460 ft.‡ At both ends this gallery sweep ends in a tower, but the towers differ in size.

From the Octagon exactly at r. angles runs the one-storeyed conservatory, and this axis ends in the middle of the cross-bar of the T-Drawing Room. This room, which had a pre-Pugin

---

* Would *Pugin* have permitted that?
‡ STAINED GLASS by *Willement*.

Gothic interior, forms the SE end of the actual domestic block of Alton Towers; for most of the area was for display rather than use. The centre of this domestic block is the BANQUETING HALL, set by Pugin into the existing block. The hall is in a sad state, totally given up and only reached along a tunnel and across rubble. It is impressively high. Its roof with windbraces and its lofty N bay window in the end wall (between turrets) are there, even with the heraldic STAINED GLASS by *Hardman*. The two chimneypieces* and two doorways still give an idea of the sumptuous decoration (executed by *Crace*) once lavished over everything. The S façade of the domestic block (towards the conservatory) is truly domestic-looking, symmetrical, but convincingly Pugin in style and detail.

Extending E from the domestic block is the CHAPEL. According to the print of 1830 it must have existed then, though *Pugin* apparently remodelled or completed it. It is marked by the high, slim Chapel Tower whose top stage is over-decorated – too wildly for Pugin. The interior, now divided horizontally, is again impressively high with two W galleries. Low E polygonal apse between two turrets. The roof corbels are large kneeling angels, reading. They are very naturalistic – too much so for Pugin, though the decorative colouring is probably his. Externally the chapel has decorated parapets.

Not far from the building is the isolated FLAG TOWER, of before 1830: four storeys, rock-faced, with rounded angle buttresses or turrets.

The ALTON TOWERS GARDEN was created by the fifteenth earl in a densely planted dell N of the house with plenty of rocks. He put in far too many buildings, in far too many styles, far too close together. The result suits the present use to perfection. As for gardens with buildings, they had ever since 1750 been more sparing, allowing each building its full effect. Stourhead is the ideal. On the other hand it has been argued (Mr Hubbard) that by such closely packed variety the earl was not backward- but forward-looking – to Loudon's Gardenesque introduced by Repton in his later years, i.e. the second decade of the C19 – admittedly in planting rather than buildings.

---

* Mr D. S. Bagshaw tells me that besides these, which are approximately 10 ft above the present floor level, there is another one at the lower level. This was probably the original level of the floor, and the two ornate chimneypieces must be later additions.

Here then is a conducted tour of most of them. First, sw of the house the FLAG TOWER – see above. Then NE from the house to the STABLES, which must be among the earliest buildings at Alton Towers – Gothic but symmetrical, i.e. Gothic features on a Georgian body. On the way one passes a fine seven-arch BRIDGE, probably by *Papworth* – not really a bridge but the end of a lake. Between bridge and stables in the trees the little STONEHENGE, very much an abridged version.

The main area of garden buildings is below in the dell. It is demarcated by a WALL of lobed skyline and dominated by the white MEMORIAL to the fifteenth earl, a replica of the Choragic Monument or Monument to Lysicrates (cf. Shugborough, pp. 236–7). The buildings close by are as follows: a former ORANGERY, now lavatories, with two end bays with glass domes and glazed four-centred, i.e. Gothic, arches between. Higher up on the opposite bank the HARPER'S COTTAGE by *Fradgley* appears in the trees, the house for an old retainer whose harp was to contribute to the emotions on entering Alton Towers. It has two steep bargeboarded gables. The main CONSERVATORY by *Abraham* conjures up the 'Arabian Nights' with its seven glass domes. The façade breaks forward and backward. At its far end a stone ROTUNDA and a little further and higher the SCREW FOUNTAIN, four tiers of shelves and short spiral-fluted pillars diminishing in girth. Yet higher and in fact out of the dell the PROSPECT TOWER,* the most attractive garden ornament (by *Abraham*). It is of three storeys of diminishing size and Gothic in the details – but still entirely the playful C18 Gothic – leagues apart from the sixteenth earl's. Clustered shafts, four-centred arches, and a glazed ogee cap. Much use is made of cast iron. Even at this top level a made lake is near the Prospect Tower.

Now down to a lower level. A stone LOGGIA of nine arched bays with a top balustrade, a delightful miniature iron BRIDGE, with chains, but not a chain-bridge, and – the end of the tour – the PAGODA in a lake, with Chinese roof and little bells (in fact a fountain). It is by *Abraham* and of 1827. Mr John Harris notes that it is a copy of the To-ho pagoda in Canton, as illustrated by Chambers. Nothing could tell more eloquently of the fifteenth earl's conservative attitude to gardens and landscape. Chinoiserie was a passion or fashion of the rich in

---

* Also wrongly called the Chinese Temple.

the C18, dead and buried by the time the earl set out to create his gorgeous gardens.

On the way out an Italianate LODGE and the grander Tudor lodge, already referred to and according to its style and serious solidity no doubt *Pugin*'s. For QUIXHILL LODGES *see* Quixhill.

ALTON CASTLE. Alton Castle and the Hospital of St John are one composition, separated only by the deep ravine-like moat of the medieval castle. For Alton had a medieval castle built about 1175 by Bertram de Verdun, the founder of Croxden Abbey. Quite a substantial part of one tower remains in the forecourt of the new building, the building begun by *Pugin* in 1847. Whom it was built for does not appear known. The earl's nephew and heir? The fifteenth earl's widow? The size seems excessive for either purpose. It is an amazing performance, four storeys high, with three towers and a chapel projecting E from the L-shaped house, converting it into a T. The vision of such a castle high up on the wooded rock must have come to the earl in Germany. As soon as one is near, the romantic apparition recedes, and we stand in front of a house from which all the imposed symmetries of the neo-Gothic mansions of the early C19 are absent. The fenestration seems arbitrary but is in fact functional. That is particularly remarkable on the E side, where the windows are at least all of one kind, transomed and with each light having a two-cusped arch. Pugin varies their widths much as the architects of the 1960s liked to do. The principal room is the CHAPEL, with its roof in coloured tiles, again as seen on the Continent, and with a polygonal apse. The window tracery is of course geometrical. The chapel consists of an ante-chapel of two bays, raised to a height greater than the chapel proper and lit by a lantern, and the chapel proper, which is long, high, and narrow. Also – which is remarkable – it is rib-vaulted in stone. The vaulting shafts stand on angel corbels except for the westernmost, which have nobbly leaves to stand on – a type of foliage later than the tracery. It is a room which inspires worship.

HOSPITAL OF ST JOHN. The hospital was begun seven years before the castle but built more slowly. It is of three sides of a quadrangle, open to the castle. The l. range and half the middle range were ready in 1843, when Pugin illustrated and discussed them. The r. wing came later and is different in character. The hospital, to quote *Pugin*, was to 'consist of a chapel, school, lodging for the warden, common hall, kitchen, chambers and library, ... lodgings for the poor brethren, and a residence for the schoolmaster', i.e., to quote Pugin again, 'the true thing'. Pugin was prouder of this and of Cheadle church than of any of his other buildings. The schoolmaster's house is separate, and no more than a self-effacing adaptation of two existing cottages. The chapel is in the l. wing, and the warden's house is attached to it. It has a tower which is the most prominent feature. The back range is lower and composed truly informally. The centre is the entrance, with an oriel and a gable. The l. half differs from the r. half, but then the r. half was not done to the published design. The plain small Elizabethan windows in fact make it very unlikely that this part should be Pugin's design. The r. wing, with the guildhall, a village hall, as it were, for Alton, resembles in its fenestration the castle and is either by *Pugin* as late as that or not by him at all. The local architect who worked for the earl was *Fradgley* of Uttoxeter. The name comes to mind for the guildhall tower which in its upper part at least seems impossible for Pugin.* The hospital windows incidentally are straight-headed with ogee-arched lights. The CHAPEL is a nave, originally used as a schoolroom as well, and a chancel. Fine chancel roof. Ornate alabaster REREDOS by *Pugin*. His SCREEN has been removed to the Birmingham museum. – STAINED GLASS. The E window is by *Willement*, 1840 (so Mrs Stanton reports). – MONUMENTS. Brasses to the sixteenth and seventeenth, the last Catholic, earls; † 1852 and 1856. Pugin died in 1852 himself.

AMBLECOTE

HOLY TRINITY. 1841–4 by *Samuel Heming* (CPDD). Yellow brick, lancets, w tower. Wide aisleless interior with a thin timber roof. – MONUMENT. Anna Amery † 1844. Large tablet with a putto by a sarcophagus. He extinguishes a torch.

CORBETT HOSPITAL.‡ The nucleus is a Late Georgian brick house of nine bays, plain to the front (and altered), but with a

---

* According to White (1851) the Guildhall was completed in 1847, i.e. at a time when Pugin and the earl were in full collaboration. However, the building as existing differs from Pugin's project illustrated in the *Dublin Review*, 1842 (*Present State*, following p. 92) and Mrs Stanton thinks that it may not be by A. W. Pugin. She notes that *E. W. Pugin* was working at Alton in 1854, and the tower at any rate seems consistent with his style (EH).

‡ The hospital is actually in Worcestershire.

Venetian window to the back. It lights the handsome staircase, which has thin twisted balusters. To the N is another Late Georgian building. This is of seven bays with a three-bay pediment and a pedimented doorway.

AMINGTON*

ST EDITHA (of Polesworth). 1864 by *G. E. Street*. Sandstone, rock-faced, of nave and chancel, with a bellcote at the end of the nave, and a S aisle. Typical plate tracery with very flat mullions – quite a severe motif. – STAINED GLASS. The E window is very early *Morris* glass, of 1864, and some of the finest Victorian glass in the county. It was designed by *Burne-Jones*, who also designed the window with St Editha in the chancel. The general impression is as convincing as the details studied from close by. The Crucifixus with two white and gold angels below, the Virgin and St John large figures set against tall sea-green shrubs. Below are three scenes, the Magi, the Nativity, and a delightful group of three Shepherds in the front and angels behind. It is all perhaps less strong than Street's architecture but undoubtedly more sensitive.

(AMINGTON HALL. Georgian, ashlar-faced, quite large.)

APEDALE
2½ m. NW of Newcastle-under-Lyme

(WATERMILLS COLLIERY. Only the base of the chimney remains. Red brick with some vitrified brick diapering. Recessed panels with mottoes and the date 1840.)

AQUALATE HALL *see* FORTON

ARMITAGE

ST JOHN. On a rock above the Trent. Short W tower of 1632. The rest Norman of 1844–7, very thoroughly done and replacing a genuine Norman church of whose S doorway re-tooled pieces are incorporated in the CHURCHYARD CROSS. The architect of the new building was *Henry Ward* of Stafford (D. Robinson). He must have enjoyed himself in his sumptuous S doorway, his stylish windows with zigzag arches, and his round piers. His aisles of course are too wide to be correct. – FONT. An important Norman piece, with pairs of very

---

* Formerly in Warwickshire.

elementary figures under arches. – PLATE. Chalice by *John Cory*, London, 1697.

HAWKESYARD PRIORY. A Dominican priory built in 1896–1914 to designs by *E. Goldie*. The Dominicans had arrived in 1894 and first settled in the C18 house which already existed on the estate. This had been begun in 1760 by Nathaniel Lister and was called Armitage Park. In 1839 Mrs Spode, widow of Josiah Spode III, bought it. Josiah was the son of the more famous Josiah II who took William Copeland into partnership. The house is Gothick in style – an early case considering the date 1760. Before the Spodes it was of five bays with the entrance in a canted bay in the middle. This is still so, but the whole l. part and the continuation round the l. corner are an alteration of 1839. This is stone, the C18 part brick stuccoed. The top of the house is battlements and pinnacles, but the tall chimneys were removed in 1963.

Inside is a large staircase hall with a lantern. Several rooms have stucco ceilings of *c.*1839, Jacobean rather than Gothic. The service part is, thanks to the steep fall of the land, three-instead of two-storeyed, and so as access to the level of the living quarters a fascinating arrangement has been made. There is a giant loggia of three four-centred arches, and inside it a double staircase rises to the appropriate upper level. At the low level are the river and the Trent and Mersey Canal (of 1766–77), which had a short tunnel here.

The CHAPEL is a large brick building, competent but impersonal. Eight bays of large Perp windows. The façade is of the Royal Chapel type. A fan-vaulted chapel on the s side. Hammerbeam roof. – The ORGAN CASE is a spectacular piece of 1700–1 and comes from Eton College.

The PRIORY BUILDINGS are Early to Late Tudor.

HIGH BRIDGE. *See* Mavesyn Ridware.

ASH BANK *see* WERRINGTON

ASHCOMBE PARK *see* CHEDDLETON

THE ASHES *see* ENDON

ASHLEY

ST JOHN BAPTIST. The w tower is assigned to the early C17. The rest of the church is by *J. Ashdown* of London, 1860–2, and cost £30,000. The style ranges from the late C13 to the early C14. The surprise is the interior, not by architectural means, but because it is so oppressively over-furnished. As for SCREENS, gilded REREDOS, ORGAN GALLERY, marble FLOORING, sixteen brass CHANDELIERS, and divers other objects, this is all obviously Bodleian. It is indeed by Bodley's successor *Cecil Hare*, of 1910, and F. G. Lindley Meynell (cf. Hoar Cross, p. 150) paid for them. As for monuments, it is the Kinnersley family who piled marble into the church. Of that anon. – FONT. Of cauldron shape with elementary emblems typical of the C17. – MONUMENT. Sir Gilbert Gerard † 1592 and his wife † 1608.* He started the over-crowding of the church. Very large alabaster *machine*, with four columns below, obelisks above, and two recumbent effigies behind an arch and under a ribbed vault. Two children, a big man, and another kneel at head and foot, two little children kneel frontally on the ground, four women frontal in relief against the back wall. The Kinnersleys could claim precedent. – Hugo Meynell † 1800 by *Nollekens*. Big tablet with mourning putto (chancel). – Elizabeth Ingram † 1817. Standing putto by an urn. – The rest in this summary record is Kinnersleys. Thomas, by *Noble*, 1859, the most demonstrative. Two life-size angels sit l. and r. of a rock on which stands a third. – Thomas, by *Chantrey*, 1826, semi-reclining effigy holding a book. – Anne † 1843, weeping woman with child by an urn. – Harriot † 1843. Standing woman by an urn. – William Shepherd † 1823, by *Ternouth*. Medallion suspended from a column. – Elizabeth † 1865 by *Hollins*. Two standing putti; above, an urn and three putto-heads.

OUR LADY AND ST JOHN (R.C.). 1823. A lovable little building, so naive that you would expect it in some *dorp* in South Africa rather than in Staffordshire. White, with motifs indicating but only indicating Gothic. May it not be replaced by some fashionable piece of the 1970s!

ASTON

ST SAVIOUR. 1846 by *James Trubshaw*, but the steeple 1870 by *J. R. Botham* (CPDD). – REREDOS. With stone mosaic. – STAINED GLASS. The E window by *Gibbs*, 1860. By the same c.1863 the nave SE and NE (CPDD).

---

* The Rev. M. F. L. Clarke writes that the monument is to Sir Gilbert and not the Lord Gerard.

AUDLEY

ST JAMES. Mostly Dec and with an excellent chancel. It has a tomb recess outside and another in the usual donor's position, i.e. the N side opposite sedilia and piscina, with ogee arches and crocketing. The chancel arch is splendidly high. The tower is Dec too – see the continuous mouldings of the arch to the nave. Perp arcades and aisle windows. The clerestory is Victorian. *Scott* indeed partially rebuilt the church in 1846. His is apparently also the elaborately Dec chancel E window. – STAINED GLASS. The E window is by *Wailes*. – TILING. The dado of the chancel probably also *c*.1846. – MONUMENTS. The 5 ft brass of Sir Thomas de Audley † 1385 was uncommonly good. Only part of the canopy remains. – In the N recess in the chancel stone effigy of a Knight, his legs not crossed. Later C14.* – Edward Vincent † 1622. Recumbent effigy of a parson.

NW of the church some remarkable HOUSES WITH SHOPS. They are by *William White* and were illustrated in *The Builder* in 1855. How they must have pleased young Philip Webb! They are indeed something quite extraordinary – a group of three shops, an archway, and a house, brick and all Gothic, but Gothic reduced to essentials – pointed arches of various sizes, pointed relieving arches, and no ornament or decoration at all except for a little polychromy. It is a great pity that modern shops have intruded.‡

WEDGWOOD MONUMENT, 1 m. NNE. A tall obelisk commemorating John Wedgwood. It was, according to the CPDD, erected in 1839.

AUDLEY'S CROSS see HALES

BAGNALL

ST CHAD. 1834; the chancel by *J. Beardmore*, 1879–81. Small w tower. Nave windows with Y-tracery under four-centred arches. – STAINED GLASS. The three panels in the chancel s window are very probably of *c*.1835.

BAGOT'S BROMLEY see BLITHFIELD

---

* The Rev. E. K. Victor Pearce tells me that by way of heraldry the Knight has recently been identified as Sir John Delves.

‡ It was Dr Muthesius who drew my attention to this terrace.

BALL HAYE HALL see LEEK

BALTERLEY

CHURCH. 1901 by *Austin & Paley*, and certain small touches betray the brilliance of the architects, even if the building at first appears quite workaday. Red brick and red stone. Nave and chancel in one. Gothic windows, one of them rising dormer-wise higher than the others. But the tallest has a semi-circular top. Inside exposed brick and a roof of heavy timbers.

HALL O' WOOD, ½ m. E. One of the most delightful black and white houses in the county. The suggested date 1557 must be too early for so much joyous decoration, even if the motif is all the same: not strictly quatrefoils but rather five overlapping circles. The façade is symmetrical with two large gables and between two porch-like projections with smaller gables and a recessed centre bay. Overhangs up to three in the porch-like parts.

BANKS FARMHOUSE see ROCESTER

BARLASTON

Wedgwood's in 1936 decided to move away from Etruria and build a new factory and a model village in a park setting. They chose *Keith Murray* as their architect on the strength of vases etc. designed for them by him in modern shapes. The buildings erected in 1938–40 are indifferent architecturally, though at the time they were welcomed as a step in the right direction – a factory in parkland. More buildings since, but nothing of distinction. So the architectural thrill on the new Wedgwood estate was Barlaston Hall alone, a great asset, but a liability too.

BARLASTON HALL. Built *c.*1756. Dr Gomme's attribution to *Sir Robert Taylor* is convincing. Brick, tall for its size. Five bays, two and a half storeys. The three middle bays project and carry a pediment. Lozenge-shaped window panes. Single doorway with Tuscan columns, a triglyph frieze, and a pediment. On the garden side a central bow, on the other two sides a canted bay and above it an outsize over-arched Venetian window. The interior has or had a fine staircase and good plasterwork and other features. Had – for Wedgwood's have allowed it to fall into complete disrepair, and it is at the time of writing neglected and empty.

ST JOHN. Medieval w tower, the rest 1886–8 by *C. Lynam*. A very good vestry has recently been added (1969 by *A. G. Capey* of *Wood, Goldstraw & Yorath*).

BARTON-UNDER-NEEDWOOD

ST JAMES. The church will not easily be forgotten. It has the rare virtue of total architectural unity and, especially from the E, shows that at once in the battlements on all parts. It was built by Dr John Taylor, whose initials and the date 1517 are on the tower s wall. Taylor was chaplain to Henry VIII, present at the Field of the Cloth of Gold, and led embassies to France in 1526 and 1531–3. In 1527 he was made Master of the Rolls. He died in 1534. Stubby W tower with eight pinnacles. Nave and aisles, clerestory, polygonal apse. In the chancel N wall is a blank arch, and it has been suggested that here a chantry was intended with Taylor's tomb. Five-bay arcades with short octagonal piers. The chancel arch is more interesting, with concave-sided responds.* – COMMUNION RAIL. About 1700. – PAINTINGS. Inscriptions in shields in the spandrels of the arcade. They refer to John Taylor, who in one of them is called 'Decretorum Doctor et Sacrorum Canonum Professor Archidiaconus Derbie et Buckkynghamnec non et Magister Rotulorum illustrissimi Regis H.VIII'. – STAINED GLASS. The E window of c.1860–5, but with a C16 Crucifixion.‡ – PLATE. Elizabethan Chalice. – MONUMENT. Joseph Sanders † 1691. Pretty tablet with intricate leaf trails.

VICARAGE, SW of the church. A curious house with an Ionic porch in the middle and l. and r. slightly projecting bays with segmental gables. The windows in these bays are vertically connected by bands, widening from the upper to the lower windows.

DOWER HOUSE. This house and the next are N of the church, on the road to Dunstall. Early C19, rendered. Two trellis verandas and a porch of Greek Doric columns also built up of wooden sticks.

BARTON HALL. Georgian, of eleven bays and two storeys. Doorway with lugs. (Also a deer-shelter is preserved. It is dated 1724. Timber with an ambulatory of brick pillars. Enclosure for hay l. and r. DOE)

---

* Canon Clarke told me of a faculty dated 1862 to demolish the N and s walls in order to widen the church. Architects *Stevens & Robinson* of Derby.
‡ The window is not mentioned in the faculty.

Blakenhall Farmhouse, 1 m. sw. The NMR has a photograph of a roof evidently pre-Reformation.)

BASFORD

St Mark. 1914 by *Austin & Paley*, the w end added in 1969–71 by *Charles Lewis*. The interior has round piers with chamfered arches dying into them and the typical Austin contrast between the chancel N and the chancel s elevation.

BATCHACRE HALL

Later Georgian façade, but an earlier building – see the very odd chimney flues and the mullioned basement windows. The façade is of brick with a middle porch projection which has on the first floor a Gothick tripartite window and a single pointed window over. Inside, a fine early C18 chimneypiece with open curly pediment and another with volutes l. and r. and a plain open pediment.

In the wood s of the house, hard to find and forlorn-looking when found, is the porch of Gerards Bromley Hall (*see* p. 81). This is dated 1584 (CPDD). Two pairs of fluted Ionic columns. Strapwork on top with device. Inner doorway with diamond-cut stones.

BEAUDESERT

This splendid mansion of Thomas Lord Paget and later the Marquesses of Anglesey was all but demolished in 1932 – a grievous loss to Staffordshire architecture. All that is left is the GRAND LODGE of the early C19 (perhaps by *John Shaw*, 1814) and the fragment of a medieval GREAT HALL with three Late Perp windows. They are of four lights and have transoms. The lodge is of brick, with long lower wings l. and r.

BEDNALL

All Saints. 1846 by *H. Ward*, the sw steeple of 1873. Of that date probably also the w and e windows.

BELMONT HALL *see* IPSTONES

BENTLEY *see* WALSALL, p. 297

BERESFORD DALE

Izaak Walton's Fishing Lodge. 1674. Built by Charles Cotton, the poet and squire of Beresford Hall, of which only scanty fragments remain. The lodge is a square with big pyramid roof and two windows to the l. and r. of a round-headed doorway with flanking Tuscan pilasters.

BERTH HILL *see* MAER

BETLEY

St Margaret. Essentially a timber church; for the arcades are of wood (octagonal piers and arched braces instead of arches) and so is the (C19) clerestory. The roof timbers of the nave are heavy and include cambered tie-beams. The chancel roof is of 1610. The timbers are less in scantling, and decorative pendants are used. The chancel was in fact rebuilt in 1610. But the whole exterior was over-restored by *Scott & Moffatt* 1842 – an early Scott job (cf. Stafford, p. 241). The W tower is said to be C17, but that is no longer visible. – Pulpit. Jacobean, with two tiers of the usual blank arches. – Screen. To the N chapel. Perp, with single-light divisions. – Plate. Paten, 1721 by *William Darkeratt*; Chalice and Flagon, 1727 by *John Eckfourd*. – Monuments. Ralph Egerton † 1616. Two kneeling figures facing one another. Columns l. and r. back wall with shields. Top with a semicircular up-sweep in the middle. Large strapwork at the bottom. – George Tollet † 1768. Finely detailed architectural tablet.

Betley Court. An early C18 house of five bays, with a boldly raised, shaped gable in the middle. One may well be tempted at first to write the house off as bogus because of the big C20 porch, but one would be wrong. Later bow windows round the corner. Fine iron Gates to the road.

(Betley Old Hall is timber-framed and has a chimneypiece dated 1621.)

Buddleigh, 1 m. NW. There is a good timber-framed house here as well, dated 1622. The Beehive close to it has exposed cruck timbers.

BIDDULPH

St Lawrence. E.E. four-bay arcades with standard elements. Perp NW tower, the rest externally mostly of 1833 by *T. Tru-*

shaw. His are the windows of Late Perp type in aisles and clerestory, and his is the stone chancel with its internal stone wall-panelling. Some alterations were made by *Lynam* in 1894, and the S (Heath) chapel was added by *Ernest Bates* in 1873 to secure spectacular lighting from above for the monument for whose sake the church ought to be visited. – MONUMENTS. William and Mary Heath, 1872 by *Matthew Noble*. White marble. Two life-size figures l. and r. and hovering above them Jesus Christ, a figure inspired by Blake. – Sir William Bowyer † 1640 and wife. Tomb-chest with shields on the sides. Helm and gauntlets above. – Incised slabs outside the church. All have crosses, some also a sword. They must have been monuments to the Knipersley family. – STAINED GLASS. In the W window an excellent Flemish early C16 scene. – In the E and other windows ancient fragments. – PLATE. Chalice by *H.C.*, 1588; silver-gilt Cup, 1599; Paten, 1684.

T JOHN EVANGELIST, Knypersley. 1848–51 at the expense of John Bateman of Biddulph Grange. NW steeple with porch and unfortunately detailed lucarnes. Mr Bateman also paid for the exceptionally large PARSONAGE, neo-Jacobean, with at the back stables and coach house, and for the SCHOOL (in Newpool Road) which is dated 1850 and is symmetrical except for the turret. The architect for the whole group was *R. C. Hussey* (CPDD).

IDDULPH GRANGE. Mr Bateman's great achievement was his gardens. He started on them about 1845, and they are still a prime document of Early Victorian garden layout. They were described in detail in the *Gardener's Chronicle* in 1857–62.* They include a long Wellingtonia avenue, running E, the Egyptian Court (with a temple entrance and two pairs of sphinxes), the Great Wall of China, and the Chinese Pavilion and Bridge. The house is largely of 1896, i.e. built for John Bateman's son. The architect was *Thomas Bower*. Of the preceding house destroyed by fire are the porte-cochère, the outer hall, and, on the garden side, the low end parts l. and r.

IDDULPH OLD HALL. A late C17 house of no pretension is attached to an Elizabethan mansion, sacked in the Civil War. The ruins stand up in considerable parts and ought to be examined. The house had an inner courtyard. The entrance (s) range was symmetrical with an archway with tapering pilasters dated 158? (1588 or 1589), a window with tapering

---

* Mr Hubbard discovered this valuable document.

pilasters l. and r., and five-eighths bay windows in the end bays. The kitchen in the range is recognizable by a huge fireplace. The N range was probably the hall range, although evidence here is confusing. The high tower with ogee cap no doubt contained the staircase. Was there a long gallery on the top floor with a polygonal bay window in the tower?

BIDDULPH MOOR

CHRIST CHURCH. 1863 by *Ward & Ford*. Neo-Norman with an apse.

BILSTON

2½ m. SE of Wolverhampton

ST LEONARD. The very hub of the town. A medieval foundation rebuilt by *Francis Goodwin* in 1825–6 to a classical, not a Gothic, design. The present rendering is of 1882–3. Long round-arched windows along the sides, broad five-bay front with two tiers of windows and a square, chamfered turret, a little Soanian in detail. Set into the doorway two cast-iron objects which may remind one of bollards. The apsidal chancel and the interior are by *Ewan Christian*, 1883–93. But the shallow segmental vault is no doubt original. – FONT. 1673. A shallow, fluted bowl. – PLATE. Set of 1826. – MONUMENTS. Mrs Willim † 1834. Standing female figure by an altar. – Mr Riley † 1835 by *William Weale*. Medallion with an angel conducting her to Heaven. Drapery on the l.

ST LUKE, Market Street. 1851–2 by *Johnson & Son* of Lichfield. A Commissioners' church. Stone, decaying, with lancet windows and a SE tower.

ST MARY, Oxford Street. Also by *Goodwin*, but a little later 1827–9. This is also a Commissioners' church, and it is Gothic. Nave and aisles, W tower with diagonally set entrance bays and an octagonal top with eight pinnacles. Polygonal apse and no structural chancel. Tall two-light windows with Y-tracery. Three galleries on iron columns.

HOLY TRINITY (R.C.), Oxford Street. Aisleless, with lancets and a short chancel. 1883–4, but the chancel 1846 by *Pugin*. It has a three-light E window with Late Geometrical tracery. – STAINED GLASS. In the E window by *Wailes*.

* So Mr Evinson tells me.

TOWN HALL. 1872–3 by *Bidlake & Lovatt*. With a tower. What can one call this style? Segment-headed windows and Early Gothic capitals?

CENTRE HEALTH CLINIC, Wellington Road and Prouds Lane. By *Lyons, Israel & Ellis*, 1938–9. Small. Light brick and horizontal windows. The moment of Dudok inspiration in England.

No perambulation, but a number of worthwhile houses. Farthest away from the centre and oldest is the GREYHOUND INN in the HIGH STREET, timber-framed, with closely set uprights, i.e. *c.*1450 or so. Two gables not in line. Inside, a nice Jacobean plaster ceiling with thin leaf scrolls.

The rest is all near St Leonard. The best house is the former PARSONAGE, N of the church, also by *Goodwin*. Three wide bays, stuccoed, with giant pilasters, a composition a bit out of the ordinary.

The largest house is at the junction of LICHFIELD STREET and Oxford Street, mid C18, brick, of five bays and three storeys. Pedimented doorway.

In CHURCH STREET is the OLD PHARMACY, a small and funny front, but with the original shop window and interior.

Stuccoed early C19 or Early Victorian houses also in MOUNT PLEASANT, and two attractive doorways in WELLINGTON ROAD.

BISHOPSWOOD

ST JOHN. Consecrated 1851. By *G. T. Robinson*. S tower with a characteristically early C19 thin, tall doorway. Lancet windows, wide transepts, short chancel, i.e. all still in the Commissioners' tradition. Tricky timbering over the crossing bay.

BISHTON HALL *see* COLWICH

BLACKBROOK FARMHOUSE *see* WEEFORD

BLAKENALL HEATH *see* WALSALL, p. 295

BLAKENHALL FARMHOUSE *see* BARTON-UNDER-NEEDWOOD

BLITHBURY

There was once a Benedictine priory here, founded *c.*1140 by Hugh de Ridware.

BLITHFIELD

ST LEONARD. The church lies immediately N of the house. It has a C13 to C14 nave and a C13 to C14 chancel, the chancel later than the nave. The arcades are of round piers with round capitals and double-chamfered arches. The S capitals differ from the N capitals. The chancel windows are typical of the end of the C13 (Y-tracery and intersecting tracery). the SEDILIA are plain, but the PISCINA has an ogee arch. Is all this then early C14 and not late C13 ? The chancel was restored by *Pugin* in 1851, but the tradition is that he reproduced faithfully what had been there. The aisle fenestration is Dec anyway (ogee-arched lights under straight heads). Late Perp clerestory. The polygonal vestry is of 1829–30, built as a Bagot mortuary chapel. The S porch is by *Street*, 1860. He may also have had something to do with the W tower, which is Dec below, Perp above. – PULPIT. Said to be by *Pugin*, 1846. It does not look it. – SCREEN. Perp. One-light divisions, top frieze and cresting. Much restored by *Bodley*, 1881. – BENCH ENDS. The largest set in the county – twenty-one traceried ends with poppyheads. By no means all are original. – PILLAR PISCINA. Norman (by the S entrance). – STAINED GLASS. In the chancel grisaille and heraldic glass of the time of the building. – In the W window of *c.* 1526, Sir Lewis Bagot and his wives. – In the S clerestory some glass probably by *Hardman & Powell*, 1848–9. Probably designed by *Pugin*. – PLATE Chalice and Paten by *P.B.*, 1671; Set of 1707 designed by *John Jackson*, London; Almsdish of 1717, by *Samuel Paten* London. – MONUMENTS. In an outer recess effigy of a Priest, early C14. – Sir Lewis Bagot † 1534 and wives. Incised slab (chancel N). – Thomas Bagot † 1541 and wife. Incised slab (chancel N). – Francis Aston † 1593 and wife. Incised slab (chancel floor). – Sir Richard Bagot † 1596 and wife; recumbent effigies (chancel N). – Hervey Bagot † 1655 aged thirteen. Cartouche; very characteristic of the mid C17. – Several large architectural late C17 to early C18 tablets, one with looped-up curtains († 1686), one with curtains pulled back. – In the vestry Lady Bagot † 1695. By *William Stanton*; no figures.*

BLITHFIELD HALL has been Bagot property since 1367. It is a large house, but without any monumentality and indeed any compositional order. In its informality it is picturesque al-

---

* Mr Paul Joyce tells me that the SCHOOL and MASTER'S HOUSE are of 1856–7 and by *Street* too.

right, but even that only in picture after picture and not as a whole. As one approaches from the s, one has the large STABLES on the r., the s range of the house on the l. The style is castellated Tudor, rather like say Sidney Sussex College. The date is in fact 1820–4.* The architect was possibly *John Buckler*. As one proceeds a little, the gatehouse to the stables is on the r., the kitchen court with the E range of the house in front. To reach the s range one has to cross another gatehouse. This one has turrets and a rib-vault inside. The l. end of the s range is of 1769, but tudorized. It has inside a modest stucco ceiling. In the middle of the s range is a Tudor entrance hall with a panelled ceiling, and from here one reaches a rib-vaulted cloister open towards the centre of the house, which is the courtyard. In appearance this, like the s range and the cloister, is of c.1820, but a blocked doorway with a four-centred head and decorated spandrels establishes the pre-Reformation date of the house. The w range into which this doorway led is altogether the oldest part of the house. It is externally all cottagey, with irregular gables, but has C16 timber-framing inside.

The N range is what in the C17 and C18 was called a double pile, i.e. the N side is c. 1740 (*Richard Trubshaw* is recorded to have worked at Blithfield in 1738), except for the r. end bay, which has a low blank doorway and a large churchy Perp window over, clearly an alteration of c.1820. But the s side of this N range, i.e. the side towards the courtyard, is initially medieval, even if in appearance 1820. It contains the great hall with traceried windows, very tall canopied niches, an elaborate lierne-vault with pendants, and a screens passage. *Bernasconi* did the decorative work here. Above the plaster vault is still the C16 roof. Also in the N range is the staircase. It is re-set from the screens end of the hall and was there differently arranged. It is of c.1660–70 and has openwork feathery leaves and other more stylized motifs.

Other interesting internal features are Lady Bagot's study in the E range with late C17 panelling, and the library of c.1740 with pilastered panelling. The library lies E of the hall on the upper floor, i.e. in the position of the solar or chamber.

ORANGERY, N of the N range. By *James Stuart*. Eleven bays, the end bays tripartite with pediments.

GAME LARDER, NE. Octagonal. Of 1895.

* The house was illustrated in Neale's *Seats* already in 1820.

LODGES, s. Two identical pairs, Cubic but Gothic.

WELL, w of the w range. Square, with open four-centred arches. Dilapidated at the time of writing. Good view to the w.

MONUMENT, Bagot's Bromley, 1¾ m. NE. 1811. Just a base with inscription to mark the site of the manor house of the Bagots.

CALLOW HILL, 1⅝ m. NNE. Timber-framed and gabled. Brick at the back. Little of decorative treatment of the studs and braces. An outer stone staircase leads to the porch. Elaborately carved handrail.

GOAT LODGE, 2½ m. NE, N of Dunstall Farmhouse. 1839 by *Trubshaw* (CPDD). Crazily over-decorated. Porch with a row of goats' heads above it, bargeboarded gables, ornamental chimneys.

BLORE

ST BARTHOLOMEW. Of complex outline and with a mixture of windows. The majority, however, are late, and the date 1519 reported for a remodelling would fit well. The chancel E window looks Victorian.* The arcade is Perp too, but the wall between chancel and chapel seems Dec. Good Perp roofs, especially in the N aisle. – Much Jacobean WOODWORK, notably the BENCHES with minimum poppyheads, the simple PULPIT, the COMMUNION RAIL with balusters turned bobbin-wise, and the chancel PANELLING and STALLS. – Perp and with a great resourcefulness of tracery motifs the SCREEN to the N chapel. – FONT. Perp, octagonal, with quatrefoils. – SCREEN. The gates are of wrought iron, High Victorian and very elaborate, taking advantage of the third dimension to a degree exceptional in ironwork. – STAINED GLASS. In the chancel windows several figures, e.g. a charming Virgin as a girl and the kneeling figures of the two donors. – MONUMENT. William Bassett, late C15 brasses, 36½ in. figures. – William Bassett † 1601 with wife † 1640 and son-in-law † 1616. William lies in the middle above the others. At their heads two kneeling daughters, one showing unmistakable sorrow. At head and foot screens of four columns with shields on top.

BLORE HALL. The house has two late C15 or early C16 two-light windows, uncusped.

---

* Glass of 1865 (CPDD).

BLOXWICH see WALSALL, p. 294

BLURTON see STOKE-ON-TRENT, p. 266

BLYMHILL

ST MARY. E.E. S arcade (octagonal piers), Perp w tower, and Dec chancel with a tomb recess. Note the sunk-quadrant moulding. Nearly all the rest is *G. E. Street*, 1856–9, and Street at his best. The style is E.E. of course. Only the N porch is, as an attempt at being playful, not so successful. The N windows all different, the s windows in a rhythm of 1-2-1-2-1 lights, the two-lights having plate tracery. One huge gargoyle at the E end of the S aisle. The S dormers are of 1876, not by Street. By Street again the N aisle E window, a quatrefoil of four trefoils high up. Roof with big arched braces and windbraces. – FONT, PULPIT, extremely low stone SCREEN, fine iron SCREEN on the chancel N side, STALLS, COMMUNION RAIL, and more designed by *Street*. – (STAINED GLASS. In the aisles by *Wailes*, in the chancel N by *Hardman*, the E window by *Burlison & Grylls*.*) – PLATE. Chalice, 1562 by *John Freeman*, London; Paten, 1562; Bread Tray, 1745.

RECTORY. Partly by *Street*, but also partly demolished.

SCHOOL. 1855–7, by *Street* too. Characteristic half-hipped dormers.

BRADFORD ARMS, 2 m. SE. Late Georgian. Six bays, two storeys, with Gothic glazing bars.

BOBBINGTON

HOLY CROSS. A church of quite some interest. The N arcade is mid-Norman, four bays, round piers, square many-scalloped capitals, single-step arches (cf. Enville). The E pier has an undecorated capital. This last bay of the aisle has a lancet in its E wall.‡ The masonry of the bay differs from that of the rest of the church, and there are other noticeable differences in masonry. Most of the windows are renewed or outright Victorian, but the only totally Victorian piece is the uninspired S tower. *Sir Arthur Blomfield* restored the church in

* I owe this information to Paul Joyce, who also told me of a piece of SCULPTURE executed by *Street*. It represents the Magi. N aisle W window.

‡ According to the Rev. John Gibbons the aisle W window is an original lancet too.

1878. – FONT. Big, octagonal, C14 or C15. – MONUMENTS. In the porch effigy of a Civilian (a lady?) holding a shield; C13. – Good cartouche to Thomas Dickins, 1701.

BOBBINGTON HALL, ¾ m. SW. Brick, C17. Stepped gables and mullioned windows.

LEATON HALL, ½ m. SE. Stucco-faced, 1817. Of eight bays and three storeys, symmetrical, with a porch of paired Tuscan columns.

BOLE HALL see TAMWORTH

BONEHILL HOUSE see FAZELEY

BOOTHEN see STOKE-ON-TRENT, p. 263

BRADFORD ARMS see BLYMHILL

8010
BRADLEY

ST MARY AND ALL SAINTS. Mostly late C13 and early C14. Of the former the N chapel and the chancel, of the latter the chancel E window with its flowing tracery and the three-bay N arcade with quatrefoil piers and thin extra shafts in the diagonals and arches having sunk-quadrant mouldings. Perp W tower top, but the arch to the nave probably Dec. – FONT. Norman, high drum-shape with bands of decoration including stars and Greek key. – REREDOS in the chancel E wall. Dec. A broad strip of a cusped wave, as in friezes at the top of towers or along parapets. – NORMAN STONES. Tower W wall. – Head of a CHURCHYARD CROSS. Also under the tower. – STAINED GLASS. Some fragments in a S window. – PLATE. Chalice, 1756–7, by *Thomas Wright*, London; Paten, 1764, by *Fuller White*, London; Paten, 1767. – MONUMENT. Thomas Browne † 1633. Two kneeling figures facing one another; detached columns l. and r.

(LITTYWOOD, I m. NE. A timber-framed manor house faced in brick but containing a timber-framed hall of *c.*1400 formerly open to the roof. It is of two bays plus the screens passage. The W truss of the hall has crucks. To the W of it was the solar. The mid-truss of the hall has arched braces to a collar-beam.)

BURY RINGS HILLFORT, 2 m. NNE. An oval, univallate hillfort covering some 7 acres. The broad gap on the S may be original but is so wide as to suggest either that the site is unfinished or that it was altered at a later date.

BRADLEY see WOLVERHAMPTON, p. 322

BRADLEY-IN-THE-MOORS

St Leonard. Built in 1750 and architecturally unaltered, which is a rarity. Tower, nave, chancel. Arched windows, and above the doorways lunette windows. – Baluster FONT.

BRADMORE see WOLVERHAMPTON, p. 324

BRADWELL HALL see WOLSTANTON

BRAMSHALL

St Lawrence. 1835 by *Thomas Fradgley* of Uttoxeter, at the expense of Lord Willoughby de Broke. Ashlar, with a substantial w tower provided with the typical narrow and steep doorway of Commissioners' churches. Again, like many of these churches, that of Bramshall has Perp windows with Y-tracery. Nave and chancel are in one. – STAINED GLASS. Substantial fragments fill one window. – PLATE. Chalice and Paten, 1793 by *Edward Fennell*; Chalice, 1829 by *Hester Bateman*.

BRANSTON

St Saviour. 1864 by *Street*,* enlarged 1891 (Kelly). Brick walls, big roof. Plate tracery. Small bell-turret.
Sinai Park, 1½ m. N. Accessible from Shobnall Road, Burton. Totally derelict at the time of writing. It was probably a summer house of the abbots of Burton. Built about 1500. Three sides of a courtyard. Timber-framing and brick.

THE BRATCH see WOMBOURNE

BRERETON

Brereton is really the SE end of Rugeley. In Main Road, Brereton, is Brereton House, a handsome five-bay brick

---

* According to Mr Paul Joyce.

house of the late C18 with a pedimented doorway of Tuscan columns and good rusticated stone gatepiers.

ST MICHAEL. 1837 by *Thomas Trubshaw*, but much enlarged and improved by *Sir George Gilbert Scott* in 1877–8. Moreover, the octagonal top stage and the spire of the NW tower or rather turret is by *John Oldrid Scott*, 1887. The plan of the church seems complicated in that Scott added the transepts as well as the chancel. His are the shafted lancets and the groups of three. – Inside a very fine painted FRIEZE by *Heywood Sumner*, 1897. Vine trails and large drop-shaped medallions with figures of angels.

BREWOOD

Brewood, pronounced Brood, is an engaging little town, even if only four houses qualify for a mention here. The peach is SPEEDWELL CASTLE in MARKET PLACE, looking down Stafford Street. This is a delectable folly, Gothick, of c.1750, brick, three-storeyed, with two canted bay windows, round-arched and ogee windows, and an ornate ogee doorway. Battlements of course. The house was built out of the proceeds of betting on 'Speedwell', the Duke of Bolton's horse. (Inside, elaborate plaster ceiling and Chinese-Chippendale staircase.) The other houses are in DEAN STREET, S and SE of the church, all three of brick. THE CHANTRY is of five bays, with a pedimented doorway. WEST GATE is Early Georgian (dated 1723) of five bays and two storeys. Doorway with moulded surround and window with volutes over. DEAN STREET HOUSE is Late Georgian and has tripartite windows.

ST MARY AND ST CHAD. Perp W tower with a recessed spire. Early C13 chancel, long, with six lancets along the sides. The E windows are Victorian. The N aisle has Dec windows. But the S aisle was restored and to a certain extent reconstructed by *Street* in 1878–80. He had evidence that cross-gables had existed. So he built them, but in order to find a place for them, he created a narrow outer aisle with piers and arches in continuous mouldings. The window under each gable is a stepped lancet triplet. It makes a fine effect. The arcades between nave and aisles have tall octagonal piers, probably C13, but heightened early in the C16. There is no clerestory. – FONT. Cauldron-shaped. Just with panels framed by a roll. It is later C16? – REREDOS by *Caröe*, 1911. – PULPIT. By *Street*. Also LECTERN and STALLS (P. Joyce). – STAINED GLASS. Two chancel lancets by *Bryans*, a close imitator of Kempe, one signed (a hound). – PLATE. Silver-gilt Chalice and Cover, 1654; silver-gilt Paten, 1705 by *John Bodington*, London; Paten, 1718 by *Joseph Clare*, London. – MONUMENTS. In the chancel four large alabaster monuments, all of Giffards of Chillington, all husbands and wives, and all four men bearded. Sir John † 1556 with two wives. On the tomb-chest thirteen babies in swaddling clothes and one son and four daughters (s). – Sir Thomas † 1560 and two wives. On the tomb-chest 24 frontal figurines and primitively twisted colonnettes (N). – John † 1613 and wife, with fourteen figurines against the tomb-chest (N). – Walter † 1632 and wife. Arcaded tomb-chest without figures (s). – Also incised slab to Richard Lane † 1518 and wife. – Tablet to Matthew Moreton † 1669 and wife and parents (?). Two tiers of kneeling couples facing one another.

ST MARY (R.C.). By *Pugin*, 1843–4. Not as starved as most of his churches, but certainly not thrilling either. Thin w steeple with broach-spire. Nave, aisles, and lower chancel, slate-roofed. The style is Middle Pointed, i.e. *c*.1300–30. Four bays of octagonal piers. – STAINED GLASS. One light of the N aisle E window by *Wailes* was given by Pugin.

Pugin also did the PRIEST'S HOUSE and the SCHOOL. They are plain gabled brick houses with mullioned windows, without anything done for display, nor with any symmetry for its own sake. In fact a house like this priest's house anticipates Butterfield and Street, and so Webb and Red House.

(AVENUE BRIDGE. By *Telford*. Stone, rusticated, with excessively tapered pilasters and a balustrade parapet. NMR)

BLACKLADIES. The house incorporates* remains of a Benedictine nunnery in existence *c*. 1140. T-shaped plan. Brick. A symmetrical façade, but the fenestration still asymmetrical so as to emphasize the position of the hall. Two canted bay windows and a (later) porch. Mullioned and transomed windows. Two large stepped dormers, and also stepped end-gables. One wants to know more about the house.

THE ROMAN SETTLEMENT of Pennocrucium lay partly in this parish and partly in that of Penkridge. It consisted of a straggling roadside village on the frontages of Watling Street. On the S fringe of the settlement lay the ENGLETON ROMAN VILLA, a porticoed house with a small bath wing. It was occupied from the C2 to the C4. Astride Watling Street lay a rectangular defended enclosure, measuring 700 ft by 450 ft,

---

* So the DOE says.

BRIERLEY HILL

2½ m. sw of Dudley

St Michael, Church Street. 1765. Brick. The w tower restored and largely rebuilt in 1900. The top is hardly facsimile. Side of four bays with the two middle ones projecting and pedimented. Two tiers of windows, arched below and small and segment-arched above. Brick quoins. The chancel more ornate inside. It must belong to the restoration of 1873–88. The church faces ten new high blocks of flats. As if a place like Brierley Hill needed any.

Christ Church, High Street, Quarry Bank. By *Thomas Smith* 1845–6. A Commissioners' church. Yellow brick, lancet-Gothic transepts, chancel of 1900. Thin hammerbeam roof.

St John, High Street, Brockmoor. By *Thomas Smith*, 1844–5. Also a Commissioners' church. Neo-Norman, of plum and yellow brick. Bellcote; no tower. Transepts and a short chancel.

(St John, Dudley Wood. 1931 by *Sir Charles Nicholson*. GR)

St Mary (R.C.), High Street, E of the parish church. 1872–3 by *E. W. Pugin*. Brick, nave and chancel in one; no tower. Windows to the (ritual) s with plate tracery. A typical asymmetrical, busy E.W.P. front, and inside typical E.W.P. capitals.

Civic Buildings, Bank Street. Of brick, large and not symmetrical. By *J. P. Moore*, early fifties to 1962.

BROCKMOOR see BRIERLEY HILL

BROCTON

Brocton Hall. Early C19 house of five by five bays, rendered. Top storey removed after a fire in 1939. The main front is very impressive. It has a central bow with the porch set in it. The porch has giant Tuscan columns, and columns continue detached along the bow, three l., three r. Fine circular entrance hall and behind it a fine staircase, through both floors, with a dainty iron trellis handrail. The staircase has a Venetian window and above that a tripartite lunette window. Near the house an octagonal Dovecote, made Gothick by pointed and quatrefoil windows. Also between kitchen garden and pond

Gothick arrangement of two arches. They are genuine Gothic arches, one for a window with most of the tracery broken out, the other for a doorway. They are said to come from St Thomas's Priory near Stafford.

BROUGHTON

ST PETER. 1630–4, Gothic, but Gothic of that debased kind. Windows straight-headed with round-arched lights. Two-bay arcades. – (FONT. Small basin set in a niche at the w end of the church. Jeavons) – High BOX PEWS, a rare sight nowadays. – COMMUNION RAIL. Georgian. – STAINED GLASS. C15 glass, including whole figures, in the E window. – Good later heraldic glass in the chancel N windows. – S aisle by *Kempe*. – PLATE. Chalice and Paten by *F.S.*, 1672; Flagon and Paten by *E. & Co.*, 1812. – MONUMENTS. Many tablets, the best the cartouches to William Bagot † 1687 and Spencer Broughton † 1702/3. – Also, of several marbles, Sir Brian Broughton † 1766.

BROUGHTON HALL. The most spectacular piece of black and white in the county, made more spectacular in 1926–39 by *W. & S. Owen*, who doubled the size of the house and interpolated a great deal of stone architecture as well, e.g. the great hall (now chapel) with its huge window. The original work is dated 1637. It is of three storeys with gables over the l. and r. end bays and plenty of cusped concave-sided lozenges and a few similar motifs. On the ground floor are shafts carrying ornamental tablets, on the first floor the windows are boxed out on carved brackets. For the overhang of the second floor, which contains the long gallery, there are grotesque corbels as supports. The staircase is typical 1630s, but the wood-carved urns on the newel-posts must be c.1660. They are said to come from Holland. The long gallery has a frieze with stories, beasts, and monsters.

GERARDS BROMLEY HALL, 1¼ m. NE. The present house has good C17 gatepiers and a C17 barn with mullioned windows. The masonry of the house must partly be that of Sir Gilbert Gerard's mansion of c.1575, of which only the porch remains, transferred to Batchacre Hall (*see* p. 67). The mansion was called by Plott 'the most magnificent structure of all this county'. Plott's illustration shows a high block of nine bays of which the angle bays are solid and have normal windows in two tiers, whereas the rest have only one tier – but they are very high, of four or even six lights, with four transoms. The range has shaped gables, and behind seem to have been four turrets with ogee caps. The gatehouse was two-storeyed with polygonal towers.

CHARNES HALL, ⅞ m. E. Early Georgian,* a nine-bay front with quoins of even rustication. The middle bays project, and at the top behind them a big segmental pediment appears. Porch of four Tuscan columns.

BROWN EDGE

9050

ST ANNE. 1844 by *J. & C. Trubshaw*. Norman, with a very short chancel. In 1854 H. H. Williamson donated a NE steeple. The architects were *Ward & Son* of Hanley (CPDD). They certainly had a lot of self-confidence, little bothered about antiquarian accuracy: just note the way the turret with conical roof gets mixed up with the square (not octagonal) spire. Or where could one see spire lucarnes in pairs? Small but sumptuous w doorway into the tower (Mr Williamson's doorway) and large sumptuous arch between tower and nave. – STAINED GLASS. A beautiful *Morris* window of 1874. The Ascension and fine single figures, the latter placed against a background of vine. Figures by *Burne-Jones*, foliage by *Morris*. – To the N of the church Mr Williamson built himself a small two-storeyed range for horse and carriage below, for himself between services above.

The PARSONAGE is probably mid C19 too.

(KNYPERSLEY WATER MILL, NNW of Brown Edge. Dated 1827. Stone, the windows segment-headed with raised ashlar surrounds.)

BROWNHILLS

0000

Brownhills has over 26,000 inhabitants. Yet it is not an entity, let alone a town.

ST JAMES. 1850–1 by *G. T. Robinson* of Wolverhampton. Aisleless, with pairs of pointed trefoiled windows. Transepts and a half-projecting w tower with a short spire and a w porch. A three-light E window with geometrical tracery. – STAINED GLASS. Art Nouveau in the w window.

BUCKNALL *see* STOKE-ON-TRENT, p. 266

BUDDLEIGH *see* BETLEY

---

* Or *c*.1680 according to Dr Gomme, who refers also to Georgian alterations to the top storey and the interior.

BURNTWOOD

CHRIST CHURCH. 1819–20 by *Joseph Potter*, the N aisle 1869 by *Stevens & Robinson* of Derby. Light brick, W tower, windows with Y-tracery, short chancel.

MAPLE HAYES, 1¾ m. ENE. *See* p. 201.

BURSLEM see STOKE-ON-TRENT, p. 253

BURTON-ON-TRENT

There is plenty that is dreary at Burton, terraces of dreary brick cottages and big dreary industrial premises behind high walls. But there are two visually redeeming features – the leafy stretch by the river Trent right in the centre and the suburban churches. That they are large and dignified is due to the brewers who built the dreary breweries and often also the dreary cottages. As for the BREWERIES they are not without interest from the point of view of industrial archaeology and even of architecture, and the County Planning Department has had the kindness to provide some special paragraphs on them. They will be found on pp. 88–91. Burton-on-Trent has only just over 50,000 inhabitants. So the description here will be divided into an Inner and an Outer Burton, but the Outer needs only elementary subdividing.

INNER BURTON

ST MODWEN. 1719–26 by *William & Richard Smith* of Tettenhall, completed by *Francis Smith*. Almost identical with the Smith church at Whitchurch in Shropshire. The Burton parish church is handsomely set against the trees along the bank of the river. Powerful W tower with balustrade and urns, very large windows, entrances in the W bays of the nave; E apse. Interior with big Tuscan columns and the parapets of the wooden galleries set between them. The interior was remodelled in 1889 by *W. Tate*. The decoration of the sanctuary is by *Powell*'s, the plasterwork by *Battiscombe & Harris*, the REREDOS by *Farmer & Brindley*. The most recent redecoration is the work of *Campbell Smith* (1961). – FONT. Octagonal bowl, Perp, with arches and tracery patterns. – COMMUNION RAIL. Probably of c.1730. – ORGAN CASE. A splendid piece of neo-classicism of 1771 (and 1902). – STAINED GLASS. Mostly by *T. F. Curtis* of London; it looks c.1900.* – CHANDELIER.

* Mr H. H. Pitchford however writes that the glass is of 1865.

Of brass. Inscribed 1725. – PLATE. Chalice and Paten, 1662 by *W.M.*; Paten, 1694; Paten, 1699–1700 by *John Downes*, London; Flagon, 1726; Flagon, 1727 by *R.B.*; Chalice, 1795 by *Emes & Edward Barnard*; two Chalices and a Flagon, 1796 by *Thomas Howell*, London. – MONUMENTS. Lady Fowler † 1825 by *Sir Richard Westmacott*. Seated woman by a pedestal. – Thomas Fosbrooke Salt † 1864, with Faith, Hope, and Charity. High Victorian Gothic. – William Worthington † 1871. Gothic, with three seated allegories.

CHRIST CHURCH, Uxbridge Street. 1843–4 by *Joseph Mitchell* of Sheffield. A Commissioners' church. It cost over £3,200, and is very typical of major Commissioners' churches. W tower, pairs of lancets in the nave between thin buttresses, transepts, and a short chancel.

ST MARY AND ST MODWENA (R.C.), Guild Street. 1878–9 by *Morley* of Burton. Brick NW tower with a tricky top and short spire.

HOLY TRINITY, Horninglow Street. 1880–2 by *J. Oldrid Scott*.* Large and ambitious, the money coming from the Allsopp family. E.E. style with free details. Proud NW steeple, transeptal projection, a porch by the steeple, and windows with Kentish tracery between porch and transeptal feature. S aisle with twice as many windows as piers. Big chancel arch, very large E window, high openings to chancel chapels. – (STAINED GLASS. From the old church of 1823–4.) – PLATE. Set of 1824 by *Robert Gainsford* of Sheffield.‡

TOWN HALL. *See* Outer Burton, p. 86.

ART GALLERY AND MUSEUM, Guild Street. 1914–15 by *Henry Beck* of Burton.

LIBRARY, Union Street. 1878. High and narrow; Gothic.

MAGISTRATES' COURT, Horninglow Street. 1909–10 by *Henry Beck*. Small, of white artificial stone, symmetrical and with a dome. It might be a variety theatre. The Baroque style inspired by Rickards.

MARKET HALL, next to the parish church. 1883–4 by *Dixon & Moxon* of Barnsley.

TRENT BRIDGE. 1863–4. Partly of iron.

PERAMBULATION. Much new shopping, including two precincts, has recently been provided, but a number of older worthwhile houses remain – not however the oldest, Lady

---

* Demolished in 1971.
‡ HOLY TRINITY SCHOOL and MASTER'S HOUSE, Hawkins Lane. According to Mr Joyce by *Street*, 1859–60.

Paulett's Almshouses of 1593. They have fallen victim to the new SHOPPING CENTRE by *S. Greenwood*. The other is called BARGATES and is by *Willoughby, Fletcher & Associates*. Only two walks are needed: from the bridge w, and from the bridge s.

First w. At once in BRIDGE STREET No. 22, a house with a pedimented doorcase on Tuscan demi-columns, and opposite TRENT HOUSE of five bays with an Ionic entry *in antis* and a pedimented window over – early C19. Then in HORNINGLOW STREET No. 5 with a Tuscan doorcase as before opposite No. 181, much finer, three bays, doorcase with Adamish columns and pediment, tripartite windows l. and r., decorated mid-window. No. 180 is earlier. It has windows with moulded surrounds. No. 6 opposite has a pretty tripartite doorway. No. 167 is of five bays with an ornamented doorcase and mid-window and a one-bay pediment. To its r. a link, then a three-bay building with two pediments.

Back to the bridge and s down the HIGH STREET. The old houses are smaller here. What dominates the beginning of the street is the BASS BREWERY ranges of simple Jacobean type. Of Georgian buildings it is sufficient to mention No. 102 at the corner of Horninglow Street for its shop windows and Egyptian lettering. Nos. 61–2 have a pair of small doorways with broken pediments. No. 54 is of four bays with a doorway of Tuscan demi-columns and a triglyph frieze. Opposite No. 146, the best house, set back, *c*.1760, five bays with one-bay pediment, a tripartite lunette window below, and a Venetian mid-window. Staircase of alternating turned and twisted balusters.* Finally No. 148 of six bays with another Tuscan doorcase. The High Street then meets the Market Square.

In continuation of the High Street Nos. 9 and 10 LICHFIELD STREET, a pair, even if not identical. Both are of three bays and have tripartite ground-floor windows, i.e. early C19. In the gardens of Lichfield Street is the bronze WAR MEMORIAL (by *Henry C. Fehr*, *c*.1922). To end with, between the Market Hall and the river the ABBEY (now a club), a rambling Victorian house in its grounds, built into and over the INFIRMARY of the Benedictine Abbey. BURTON ABBEY was founded for Benedictines in 1004. The church N of the present site, 228 ft long, seems to have had two transepts and two crossing towers – German rather than Anglo-French. But the oldest illustrations are hard to interpret and contradict each

---

* On Bass's brewery and on the High Street *see* p. 89.

other.* Excavations have produced the doorway from the E end of the S aisle to the cloister and traces of the S, i.e. refectory, range of the cloister.‡ What is still upright belongs to subsidiary buildings. There are two ranges only, forming an L. Both were parts of the infirmary. One has a roof of six trusses with wind-braces, the other was the chapel. This has to E and W a window of three stepped lancet lights. In the corner of the site by the parish church is a re-erected arch.

OUTER BURTON

(A) The Town Hall Area

This area must at once be singled out; the rest can be lumped together (plus an extra section on the breweries). For Town Hall, St Paul, and some other buildings close by form a centre competing with the old. The site for the Town Hall seems oddly chosen, so far out, but it was first built as the St Paul's Church Institute, and became the Town Hall only in 1894.

TOWN HALL, King Edward Place. 1878 and 1894. The work of 1878 was done at the expense of Michael Thomas Bass, the work of 1894 at the expense of Michael Arthur Bass, first Lord Burton. Not very large. Gothic, with a closely decorated flat front and a projecting tower at the l. end, rather disjointed. There is an extension to the l. and a depressing extension of 1938–9 by *Thomas Jenkins* to the r. Of 1894 are the Municipal Offices, the Council Chamber with its ornate plaster ceiling, the rest of the Council Suite, the Concert Hall, and the Staircase. The latter with its iron balustrade is lively and impressive. It goes up through two storeys and is sky-lit. – INSIGNIA. Mayor's Chain and Badge, presented in 1878 by W. H. Worthington, the first Mayor. In the Square STATUE of the first Lord Burton by *F. W. Pomeroy*, unveiled 1911. Facing the square is the E end of St Paul's – *see* below.

Close to the square in WELLINGTON STREET the Gothic brick ALMSHOUSES of *c*.1875. Three ranges, U-wise. One-storeyed with wooden porches, but a two-storeyed centre with an oriel. Asymmetrically set turret.

ST PAUL. 1874 by *J. M. Teale* and *Lord Grimthorpe*. Built at the expense of Michael Thomas Bass (who also paid for St Margaret, now demolished). Large and expensively done.

* The church area is now market place and parish church.
‡ Where the cloister was is now the Market Hall.

Geometrical style, with a crossing tower and transepts; five-bay arcades with naturalistic capitals. By *Bodley* the huge overdecorated ORGAN CASE, the ceiling PAINTING of the chancel, the wooden SCREENS, and the whole S chapel.

(B) The Rest

ST AIDAN, Shobnall Road (NW). 1884 by *Giles & Brookhouse*. Brick, not large.

SHOBNALL GRANGE, SW of the church, has a C17 part with old brickwork and mullioned and transomed windows.

ALBION BREWERY, Shobnall Road. *See* p. 89.

ALL SAINTS, Branston Road (SW). 1903–5 by *Naylor & Sale* of Derby. Dec style. A large building paid for by William Bass. Tall NW tower, low baptistery with a large nave W window over and a porch on the r. of this. Five-bay arcades, high chancel arch, seven-light E window. The details are Arts and Crafts Gothic, though the architectural conception is still Victorian. See especially the vestry entrance and the FONT, the PULPIT, and the low stone SCREEN.

ST CHAD, Hunter Street (N). The best building by far in Burton, and one of *Bodley*'s late masterpieces. Designed in 1903 and completed after Bodley's death by *Cecil Hare* in 1910. The most brilliant invention is the NW tower separated by a rib-vaulted corridor from the N aisle and thus standing, tall and erect, almost on its own. The walls are sheer, as are the church walls. The entrance alone is allowed decorative ease: the doorway, a canopied niche, and the window above form a unity. To the W the polygonal stair projection is attached to the middle of that side, and the flanking buttresses have no set-off until they have reached the top of the projection. The E view of the church is convincing, though it cannot be fully taken in. A N chapel taller than the aisle with a reredos-like composition on its E wall and then stepped-back chancel, S chapel, and a polygonal chapter-house-like vestry. The prevailing style is Bodley's Dec throughout. The interior has five bays with slender piers and the aisle windows in deep reveals. This magnificent church was built at the expense of the first Lord Burton. It cost £38,000. – REREDOS in the N chapel, as typical of Bodley as the tower. Yet the grandeur of the tower and the busy-ness of the reredos don't easily make up into one personality. – PLATE. Silver-gilt Paten and two Almsplates by *Thomas Howell*, London, 1796.

ST JOHN THE EVANGELIST, Horninglow Road (N). 1864–6 by *Edwin Holmes* of Birmingham. SW steeple, geometrical tracery, French Early Gothic capitals. Run-of-the-mill, but also large and expensively done.

ST MARGARET, Shobnall Street. 1881 by *Reginald Churchill*, at the expense of Michael Thomas Bass, father of the first Lord Burton; late work by *Bodley*. Demolished in 1968.

ST MARK, Church Hill Street, Winshill (E). 1869 by *Holmes*. Again large and ambitious SW steeple with broach-spire. Geometrical tracery. Curious arcade piers. The money for building the church was given by John Gretton.

ST PETER, Stapenhill Road (SE). 1880–1 by *Evans & Jolly* of Nottingham. SW tower with a top of different stone. The top is ornate, the rest of the church remarkably matter-of-fact. All side windows are small and straight-headed and of the same pattern. In the clerestory are two windows to each bay. The chancel arch is omitted. – (MONUMENT. An incised slab of 1497. Kelly)

CEMETERY, Stapenhill Road (SE). 1865–6. Uninteresting chapel, but an enterprising gateway.

Finally, not a church, but the most prominent tower: the square brick WATER TOWER of 1907 on the hill E of the cemetery.

(C) *The Breweries of Burton**

Burton beer was known in London in the C17, and by the end of the C18 it was being extensively exported from Hull to the Baltic. Few early buildings associated with the brewing industry survive, owing to the great expansion that followed the arrival of the railway in 1839. Within thirty years the breweries covered 174 acres, and there were 76 ale-stores, 20 cooperages, and 104 malt-houses, quite apart from pumping-houses, water-towers, and offices. Although the gypsum in the water gave the beer its special quality and although the union system of fermentation was characteristic of the Burton area, the architecture of the breweries was not itself distinctive, and non-local architects such as *George Scamell* of London were employed. The typical brewery of the late C19 emphasized by its architecture the duality of function: the tall, irregular part was where the many separate processes of brewing were piled on top of one another to exploit the force of gravity; the large uniform part was divided

* The County Planning and Development Department kindly provided this account.

into rooms for cooling, fermenting, and racking. Both parts of the brewery invited cast-iron construction, the former because of the fire risk, the latter because of the spans that were needed.

Most of the late C19 Burton breweries were in the centre of the town, in continuance of an existing tradition, but not so the malthouses. So long as the germination of the barley was controlled by spreading it with shovels and ploughs the floor areas of malthouses were immense. They were therefore relegated to the outskirts of the town, the disadvantage of separation being reduced by the private railway system that until 1967 crossed and re-crossed the Burton streets. The architecture of the malthouses matched that of the breweries, the greatest opportunity for variety being provided by the roofs of the kilns.

Since 1950, changes due partly to technology, partly to organization, and partly to drinking habits have transformed the Burton scene even more radically than the coming of the railway. The best groups of early malthouses now to be seen are those erected by Bass in Wetmore Road (1863–4) and off Shobnall Road (1873–91). A malthouse (c.1883) in Clarence Street is remarkable for having an octagonal kiln, the answer to the use of steam-powered machinery. The earliest brewery in operation is that of Bass in Station Street (opened 1864). Black Eagle Brewery, Derby Street (by *George Scamell*, c.1875), and Albion Brewery, Shobnall Road (by *W. & S. T. Martin* of Nottingham, 1875) illustrate the typical design of the late C19. The Bass town house, the Tudor-style offices (c.1880), and the 120-ft-high water-tower (1866) are all that is left in the area of Bass's Old Brewery.

ALBION BREWERY, Shobnall Road. Designed by *W. & S. T. Martin* of Nottingham in 1875 for the London-based firm of Mann, Crossman & Paulin. The brewery proper stands at the centre of the site; it is of red brick and impressive, and the semicircular-headed panels all round make the exterior unusually uniform. It overshadows the cooperage (now the engineer's shops) at the NW corner of the site, and the stables (now stores) along Crossman Street. On the rest of the estate, Mann, Crossman & Paulin built a MODEL VILLAGE with cottages, houses, a hotel, and the church of St Aidan; Shobnall Grange was used as the manager's house. For the church and the Grange, *see* p. 87.

BASS BREWERIES, High Street etc. Bass's first brewery, like many others at Burton, began as the adjunct to a town house. The house, bought in 1777, was the building now known as

No. 136 High Street, and its grounds extended towards the river Trent. The OLD BREWERY, as it continued to be called despite reconstruction in 1884–5, was demolished in 1971, and the only other buildings to remain in this part of the town are the Tudor-style offices that date from about 1880 and the 120-ft-high tower, dated 1866. A steam-engine pumped the water to a 60,000-gallon tank in the tower.

The MIDDLE BREWERY was built in 1853. The brewhouse was demolished in 1960, and since then the fermenting buildings have been adapted to receive other plant. The engineer's office and the extensive ale and hop stores are dated about 1853 and 1865 respectively. In the yard north of 'The Middle', the three-storey joiners' shop dates from 1866. The Electric Cooperage, formerly the Steam Cooperage, was built in 1864, and two of its machines are now in the County Museum at Shugborough.

NEW BREWERY ('Bass No. 2 Brewery') on the opposite corner of Station Street and Guild Street started production in 1864 and has thus become the oldest of Bass's Burton breweries. The two shortened stacks are dated 1863.

BASS MALTINGS, Wetmore Road. On the W side of what was formerly Anderstaff Lane six malthouses run parallel to one another. Nos. 16 and 17 at the N end comprise a single range, three storeys high and inscribed 'ERECTED 1863'. The barley intake is at the centre, and the production proceeds thence to the opposite ends of the range. Nos. 18–21, inscribed 'ERECTED 1864', are single houses and have the barley store incorporated over the top of the working floors. The building to the W of malthouse No. 18 is an empty engine-house. Floor malting continued at Wetmore Road until about 1965.

BASS MALTINGS, Shobnall. In 1887 the range of maltings at Shobnall was said to be the largest in the world belonging to any one brewery. Nos. 1, 2, 3, and 4 date from 1873; Nos. 5 and 6 from 1874; No. 7 from 1875. They are all four storeys high. Nos. 1–7 were designed by *William Canning*, the company's chief engineer, and the total cost was nearly £100,000. An eighth malthouse, designed by *Herbert Couchman*, has compound riveted steel joists and was added at a distance to the S in 1891. Nos. 4 and 5 malthouses are separated by a pumping station, and there is a second station beside No. 8.

Despite their wide-flung distribution, a common architectural treatment, substantial construction, and a high standard of craftsmanship unify the buildings that were erected by Bass in the second half of the C19. Externally the red brick walls are relieved by round-headed panels linked at spring-level by a stone string-course. Internally there is prodigious use of deal* and a partiality for queen-post roof trusses.

BLACK EAGLE BREWERY, Derby Street. Truman, Hanbury, Buxton & Co. Ltd, a London-based firm, in 1873 bought a small existing brewery beside the main railway and proceeded to build a new one, which was designed by *George Scamell* of London. The block, 280 by 75 ft, is of red brick. The taller part, surmounted by a turret, is the brewhouse. The first floor of the engineer's shop and laboratory was formerly a reading room, workmen's hall, and mess-room. Other provision for the staff is seen in the eighteen foremen's cottages, Nos. 219–228 Derby Street, and in the head brewer's house, now the offices, at the entrance to the brewery forecourt.

CLARENCE STREET BREWERY (former). A reset stone tablet records that Clarence Street Brewery was erected in 1883, and that *Scamell & Collyer* of London were the architects. The brewery itself ceased to be used as such about 1925 and has since been reduced in size and altered internally. But the maltings were not converted to grain stores until 1967 and they still possess some of the features that made them unusual. The striking oddity is the octagonal kiln, surmounted by a goat-shaped copper vane, at the Clarence Street end of the northern malthouse. It was circular inside originally and was the only one of this shape noted by Alfred Barnard. The shape was determined by the use of steam-driven prongs and brushes for turning of the malt. The 5 h.p. steam engine has been removed from alongside the kiln, but the recess to receive part of the flywheel shows where it stood.

BURY BANK see STONE,

BURY RINGS see BRADLEY

BUSHBURY see WOLVERHAMPTON, p. 320

BUTTERTON

3 m. SW of Newcastle-under-Lyme

ST THOMAS. 1844 by *Thomas Hopper* of London (CPDD). Neo-Norman and very substantial, though not big. Crossing

---

* The deal would have been supplied by the timber-merchant, William Bass, who was a brother of Michael Thomas Bass.

tower with a pyramid roof and a plaster rib-vault inside. – Several BOX PEWS. – MONUMENTS. Mary Milbourne Swinnerton † 1854, with a standing female figure, and Sir William Milbourne Milbourne Swinnerton Pilkington † 1855, with a draped urn. Both by *G. Lewis & Co.* of Cheltenham.

BUTTERTON GRANGE, 1 m. E. A square red-brick farmhouse, by the great *Soane* himself, and as idiosyncratic as any of his late buildings. The date here is 1816–17. The front is of only three bays, the side of two. Each bay has two giant pilasters, but they are slightly set in from the angles, and at the end of the façade the real angles are canted. The middle bay is recessed, and the giant pilasters here look at one another. One is immediately reminded of some of the neo-neo-classicists of the Reilly moment. Soane's designs for the interior were not carried out.

BUTTERTON
Near Wetton

ST BARTHOLOMEW. 1871–3 by *Ewan Christian*. But the W spire, the only more than adequate part of the building, is of 1879 by *Sugden*. The style of the chancel is late C13 to early C14. – FONT. Dec, with representations of windows with three-light intersecting tracery. – STAINED GLASS. E 1872 by *Powell*, designed by *Wooldridge*. – PLATE. Paten with head of Christ, *c.*1475.

BYRKLEY LODGE *see* RANGEMORE

CALDMORE *see* WALSALL, p. 293

CALDMORE GREEN *see* WALSALL, p. 294

CALLOW HILL *see* BLITHFIELD

CALTON

ST MARY. 1839. Nave and short chancel; bell-turret, widely spaced lancet windows. – COMMUNION RAIL. Two panels and one loose one of *c.*1670. Juicy openwork foliage. No doubt imported.

BANK HOUSE, a little W of the church. 1743 and very conservative. Three wide bays, two and a half storeys. Symmetrically arranged windows in the rhythm 2-1-2 lights. The windows are still mullioned, but the doorway has a pediment.

ROUND CAIRNS, ½ m. E, on Marsden Low. Four, of the Bronze Age; the largest (w) is 70 ft in diameter. All were excavated in the C19 and covered Bronze Age inhumation and cremation burials and a number of secondary Anglo-Saxon interments.

CALWICH ABBEY see ELLASTONE

CANNOCK

Cannock for its size – 55,000 inhabitants – and for its position as a centre of Staffordshire coal mining has remarkably little to offer in the way of notable buildings. The DOE allots Grade II to five and altogether lists only eight.

ST LUKE. A large town church, but only the w half is medieval. The two E bays of nave and aisles, the chancel, and the vestry date from 1878–82 (*N. Joyce* of Stafford), the s chapel from 1949. As for the medieval parts, there is some late C12 or early C13 masonry in the N aisle; the w tower is clearly C14 (ogee-headed doorway to the N); so are the arcades (octagonal piers, arches with sunk-quadrant mouldings); and the s aisle fenestration is Late Perp. – PLATE. Elizabethan Chalice; Dish of 1680 by *R.H.*, London; Flagon by *Frank Spilsbury*, London, 1733; two Dishes by the same, 1741; Paten by *P. & W. Bateman*, 1806.

Close to the church in HIGH GREEN are the COUNCIL OFFICES, a Mid Georgian house behind splendid iron GATES (attributed to *Bakewell*). Stuccoed five-bay front of two storeys with a parapet curving up on the gable sides. Doorway with elegant pediment. Close to the house the TANK TOWER, a conduit house. Octagonal, of stone, with a peaked roof – quite small.

LONGFORD HOUSE, 1¼ m. SW, at the junction of A 5 and A 460. Three bays and two storeys with low one-bay wings surmounted by shaped gables. Brick and brownstone. Probably c. 1840.

CASTLE RING, ½ m. N of Cannock Wood. A multivallate contour fort enclosing 8 acres and defended on the weaker (s) side by five lines of ramparts and elsewhere by two. Inturned entrance on the E.

CANNOCK CHASE

POST OFFICE TOWER, Pye Green. This is the most conspicuous object of Cannock Chase. It serves telephone communication by air. Round concrete pillar, and above the necessary excrescences which, although strictly functional, look with their shoots and trumpets like the fantasy of a sculptor of 1970. The whole is 258 ft high.

(GERMAN MILITARY CEMETERY. This excellent piece of work was designed by *Diez Brandi*.)

CANWELL

Canwell had a Benedictine priory. It was founded by the widow of Geoffrey Ridal *c*.1140.

ST MARY, ST GILES, AND ALL SAINTS. 1911 by *Temple Moore*. Not large, but very much a complete unit. Short W tower, nave with three-light Dec windows and broad buttresses without set-offs. The chancel projects very little. Complex NE group with the vestry. (Beautifully simple and clear interior. It is of ashlar and rib-vaulted. No aisles, and no structural division between nave and chancel, though the chancel windows are slightly emphasized. The vaults are quadripartite and have carved bosses. – PANELLING to the lower part of the walls. – STAINED GLASS. E and W windows by *E. V. Milner*. – Nave N window by *Geoffrey Webb*, 1938. EH) – Excellent GATEPIERS of elementary geometry.

(CANWELL HALL. The house consisted of a centre and two wings which were added by *James Wyatt*. Only one wing remains.)

CASTERN HALL see ILAM

CAULDON

ST MARY AND ST LAWRENCE. 1781–4, the chancel with some earlier work. W tower. The nave has quoins and large arched windows. A N aisle is divided from the nave by square pillars. – PLATE. Elizabethan Chalice and Paten.

OLD VICARAGE. Late C17. Stone, of two and a half storeys. Regular fenestration of 3-2-3 lights. Doorway with straight hood.

CAVERSWALL

St Peter. Low Perp w tower built into the earlier nave. The church basically late C12 (see the one N lancet*), the arcade basically C13 (see the piers); but the round arches are a surprise and may be connected with some rebuilding that went on in the early C17. To this obviously belongs the clerestory, and probably the large windows with intersected tracery, although that also is a late C13 motif which would go with the arcades. The chancel arch is of 1880 by *Lynam*. – PULPIT. Jacobean with the usual blank arches, though they are unusually small. – STAINED GLASS. By *Kempe* of 1880 the glass in the clerestory and more. – By *Holiday* N aisle E. – S aisle E by *Selwyn Image*, 1907.‡ Two figures remarkably stylized for their date. – CHANDELIER. Of *c.*1820 (cf. Abbots Bromley).§ – PLATE. Silver-gilt Portuguese dish, *c.*1500; silver-gilt Flagon, 1614; Tray by *Richard Gurney & Co.*, 1714; silver-gilt Chalice and Paten by *Richard Gurney & Thomas Cook*, 1760. – MONUMENTS. George Cradock † 1642. Pedestal and urn, astonishingly classical for its date. Indeed a foretaste of the C18. – Two triptych tablets to members of the Parker family; late C17. – Sir Thomas Parker † 1784. Standing woman by an urn. – Countess of St Vincent. By *Chantrey*, 1818. White marble figure of a kneeling young woman in the round.

Caverswall Castle. Licence to crenellate was given in 1275. That fits the shape of the castle – a roughly oblong enclosure with four polygonal angle towers. They and the walls do not stand to full height. The towers were terminated by balustrading at the time, *c.* 1615, when Matthew Cradock built a house into the castle. This is attributed by Dr Mark Girouard to *Robert* or more probably *John Smythson*. It is a fine building, high and even, three-storeyed and fully symmetrical. Centre of three bays, and close to the angles a canted bay on either side. The windows are mostly of three lights with one transom. Round the corner a higher staircase tower. The top balustrade was replaced in the C19 by crenellation. Inside much brought-in C17 woodwork.

Close to the castle St Filomena (R.C.). 1863–4 by *Gilbert Blount*.

---

* Part of a C12 tympanum was discovered in 1962 but not exposed. It formed part of the sill of the N aisle E window and may have had a representation of Daniel in the lions' den or Alexander carried by eagles.

‡ I heard of this from Mrs Tickner.

§ Mr Sherlock told me of this.

CHAPEL CHORLTON

ST LAWRENCE. The W tower is medieval but was remodelled by *James Trubshaw Jun.* in 1826–7. The nave and chancel are by Trubshaw, not large, though the nave has five windows along the sides. The E window is tripartite with a lunette over, and the whole tripartite part is blank. – PULPIT. Jacobean, with the familiar blank arches and also panels with rosettes.

CHARNES HALL see BROUGHTON

CHARTLEY HOLME

CHARTLEY CASTLE was built by Ranulph Blundeville, Earl of Chester, in the early C13. It is in ruins. Round keep on a motte. Only foundations of this survive. Also curtain wall with two round towers out of originally five. Traces of earthworks earlier than the C13.

CHARTLEY HALL. Elizabethan. Built after a fire which took place in 1847.

(CHARTLEY FARMHOUSE. A symmetrical C17 house. Timber-framed gables with decorative motifs. NMR)

CHASETOWN

ST ANNE. Founded by John Robinson McLean, one of the pioneers of the working of the Cannock Chase coalfield (CPDD). The church was built in 1865 to the design of *Edward Adams*. He worked for the South Staffordshire Railway Company and the South Staffordshire Waterworks (CPDD). His is a church which hits hard. It is in an idiom uncommon in the sixties and used with conviction. Neo-Norman of brick with black brick decoration. No tower. Nave and chancel in one and a lower apse. Two two-light windows per bay, the arches with jagged cut-brick decoration. In the apse the windows high up are reminiscent of Italian or Rhenish dwarf galleries. Wide nave, thin brick columns with free Romanesque capitals inlaid in black; jagged arches. Open timber roof. Very odd clerestory windows. In the wide apse large panels in various marbles. – STAINED GLASS in abstract patterns. – PAINTING. Christ and the Children. Is it English of *c.*1800 ?*

---

* The church had electric light in 1883. That is remarkably early (but cf. Ingestre).

ST JOSEPH (R.C.), New Street. 1882–3.

CHEADLE

ST GILES (R.C.). 1841–6. Cheadle is *Pugin*-land. The Anglican parish church may be quite a substantial building, but what haunts you for miles around is the raised forefinger of Pugin's steeple pointing heavenward. Cheadle, Pugin wrote, is 'a perfect revival of an English parish church of the time of Edward I'. He said so not to praise himself but to praise the Earl of Shrewsbury, at whose expense the church was built. Only here and at St Augustine in Ramsgate, where he paid himself, was he free of financial stringency. St Augustine is simple and solid and antiquarianly correct – no more; Cheadle is decorated wherever decoration could find a place. But then Pugin was an affluent man, Lord Shrewsbury a very rich man. The Cheadle W steeple (the directions always meant in the ritual sense) is one of the most perfect pieces of C19 Gothic Revival anywhere, especially the sharp spire with two sets of pinnacles. The style is Dec, and Pugin, as we have heard, uses that style throughout the church. The E window is of five lights, with the four-petal motif at the top. Nave and aisles, lower chancel, and a N vestry annexe with a powerful staircase projection. Arcades of five bays with octagonal piers and moulded arches. In the chancel are SEDILIA and PISCINA, and opposite is the EASTER SEPULCHRE recess. The S porch has a pointed tunnel-vault with transverse arches. The church is painted all over: walls, even the piers, and the floor tiles are patterned too. Designed by *Pugin* also was the FONT, probably the FONT COVER, the REREDOS with the Coronation of the Virgin and six angels, the PULPIT with carved scenes, the SCREEN with coving, parapet, and rood (the STAINED GLASS is by *Wailes*).* Did he also design the SCULPTURE l. and r. of the E window: the Virgin and St Giles? – No doubt he did the high crocketed CROSS in the graveyard.

St Giles does not stand alone. To its SE (ritually) is the SCHOOL, of brick, very typical of *Pugin* in its combination of a picturesque asymmetrical front and a frankly utilitarian back wing with buttresses and regular fenestration. The turret is very Pugin too, with a truncated pyramid and a spirelet on the top. S of the steeple is the CONVENT OF ST JOSEPH, also of brick, with a tower with saddleback roof and a little wooden

---

* Recently thinned out by introducing clear glass round figures.

cloister of only two sides. The main wing is much altered but still has a few of the straight-headed two-light Pugin windows. The former PRESBYTERY is a little way away, in Chapel Street. Brick again, asymmetry again, mullioned and transomed, not Gothic windows. Typical Pugin chimneys.

ST GILES. The Anglican church, quite large too, was built in 1837–9 to the design of *J. P. Pritchett*. High, embraced w tower. Nave of six bays with tall two-light Perp windows with a transom, and with battlements. Short chancel. Thin octagonal piers. Of the three galleries only the W gallery remains. Open timber roof. The columns attached to the piers originally supported galleries. Some head-stops of hood-moulds come from the former church. – COMMUNION RAIL 1687, with twisted balusters. – PLATE. Set of 1807 by *Crispin Fuller*.

In WATTS PLACE is the former WORKHOUSE, mutilated. It is of brick and was built in 1775.

In TAPE STREET is CHEADLE MILL, formerly of J. & N Philips (cf. Tean). The oldest special buildings were of the 1790s, and the N end of the Tape Street front may belong to that date. The main building, moving back from Tape Street is of *c*.1823. It is of 114 by 51 ft and three storeys high. Three rows of iron columns on each floor inside. An extension built on the same system faces Tape Street. Iron roof trusses are preserved.

The MARKET PLACE is just an opening off the High Street. The far side is one Late Georgian terrace of ten bays and three storeys, dated 1819. It is of brick, with on the ground floor shop-windows in the form of wide, shallow bows. In the HIGH STREET also a number of houses worth looking out for. First the POLICE, with an ashlar front of three bays, a doorway with fluted capitals, and l. and r. Venetian windows: at the top a pediment right across. The WHEATSHEAF has a Tuscan porch and one of the best of Cheadle's enormous inn signs. Then the MARKET CROSS, an octagonal shaft on steps, probably C17. No. 77, farther out towards the parish church, is timber-framed. On the r. part some decorative motifs.

HALES HALL, 1 m. NE, is dated 1712. It has an exceptionally swagger front. Brick, of five bays and two storeys with stone quoins of even lengths, moulded window surrounds, a doorway with pilasters with sunk panels and an open scroll pediment, a mid-window with volutes at the foot and garlands

and three dormers with one open scrolly pediment and two
open concave-sided ones. Round the corner also five bays, also
a doorway, also even quoins, and also windows with moulded
surrounds. (Good staircase.)

CHEBSEY

8020

ALL SAINTS. A Norman church – see the chancel N window,
one nave N window splayed oddly diagonally, the (Late
Norman) N doorway, several of the typical shallow buttresses,
and the masonry. Of the E.E. period the four-bay S arcade
(round piers, double-chamfered arches), the S doorway (big
quadrant moulding), and the chancel arch. The tower arch
stands on the heads of a monster and a woman with caricatured
head-gear. Perp W tower with eight pinnacles. – COMMUNION
RAIL. 1682. With twisted balusters. – STAINED GLASS.
Several *Kempe* and *Kempe & Tower* windows. – In the churchyard remains of an Anglo-Saxon CROSS. Undecorated fat
round shaft turning square and then decorated, mainly with
(decayed) interlace.

WALTON HALL, ½ m. SW, in Eccleshall parish. A Late Classical,
but clearly Early Victorian house. White indeed dates it 1848.
The motifs subdued, the ashlar masonry fine. Front of five
bays with a canted middle bay window. At the back an
enormous porte-cochère with Tuscan columns.

CHECKLEY

0030

ST MARY. A very curious church; for much of what we see, be it
apparently Perp or be it apparently earlier, is done or re-used
by early C17 masons. We start with the puzzling W tower.
There is here a flat Norman buttress, the tower arch is Dec, the
top with the pretty bell-openings Perp. The embattled
clerestory has three-light windows of a Dec and Perp type, but
is all C17. The same windows appear in the S aisle. The N aisle
windows are more bluntly and undisguisedly C17. But the S
doorway is of *c.*1300 and no mistake. It has three orders of
columns. The porch on the other hand with its rib-vault must
remain doubtful. Finally the chancel. Here we are on safe
ground. These windows with intersected tracery, three lights
N and S, five lights E, are, in spite of the uncommon motif of
rosettes at the points of intersection, pure late C13. As for the
interior, the chancel arch goes with the chancel. The arcades
look fine, Late Norman to E.E., but they are probably re-used

and heightened. The E.E. N arcade is less problematic and ma[y] be in order; the S arcade is not to be trusted in the shape o[f] the piers and the shapes of the capitals. The low-pitched roo[f] is entirely C17. – FONT. Norman, of drum shape, with coars[e] ornament and a donkey. – SCREEN. To the S chapel. Of 192[?] by *Comper*, very pretty. – STALLS. Datable to *c*.1535; yet n[o] Renaissance details. Very summary poppyheads; linenfo[ld] panels. – STAINED GLASS. Good figures of the later C14 in th[e] chancel E, NE, and SE windows – saints, an evangelist, and [a] prophet – and in the E window also scenes: the Stoning of S[t] Stephen, the Sacrifice of Isaac, the Crucifixion, St Margar[et] and the Dragon, the Martyrdom of St Thomas Becket. Als[o] many coats of arms. – In the N aisle an anaemic St George b[y] *Comper*. – PLATE. Chalice of 1803 by *P., A., & W. Bateman*[;] Chalice of 1805 by *T. Phipps & E. Robinson*. – MONUMENT[S.] Cross-legged Knight, early C14, – Godfrey Foljambe † 15[..] and wife. Alabaster couple on a tomb-chest with shields. – ([In] the churchyard, *c*.25 ft from the S porch, two Saxon fragmen[ts] of a CROSS SHAFT or two cross shafts: interlace as well [as] figures. Also an undecorated fragment.)

CHEDDLETON

9050

ST EDWARD. Thomas Wardle, William Morris's friend, was [a] churchwarden here, which explains certain remarkable thing[s] about the church but not all. It has an E.E. N arcade of thre[e] bays with round piers, octagonal abaci, and double-chamfere[d] arches. The S arcade is Perp, the W tower Perp too. Fine D[ec] chancel with ogee-headed PISCINA and SEDILIA. Ballflow[er] in the mouldings. Ogee-headed also the priest's doorway. T[he] windows are Dec, but the large E window is by *George Gilbe*[rt] *Scott Jun.*, who restored the church in 1863–4. The S ais[le] windows must also be his.* – FONT. Alabaster, pre-1876. [–] REREDOS. A Flemish relief of the Deposition, but the wings make it a triptych by *Morris, Marshall & Co.*, pre-1866. T[he] wings have the Annunciation and on the back a flower patter[n.] Scott wrote to a churchwarden, presumably Wardle, in 186[?:] 'You are quite before the age in possessing such a work, as [I] do not know of any other church in England where such [a] thing is to be seen.'‡ Comments: no. 1, Scott Jun. was qui[te]

---

* The local architect for Scott was *Robert Edgar* of the Wedgwo[od] Memorial Institute at Burslem (*see* p. 254).

‡ I owe this quotation to the Ferriday Index.

before the age of Scott Sen., and no. 2, Scott Jun. did not know the early Bodley churches with Morris decoration. – STAINED GLASS. Much by *Morris*, and showing the important development from 1864 to 1869, from an early to a mature style. Of 1864 the delightful eight small figures (designed by *Ford Madox Brown*) in the chancel, of 1865 the two-light Baptism of Christ s aisle w, of 1869 the three large angels by *Burne-Jones*, s aisle s, with their ruby wings and their agitated drapery.* By Morris also N aisle E and N aisle NE. – LECTERN. A spectacular brass eagle, not English, but Flemish. – PLATE. Chalice of 1703 by *F.A.*; Paten 1706 by *D.*; two Chalices and Paten 1743 by *Richard Bayley*. – MONUMENT. Fynney family. Imaginative Gothic tablet with two head corbels. – The painted decoration of the chancel roof may be ascribed to *Scott* too. The charming decoration above the organ in the tower is recent. – In the churchyard high CROSS, the upper part by *Scott*, but the Instruments of the Passion designed by *Morris*, again pre-1876.

Scott Jun. designed the solid stone LYCHGATE with its saddleback roof, and also the SCHOOL and LIBRARY, where he used existing old parts. The school has two-light mullioned windows, but also a Dec window and a Dec doorway. Both jobs were done before 1876.

STATION. Picturesque Tudor on a small scale. The line was opened in 1849.

ASHCOMBE PARK, ¾ m. s. 1807–11 by *James Trubshaw Jun.* Ashlar, of two storeys and four bays. The bays project and have a three-bay Tuscan porte-cochère.

COUNTY MENTAL HOSPITAL, ¾ m. N. The centre block of brick, Elizabethan, symmetrical, with a middle tower, is by *Giles & Gough*, of 1895–9.

HAZLEHURST BRIDGE. *See* Endon.

FLINT MILLS. Flint powder is used in ceramic ware. The North Mill dates from 1756–65 and was probably designed by *Brindley*. The South Mill first served the grinding of corn. The mills were opened to the public in 1969.)

CHESTERTON

HOLY TRINITY. 1851–2 by *H. Ward & Son* of Hanley. With a s steeple. Lancets and also bar tracery. Some more personal motifs inside. – STAINED GLASS. E window by *Wailes* (TK).

* The dates kindly provided for me by Mr Sewter.

A ROMAN FORT lay at Mount Pleasant, on a flat-topped hill. It appears to have been occupied in the later C1, but nothing is known about its internal planning.

CHETWYND BRIDGE see ALREWAS

CHILLINGTON HALL

The Giffard family, owners of Chillington, have held the estate ever since c.1180. The mansion is fine to look at and interesting to the historian, but the chief attraction is the beautiful grounds and the small buildings set up in them in strategic positions. As for the history of the mansion, three phases can be distinguished: the work of Sir John Giffard, who died in 1556 and who in all probability put up a courtyard house whose former courtyard can still be distinguished; the work of Peter Giffard, which has rainwater heads with the date 1724 and the work of Thomas Giffard of 1786–9. Peter's architect in all probability was *Francis Smith* of Warwick, Thomas's was *Soane*. Of Peter's time is the s side, of Thomas's the E façade.

The s side is of brick with stone dressings including quoins of equal length. There are eight bays and two and a half storeys. The windows have aprons. Top parapet with balustrading in the window axes. Affinities with Mawley in Shropshire and Sutton Scarsdale in Derbyshire are evident.

Soane's E front is of nine bays with a three-bay giant portico of unfluted Ionic columns carrying a pediment. The end bays l. and r. are heightened *à la* Wilton and Holkham (Soane knew Norfolk well), a device to achieve a visual link with the s side. Round the N corner the proportions of Soane's end pavilion continue for seven bays.

Inside, the finest room of c.1724 is the staircase hall, a spacious room of stylish details. The staircase itself has three balusters to the tread and lusciously carved tread-ends. On the walls are stucco panels with busts and whole figures. There is also heraldic stained glass of c.1830 by *John Freeth* of Birmingham. In the Morning Room is a splendid stucco ceiling with an allegorical figure in the centre. The style of the stucco is close to that of *Artari* and *Vassali*. Queen Anne panelling on the first floor and also a mahogany lavatory niche.

Soane's entrance hall has two very Soanish chimneypieces and, at its back, a screen of two slender Ionic columns. The area thus separated communicates with a cross corridor

CHILLINGTON HALL

Another cross corridor is on the first floor, and this has two glazed domes to scan its length. But Soane's principal apartment is the Saloon, which has taken the place of the Tudor courtyard. It is oblong and has as its centre an oval dome with a lantern. The dome stands on typical Soane segmental arches. The decoration is far from conventional. To the l. is an extra bay with a segmental tunnel-vault. The corresponding r. bay was never built. The chimneypiece is very puzzling. It tells a family story – Sir John shooting a panther – and the style seems a rustic 1830 trying to look ancient. To the r. of the entrance hall is the three-bay Dining Room, to the l. the Drawing Room which must be of *c*.1820–30.

Of the buildings in the grounds the earliest is the BOWLING GREEN ARCH, a tripartite, smoothly rusticated gateway of *c*.1730 with quoins of equal length, two fluted pilasters not touching the frieze, and two niches, rather jerkily composed. The iron GATES are in the *Bakewell* style. The Bowling Green Arch is W of the SW corner of the grounds. Also of *c*.1730 is the swagger octagonal DOVECOTE by the stables. It has quoins, round windows in the roof, and a cupola.

The GROUNDS were laid out by *Capability Brown c*.1770, but to the NE is still the long avenue of *c*.1720, divided into the UPPER AVENUE, *c*.1 m. long, and the (abandoned) LOWER AVENUE, *c*.1¼ m. long. Half way is *Telford's* classical CANAL BRIDGE of 1826. To the SW is the magnificent LAKE, continued towards the house as a wide winding canal. At the junction of lake and canal is a classical BRIDGE by *Paine*. Niches in the piers, medallions in the spandrels. By the lake is the GOTHIC TEMPLE, at the time of writing a sad sight. The temple has polygonal turrets l. and r. In the centre is a Gothick window, but the rooms are in the classical style of *c*.1770. Also close to the lake is the IONIC TEMPLE, built probably in 1771, Adamish in style.* Five bays, centre with unfluted Ionic columns carrying an attic. The dome has recently been reinstated (in fibre-glass). The side bays have an aedicule each. The temple masks a cottage. A view from it has in the distance a SHAM BRIDGE. (Near that, in the wood, difficult to reach, is the GRECIAN TEMPLE. This has Roman Doric columns. It is not kept up.)

WHITE HOUSE. This, dating probably also from the 1770s, stands just outside the park proper, but was originally meant

---

* And indeed *Robert Adam* prepared plans for both rebuilding and remodelling the house itself.

CHURCH EATON

ST EDITHA. The church has a late C12 to early C13 W tower, the W wall of it with two small Norman windows and clasping buttresses, the arch to the nave wide, with one order of shafts with shaft-rings. The bell-openings are twin, pointed, but under one round arch. The recessed spire is C15 work. E.E. the N arcade with round piers and round abaci. Dec N wall and straight-headed windows, Perp N chapel. Perp also the seven-light chancel E window. Small C17 N vestry. – FONT. A broken Norman font, with broad bands of ornament, very similar to that of the Bradley font. – STAINED GLASS. Mostly by *Kempe* 1893–1906. – MONUMENT. Maria Wright Crockett † 1812. Semi-reclining. Her husband supports her and their child clings to the father.

RECTORY. 1712. Brick, five bays, with strongly segmental window-heads and door-head.

WOOD EATON HALL, ¾ m. NW. By *William Baker*, 1754–5. Brick. Three bays, the middle one with an embellished gable.

LITTLE ONN HALL, 1½ m. SW. Built *c.*1870–5, but altered and enlarged later. Large, rock-faced, a free asymmetrical composition with a turret and stepped gables. Gardens by *Mawson*.

CHURCH LEIGH see LEIGH

CLANFORD HALL see SEIGHFORD

CLAYTON see NEWCASTLE-UNDER-LYME

CLIFFE PARK HALL see RUDYARD

CLIFTON CAMPVILLE

ST ANDREW. The church has an uncommonly fine steeple. The details are Dec. The recessed spire is supported by flying

CLIFTON CAMPVILLE

buttresses. The arch to the nave is high, and there is a rib-vault at that level. The chancel is E.E. – see one lancet – but the E window (five lights; reticulated tracery) and one N window are Dec. The S chapel is of about the same time or perhaps a little earlier. Plain intersected tracery in the E window. The arcade piers to the chancel (three bays) are quatrefoil with fillets. Again of that time is the two-storeyed NE annexe with a stepped group of lancet lights to N and W. The lower storey has a quadripartite rib-vault with single-chamfered ribs, the upper storey a garderobe. So it seems to have been a dwelling. Now the S aisle. The piers are of an odd shape, not round with fillets, but shallowly quatrefoil with the fillets projecting between the lobes in the main direction. The aisle windows are all Dec. In short, it is a church largely of c.1300–50. – SCREENS. The rood screen is good Perp work, with single-light divisions. – Much more interesting the S chapel screens. They are of the time of the chapel, i.e. very early. Dado with two tiers of punched-through quatrefoils. Colonnettes instead of muntins. Intersecting tracery. – A third chapel screen transfers these forms into the Jacobean, keeping however the colonnettes. The screen is dated 1634 – so is the door in the chancel screen. – STALLS with seven MISERICORDS, early C14. Naturalistic foliage and heads. – PAINTING. In the S aisle a large semicircular recess, too high to fit under the window. Painted in it Christ seated in Glory and two kneeling donors. The painting is mid C14. – STAINED GLASS. A little old glass in a N aisle window. – MONUMENTS. Palimpsest brass. A lady of c.1360, 22 in. long, and at the back fragment of a Knight. – Sir John Vernon † 1545 and wife. An outstanding alabaster monument. Against the tomb-chest on one short side two kneeling children, against the other three bedesmen. Against the long side figures and also shields with supporters. Twisted shafts, pretty frieze of beasts and birds on the base. – Sir Charles Pye † 1721. Also Sir Richard † 1724 and Sir Robert † 1734. Both monuments by *Rysbrack* and both made in 1736. Both are architectural without any figures. – Charles S. Watkins † 1813. By *Westmacott*. Kneeling woman. – Rev. John Watkins † 1833. By *Behnes*. Seated young man, mourning.

CLIFTON HALL. Two monumental wings of the early C18. The main range between seems never to have been built. The owner at the time was Sir Charles Pye. The architect was probably *Francis Smith*. Each wing is seven by five bays and has two doorways. Those of the end walls have segmental pediments, those to the *cour d'honneur* yet more lavish details, moulded surrounds, brackets, open curly pediments.

MANOR FARMHOUSE. The house has a big square DOVECOTE and a square GAZEBO.

COBRIDGE, see BURSLEM, STOKE-ON-TRENT, pp. 255, 256

CODSALL

ST NICHOLAS. Norman S doorway with zigzag at r. angles to the wall, on one order of colonnettes, their capitals decorated with beaded trails. The W tower is over-restored but Perp. The rest of the church is of 1846–8, by *E. Banks* of Wolverhampton. The style he chose was Dec. – STAINED GLASS. N aisle, second window from E by *O'Connor*, c.1870. – S aisle one window also by *O'Connor*, 1873, rather French than British. – Chancel S by *Bryans*, c.1900. – PLATE. Chalice, 1592; Salver by *Ebenezer Coker*, London, 1767; Cup with lid by *D.W.*, London, 1771–2. – MONUMENT. Walter Wrottesley † 1630. Recumbent effigy. Arched back panel with fret decoration. Against the tomb-chest kneeling figures.

Suburban Wolverhampton is winning against the village.

WERGS HALL, 1¾ m. SSE. Asymmetrical Italianate with a tower. *Circa* 1840?

WHITE HOUSE FARM. *See* Chillington Hall.

(OAKEN HOUSE. Late C18. Brick, three bays, three storeys. Pedimented doorway. Shaped parapets to the gable ends. DOE)

COLTON

ST MARY. The church is by *Street* (1850–2), except for the short E.E. tower with twin lancet bell-openings (and eight Perp pinnacles)* and the late C13 S chapel with lancets, quatrefoil piers with thin shafts in the diagonals, and plain SEDILIA. Three MISERICORDS, from Tenby. One has a Janus head, the other two wyverns. – CORONA. S chancel aisle perhaps 1851–2, nave (by *Hardman, Powell & Co.*) 1892. The latter still looks 1851–2 in style. The earlier corona and FONT, PULPIT, LECTERN, low SCREEN, STALLS, etc., all by *Street*. – STAINED

---

* Street intended a spire (P. Joyce).

GLASS. By *Wailes* E, one chancel N, N aisle E; 1858. – PLATE. Paten of 1734. – MONUMENT to the Rev. Abdeli Seaton and his wife who died in 1857 and also monument to James Oldham Oldham † 1857. Both by *Street*. Both are outdoors.

COLTON HOUSE. Nine-bay brick front in the rhythm 2-5-2. Quoins; doorway with broken pediment. Of c.1730, according to Dr Gomme.

LITTLEHAY MANOR HOUSE. A pair of C16 chimneystacks survives from an older house. DOE)

COLWICH

ST MICHAEL. High W tower dated 1640, but still entirely in the Gothic tradition. The rest of the exterior largely Victorian (by *Stevens* of Derby, completion of the work 1856; CPDD). The arcades inside seem to be E.E. (standard elements). The tower is built into the W bay of the N arcade. Ornate Victorian chancel interior, including STALLS with canopies. – STAINED GLASS. The W window by *Wailes*, 1859. – PLATE. Paten by *T.H.*, London, 1793. – MONUMENTS. Sir Robert Wolseley † 1646. Alabaster; standing monument, recumbent effigy; above, against the back wall, two standing children holding skulls. Also two angels. – Gabriel Wood † 1706. Large tablet of diptych type. The mid-column is twisted. – Charles Trubshaw † 1772, the architect builder, has a plain tablet. – Elizabeth Sparrow † 1841 by *Baily*. Three female figures hovering over a sarcophagus. – Lady Chetwynd † 1860. Christ, a kneeling angel, and two Roman soldiers. By *Matthew Noble*, 1862.

To the N of the church is the SCHOOL. It is of 1860* by *Christian*.

The STATION is by *Livock*, 1847, and has his characteristic shaped gables.

ST MARY'S ABBEY, built as MOUNT PAVILION by Viscount Tamworth c.1825. The nuns moved in in 1834, and much was altered then and later. On the entrance side the one bay with a ground-floor bow is still Gothick, i.e. with fancy motifs such as round window arches with crocketed ogee gables over. (The main front long and castellated, with a symmetrical Tudor Gothic centre. EH). On the S side, a view to the hills and Shugborough.

WOLSELEY BRIDGE, 1 m. ESE. By *Rennie*, c.1800. Three elegant arches.

* Information from Mr W. Bourne.

BISHTON HALL, 1 m. E. Georgian, rendered, of seven bays, with a three-bay pediment. Porch of four Tuscan columns. An Early Victorian addition with a convex front on the l., another only one-storeyed on the r.

COMPTON see WOLVERHAMPTON, p. 326

CONSALL

(OLD HALL. Small, gabled, late C17.)
(NEW HALL. Brick, c.1810. Close by a GROTTO. This was transferred here from Wootton Hall, where Rousseau spent a year, having arrived in March 1766.)

COPPENHALL

ST LAWRENCE. A perfect C13 village church, small but of great dignity. Nave and chancel only. The weatherboarded and shingled bell-turret is of course Victorian. w doorway with a continuous roll-moulding. Three stepped lancets over. Lancets along the nave, smaller lancets along the s side of the chancel. Fine E composition of three widely spaced lancets and a round window over. Chancel arch with simple half-column responds. The capitals also extremely simple. – PLATE. Chalice and Paten, Elizabethan.

COSELEY

3 m. N of Dudley

CHRIST CHURCH, Church Road. 1829–30 by *Thomas Lee*. Tooled ashlar, lancet windows. w tower with pinnacles. Slim Perp piers, three galleries, flat ceiling. The nice E chapel by *A. T. Butler*, 1910.
ST MARY, Gorge Road, Hurst Hill, 1½ m. E of the above. 1872 by *G. Bidlake*, the chancel 1882 by *Fleeming*. Quite large; no tower.
EBENEZER BAPTIST CHAPEL, Birmingham New Road, s of Ivyhouse Lane. Built in 1856. Three bays with giant pilasters and pediment; stuccoed.
SWIMMING BATHS, Pear Tree Lane, s of Christ Church. By *Scott & Clarke*, 1961–3.
WINDMILL, Oak Street, ¾ m. sw of Christ Church. Roughcast white. No sails. Converted into a house.

COTES HEATH

ST JAMES. 1837 with a chancel of 1891 (by *C. Lynam*). Low, nave with a bellcote.

COTON-IN-THE-CLAY

COTON HALL. A handsome Late Georgian* front, stuccoed. The end bays have tripartite windows, the doorway has columns with reeded capitals and a pediment.

COTTON

ST JOHN. 1795. A sweet building, humble close to the Catholic ambitions next door. Brick, just oblong, but with two canted transeptal bays midway along N and S. The E and W ends have rising battlements and pinnacles and a circular window. The other windows are pointed. Plaster rib-vault inside. – PLATE. Chalice and Paten, 1794 by *Edward Fennell*.

ST WILFRID'S COLLEGE (R.C.), better known as Cotton College. A Georgian house, on the site and still existing, was in the first place bought by the Earl of Shrewsbury for his nephew. It was then, in 1846, given to Father Faber and his Brothers of the Will of God. They joined up with the Oratorians, who moved from Birmingham to Cotton. Newman was the first Superior. In 1849 the Oratorians went back to Birmingham, and in 1850 Cotton was taken over by the Passionists. After a short time they left, and in 1868 the school moved in.‡

The CHAPEL is by *Pugin*, 1846–8, lengthened in 1936–7 by *George Drysdale*. SW steeple with broach-spire. Long nave and S aisle. The features all in the style of 1300, i.e. cusped Y-tracery, but also many trefoils and quatrefoils. – STAINED GLASS. By *Hardman* probably one S aisle window.

The buildings of the college are of many dates. There is the Georgian nucleus. *Pugin* designed the earliest new range, the stone range with three gables and two-light windows with ogee-headed lights and the more utilitarian brick range to its l. Additions 1874–5, 1886–7, and 1931–2.

---

* White mentions the date 1790.
‡ Information given me by the staff of the VCH.

COVEN

ST PAUL. 1857 by *Banks*. Nave, transepts, chancel, and a SW bell-turret.

GROVE HOUSE FARM, W of the church. Timber-framed. The cross wing is late C16 or early C17 and has the very unusual decorative motif of little arches on columns.

BLACKLADIES. *See* p. 79.

CRAKEMARSH HALL *see* UTTOXETER

CRESSWELL

ST MARY (R.C.). 1815–16. Brick, with lancet windows. – STAINED GLASS. The two-light window of the Annunciation was designed by *Pugin*. – White also attributed to him the CROSS in the graveyard.

CRESWELL

CHURCH. A ruin in a field. The N wall remains fairly intact, with two lancet windows, and the E wall with the outline of the E window.

CROSS HEATH *see* NEWCASTLE-UNDER-LYME

CROXALL

ST JOHN BAPTIST. Chancel of *c.*1200 – see the priest's doorway and one small S lancet.* Another S window Dec, a N window of *c.*1300. Of the same date the S windows re-set in the blank arches of a former S arcade. Good Perp N windows. The W tower is said to be C13 below, Perp above. – COMMANDMENT BOARDS. Early C19 probably. – MONUMENTS. More incised slabs than can here be enumerated. Greenhill counts twelve. They almost pave the chancel and run from *c.*1480 into the C17. They are mostly to Curzons or Hortons. Three babies are among them. – More tablets also than can here be enumerated. Amongst them are the following. Eusebius Horton † 1814. By *Chantrey*, 1823. A beautiful group of two standing women. – Frances Levett † 1835 by *Reeves* of Bath. Tablet with luxuriant weeping willow. – Margaret Prinsep † 1837. By

---

* Also two aisle W lancets.

the same, and the tablet the other's big brother. – Sir Robert Wilmot Horton † 1843. By *Denman*. Grecian.

CROXALL HALL. Brick, of the late C16, but altered and enlarged by *Potter* of Lichfield, 1868. L-shaped but originally U-shaped. Mullioned and transomed windows. (One good plaster ceiling. DOE) Square DOVECOTE with cupola.

CROXDEN

CROXDEN ABBEY was founded by Bertram de Verdun in 1176 for Cistercians. The colonization was made from Aunay in Normandy. The first settlement was at Cotton; emigration to Croxden took place in 1179. The buildings are in ruins but date with a few exceptions all from c.1179 to c.1280. A first church consecration is recorded for 1181, the final consecration for 1253.

To find one's bearings in the impressive ruins one can be guided by the two most impressive fragments still standing upright: the S wall of the S transept and the W wall of the nave. Both have the superbly long lancets so much beloved of the North Country abbeys and cathedrals. Further E than the transept the plan of the CHOIR is known and set out in the grass. It is very unusual for Cistercians; for it is the French *chevet* type, i.e. an apse, an ambulatory, and radiating chapels. The scheme is that of Aunay, and it represents a loosening of the Cistercians' rigidity of straight-headed choirs and straight-headed chapels. Of all this only some walling of the first (NW) chapel remains, with a respond exhibiting keeling and the start of a rib-vault. Near by is evidence of the N TRANSEPT. It had an E aisle of two bays, and the piers were of four major and four minor shafts. For more evidence on the transept we must go to the S. The glorious S wall has two lancets, and the W wall one more. Buttresses are canted. The S respond of the E aisle is triple, and the main shaft is again keeled. The capital is moulded. There is also one jamb of the upper SE window. In the S wall is a small doorway into the sacristy (*see* below), and this has a round arch with two continuous slight chamfers, the oldest surviving feature of the church. The upper doorway in the S wall led into the dormitory. Vaulting shafts of the S and W walls prove that a rib-vault existed. The S wall of the S aisle also survives, without any window, even above the line of the cloister roof. Inside there are vaulting shafts again for rib-vaults. The WEST WALL is magnificent, but it is also odd. It has a sumptuous portal of four orders with moulded capitals and many-moulded arches, and it has three lancets, the middle one not having enough space to reach as low as the others. The w responds of the aisle arcades are odd too. They have one main keeled shaft and two canted surfaces on the side. There is a small doorway into the s aisle.

Of the CLOISTER nothing stands up. From the E bay of the s aisle the cloister was reached by a rich PORTAL of three orders with stiff-leaf capitals and a many-moulded arch. In front of the chapter house is an unexpected widening, its destination unknown. The room s of the transept has a later tunnel-vault. It had the book-room opening to the cloister and the sacristy E of it. Then follows the CHAPTER HOUSE with its two windows and one doorway to the cloister all exuberantly shafted and provided with stiff-leaf capitals. The room was of five by three bays, vaulted. The piers had eight shafts. The PARLOUR is of two bays, vaulted. Round the entrance arch an enrichment of lobes in shallow relief. The SLYPE has a pointed tunnel-vault with transverse arches. The next room was the UNDERCROFT of the DORMITORY, which filled the upper floor of the E range. At first it did not go as far N nor as far s as later. To the N was at first a corridor from the upper doorway to the chapter house N wall. In the C14 the area was filled in. Hence the traces of a roof cutting into the transept lancets. To the s also the undercroft was lengthened in the C14. The division between the old and the new is clearly visible. SE of the dormitory is the REREDORTER or lavatories. The flushing channel has recently been exposed.

The s range is less easily understood. The REFECTORY ran N–S, not E–W; that was a Cistercian custom. So we find from E to w at first the spiral DAY STAIR to the dormitory and then the WARMING HOUSE with its big fireplace and two straight-headed windows. The w range had a vaulted undercroft too. Four and a half by two bays remain.

SE of the E range was the ABBOT'S LODGING, built in 1335–6. It was of four bays with three central piers. The three E bays were rib-vaulted, but the w bay was of two storeys and divided off by a wall. Spiral staircase in the NW corner. N of the abbot's lodging are the remains of the INFIRMARY. It was seven bays long (the three N bays are under the present road) and rib-vaulted. The ribs rested on inner buttresses or projections. Beds no doubt stood at r. angles, each one flanked by two of the projections. There was also a pair of stone tables rests in each bay. One pair is intact. A two-bay chapel, also rib-vaulted, projected to the E.*

ABBEY FARMHOUSE, overlapping into the W range, has a Georgian front of five bays with a doorway with straight head.

ST GILES. 1884–5, replacing the chapel *ante portas*. A good design, and one would like to know the architect. The building was paid for by the Earl of Macclesfield. Rock-faced, of nave and chancel. Two W lancets, a mid-buttress between on which a shaft, helped by two corbels, suggests the bellcote. The features are early C14. Ashlar facing inside. The S chapel has a fireplace and was no doubt the Earl's pew. – PLATE. Chalice and Paten by *C.R.*, 1733.

CROXTON

ST PAUL. By *Ewan Christian*, 1853–4. An attractive piece of work, not entirely routine – see that one tall transomed S aisle window. Nave and chancel, bellcote, aisles, polygonal apse. The style is Dec.

CUTTLESTONE BRIDGE see PENKRIDGE

DAIRY HOUSE see HORTON

DARLASTON see WALSALL, p. 296

DENSTONE

ALL SAINTS. Built for Sir Thomas Percival Heywood.‡ His architect was *Street*, and here indeed is young Street at his very best – young Street, for he was thirty-six when he designed Denstone in 1860. The building, consecrated in 1862, is in the Middle Pointed, the style of the later C13 and the early C14, the style Street – like Scott and like the Ecclesiologists – believed to be the best Gothic, but it is highly original in the handling, and it is not provocative, as Butterfield liked to be. Street's elements are the simplest: nave, chancel and rounded

---

* I am grateful to Mr M. W. Thompson, Inspector of Ancient Monuments, for the information on the abbot's lodging and the infirmary.

‡ Of the Manchester banking and church-building family.

apse, N tower. But watch what he does with these elements. The apse e.g. has large windows with plate tracery – Street always preferred the flatter and more solid plate tracery to the wirier and more elegant bar tracery – and massive buttresses, but the buttresses stop at the sill level of the windows. The main windows altogether have plate tracery. In the nave S wall there are three, widely spaced, and of differing patterns. Their arches have alternating cream- and rose-coloured voussoirs, and the walls also had rose bands – the kind of polychromy Butterfield was carrying to extremes. In the chancel Street breaks the order of the windows and suddenly inserts (for inner reasons) two small quatrefoils high up instead of a proper window. On the N side there are only small single lights except for one large quatrefoil which gives light to the font. On the N side also is the tower, and it is round with a conical top, but grows out of an oblong base zone, the vestry, and is reached by an outer stair. This is the one place where the design strikes one as clever rather than organic. On the S side the porch projects, characteristic of Street by its roof starting very low. The interior is faced in rough stone, not ashlar, but with smooth dressings and again restrained polychromy. The small windows have deep slopes below. The chancel windows are black-shafted. – FONT. Also by *Street*, with carving by *Earp*. The bowl has four angels in long robes holding reversed jars symbolizing the four Rivers of Paradise. The style of the figures derives from Giovanni Pisano. Street of course knew Italy. – By *Street* also the REREDOS, the very low stone SCREEN, the circular stone PULPIT, the iron SCREEN to the organ, the STALLS, the ORGAN CASE, and the ironwork of the DOOR. The sculptural work is by *Thomas Earp*. – All the STAINED GLASS is by *Clayton & Bell*, much brighter than their later work.

Street also designed the LYCHGATE (1862), with its elementary construction, the churchyard CROSS (1862), and the SCHOOL (1860–2) with its roof starting low, its typical chimneys with a set-off, and its half-hipped roof in a specially emphasized place. The same elements in the VICARAGE (1860–2). Church, school, and vicarage lie strung up, but they do not form a group.

DENSTONE COLLEGE, ¾ m. WSW. The Rev. Nathaniel Woodard was a man of social conscience, great energy, and organizational talent. He wanted to achieve the 'union of classes by a common system of education'. It was especially the poorer

DENSTONE

middle class that should benefit. Woodard visualized three classes of schools: for clergy and gentlemen, for substantial tradesmen, farmers, clerks, etc., and for petty shopkeepers, skilled mechanics, etc. – a very Victorian vision of common opportunities of education. He started on a small scale in 1848 at New Shoreham, because he was curate there. In 1850 he gave up his curacy, and in 1851 the first of the Woodard Schools was started at Hurstpierpoint. This was followed by Lancing: 1854, Bloxham: 1860, Ardingly: 1870. His original architect was *R. C. Carpenter*, who unfortunately died young in 1855. His partner *Slater* carried on, later himself in partnership with Carpenter's son *R. H. Carpenter*. Denstone College was begun in 1868 by *Slater & Carpenter* and completed in 1873. Only the chapel and the hall came later. The former is by *Carpenter & Ingelow* and was begun in 1879 and consecrated in 1887. In 1888–91 the hall was built. The college started with 46 boys and now has *c*. 325. The site is fine, the composition is sweeping and has never been destroyed. It is an H with shorter wings to the front, longer to the back. The centre range is of five widely spaced bays, Gothic of the Middle Pointed kind, and not at all ornamental. The ground floor has the entrance and small lancets in pairs, above large two-light windows with plate tracery rising as dormers. Behind them was originally the main school room. The CHAPEL (opened in 1879) is in the l. projecting wing. It is large, very high, and was meant to have two towers flanking the polygonal apse. Inside, the towers open to the W into the nave in one long lancet. All windows of the chapel are large and are placed high up.* The HALL is in the wing corresponding to the chapel. It has five large three-light windows with two foiled circles over. The walls are brick-faced. The STAIRCASE leading up to the hall and the schoolroom is amazing. It is not at all Gothic in any accepted Victorian sense. It is as free and as simplified as Berlage's Exchange, Gothic in spirit perhaps, but no more. It was, in fact, built in 1939 (architects: *Collcutt & Hamp*), together with the entrance hall and the impressive corridor set in front of the other side of the centre range. The wings on that side project far, are of great height, and either ends in two towers not much higher than the wings. There are also two less successful water towers l. and r. of the centre range. The wings house classrooms, dormitories, etc.

---

* PLATE. Cross, Abyssinian, C17.

STONE HOUSE, on the way up to the College. Dated 1712. The front is symmetrical, though the windows were (and some are still) mullioned.

BARROWHILL HOUSE (Corbellion Restaurant). 1780. White, with a central canted bay and single-storey wings.

DERRINGTON

ST MATTHEW. By *Henry Ward* of Stafford (CPDD). Completed in 1847. Nave with bellcote and chancel. Late C13 details. Timber roof on large heads and angel busts. The SEDILIA happily overdone, three N and five S, the latter with nodding ogee arches. The rector at the time, as his son wrote much later, received 'much valuable advice' from the Cambridge Camden Society.

DEVIL'S RING AND FINGER see OAKLEY HALL

DIEULACRES ABBEY see LEEK

DILHORNE

ALL SAINTS. The church has one of the few octagonal W towers in the country. It is early C13 in its lower parts and Perp above. The arcades of four bays are late C13. The chancel is late medieval but over-restored (by *Christian*). The aisles date from 1819. Windows with Y-tracery. The doorways in their rusticated surrounds look C18, not early C19. – COMMUNION RAIL. Jacobean. – PLATE. Chalice, 1722 by *Nathaniel Gulliver*; Paten, 1723 by *Thomas Bamford*.

N of the church ARCHWAY and LODGES to the former Dilhorne Hall, which was rebuilt in 1830. The archway is high and has polygonal turrets. The small lodges have shaped gables.

(OLD PARSONAGE. Three bays, four storeys, with a semi-circular porch and elementarily treated Venetian windows. NMR)

STANSMORE HALL, 1 m. WNW. Early C17; stone. Three gables front and three back. Mullioned windows.

HEYWOOD GRANGE, 1¾ m. NW. Dated 1672. The porch has indeed the ovals, horizontally placed, which are a hallmark of *c.*1670. The upper porch window on the other hand has arched lights, which is a decidedly reactionary motif for 1670.

DOSTHILL*

ST PAUL. 1870–2 by *Holmes* of Birmingham. Of sooty brown stone with a s tower with 'a most extraordinary baby broach spire' (Goodhart-Rendel) starting at a height of about 15 ft. The chancel arch corbels have naturalistic vine and lilies, a favourite among the High Victorians. – STAINED GLASS. The E window looks *Hardman*.

OLD CHURCH, to the NE. Plainly oblong, with Norman S and N doorways and S and N windows. The former chancel arch is blocked and a four-light window has been set in it naively.

BARN, N of the former. C15 (or earlier?). With impressive cruck-trusses.

(DOSTHILL HOUSE. 1830, with a nice porch.)

DOVE CLIFFE see STRETTON

DRAYCOTT-IN-THE-MOORS

ST MARGARET. Broad w tower, early C13 and later. The N chapel late C13 (one lancet, Y-tracery, intersected tracery), the nave and chancel Dec (E window with the four-petal motif, S windows of the nave with flowing tracery, S arcade with arches with the sunk-quadrant moulding). – STAINED GLASS. One N window by *Kempe*. – MONUMENTS. In the Draycott Chapel. Cross-legged Knight, c.1300. – Sir Philip Draycott † 1554. Two recumbent effigies. Many upright children against the tomb-chest. – Richard Draycott † 1544, Philip † 1604, John † 1600 with wife. They are one group and were probably made at the same time. All have shields against the tomb-chest. The middle one has two recumbent effigies, the other two just a large cross. – Richard † 1662. Effigy, and space for that of his widow. The ornament confirms the date. – Several incised slabs.

DRAYTON BASSETT

ST PETER. Perp w tower. The nave of 1793 (CPDD). It has two-light windows with reticulation units. The short chancel of c.1855 (CPDD). – PLATE. Chalice and Paten by *R.S.*, 1664. – MONUMENT to Sir Robert Peel, the statesman, † 1850. Inscription in black letter and a florid Gothic canopy over. By *White* of Vauxhall Bridge Road.

---

* Formerly in Warwickshire.

DRAYTON MANOR, which does not exist any longer, was built c.1820–35 by Sir Robert Peel's father (cf. Fazeley), who was a textile millionaire in the twenties and thirties, and was enlarged by Peel himself. It was designed by *Sir Robert Smirke* in the Jacobean style with broad short angle towers. *Gilpin* laid out the garden, and something of that remains.

Gothic ESTATE HOUSING.

(CANAL BRIDGE with circular Gothic brick towers, N of Drayton Bassett. It is a footbridge.)

DUDLEY

Dudley is now a county borough. In fact it is a town with a castle and the ruins of a priory surviving from the Middle Ages and around the town an assembly of former villages all grown together. There are, however, within the borough still open fields and even an occasional patch of wood. In fact Dudley, though part of the Black Country, has not the black-country character. The hills of course help, and there is much cheery suburban housing. Dudley belonged to the Sutton family. John Dudley, Viscount Lisle, Earl of Dudley, and Duke of Northumberland, bought it in the first half of the C16. After a short time it went back to Edward Dudley, son of the last Sutton. The Suttons were followed by Humble Ward, son of a London goldsmith, who became Lord Ward in 1644. The eighth Lord Ward died in 1823, the eleventh became Earl of Dudley in 1860. The industrial importance of Dudley dates back to the time after Dud Dudley, illegitimate son of Edward Lord Dudley, had discovered that iron could be smelted with coal instead of charcoal. But it still took a hundred years, till the mid C18, for the use of coal to become accepted.

For Amblecote *see* p. 60, for Brierley Hill p. 80, for Coseley p. 108, for Kingswinford p. 164, for Lower Gornal p. 199, for Netherton p. 208, for Pensnett p. 222, for Sedgley p. 232, for Upper Gornal p. 289, for Wordsley p. 329.

THE CASTLE

Dudley Castle lies on a wooded hill and is dominated by the so-called keep. It was founded in the C11 and is mentioned in Domesday. The earthworks are indeed assigned to that time. Of stonework very little is Norman: the walls of the inner gatehouse and possibly its tunnel-vault. There is also one arch in the N wall of the buttery (*see* below). The C13 is not represented, but the early C14 substantially. The INNER GATEHOUSE, except for the Norman parts, belongs to those decades. The entrance and exit arches are depressed and have three convex quadrant mouldings. The portcullis groove also survives. The BARBICAN with its two round towers is a later C14 addition. But the main early C14 contribution is the so-called KEEP, an oblong structure with one room on each floor and thick round angle towers, much like Nunney in Somerset. The ground floor is vaulted, the hall is on the first floor. The N part of the keep stands up high. Here the two towers have staircases, and there is in the middle a doorway with the same details as the archways of the gatehouse. Much of the E wall of the castle is early C14 too, but the chapel block NE of the gatehouse is about twenty or thirty years later. The CHAPEL fills the S half of the block. It is 50 by 23 ft in size and stands on a tunnel-vaulted undercroft. There are an ogee-headed upper doorway to the S, and the remains of a W window with tracery.

The rest is mostly C16; only the two-storeyed range between keep and gatehouse is later. By the cross-windows one can date it to the later C17. The C16 work is largely still Perp, but the first signs of the Renaissance in Staffordshire architecture appear here. The work dates from the time of the Duke of Northumberland who was executed in 1553. The main addition he made to the castle is the GREAT HALL, of remarkably original design. It probably stands on the site of the medieval hall. The hall is 78 by $31\frac{1}{2}$ ft and has mullioned and transomed windows. W of the hall is a former LOGGIA of five bays with Ionic columns. The demi-columns of the responds are still there. The arches are four-centred, not yet round, and the loggia rests on four transverse tunnel-vaults. The middle bay has the outer staircase up to the hall instead. The loggia stretched between two projections. The N one had the porch, the S one belonged to the dais end of the hall. At the N end of the hall the three usual service doorways survive. Certain details in conjunction with a letter of June 1553 place this work accurately. The letter was written by Sir William Sharington of Lacock to Sir John Thynne of Longleat. Sharington apologizes to Thynne for having been unable to send him *John Chapman*, a mason; however, Chapman had been sent for by the Duke of Northumberland and would be leaving Lacock presently. Indeed the doorways from the terrasse with the colonnade to the wings projecting from the hall and also the mullioned windows, especially those on the ground floor with their sills on brackets, can be matched exactly at Lacock. NW of the hall are BUTTERY, PANTRY, and KITCHEN. The details here are too complicated and not important enough to be described here. It must however be said that the bow window of the buttery cannot be as early as c.1550. It must be a later alteration. It runs through two storeys, and there were the best bedrooms on the upper floor in this range, which explains the existence of the bow. Behind them, on the E side, ran the LONG GALLERY, 72 ft long. The windows of the range have mullions and transoms and two big gables. The kitchen, as usual, runs through both storeys. It has two large fireplaces. Round the corner, i.e. to the N, are minor rooms and the POSTERN GATE. There were also ranges along the W side – see one upper fireplace.

THE PRIORY

Dudley Priory was founded for Cluniac Benedictines by Gervase Pagnell c.1160. It was subject to the lords of the castle and lies at the foot of the castle hill. It was never a large house. We hear at no time of more than four monks. Considering that, the size of the premises is surprising. What is preserved to very different degrees shows an aisleless nave, a S transept, a straight end to the choir, two chancel S chapels, the outline of the cloister, the W wall of the W range projecting W of the W front of the church, and a spiral stair in the E range. Of details not much need be said. The nave is of the early C13 – see the N windows – but the much damaged W doorway placed under a gable and the W window above the gable are a hundred years later. The S windows of the nave are of the latter period too. The responds of the arch for the S transept to the SW chapel may be early C13 again, but could well be late C12 instead. The SE chapel was of three bays, vaulted, and the E window is Late Perp. There are image niches l. and r.

PRIORY HALL. Built in 1825. The style used is Early Tudor, and the plan is asymmetrical.

THE TOWN

ST EDMUND, Castle Street. 1722–4. Brick and stone, very typical of its date. Nave, aisle, and unusually long chancel.

Arched windows, w tower with a big stone portal, eared and pedimented, and stone aisle portals with horizontal ovals over. The E window was originally much larger than it is now, and probably Venetian as it now also is. Large wooden portal from tower to nave. The interior has three galleries, but was altered in 1858 (1864?) in rather unfortunate ways.* – MONUMENTS. Tablet to Edward Dixon † 1806. By *King* of Bath. Standing female figure by an urn, easily recognizable as by King. – Big tablet to Thomas Badger † 1856. By *Peter Hollins*. Seated young woman by an urn on whose base the head of the deceased in relief. – PLATE. Cup and Paten, 1748; Chalice, given in 1801.

ST AUGUSTINE, Hallchurch Road. 1884 by *H. D. W. Drinkwater*. Brick, quite large, but without a tower. Lancet windows.

ST JAMES, St James's Road. 1840. Close to some unnecessary high blocks of flats. Of small stones. W tower and lancet windows. The surprise is the piers between nave and aisles which are columns with rings and French Early Gothic foliage capitals – looking for all the world like Clutton in the 1860s. – MONUMENT. J. Stokes. In the churchyard. Very large and black. A broken column on a high pedestal.

ST JOHN, St John's Road. Also 1840 and almost identical with St James, especially in the curious piers.

OUR LADY AND ST THOMAS (R.C.), St Joseph's Street and Trindle Road. By *Pugin*, 1842. Like most Pugin churches, a disappointment. Nave and aisles and chancel; no tower, lancets, large W and E, small in the aisles, and clerestory. Short chancel, octagonal piers. – STAINED GLASS. The Virgin in the l. chancel chapel is by *Pugin* too, and probably also the abstract patterning in the chancel E window.

ST THOMAS, High Street. 1815–18 by *William Brooks*. An uncommonly interesting and attractive building of its date. W tower with recessed spire, nave of three bays with the middle one treated transeptally to the outside and with the W bays continued towards the tower by a canted extra bay. Short chancel. The style is Perp.‡ Internally nave and aisles and again short extra bays to W and E which are canted. Slim Dec piers, plaster tierceron-vaults. Three galleries. – STAINED

---

* According to Mr Bartlett the church is only the E half of a much larger medieval church. Masonry of this has been found, and a crypt below the C18 tower crypt.

‡ The window tracery is of iron; so Mr Hoyle, Director of the Dudley Central Library, told me.

GLASS. In the E window Transfiguration by *J. Blacker*, 1821, the Christ from Raphael's famous painting, below larger standing figures, the whole still entirely in the C18, say Reynolds, tradition, painterly and with much brown. – PLATE. Cup, 1571; Paten, 1594; Cup, 1626; Paten, 1721; Flagon, 1724? (given in 1743); Paten, given in the late C18.

COUNCIL OFFICES, Priory Street. 1935 by *Harvey & Wicks*. Brick, large and symmetrical, with cross-windows but in the centre a semi-Romanesque loggia *à la* Östberg. To its r. the former DISPENSARY, of 1862, small and in a wild Gothic, totally asymmetrical. Behind the Council Offices the former POLICE BUILDINGS, big, of brick, with a dominant gatehouse motif. 1847. Castellated. At its end a tower of 1928, again by *Harvey & Wicks*. (INSIGNIA. Mayor's Staff presented in 1798.)

COUNTY COURT, Priory Street. Stone, Italianate, 1858.

CENTRAL LIBRARY, St James's Road. 1909 by *George H. Wenyon*. In a fine early C18 English Baroque.

TECHNICAL COLLEGE, The Broadway. 1933–6 by *A. T. & G. Butler* with the County Education Committee Architect, *G. C. Lowbridge*. How can so unrelievedly utilitarian a brick block have been accepted bang between the priory ruin and the castle hill?

GRAMMAR SCHOOL, St James's Road. 1897–9 by *Woodhouse & Willoughby*. Flaming red brick.

GIRLS' HIGH SCHOOL, Priory Road. 1910 by *J. Hutchings*. In a free William-and-Mary style.

MARKET PLACE FOUNTAIN. 1867 by *James Forsyth*, sculptor of the Perseus Fountain at Witley Court, Worcs. The Dudley fountain was exhibited at the Paris Exhibition of 1867.* The Earl of Dudley paid for it. It is a lush and very enterprising design, in a free Italian Renaissance, with two busts of horses on two prow-like corbels and with a figural finial.

DUDLEY ZOO, Castle Hill, and happily mixed up with the outer bailey of the castle. The mixture comes off well, however savagely the Royal Fine Arts Commission, if it were today, would oppose the outrage. After all, medieval castles sometimes had wild beasts in the moat. Only today they are better housed. This is due to Messrs *Tecton* who did the buildings for the zoo in 1936–7, having made a name by their buildings for the London Zoo, of which the first were designed in 1934. The style of Tecton's zoo buildings is remarkable indeed, even

---

* I am very grateful to Mr John Hoyle for this information.

internationally speaking. For it was not the International Modern of the thirties, crisp and clear, rectangular and rational. On the contrary – it indulges in bold curves and their interplay, preparing the ground, as it were, for the fifties and the sixties. This attitude of hostility against what is merely sensible faces you at once. The GATES with the five guichets have a number of canopies independent of each other, but interlocked. Each canopy is a shallow horizontally placed S. The same character is evident in the SEAL ENCLOSURE, the PELICAN BAR, some kiosks, and the more dramatic, especially successful POLAR BEAR PIT. Altogether Tecton did some fifteen buildings, and as the site, being the castle mound, rises steeply, another attraction is differences of level between beasts and viewers. At the time of writing the buildings are not at all well kept, which is deplorable, as this kind of concrete architecture requires an even finish and clean surfaces.

PERAMBULATION. The centre of Dudley has little to encourage perambulations. Only a few streets and buildings need be singled out. In BIRMINGHAM STREET Nos. 2–6, the CONSERVATIVE CLUB, red brick, of five bays and two and a half storeys, with a three-bay pediment and a pretty semicircular Ionic porch. In TOWER STREET, off New Street, which is off Castle Street, BAILIES' CHARITY SCHOOL (now Youth Centre) of *c.*1732. This has three bays, one-storeyed, rendered. The school has two porches with two porcelain bluecoat children. In PRIORY STREET, just NW of Tower Street, No. 7, dated 1703. Low, brick and stone dressings. Five bays with a three-bay pediment. Doorway with a bolection moulding and a pediment. In PRIORY ROAD, the NW continuation of New Street, the stuccoed Latest Classical PRIORY HOUSE. In WOLVERHAMPTON STREET, leading W from the S end of Priory Street, the Victorian Gothic LLOYDS BANK, and opposite several Georgian brick houses. FINCH HOUSE is a double house, semi-detached. It is of eight bays and two storeys and has a four-bay pediment.

DUDLEY WOOD see BRIERLEY HILL

DUNSTALL

ST MARY. By *Henry Clutton*, 1852–3, for John Hardy of Dunstall Hall.* A typical estate church, standing on its own.

---

* But the foundation stone was laid by Peter Arkwright – *see* below.

Prominent tower with a round staircase projection stopping below the top frieze. Awkward junction of tower and spire. Steep s porch, impure late C13 to Dec tracery. But all to a substantial scale with plenty of bare wall. The tower is at the sw corner. It is vaulted inside. The porch also is vaulted – a pointed tunnel-vault with transverse ribs. Nobbly leaf capitals to the s arcade. In the s aisle along the wall a stone bench ending in a lion couchant. The chancel is all alabaster-lined. – CANDLESTICKS of polished peach marble with white marble angels on top. – STAINED GLASS. The E window signed by *Willement*.

Clutton also did the SCHOOL, matter-of-fact but with one playful half-hip, and the RECTORY, of brick, with a few more 'rogue' details.

DUNSTALL HALL. Little is known about the building. Ashlar. The garden side is of ten bays with a recessed four-bay centre which was originally the whole house. The wings came later and the more ambitious entrance side later still – about 1850, rather earlier than later. The house had gone to the Arkwrights in 1814, the Hardys in 1851. The entrance side has a deep porte-cochère and a dramatic centre top with a turret-like attic and a pediment in front of it, a little below the top. One might call it reminiscent of Cockerell. The inside of the house is interesting for other reasons. Firstly, the central hall has a genuine Roman floor mosaic (Cerberus in the centre) said to come from Tivoli. The staircase in this hall was carved by *Edward Griffiths* c.1900 with lush foliage and all kinds of zoo animals. By the same the glorious front door, dated 1898, which has a landscape with galloping horsemen, trees, a castle, and many humans and beasts all spilling over the panels of the door. The metal door furniture is in the Arts and Crafts taste. Then there is the stained glass, especially the leaf and flower patterns interspersed with shields in a corridor, and the figures illustrative of Music in another place. Their artist is not known, but another glass picture, probably by the same hand, is known to be the work of one *Rowlands*. Attached to the house is a seven-bay ORANGERY with some iron tracery inside.

DUNSTON

ST LEONARD. A large church of the estate type, i.e. a town church in the country. 1876–8 by *W. D. Griffin* of Wolverhampton. Rock-faced, with a W steeple and geometrical tracery.

DUNWOOD HALL see LONGSDON

ECCLESHALL

HOLY TRINITY. This is one of the most perfect C13 churches in Staffordshire. The century appears at once in the strong W tower with its very simply detailed windows with Y-tracery and the beautifully long chancel with its five lancets along the sides. The climax is the E wall with five stepped lancets, but that climax is due to *Street*, who restored the church in 1866–9, and not to his colleague of six hundred and fifty years before.* The priest's doorway incidentally, with its many continuous mouldings, is set in the middle of the S wall of the chancel, a touch of classicity. Of the C13 also the N vestry – and of course the arcades. The nave is wide, and the aisles are wide. The arcades are of five bays and have round piers with stiff-leaf capitals. The N arcade came first. The capitals are typical early E.E., with the leaves confined to an upper band leaving the bell-shape partly exposed. This applies to the S arcade as well, but N has slight chamfers, S mature chamfers. The tower arch is yet later – see the richer stiff-leaf capitals, the sunk-quadrant mouldings, and of course the Y-tracery. Though the chancel area is by *Street*, SEDILIA and PISCINA are original. *Street* added vestries N and S of the tower, in the lancet style too. The Perp S porch *Street* restored, or rather rebuilt. But genuinely Perp and essential to the total external and internal effect of the church is the large clerestory of three-light windows. The clerestory, and also the S aisle, has battlements and pinnacles. The tower top is Perp too. Pairs of two-light bell-openings under one ogee arch, lozenge frieze, eight pinnacles. – FONT. C13; moulded. – The ALTARPIECE with canopy in the N chapel, the enormous ORGAN CASE, and the N chapel SCREEN, all most ornately early C20 Gothic, are in fact by *Caröe*, 1931. – REREDOS. By *Champneys*, 1898. – PULPIT. High Victorian. Stone, open sides, two tiers of columns. – SCULPTURE. L. and r. of a vestry window two Saxon fragments of a cross shaft: Adam and Eve and a horseman with a spear (St Chad?). – STAINED GLASS. E, S aisle E,

---

* I hear from Mr Joyce that Street proposed a second pair of transepts but was thwarted in this by Lord Grimthorpe.

and evidently also s aisle SE all by *Clayton & Bell*, c.1870. – s aisle one s window *Bryans*, c.1898. – PLATE. Set of 1777 by *James Young*, London. – MONUMENTS. Bishop Overton † 1609. Stiff alabaster effigy, recumbent. Behind and above under an arch his two wives kneeling. Tomb-chest with shields in strapwork, and flanking them caryatids. – Two incised slabs on tomb-chests (in Street's vestries): Bishop Sampson † 1554 and Bishop Bentham † 1578. – Bishop Bowstead † 1843. Alabaster effigy in a low recess (chancel N). – LYCHGATE by *Champneys*, 1892.*

Eccleshall has the HIGH STREET of a small town, not a village.‡ It is an attractive street, even if it has no houses to make you stop. There are two of brick with three-bay pediments (Nos. 46–48 and 17–21), two neighbouring hotels each with a plain five-bay arcade to keep the rain off the pavements, and a five-bay house with a porch of pairs of Tuscan columns (No. 45).

ECCLESHALL CASTLE. Eccleshall became an episcopal residence under Walter Langton in the late C13, and soon after that the castle must have been rebuilt. It is true that an episcopal predecessor obtained licence to fortify about 1200, but that cannot apply to the present building. The main survival is a nine-sided corner tower with small pointed-trefoiled windows. Plans of after the Civil War during which the castle was slighted show that there was a second tower and that the hall and chapel range connected them. Excavations are now exploring this second tower. As the house is surrounded by a moat – the BRIDGE which crosses it is assigned to the C14 – we may assume a layout with four angle towers *à la* Bolton, or Bodiam or indeed Harlech. However, some medieval masonry (re-used?) has also been exposed at the back of the house which Bishop Lloyd built inside this enclosure about 1695. It is a spacious house of L-shape with a thirteen-bay façade with two projecting wings. Inside, the best feature is the late C18 plaster ceiling in the drawing room.

WALTON HALL. *See* Chebsey.

ECTON

The *Gent. Mag.* in 1769 mentions the copper mines here, and *The Beauties of England and Wales* in 1813 tells more of copper

---

* The SCHOOL is by *Street*, 1862 (Paul Joyce).
‡ Mr Palliser reminded me that Eccleshall is indeed a lapsed borough.

and also lead mining. One small building at the Deep Ecton Mine was erected as early as 1788 to house a Watt rotative engine – four years after their first introduction. One house of interest, halfway up the hill, quite big, with a copper spire and Gothic touches. It was built in 1931–3 as a castle folly.*

EDINGALE

HOLY TRINITY. 1880–1 by *C. Lynam*. Brick, NE tower with pyramid roof. Square lancets N and S. The vestry E window has a Saxon head.

Near the church CHURCH FARM HOUSE has a date 1664. It is still in the common timber vernacular.

ELFORD

ST PETER. The W tower looks Perp but has a date 1598. The rest of the church is by *Salvin*, 1848–9, except for the S aisle and S (Stanley or Howard) chapel, which were rebuilt by *Street* in 1869–70. – COMMUNION RAIL. Victorian; good. – DOOR with blank arches; C15. – STAINED GLASS. S aisle W c.1525, probably Netherlandish. – W window 1841 by *Wailes* (CPDD). – (S chapel E by *Ward & Hughes*, 1870.) – PLATE. Chalice and Paten by *T.R.*, 1767. – MONUMENTS. Most of them are in the Stanley Chapel, which was founded as a chantry in 1474. It is known that *E. Richardson* restored the monuments in 1848. It is important to remember this fact; for it explains the appearance of the popular favourite of the monuments: John Stanley, a child killed c.1460 by a tennis-ball. The face and hair of the child are entirely late C13 in style and inspired by the so-called effigy of Jean, son of Louis IX, at Saint-Denis. – The other monuments are: Knight of c.1370 in the typical armour and costume. The bogus-Gothic inscription calling this Sir John Stanley † 1474 shows what Richardson was capable of. – Sir Thomas Arderne † 1391 and wife. Against the tomb-chest figurines and angels. – Sir William Smythe † 1525 and wives. Against the tomb-chest standing figurines under canopies and shields under canopies. – William Staunton ?, c.1450. Choir N wall. Only the upper and lower thirds are carved. They are sunk, and in the middle the

---

* Information from Dr J. A. Robey.

stone surface is left untouched.* — Also the re-cut incised slabs of Ladies.

ELKSTONE

(ST JOHN BAPTIST. 1786–8. Small, towerless and aisleless. – PULPIT. A kind of three-decker. – STAINED GLASS. One window is by *Morris & Co.*, but as late as 1922.)
ST LAURENCE. *See* Warslow.

ELLASTONE

ST PETER. The N arcade and the N chancel arcade seem to be Perp, but the chancel features and at least the chapel E window with their unorthodox tracery go with the date 1588 displayed on the chancel. The W tower, also appearing Perp, has a large inscription tablet with the date 1586. The nave externally is all a rebuild of 1830. – PLATE. Chalice, 1661; Chalice, 1818 by *William Elliott*. – MONUMENTS. Sir John Fleetwood † 1590. Two defaced effigies. – Rev. Walter Davenport Bromley † 1882. Bronze portrait.
ELLASTONE OLD HALL (Bromley Arms). Fine late C17 house of five bays with upright two-light windows. Doorway with pilasters. Quoins of even length.
CALWICH ABBEY TEMPLE, ¾ m. E. Calwich Priory was an Augustinian house founded *c.*1130. Nothing of the priory remains, and the house built in 1849–50 has also been demolished. But the delightful temple by the river remains. It must date from *c.*1790 and has a portico of detached columns, Wyatt-type tripartite windows with a blank segmental arch, a copper dome, and a back door with steps direct to the water. The dome is surrounded by four a little clumsy square pinnacles with ball finials.
(ELLASTONE BRIDGE. Of two segmental arches with cutwaters. Dated 1777. DOE)

ELLENHALL

ST MARY. The W tower of brick with pointed bell-openings is probably the contribution of *William Baker*, 1757. Brick also

* The earliest case known to me of such a divided image is at Marseille and dates from the C12.

the S side of the nave, but chancel and N side stone, and in the chancel a Norman N window. The rest Perp. – PLATE. Elizabethan Chalice.

ENDON

ST LUKE. Small C17 W tower. Or can the date 1730 apply? The rest is 1876–9 by *Beardmore*.* – STAINED GLASS. By *Morris & Co.*, 1893, the E window. Three figures against fairly loosely spreading foliage, and on top a medallion of angels receiving souls. – PLATE. Paten of 1638 by *R.S.*

PLOUGH INN. Late Georgian, with three two-storeyed bows, all mullions made into columns.

(THE ASHES, ½ m. NE. C17, five bays, stone, with two projecting wings and mullioned windows. DOE)

HAZLEHURST BRIDGE, 1¼ m. E. Built in 1842 to bridge the Cauldon Canal. Cast iron with stone abutments.

ENGLETON see BREWOOD

ENVILLE

ST MARY. In a fine position on a hill, and *Scott*, who restored and enlarged the church in 1872–5, made the most of it by giving his rebuilt SW tower a fancy crown on the pattern of Dundry or Gloucester Cathedral. The Norman S arcade takes no notice of the tower. It is of four bays with round piers, square multi-scalloped capitals, and single-step arches (cf. Bobbington, not far away). In two of the arcade spandrels small Norman figures in relief, one an Orans. The N arcade is E.E., but nothing is left of original detail. The fenestration also is all Scott's Geometrical for the aisles, Dec for the E end. The foundation of a chantry in 1333 is recorded, but nothing matches it. – (STALLS. Late C15. Four MISERICORDS of high quality: Sir Ywain at the castle gate, a couple in a pew, two dogs attacking a bear, seated angel under a canopy. NMR) – (Also a very good BENCH END with two figures.) – PLATE. Silver-gilt set by *Magdalen Feline*, 1763. – MONUMENT. Thomas Grey † 1559. Alabaster. Two recumbent effigies. Upright children against the tomb-chest, including babies.)

---

* So Canon Clarke tells me.

Opposite, the village SCHOOL, really horrid High Victorian Gothic. 1861 is the date.

ENVILLE HALL. A fine house with glorious grounds. The house is of the second half of the C18, and more than that one cannot say. It has two fronts, S and N, and they are not aligned. N is normal Georgian, classical, nine bays with a pedimented three-bay centre. But the S side is Georgian Romantic, two wings and a recessed centre, turrets in the re-entrant angles, battlements, and typical Gothick motifs, i.e. ogees and quatrefoils. Now this front is really only a radical remodelling. Before, it was mid C16. The wings ended in stepped gables. The porte-cochère is of after a disastrous fire in 1904. The whole interior was then redone.

As for the GROUNDS, they were landscaped in the C18 and C19. The zest for plant cultivation in the C19 was magnificently exhibited by one of the major conservatories of England, pulled down only about twenty-five years ago. It was the most fanciful of any, with two glazed turrets or eminences. The date of the building is not recorded. The grounds are hilly, and there is a large lake with a FOUNTAIN with a triton and four horses. *Shenstone* had something to do with the first landscaping. He had made his fame as a garden fancier by his work at the Leasowes across the Worcestershire border, and he died at Enville. What precisely he did is not certain.

The CHAPEL in the woods (with a round tower with conical roof) is dedicated to him. It is placed, as *The Beauties of England and Wales* describe it, 'in thick and gloomy umbrage'. Near the chapel is the CASCADE, still going strong. Near by again the Gothic GATEWAY, three arches connected by castellated walls. The two smaller outer arches are placed at an angle. The gateway probably marked the passage from the grounds to the wood, the high-lying Sheep Walks, and the picturesque valley in which is still a TEMPLE with four alternately blocked front columns. Nearer the house is the Gothic SUMMER HOUSE, 1750 by *Sanderson Miller*. This has all kinds of not quite archaeologically correct motifs and is therefore particularly attractive. At the time of writing it is hemmed in by excessive growth.

Other features are or were – for they are at the time of writing very ruinous – the HERMIT'S HOUSE, once with a thatched roof, the PAGODA in the wood, and the BOATHOUSE by the lake.

STABLES. A long symmetrical brick range of nine bays with

a central arch and cupola. Giant angle pilasters, also to the centre bay. The stables are axial with the mansion. They are probably of *c.*1748–50 by *William Baker*.

ESSINGTON

ST JOHN EVANGELIST. 1932–3 by *Wood & Kendrick* and *Edwin F. Reynolds*. Pale brick with mullioned and transomed windows and a thin s tower. Internally mostly Gothic in effect. No aisles.

ETRURIA *see* HANLEY, STOKE-ON-TRENT, p. 258

ETTINGSHALL *see* WOLVERHAMPTON, p. 322

FALLINGS PARK *see* WOLVERHAMPTON, p. 321

FAREWELL

The place of a Benedictine priory founded *c.*1140 by Roger de Clinton Bishop of Lichfield (i.e. at the time of Coventry).

ST BARTHOLOMEW. Chancel of *c.*1300, the E window with intersecting tracery. The rest of 1745. Brick, with a short W tower and arched windows. – STALLS. Late Perp with MISERICORDS. The ER on the misericords must mean Edward VI or Elizabeth I, i.e. a mid C16 date. Also foliage decoration. – COMMUNION RAIL. Late C17, with twisted balusters. Or can they be as late as *c.*1745? – PLATE. Chalice and Paten by *Fuller White*, London, 1748.

FAREWELL HALL. Late C17, of brick, five bays, two storeys, wooden cross-windows and a hipped roof. The doorhead is a shell, oddly vertically elongated. Two panelled chimneystacks. (Good staircase. DOE)

FAZELEY

ST PAUL. 1853–5 by *H. J. Stevens* of Derby, built at the expense of Peel (*see* Drayton Bassett). Nave and chancel in one, bellcote two bays E of the W end. Lancets and some plate tracery.

(BONEHILL HOUSE. Early C19. Five-bay front; porch of four Doric columns. DOE)

Terraces of workers' houses on both sides of the main N–S street.

MILL (WILLIAM TOLSON LTD). The oldest part was originally one of the cotton mills built by Sir Robert Peel in the late C18. Three storeys, at first eight bays. Large addition of 1883, five storeys, twenty-nine bays, plain.

FENTON see STOKE-ON-TRENT, p. 256

FLASH

Flash is 1518 ft up and calls itself the highest village in England.

ST PAUL. 1901 by *W. R. Bryden* of Buxton.* – PULPIT. Circular, of stone, carved with naturalistic fruit (cf. Meerbrook). – PLATE. C18 Chalice.

METHODIST CHAPEL. 1821. Two bays and three tiers of windows. Outer stair to the doorway. Fancy-Gothic inscription tablet.

FORSBROOK

ST PETER. 1848–9 by *James & Edward Barr* of Putney (GR). Lancets and a bellcote. The N aisle is of 1912, by *J. H. Beckett* of Longton.‡

FORTON

ALL SAINTS. A medieval W tower and a nave S wall of 1723 with arched windows, their arches keyed in. The rhythm of the S side is 1-4-1, the ones representing a doorway and a keyed-in round window over. But there is much more than this one impressive contrast to the church. The W tower, to start with, is early C13 below, Perp above, with a decorated frieze and eight pinnacles. A little earlier still than the tower must have been the chancel – see the one small N window. But the Perp E window is Victorian. The N windows are all Dec. And finally, go inside and you will see instead of a medieval arcade, an arcade of 1723 with Tuscan columns on high plinths and of course round arches. – FONTS. A baluster no doubt of *c.*1723. – (Also part of a Norman font with two volutes in a Celtic style. Jeavons) – PULPIT. Plain C18. – PLATE. Chalice and

---

* Information given by Dr D. B. Robinson.
‡ So Dr D. B. Robinson tells me.

Paten by *G.G.*, 1691; Paten by *I.C.*, 1691; Flagon by *David Willaume*, 1698; two Almsdishes, 1731. – MONUMENT. Sir Thomas Skrymsher † 1633. Two alabaster effigies. Flat canopy on four columns. Children against the tomb-chest (Jeavons). The monument is by *Garrat Hollemans* (CPDD).

FORTON HALL lies just W of the church. It is a house of great architectural significance. The porch is dated 1665, and so, while mullioned windows and gables go on, they are now made into a completely symmetrical façade.

On the pattern of Forton Hall, the village and neighbourhood has much ESTATE HOUSING.

Less than ¼ m. SE is a BRIDGE with skew arches which carries the road and the canal over the Meese, which feeds Aqualate Mere.

AQUALATE HALL, 1½ m. SE. The house, largely by *Nash*, of 1808, was destroyed by fire in 1910. It was large, with Gothic windows, battlements, and ogee domes. After the fire a new house was built in 1927–30 to designs by *W. D. Caröe*. It is in the subdued Tudor of that date and with the oatmeal-coloured bricks also typical of that date. The C18 STABLES with pediment and cupola are of red brick and are connected with the house by a range with steep gables (of the Nash time?). The grounds were landscaped by *Repton*, c.1800, and are of exquisite beauty. In the grounds the CASTLE, a red brick house with stepped gables and an attached round embattled tower.

The LODGES may well be by *Nash*, especially the ornate SW lodge with its highly decorated chimneystacks *à la* Henry VIII. ½ m. NE of the church on another hill is another FOLLY. This is conical and in all probability started life as a windmill (CPDD). (SUTTON HOUSE is a four-bay brick house and has a 'curved porch of Doric pillars'. DOE)

FOUR CROSSES INN *see* HATHERTON

FOXT

CHURCH. 1838. Thin W tower – machicolated of all things. Nave with pointed windows. No chancel.

FRADLEY

(ST STEPHEN. 1861 by *T. W. Goodman* of London.)
ORGREAVE HALL. *See* Alrewas.

FRADSWELL

St James the Less. The church has a chancel of *c.*1200 – see the two tiny pointed windows. The chancel arch is old too, but very much interfered with. w tower of purple brick, built in 1764. Windows and doorway are pointed. The nave is brick on the N side too, but the windows were altered in 1852, when the s aisle was built (rock-faced; geometrical tracery) and the chancel remodelled. – STAINED GLASS. S aisle E by *Wailes*, 1852. – s aisle w no doubt also by him.

FREEFORD HALL *see* SWINFEN HALL

FREEHAY

St Chad. By *Scott & Moffatt*, 1842–3 (consecrated 1846; CPDD). A nave with a bellcote and structurally no chancel at all. As the windows are all lancets, one may well at first be deceived into considering the church a Commissioners' building. On entering and taking in the triplet of E lancets with their shafting, one realizes that here First Pointed was chosen with a purpose. In fact, one can look at the building not as a nave without a chancel, but as an E.E. chancel without a nave. – STAINED GLASS. The E window by *Wailes*. – PLATE. Paten by *Robert Hennell*, 1794.

FULFORD

St Nicholas. 1825 by *C. H. Winks*. Of brick. Embattled w tower, not big, nave windows pointed, but the E window of three lights with intersecting tracery. – PLATE. Chalice, 1827 by *James Collins*.

s of the church the square brick SUMMER HOUSE of Fulford Hall. It has a pyramid roof.

GAILEY

Christ Church. 1849–51 by *G. T. Robinson* (CPDD), the chancel by *J. Fowler*, 1875–6. Nave with bellcote, transepts, steep roofs.

Canal Tower, ½ m. E on the A5. Circular, brick, embattled.

GAYTON

St Peter. A Norman chancel arch, though the features are almost entirely C19. E.E. s arcade with alternating round and

octagonal piers. Blocked Perp N arcade. In the chancel a late
C13 tomb recess and in it the defaced MONUMENT of a
Civilian. The w tower is of purple brick; dated 1732. Much of
the exterior by *Habershon & Pite*, 1870. – TILES. A number of
medieval floor tiles. – PLATE. Paten, 1703 by *John Downes*,
London; Chalice, 1717 by *Gabriel Sleath*, London; Tankard,
1794 by *William Bennett*, London.

GENTLESHAW

CHRIST CHURCH. Brick. An odd building, easily explained.
The w part is of 1839 (GR, or 1845 White, or 1837 Staffs
C.C. Map). With an embattled w tower and short nave with
transeptal chapels. Then, in 1903, a new E end was built with
its own transepts. The intention was clearly to continue w and
replace the old work. In fact an aisle arcade was begun. In the
end both halves were left standing.

GERARDS BROMLEY HALL *see* BROUGHTON

GLASCOTE*

ST GEORGE. 1880 by *Basil Champneys*, and at once recognizable
as the work of a resourceful architect of the generation after
Shaw's. The church is of brick, not at all attractive in texture.
It has a short chancel, then an oblong central bay, both these
rib-vaulted. Above the latter stands a tower with a saddleback
roof so big and starting so relatively low that it looks like a
high gable. It has, attached to it, a round stair-turret, and in the
top of the gable a three-light stone window the sides of which
continue as shafts and pinnacles. This motif repeats in the
gabled w wall. The arcade inside is uninteresting. – STAINED
GLASS. The E window of 1905 and N window of 1903 by
Morris & Co., i.e. designed by *Burne-Jones*.

GNOSALL

ST LAURENCE. Gnosall was a collegiate church; that explains its
ambitious plan. Yet it is not a large church. Externally it is
dominated by a crossing tower, Perpendicular at the top with
its frieze of cusped saltire crosses and its eight pinnacles. But

---

* Formerly in Warwickshire.

one sees at once that it must be older; for the transepts show Norman masonry and shallow Norman buttresses. And inside there is indeed some of the most exciting Norman work in the county. It is the crossing and the S transept. The W crossing arch is the most ornate, with colonnettes, flat trail capitals, and three bands of ornament in the arch, also flat. It includes zigzag. The other arches are less spectacular, though the badly preserved E arch had some decoration. The S transept is the great surprise. It had blank arcading, only partly preserved, and a proper triforium of two twin openings, not arched but straight-headed. The corners of the crossing incidentally are visible, and their continuation into aisleless nave and aisleless chancel. This aisleless nave was given aisles in the C13. Three generous bays, octagonal piers, double-chamfered arches. The position of the W lancets proves that the aisles were as wide then as they are now. The nave W front has a doorway with one order of colonnettes and a big quadrant moulding. Three stepped lancets above. Another C13 doorway is in the S aisle. It has stiff-leaf capitals. À propos this aisle doorway, what should one make of the round-headed archway of the N aisle and the shallow buttresses W of it and in the W front? Don't they prove that there was already in the C12 an aisled church of the present length? Most of the present windows have ogee-headed lights under a segmental arch. The VCH calls them Late Perp. They could, however, be Dec. Dec definitely the five-light E window with its flowing tracery, though the round-headed N niche in the chancel is again E.E. The meeting of E.E. with Norman is most instructively seen in the arch between S transept and S aisle. The S chapel is Perp – see the original arcade piers – and Perp too is the shallow chapel of the N transept. The S porch is by *Lynam*, 1893, curiously ignorant, considering that he was a learned archaeologist. – STAINED GLASS. Old bits in a S chapel S window. – PLATE. Chalice by *W.G.*, 1690; Paten by *Thomas Robinson* of Chester, *c*.1692. – MONUMENTS. Alabaster Knight of *c*.1470. – Child, late C14 or early C15.

GOAT LODGE *see* BLITHFIELD

GOLDENHILL *see* TUNSTALL, STOKE-ON-TRENT, p. 265

GRATWICH

ST MARY. 1775. Of brick, with pointed windows and a bellcote. But the small chancel must, judging by brickwork and motifs, be early C17 and does not look like a chancel.

GREAT BARR

2¾ m. NE of West Bromwich

GREAT BARR HALL is now part of ST MARGARET'S HOSPITAL, the main buildings of which date from 1914–26 (architect *G. McMichael*) and lie in a semicircle open to the A-road. The Hall is behind, in the valley, and is a Gothick building of 1777 etc. It was built for Joseph Scott. Leigh in 1820 called it 'one of the finest and most delightful mansions in this part of the country'. He continued: 'It stands in a beautiful vale ornamented with trees of good variety and abundance.' The house has a main part of nine bays with ogee-headed windows, buttresses, and battlements. The second part is mauled but must have been equally charming. Inside is a spectacular staircase hall forming the centre of the house. The staircase has twisted balusters and goes up complicatedly in two arms. Fretwork pilasters on the arches and ribbed ceiling forming three large stars with skylights.

To the estate once belonged HANDSWORTH LODGE, on the A road, a little to the W. This also has an ornate front and ogee windows. Yet further W, again on the A road, is FAIRYFIELD HOUSE, Gothic too, of five bays, with pointed windows, but in the middle an ogee window above the pretty porch.

By the Great Barr approach to the Motorway is a five-bay house with a hood on brackets over the door.

ST MARGARET. The church, the successor of one of the time of the house, is of 1860–1 (by *Griffin*) with a steeple of 1890. Nice recessed spire. The church is late C13 in style.

GREAT HAYWOOD *see* HAYWOOD

GREAT WYRLEY

ST MARK. 1844–5 by *T. Johnson* of Lichfield. Remarkable in that it no longer has the Commissioners' character, though on the S side are paired long lancets and buttresses. But from the N, with its aisles and the long chancel, it is already a type the Ecclesiologists could have approved of. They were indeed moderately kind to the building, but criticized a number of features. The N arcade they called good, but the chancel too wide.

GREENFIELD see TUNSTALL, STOKE-ON-TRENT, p. 266

GREEN HEATH

St Saviour. 1887–8 by *F. W. Evans*. Estimate £475. Chancel 1901.

GREETS GREEN see WEST BROMWICH, p. 304

GRINDON

All Saints. 1845 by the *Francis* brothers. Quite large and in a fine position with a screen of trees. The building is a standard article, competent, correct, and uninspired. W tower with broach-spire. Nave and aisles, the chancel as low as the aisles. The features late C13 to early C14. – (FONT. Norman, with one wavy band of ornament. Jeavons) – STAINED GLASS. Old fragments, chancel N.

HALES

St Mary. 1856 by *George Gilbert Scott*. A substantial, though not a large church. W tower, nave and chancel. Middle Pointed, i.e. late C13 to early C14. Ashlar-faced interior.

Audley's Cross, 1 m. N. A medieval cross to commemorate the battle of Blore Heath in 1459. Plinth of 1765.

(Peatswood Hall, 1½ m. W. The STABLES are of brick, seven bays and two storeys. Built *c.*1900. The style is a free Queen Anne, uncommonly well detailed. Steep central pediment; square, domed cupola. Tripartite doorway and cross windows.*)

Old Springs Hall, 1¼ m. SW. Early C19. Ashlar-faced, five-bay front. Porch with closely paired pillars.

Bridge over the Shropshire Union Canal, Tyrley, 1½ m. W. By *Telford*. One flattened arch.

Roman Villa, ½ m. E of Hales Hall, on a slope above a small stream. Only partially revealed by excavation, it is known to

---

* Dr Gomme kindly sent me this description.

HALES HALL see CHEADLE

HALL GREEN see WEST BROMWICH, p. 303

HALL O' WOOD see BALTERLEY

HALMER END

SECONDARY SCHOOL. Substantial additions by *Andrew Renton & Partners*, 1963–5.

HAMMERWICH

ST JOHN BAPTIST. On an elevated site with a view to the W towards the pretty, white, castellated former WINDMILL. The church is of 1873–83, by *Newman & Billing*, far better than the average. W tower with broach-spire. Nave and N aisle, E.E. quatrefoil piers with stiff-leaf capitals. The short chancel bay and polygonal apse are stone-vaulted. Windows with pointed-trefoiled tops, mostly in pairs, low for the aisle, high and internally with detached shafts for the nave. – PLATE. Chalice by *Peter Archambo* of London, 1729.

HAMSTALL RIDWARE

ST MICHAEL. The small, low tower with its recessed spire was placed in the C14 in front of a Norman nave of whose W wall the upper window partly remains. The chancel and the N chapel are C14 too. Perp N aisle and clerestory. C18 N chapel walls. – FONT (outside). Norman, with angle colonnettes. – REREDOS. The side pieces with PAINTINGS from the life of Christ probably come from the dado of a screen or the parapet of a rood loft. The date may be late C15; the quality is poor. – SCREENS. The N chapel screen looks c.1520–30, the two open-work medallions with putti being probably even later. – The S chapel screen is simpler. – BENCH ENDS with simple tracery. – Also STALL ARMS. – STAINED GLASS. The

Apostles in the N aisle are nearly all Victorian. – Some original pieces in the S chapel. – PLATE. Silver-gilt chalice of the C14; Paten C14 too; Paten by *T.U.K.*, 1681; Chalice, London-made, 1681–2. – MONUMENT. Richard and John Cotton, 1502. The brass on the lid is missing, but against the tomb-chest are shields halved between armorial bearings and figures of the children. Above each a scroll with an inscription about their status in life. The monument stands under a panelled, four-centred arch between chancel and S chapel.

HAMSTALL HALL. The confusing remains of a major hall of the Fitzherberts dating from the C16 to early C17. The buildings were of brick with stone dressings. There was a large court and a second one to the W of it with outbuildings. What remains complete is the GATEHOUSE with two polygonal turrets with two-light windows and stone caps. Above the arch free-standing strapwork. Then there is a tower, imposing but not telling, and a very strange LOGGIA with strapwork under a gable also embellished with strapwork. It was a porch. Walls are extensive, and the present house may contain more (Inside, some re-set linenfold panelling. Also some medallions. The date is probably *c.*1530–40. NMR)

HANBURY

ST WERBURGH. Splendidly placed on a hill with clumps of trees to the N, and of course also splendid views to the N. Moreover, a handsome group near by, on the S, with a Georgian three-bay house, two yew trees, and a timber-framed house. The church has E.E. arcades of four bays with round piers, octagonal abaci, and double-chamfered arches. The high Perp W tower cuts into them. It has a five-light window, twin two-light bell openings, and decorated battlements. The top 20 ft were added in 1883 to the incumbent's design. Perp also the three-light clerestory windows. The chancel is of 1862 (by *Hine & Evans* of Nottingham*) and has noteworthy WALL DECORATION including scenes, and also decoration on the roof. The date of the N aisle is 1869. – TILING inside the tower, 1883. – STAINED GLASS. In the S aisle SE window ancient glass including a Christ crucified. – By *Ward & Hughes* the W window (1894) and – exceptionally good for this

---

* However, the Rev. W. St J. Kemm tells me that among the Hanbury papers is a design for the chancel signed by *Street* and dated 1854. It was not used. Street was paid 8 gns, Hine & Evans £40.

firm – the s aisle w window (1890). – PLATE. Chalice and Paten by *William Holmes* of London, 1778. – MONUMENTS. Cross-legged knight, early C14 (s aisle E), probably Sir John de Hanbury † 1303, and, if so, the earliest of all English alabasters. – (Stone slab with the heads of husband and wife in rectangular recesses. Below a cross in relief. About 1300. Jeavons) – Much rubbed-off brass to John Cheney, rector, † 1408, a 19 in. figure (chancel floor). – Ralph Adderley † 1595 and wives. Alabaster. Incised slab on a tomb-chest with figurines (chancel N). – Charles Egerton † 1624. Semi-reclining bearded figure under a three-centred canopy (chancel S). – Mrs Agarde and her daughter † 1628 and 1657. Frontal busts with hats in identical architectural surrounds (chancel). – A similar tablet to Dorothy Villers † 1665 (chancel N). – (Sir John Egerton † 1662. Recumbent effigy under a low arch. Jeavons) – John Wilson † 1839. By *Hollins*. With a large seated female figure.

SCHOOL. 1848. Symmetrical, of brick, mixed Early and Late Tudor, with a turret. The architect was *Fradgley* of Uttoxeter.*

HANCH HALL see LONGDON

HANCHURCH

HANCHURCH HOUSE. An Early Victorian Tudor house of great charm. Stuccoed, symmetrical, with two gables and two dormers between. Nice glazing. An outbuilding in the same style on the l. A lake in front.

HANDSACRE

HANDSACRE HALL. Derelict at the time of writing. Front of brick with timber-framed gables, probably C17. Among decorative motifs a large fleur-de-lis. Inside, an aisled structure of two and a half bays, dating from *c.*1320 and similar to West Bromwich Manor House. The structure is now horizontally divided.

METHODIST CHURCH. Gothic, of brick and stone and hardly defensible, especially as it is as late as 1894.

HIGH BRIDGE. *See* Mavesyn Ridware.

* I owe the name to Dr D. B. Robinson.

HANFORD see STOKE-ON-TRENT, p. 264

HANLEY see STOKE-ON-TRENT, p. 257

HARECASTLE FARM see TALKE

HAREGATE HALL see LEEK

HARLASTON

ST MATTHEW. The tower is of the early C13 – see the lancets N and S and the only slightly chamfered responds of the arch to the nave. The rest by *Ewan Christian*, 1882–3. Brick, nave and chancel, and half-timbered bell-turret. – PLATE. Chalice, 1818.
To the l. of the church is the MANOR HOUSE, a good late C16 or early C17 timber-framed house.

HARRACLES HALL see HORTON

HASELOUR HALL
½ m. WSW of Harlaston

The house has a gorgeous black and white front of five gables, the third rather smaller and perhaps originally a porch; for the core of the house is genuine, though most of it is of 1885. The architect does not seem to be recorded. The work has all the motifs current about 1600.* (In the house 'an elaborate carved overmantel of uncertain date'. DOE) Attached to the house is a CHAPEL of stone, which is a real medieval building. The thin W turret with spire looks C13. Yet the assumption is that the chapel was built *c.*1370.

HATHERTON

HATHERTON HALL. 1817, in a Tudor Gothic, rendered. Two storeys, battlements and pinnacles. The front is of five bays and has an ornate porch not in the middle. Round the corner a big bow flanked by single windows.
LONGFORD HOUSE, 1½ m. SE, on the A5. *See* Cannock.

---

* An elevation, drawn by Edward Ould, appears in the second volume (n.d.) of John Douglas's *Abbey Square Sketch Book*, where it is stated that 'The lower portion of Building has been much restored' and that the l. gable 'is almost entirely Modern'.

FOUR CROSSES INN, 1 m. s, on the A5. Two parts, the r. one timber-framed and dated 1636, but much restored. The l. part is of c.1700: two bays and three storeys, brick, with quoins and a parapet starting l. and r. with concave curves. So a coaching inn about 1700 felt the need for some more straightforward bedrooms than a black and white house would get you.

HATTON see SWYNNERTON

HAUGHTON

ST GILES. Mostly by *Pearson*, 1887, but the N wall is C13 – see the W lancet – and has single straight-headed Perp windows, and the W tower is Perp. It cuts into the lancet just referred to. The tower has a top frieze of cusped saltire crosses and eight pinnacles. Pearson's are the S wall with straight-headed windows with reticulation units and the E end in the E.E. style. Lancets, and the E window a triplet of shafted lancets. Very narrow two-bay N chancel chapel, the pier and respond with uncommonly lush leaf capitals. Typical of Pearson on the other hand the steep arches. Fine treatment of the sedilia. – REREDOS. 1896. Also typical of Pearson is the blunt oblong shape. The carving by *N. Hitch*. – PLATE. Chalice and Paten by *Joseph Angel*, London, 1827. – (MONUMENT. Incised slab to Nicholas Graviner † 1520, rector, exceptionally good. In the NE corner.)

HAUGHTON OLD HALL, W of the church. Late C16, timber-framed. Mostly with closely set verticals, but in the main gable also lozenges made up of short balusters.

Less than ½ m. NW of the Hall, on the other side of the road, a cruck COTTAGE.

HAUNTON

ST MICHAEL (R.C.). Entirely like a C. of E. church in its graveyard. 1901–2 by *Edmund Kirby*. Stone with strange windows, their lights with rounded trefoil tops. Timber bell-turret and porch.

CONVENT OF ST JOSEPH. The CHAPEL is by *Charles Hansom*, c.1848. Brick.

HAWKESYARD PRIORY see ARMITAGE

HAYWOOD

ST STEPHEN. 1840 by *T. Trubshaw*, enlarged by *H. J. Stevens*. Nave and chancel in one; bellcote, s aisle with Perp arcade. All the features look Stevens rather than 1840.

ST JOHN BAPTIST (R.C.). Built in 1828 by *Joseph Ireland* at Tixall and brought here in 1845. Very much the character of an ambitious private chapel. Ornate w front with a recessed high octagonal sw turret. Along the sides large transomed Late Perp windows, all straight-headed. Inside, the dado below them is stone-panelled. Rich WEST GALLERY. The new ceiling is a pity.

The HOUSING l. and r. of the street leading to the Essex Bridge is an anticipation of Shugborough. First on either side a three-bay house with pedimented doorway, then, continuing without a break, a lower terrace with two more pedimented doorways. The RAILWAY BRIDGE which follows is as formal: rusticated, and with a middle arch and two pedestrian side arches.

ESSEX BRIDGE. Probably of the C16, only 4 ft wide, with fourteen segmental arches and cutwaters to both sides.

HAZLEHURST BRIDGE see ENDON

HEATH HAYES

ST JOHN. 1902–3 by *F. T. Beck*. Brick, with low walls and a big roof. Small windows, a s porch accessible from the E, and a little turret on the junction of nave and chancel which is not expressed internally. It is a friendly building, not without originality.

HEATH HOUSE see TEAN

HEATH TOWN see WOLVERHAMPTON, p. 321

HEDNESFORD

ST PETER, Church Hill. 1868 by *T. H. Rushworth*. The w tower was never built, and the N aisle only in 1906 (*Joyce & Sandy*). The style of the church is E.E. Nave and transepts and an apse with shafted windows. A staid, creditable job. – PLATE. Silver-gilt medieval chalice, possibly Flemish.

OUR LADY OF LOURDES (R.C.). An amazingly ambitious, self-confident building, and yet one so disjointed that no architectural enjoyment is possible. The style is C13 with more French than English overtones, but there are also places where it becomes obvious that this is a belated C20 C13. The dates of the building are in fact 1927–33. The architect was *G. B. Cox* of Birmingham. Busy W front, lacking cohesion, side chapels low and projecting individually, transepts and a turret in the corner of S transept and church. Polygonal apse. Large quadripartite rib-vaults, two for the nave and one each for crossing, N transept, and S transept. – SCULPTURE. The Stations of the Cross are by *P. Lindsay Clark*.

ANGLESEY HOTEL. The hotel, at the end of the principal square of the little town, was built in 1831 as a summer house by Edmund Peel of Fazeley. A symmetrical Tudor house with two stepped gables and a recessed centre, the recession filled in by a three-bay loggia of arches with four-centred heads. The building is rendered.

(CROSS KEYS INN, Old Hednesford. Dated 1746. Timber-framed.)

HEIGHLEY CASTLE

Spectacularly placed on a high wooded rock. (The ruins are overgrown. Two lengths of walling, including one length of arcading, remain. They are assigned to the C13. DOE)

HEYWOOD GRANGE *see* DILHORNE

HIGH OFFLEY

ST MARY. The N doorway is a typical piece of *c.*1200. A little later the S arcade (round piers, round capitals, arches of one step and one chamfer). The E respond capital is a re-used Norman piece with two spirally volutes and a head, the W window is Norman too, the E window of three stepped lancet lights must be full C13. Full C13 also the lowest stage of the W tower – see the one lancet (the round head is not original) and the arch to the nave. Dec chancel E window with reticulated tracery. Good chancel roof with moulded beams. – PLATE. Paten by *Timothy Ley*, 1723; Chalice by *Thomas Farrer*, 1730.

HILDERSTONE

CHRIST CHURCH. 1827–9 by *Thomas Trubshaw*. Commissioners' type, but with a NW steeple carrying a recessed spire. The church has lancets, with flattish buttresses between, and typically clumsy pinnacles. The interior has originality – ignorance breeding originality – with its octagonal piers, each side carrying fluting or a sunk panel, and its leaf capitals. Angel corbels for the roof inform us of people connected with the new building (Ralph Bourne, the donor, the parson at the time, and the architect). – BOX PEWS. – STAINED GLASS. The E window with its glaring colours typical of its date: 1829 by *Collins* of London (CPDD). – PLATE. Chalice and Paten, 1827 by *Rebecca Emes & Edward Barnard*. – MONUMENTS. Tablets by *William Whitelaw* to Ralph Bourne † 1835 and Sarah, his wife, † 1833.

HILL RIDWARE see MAVESYN RIDWARE

HILL TOP see WEST BROMWICH, p. 304

HILTON PARK

This is a most interesting building, but one would like to know more about its history and in particular one feature. The building clearly dates from the early C18 and fits in with much other work in the county, especially at Chillington. The main front facing the lake is of a recessed five-bay centre and two short three-bay wings. There are two storeys plus an attic storey above the main cornice. The house is of brick and has even quoins. All the windows have aprons, and on the ground floor the florid keystones rise into the aprons. The climax is of course the doorway bay. Over the doorway is an open pediment, the l. half curving up to the l., the r. half to the r. – a Borromini motif, used in England at Chicheley Hall. The window above has volutes and garlands, the attic window has volutes too, and there is a charming curved pediment with vases, a shield, and garlands. Round the corner five bays. The present porte-cochère is of course Victorian. Now the problem is the attic. The DOE reports C18 illustrations without the attic, and so assigns the attic to the C19. But can that be so, even assuming that the pediment was simply raised? At what

time would the early C18 have been so faithfully carried on?*
Fine dining room, panelled, with a niche with a marble wine-cooler. Drawing room with Corinthian pilasters. Good staircase.

Across the lake to the w a very handsome Victorian CONSERVATORY, a domed structure. To the s, further away, the PORTOBELLO TOWER, hexagonal and embattled. It commemorates Admiral Vernon's capture of Portobello in 1739. The house was built for Henry Vernon.

HIMLEY

ST MICHAEL. A church of 1764, killed stone-dead by cementing W tower, nave, and apsidal chancel. Arched windows, keyed in. Beautifully curved parapet of the W gallery. – PULPIT. Plain Georgian. – LECTERN. A brass angel of 1894. – MONUMENTS. Viscountess Ednam, 1930 by *Sir W. Reid Dick*. Small statue of a young mother with her child on one shoulder. – In the Garden of Remembrance four gravestones by *Eric Gill*: John Jeremy Ward, Georgina Countess of Dudley, Rosemary Viscountess Ednam, all three 1930, and second Earl of Dudley, 1933.

RECTORY. 1769? Three bays, brick, arched doorway, also an arched window breaking into the one-bay top pediment. The bay windows are of course later.

HIMLEY HALL. The garden side tells the story of the building. The centre is early C18. Seven bays with a pedimented three-bay projection. The pediment was at that time segmental. The windows have typical sweeping-up hoods and typical aprons – all busy and jolly. The façade is continued by three-bay wings with giant Doric pilasters, and that belongs to 1824–7 and was the work of *William Atkinson*. Previously the wings, extending back to flank the entrance court, were single-storeyed and separated by links from the main façade. Round the corner Atkinson continued with a nine-bay façade of his own design. Giant portico of unfluted Ionic colums with pediment and the side parts with Doric pilasters. The entrance side has only recently lost another such portico. There are far-projecting wings on this side. All of it is by Atkinson.

Good LODGE with a centre with attached Ionic columns between two pedimented bays.

---

* Kelly refers to alteration and enlargement of 1830.

HINTS

ST BARTHOLOMEW. 1882–3 by *John Oldrid Scott* at the expense of a cotton manufacturer called Chadwick. Yellow stone (looking unfortunately like yellow brick) and red stone dressings. Nave with bellcote at its E end and chancel. Lancets – lancets again, not still – singly, in pairs, as a triplet, as a row of fours. A dignified design. – STAINED GLASS. The W lancet by *Kempe*. – PLATE. Silver-gilt Chalice and Paten, 1704 by *John Leach*; silver-gilt Chalice and Paten, 1776 by *Matthew Boulton* and *John Fothergill*, Birmingham. – MONUMENTS. Sir Thomas Lawley † 1779, the typical *King* of Bath tablet. Standing female figure by an urn. – Robert Lawley Lord Warlock † 1834. Kneeling female figure by a pedestal. – Sir Francis Lawley † 1851. By *Foley*. Large lunette with a reclining woman and a kneeling angel at her head.

HIXON

ST PETER. Consecrated in 1848 and already fully Camdenian – no wonder, as it is by *George Gilbert Scott*.* Nave and long chancel, N tower with broach-spire. Middle Pointed details (i.e. late C13).

HOAR CROSS

HOLY ANGELS. In the early seventies *Bodley* worked on two churches, Pendlebury (South Lancashire) and Hoar Cross. Both are masterly, but there could be no greater contrast. Pendlebury is austere, Hoar Cross is luxuriant; Pendlebury is blunt, Hoar Cross exceedingly refined; Pendlebury highly original, Hoar Cross essentially derivative. At Pendlebury Bodley meant to create something new, at Hoar Cross he intended to show what perfection was obtainable within the rubrics of English late medieval decoration and architecture. For it is the decoration one thinks of first when one remembers Hoar Cross. At Pendlebury it is structure. How one man in one quinquennium of his life could have done both, believed in both, remains a mystery.

The story of Hoar Cross is well enough known. Hugo Francis Meynell Ingram of Hoar Cross Hall and Temple Newsam died in 1871. His wife built the church to commemorate him. Work began in 1872, the church was dedicated in

---

* Information given me by Mr A. Shaw.

1876. Later the nave was lengthened by one bay, the Lady Chapel N* of the chancel was built in 1891, the chapel s of the chantry with the monuments in 1900, the w narthex in 1906. The latter was designed by *Cecil Hare*.

The church consists of nave, central tower, transepts, chancel, and the adjoining chapels already referred to. The style is Dec throughout – Bodley's favourite style. The tower is high and panelled in two tiers. There are only two-light bell-openings, but they repeat blank l. and r., and three times blank beneath. It is the system of Ilminster in Somerset taken over. The chancel E window is of six lights with intricate tracery. The side windows are in pairs and placed remarkably high up – to allow for all that decoration we are presently to see. The main transept windows differ, intersected N, reticulated S. The nave is subordinated, shorter than the E end, lower than the E end, and, though it has a clerestory, much less decorated. The interior is dark even on sunny days. This is due to the STAINED GLASS windows. They are all by *Burlison & Grylls*. It remains a pity that Bodley favoured them and gave up the close connexion with Morris he established at the beginning of his career. There is nothing wrong with Burlison & Grylls glass, but one is never tempted to look at it intensely or twice. The nave has Dec piers of a pattern that occurs quite frequently in the county. But the nave, even with its three bays – originally, it will be remembered, there were only two – is no more than the preparation for the chancel.

The height of the chancel will move you at once, culminating in tierceron-vaults. In the nave and transepts there are no stone vaults. The roofs are of the wagon type instead. The arrangement of the chancel N and S walls differs. On the N is the organ chamber, on the S the so-called chantry chapel. But over both sides Bodley has lavished his enrichments, blank panelling, statues under canopies, ogee arches with crockets *à la* Percy Tomb at Beverley.

Bodley designed the FURNISHINGS as well, the REREDOSES, the SCREENS, the soaring FONT COVER, and the black and white marble FLOORING. – STATIONS OF THE CROSS. By two Antwerp carvers: *De Wint* and *Boeck*. – VESTMENTS. A Chasuble said to have belonged to Pope Gregory XI († 1378). – MONUMENTS. Hugo Francis Meynell Ingram † 1871. Recumbent effigy of white marble, between chancel and chantry

---

* The directions are ritual only, N being really W.

chapel. – Emily Meynell Ingram † 1904. On the other side of the chantry chapel. This monument has a flat wooden canopy, the other an arched one of stone. By *Farmer & Brindley*, but the head by *L. J. Chavalliaud*. – F. G. Lindley Meynell † 1910. Kneeling figure by *Bridgeman & Sons*. Design by *Cecil Hare*. – Silver plaque with an inserted crucifix, to Lady Mary Meynell † 1937. By *Goodhart-Rendel*. – Tablet to F. H. Lindley Meynell † 1941. By *Sir Charles Nicholson*.

HOAR CROSS HALL. A large mansion of brick in the Jacobean style of Temple Newsam, the Ingram house near Leeds. The architect is *Henry Clutton* and the date, according to Dr Gomme, 1862–71. Nearly symmetrical garden front with three canted bays, three gables, and large mullioned and transomed windows. The entrance front is more interesting. It is also symmetrical, except for the porte-cochère projecting on the r. and the chapel projecting on the l. There are here two turrets with ogee caps and between them is the one-storeyed centre of a ground-floor long gallery. The service wing, which extended to the r., has been demolished. The CHAPEL is decorated by *Bodley*. All his typical furnishings and motifs are there.*

PARSONAGE, N of the church. Probably also by *Bodley*.

HOLBECHE HOUSE *see* KINGSWINFORD

HOLLINGTON

ST JOHN. By *Street*, 1859–61, but not of the same calibre as the exactly contemporary All Saints Denstone. Originality Hollington unquestionably has, but, at least in the apse, at the cost of jettisoning seemliness. The apse is round, yet has at the apex a three-light window with plate tracery and a dormer-like gable over it. The clash with the rotundity of the apse is painful, and Street must have known what he was doing. The church has nave and chancel in one, and the apse is not lower either. Rock-faced walls, small windows with pointed-trefoiled lights. But W of the N doorway one large quatrefoil (cf. Denstone). Steep bellcote, and steep roofs too. The interior is ashlar-faced, and the windows have rere-arches. – *Street*'s typical cylindrical stone PULPIT and extremely low

---

* This is ascribed to the 1880s by Dr Gomme, who adds that *Bodley* also apparently did the hall screen.

stone SCREEN. – Most of the other fitments also by *Street*. – (STAINED GLASS. In the apse by *Clayton & Bell*, 1861 – i.e. very early work. P. Joyce)

HOLLINSCLOUGH

ST AGNES. 1840. An odd arrangement, similar to that at Reaps Moor. A house is attached to the W end of the church under the same roof. Bell-turret over the W end of the church. Very short chancel with three funny obelisks. Three more such obelisks over the two-storeyed porch.

HOPWAS

ST CHAD. By *John Douglas*, 1881, and certainly an ingenious and entertaining building. Brick, and in the upper parts timber-framing. Nave with a big roof starting low down and wooden windows below to light the nave. Short chancel, but connecting the two parts a kind of central tower with a dormer to the S and a shingled spirelet. The interior in contrast displays no tricks. It is faced in yellow brick. The roof of the nave has big arched braces, the central tower brick W and E arches.

HOPWAS BRIDGE. Shortly after 1795. Five three-centred round arches. Double pilasters between.

HORTON

ST MICHAEL. Perp W tower with eight pinnacles. Perp aisle windows, straight-headed with ogee tops to the lights. Late Perp or post-Reformation chancel windows, straight-headed with round, uncusped tops to the lights. The E window and S arcade are by *Sugden*, 1864. The N arcade is Perp. – TOWER SCREEN. 1618, with flat balusters. – PLATE. Chalice, 1640 by *P.B.*; Paten, 1754. – MONUMENTS to Wedgwoods. John † 1589, brass plate with kneeling figures. – John † 1724, purely, indeed purely, architectural. – John † 1757, also without figures. Obelisk top. – John Fowler † 1827. By *W. Spence* of Liverpool. Rather crowded motifs.

HORTON HALL, by the church. A very fine C17 house, rather of Cotswold appearance. Recessed centre and slightly projecting wings. Three gables with ball finials. The windows, except those in the gables, all sashed in the C18, which does no damage to the façade but turns out indeed to be an asset.

VICARAGE, to the r. of the Hall. Brick front of the early C18. Five bays, two storeys, parapet. Upright two-light windows (still), doorway with straight entablature. Arched window over.

DAIRY HOUSE, ¾ m. NW. Dated 1635. Recessed centre with three small gables and projecting wings with larger gables. A porch between centre and l. wing, later extended to the r. In two of the three small gables ovals, one horizontal, one vertical.

HARRACLES HALL, ¾ m. E. A Wedgwood house. Seven-bay Georgian brick house with a three-bay pediment. Garlands in the pediment. Doorway with open segmental pediment. Hipped roof.

HUNTINGTON

In Stafford Road an entertaining contrast – the PUMPING STATION of c.1876–9 and the LITTLETON COLLIERY PITHEAD BATHS of 1941. The former is by *Henry Naden*, the latter by *W. A. Woodland*. Both are of brick, and both are utilitarian. But the main building of the former is tall, narrow, and in a Waterhouse way Gothic, the latter International Modern in the Mendelsohn way (see the glazed, semicircular projection) and Dudok way (see the long, low window band and the unrelieved cubic blocks). The pithead baths were among the first buildings in England to adhere consistently to the International Modern.

HURST HILL *see* COSELEY

ILAM

Ilam is beautifully placed in the Manifold valley. What it possesses of architectural interest is connected with the Watts Russell family of Ilam Hall, and chiefly Jesse Watts Russell.

ILAM HALL was rebuilt by Jesse Watts Russell in 1821–6 in the Gothic taste to designs by the elder *John Shaw*. It was a large, spectacular, picturesque mansion with battlements and turrets, but survives only sadly truncated, i.e. the porte-cochère, or gatehouse, and a hall with five high Gothic two-light windows now horizontally divided. At the back the symmetrical STABLES. By the drive to the entrance an octagonal TOWER. In the village much ESTATE HOUSING. This and the SCHOOL of 1854 are characterized by tile-hanging (a surprisingly early revival of this Home Counties motif), steep, bargeboarded gables, and half-timbering trellis-wise. In a strategic position the CROSS in memory of the first Mrs Watts Russell, erected by her husband in 1840. It is inspired by the Eleanor Crosses – at the same early moment at which Scott developed his Oxford Martyrs Memorial from the same source. Scott seems to have been interested in this when he visited Ilam in 1855. Like the cross, the church is a supplement to the house.

HOLY CROSS. The church is medieval, but externally looks all 1855–6, the time of *Scott*'s drastic restoration, and in any case the church is crushed by Mr Watts Russell's MEMORIAL CHAPEL, a wide, much-bepinnacled octagon attached to the church and erected in 1831 in memory of Mr Watts Russell's father-in-law, David Pike Watts. The chapel is rib-vaulted on demi-figures of angels as corbels. The church has on the s side a blocked doorway whose proportions make it likely that it is Saxon. Also on the s side a chapel dated 1618 and with straight-headed windows, their lights still ogee-headed. Scott's are of course the E wall with its E.E. shafted lancets and the saddleback roof of the tower. Below, the tower has a lancet, i.e. is E.E. The N arcade is Scott's too. – REREDOS. By *Scott*. – TILING of the chancel from the Scott years. – FONT. Of cauldron shape, Norman, with extremely barbaric figures and beasts. – SCREENS. Of wrought iron, ornate, designed by *Scott* and made by *Skidmore* of Coventry. – SCULPTURE. In the s chapel a small length of Saxon interlace. – PAINTING. St Helena and the True Cross. By *B. Viviani* (rather Ottavio Viviani). – PLATE. Silver-gilt Paten, 1719; Tray, 1737 by *John Tuite*. – MONUMENTS. Shrine of St Bertelin (cf. Stafford, p. 240). All that remains is the base with large open quatrefoils. There was no doubt once a canopy. – Robert Meverell † 1626 and his wife. Two alabaster effigies. Against the back wall one large and three small kneeling figures. Columns l. and r., top with raised semicircle. – In the Memorial Chapel David Pike Watts by *Chantrey*, 1831, all white and artfully lit. He lies on a couch, but sits up to bless his daughter, who has come with her three children. A very impressive piece; theatrical? – yes, but not at all without feeling. – In the chapel also the BUST of J. Watts Russell by *Laurence Macdonald*, 1863.

In the churchyard two late Anglo-Saxon CROSSES, a Peak District type, though closest to Beckermet St Bridget in Cumberland. One is round in its lower part, the other is rectangular throughout. Decoration in bands. In Staffordshire Checkley comes nearest.

(CASTERN HALL, 1½ m. NW. In a remote position. C18, of stone; five bays, with stone surrounds to the windows and a pedimented mid-window. DOE)

ROUND CAIRNS, on Ilam Moor, 1 m. N. Bronze Age. Some were excavated in the C19 and found to cover inhumation burials accompanied by Beaker and Food Vessel pottery.

INGESTRE

INGESTRE HALL. A mansion of the Chetwynd family until 1767 and then of a cadet branch of the Talbots which took the name Chetwynd-Talbot in 1784 when they became Earls Talbot. They became Earls of Shrewsbury in 1856. The s front of Ingestre Hall, built by Sir Walter Chetwynd († 1638), is the foremost display of Jacobean grandeur in the county – or the grandest side by side with the Elizabethan Tixall gatehouse. Behind that front lie rooms reinstated by *John Birch* after a fire had gutted them in 1882. But behind that front also are the N and W façades, and they, after having been drastically georgianized, were re-jacobeanized in 1808–10 for the second Earl Talbot by *Nash*. So much for the dates.

Now the appearance. The house is of brick with stone dressings, two floors high. The windows on both floors have several mullions and transoms. The wide angle bays project and have a big bow of ten lights and a broad shaped gable. There is also a middle projection, and this has a doorway with coupled Roman Doric columns, a round arch, and a heavy attic with short pilasters. Above is a canted bay with 2-2-4-2-2 lights. The cupola terminating the projection is a reconstruction by *Birch* after *Nash* had altered it drastically. Between the middle and the corner projections are on either side two windows, and in the re-entrant angle between that part and the angle projection the hall bay window of six by three lights on the l. and its companion piece of no functional need on the r. The contrast between the over-adorned portal and the plain grid of the rest is impressive. The N side is by *Nash*, replacing a classical design. The *Wren* office worked out a design late in the C17 with a giant portico of six attached columns and apparently sash windows.* Nash's façade is flatter than the Jacobean s front but also has the bows and the porch bay. There are more shaped gables here, and the porch bay has curious rounded angle shafts. In spite of such an incorrect

* The attribution to the Wren office was made by Dr Downes.

(archaeologically incorrect) motif, it is remarkable that Nash should have been able and willing to re-create the Jacobean so self-effacingly. The interior is all *Birch*-Jacobean. Large hall, large staircase awkwardly connected with it. The most remarkable room is the Yellow Drawing Room, in a very busy kind of free Quattrocento that deceives people into taking it for a paraphrase of the Adam style.

ST MARY. The church is close to the house, and while the house is magniloquent, the church is laconic, while the motifs of the house are hard, those of the church are urbane, though both can afford to be sparing in motifs, and while the house is brick, the church is ashlar. It is dated 1676 and attributed to *Wren*. There is no documentary proof, but Walter Chetwynd, owner of Ingestre at the time, belonged to the Royal Society, as did Wren. Moreover a drawing by Wren annotated 'Mr Chetwynd's Tower' exists. This is undeniably not enough reason; for Wren worked almost exclusively for the King (the City churches are the one great exception). But in the case of St Mary the exquisite quality speaks unequivocally. Ashlar with quoins. Projecting w tower, so that it should not ambiguously merge with the body of the church. The w doorway has three-quarter Tuscan columns and a pediment. Above this a shield with garlands. L. and r. of the clock also garlands. That is the only decoration. Top balustrade and four urns. Arched windows, keyed-in only at the top.* At the E end no Venetian window, but a less happy group of three stepped lights with two odd corbels between. Circular clerestory windows. Enter through the circular lobby under the tower, and you find yourself in a room of blissful harmony. The four-bay arcade arches stand on a cluster of four shafts grown together. There are no galleries – which helps in preserving unity. The ceiling of the nave is flat and decorated with the most gorgeous stucco of that happy moment in English decoration. The chancel has a plaster tunnel-vault with simpler motifs in panels.‡ His woodcarvers did not disappoint Wren. Magnificent yet not crowded SCREEN, tripartite, with pilasters and the Royal Arms. – REREDOS. Annunciation, and a garland. The latter is probably *in situ*, but the figures of the Annunciation were bought on the Continent c.1871.§ –

---

* The vestry bay is of 1908.

‡ The Rev. A. J. Poole writes that the panels have armorial bearings, and are later alterations.

§ Information from Mr Poole.

PANELLING around the chancel. – PULPIT with tester. – FONT. Of baluster type. – STAINED GLASS. One N window by *Morris & Co.*, 1897–8, i.e. after Morris's death. Showier than he would have been in so quiet a church. Two large angels. – Chancel N signed by *Willement*. – LIGHT FITTINGS. From the start, i.e. 1886, for electric light.* – PLATE. Silver-gilt Set by *I.B.* (Chalice and Paten, two Salvers, two Candlesticks); silver-gilt Chalice and Paten by *I.C.*, 1693; silver-gilt Christening Bowl, by *G.N. H.H.*, Chester, 1731‡; Chalice, C18. – MONUMENTS. All of Chetwynds, Talbots, and Chetwynd-Talbots. There are more in the church than is good for Wren. They impose themselves on one's attention, as of course they were meant to do. In the following account they are listed topographically. Chancel N and S four diptych tablets, purely architectural. Dates of death 1663, 1767 – 1692, 1741. The stylistic comparisons are telling. – Eighteenth Earl of Shrewsbury † 1868 by *Sir John Steell*. Recumbent effigy of marble. – Second Earl Talbot † 1848. By the younger *Westmacott*. – Francesca Tomasine Countess Talbot † 1819. By *Thomas Kirk*. Sarcophagus with two free-standing busts. – N aisle E. Viscount Ingestre † 1915. By *Lady Feodora Gleichen*, 1918. Recumbent effigy. Black marble and shiny bronze. – The Rev. John Chetwynd Talbot † 1825. By *Chantrey*. Frontally standing priest. – Viscount Ingestre † 1826. Also by *Chantrey*. Relief of his fatal accident. – Lady V. S. Talbot † 1856. By *Ernesto Cali*, Naples 1857. Relief. She lies asleep on a day-bed. – (Lady Winifred Pennoyer, by *Oliver Hill*. Slate.)

Other buildings round the house are:

NEW STABLES. By *Birch*, and a piece of unabashed display, making the house appear reticent. Entry archway with cupola and in the middle of the far wall arcading with cupola.

OLD STABLES. A humble range of the late C17. Brick, with quoins. Centre gabled rather than pedimented. Three bays l., three bays r.

ORANGERY. Late C18. Ashlar. Two pedimented end pavilions with Doric pilasters and between them nine bays of glass and Doric pilasters. A fine, unostentatious design.

(PAVILION, at some distance NW of the house. Mid C18. Rusticated and pedimented. Central recess and a screen of Ionic columns.)

---

* So Mr Sherlock told me. Cf. Chasetown.
‡ Probably a late replica.

The PARK was landscaped by *Capability Brown* in 1756.

IPSTONES

ST LEONARD. Built at the expense of John Sneyd. Briefs are dated 1787 and 1792.* W tower, nave with Y-tracery and battlements. The chancel by *Gerald Horsley*, 1902–3,‡ with a shallowly canted E wall. In its gable outside the Crucifixion. Inside, a Norman tympanum with two dragons and an outer band of ornament. – SCREEN. By *Horsley*. It fills the whole chancel opening. The side parts have close openwork panelling, the centre is wide open but has at the top good Arts and Crafts carving. – Above the screen a PAINTING of Christ in Glory and the twelve apostles. L. and r. stencilling. – MONUMENTS. On a window sill three free-standing urns: to Jane Sneyd † 1840, William Debank Sneyd † 1825, and Ralph Sneyd † 1821.

THE GROVE. Swagger mid C18 house of ashlar, three bays and two and a half storeys. The windows have moulded surrounds, the doorway a pediment. The mid-window is Venetian.

The Sneyds lived at Belmont Hall, 1 m. W, and there, by the road, John Sneyd about 1790 began a church, because he had quarrelled with the incumbent of St Leonard. In the end the quarrel was settled, and the church became CHAPEL HOUSE. Elaborate, now blank, E window of four lights with intersected tracery. Stump of a W tower.

MOSS LEE HALL, 1¼ m. NW. Dated 1640. The house has an asymmetrical façade with two canted bays. Only a few windows have transoms. Staircase with flat balusters and heavy newel-posts.

WHITEHOUGH, ½ m. N. Dated on two doorways 1620 (DOE) and 1724. Really like two houses, the r. one quite possibly of 1620 with a canted bay and at the back a three-transom window, the l. one regular, especially at the back. Three bays, with l. and r. of the doorway a three-light mullioned window and above three cross-windows. On the garden gate the date 1719.

SHARPECLIFFE HALL, 1¼ m. NW. A substantial C17 house, but mostly with windows without transoms. Front of three plus one gables.

---

* Information given me by Dr D. Robinson.
‡ But the faculty of 1876 is for *G. G. Scott Jun.* (Canon Clarke).

KEELE

ST JOHN. Rebuilt in 1868–70 by *J. Lewis* of Newcastle-under-Lyme at the expense of Ralph Sneyd of Keele Hall (*see* below). Red and much cream stone, with a SW steeple with a sharp spire. Coarse pinnacles. W and S porches. The features are Dec. The interior is plain, with four-bay arcades. – Good iron SCREEN. – MONUMENTS. William Sneyd † 1613 and wife. Recumbent effigies; tomb-chest with shields. – Ralph Sneyd † 1703. Elaborate architectural tablet with two upright putti.

VICARAGE. Red brick with patterns of blue bricks, probably of the time of the church. In similar style the SCHOOL.

KEELE UNIVERSITY.* Keele is the first of the New Universities, and visually it has suffered for that and is still suffering. The University College of North Staffordshire was founded in 1949 and took over Keele in 1950. It became the University of Keele only in 1962. (The new universities of Sussex, Essex, York, and East Anglia were founded in 1961, 1961, 1963, and 1964 respectively.) The University College of North Staffordshire was first housed in Nissen huts, but the conversion of Keele Hall was begun and completed quickly.

KEELE HALL. The first Keele Hall was built for Ralph Sneyd *c*.1580. Another Ralph Sneyd built the present one in 1856–61. His architect was *Salvin*. Twenty or twenty-five years before, *Blore* had built new stables (*see* below). Salvin's is a self-confident and, at least when one first takes it in, a showy design – super-Jacobean to keep in harmony with the old house. It is built of red stone with angle stone dressings and consists of a low ground floor and two main floors. The windows on these are mullioned and transomed. The top tends to be developed into shaped gables. The entrance side has plenty of architectural events, but nobody can say that it is busy with ornament. It is L-shaped, and the dominating motif, the staircase tower, is in the angle. The ascent of the stairs is marked by the position of the windows, and the top is an ashlar-faced lantern storey as big in dimensions as the rest. The l. wing has the character of a service wing. The fenestration is deliberately informal, for picturesque and functional reasons. In the r. wing is the porch with an upper oriel. There

---

* J. Mountford: *Keele, an historical critique* appeared too late to be used in this volume.

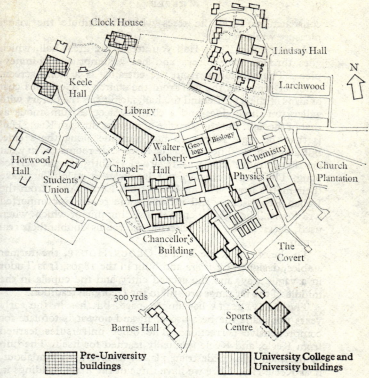

Keele University: Plan

is also a canted bay and a lower r. end attachment. The garden side (s) is nearly symmetrical, and indeed echoes the entrance façade of the Elizabethan house. The symmetry is broken by one upper canted bay window in the l. bay. The centre is recessed and has a three-bay stone arcade and ashlar also above it. There was no precedent for that in the Elizabethan house. The E side is a show side too, flanked at both ends by polygonal turrets. The chief feature here is an ornately treated canted bay window.

The university, behind and in the trees, added its REFECTORY. No one sees its exterior, mostly glass, white panels, and black metal, and inside this is a sensible room, faced with engineering bricks and roofed by a light-metal space-frame construction. It is the trees which contribute the visual pleasure while you eat.

As you enter Keele Hall you are in the great hall, which goes through two storeys and has a sumptuous chimneypiece. The separation from the entrance is a stone screen. Another separates the hall from the staircase. Gorgeous coat of arms of the C19. Behind the hall, facing s, is the library with gallery on three sides and a chimneypiece as sumptuous as that of the hall. But the surprise of moving through Keele Hall is that the state rooms do not continue along the s side, but along the E. The *enfilade* of three state rooms lies in what on the entrance side was regarded (rightly) as the service wing. The state rooms are not Jacobean in style. They take their motifs from William Kent, from Louis Seize, from the Italian Renaissance, and include some re-used or imported C18 items. The *enfilade* ends in a sliding mirror which, when used, deceives you into believing the rooms double their real extent.

To the NE of Keele Hall is CLOCK HOUSE, the former stables, designed by *Blore* and built in the 1830s. It is Tudor in a vague way, and the arched entry and the cupola in the middle of the far range are still in the Georgian tradition.

The UNIVERSITY has ample space, but has in the early years not made the best use of it, and now it is too late for comprehensive corrections. The other universities learned from Keele, and Keele gradually learned for itself. The hub of the plan is a 'pedestrian plaza', formerly a roundabout, near Keele Hall. Here we have three of the main buildings in three different moods and styles totally without connexion with each other. The LIBRARY is the earliest of the three; *Sir Howard Robertson* designed it, and it was built in 1960–1, much too late for this kind of thing. It is really a Georgian type of building, symmetrical with a clock turret, made superficially modern by the shapes of the windows and by pretty little motifs of the kind the Swedes used in the twenties. That was no good start for monumentality on the Keele campus. Much has happened since, and one cannot deny that chapel and Students' Union are up-to-date in conception and motifs. The STUDENTS' UNION, the best building so far, is by *Stillman & Eastwick Field*, 1961–3. Oblong, three-storeyed, of reinforced concrete, white. Much glass; also an irregular outer gallery and staircase with chunky parapets. Inside a staircase rises straight, with landings, up and up. The building contains a ballroom with wood cladding and a shallow vault, lounges, bars, etc.

The CHAPEL is by *G. G. Pace*, 1964–5. It is like much that Mr Pace designs, a very personal statement. It is a big, lumpish building of sombre engineering bricks with windows in the odd rhythm Mr Pace likes, mullioned windows, perhaps in deference to Keele Hall, but with the lights in groups not only of different width but also of different length. The side towards the former roundabout has two rounded towers with triangular spirelets, which, however, don't mark the entrance, as medieval buildings have taught one to expect. They house chapels. The primary conception of the building was indeed to allow congregations to assemble from a few to several hundred. So the whole is a plain rectangle (apart from the chapels). It is roofed in pitches not starting at the same level. The interior is one large room continued by one smaller which can be thrown together with the other, and the two round chapels. The details need no comment except for the curious glass screens suspended in the chapels. – PLATE. Silver-gilt Cup by *T.F.*, 1619; Paten by *James Smith*, 1723; Flagon by *J. N. Parker & Edward Wakelin*, 1769; Paten, 1769; Paten by *J. N. Wakelin & William Taylor*, 1781; Chalice by *Richard Goodall or Robert Gage*, 1806.

These three are the main buildings, but space by the former roundabout is still kept vacant for others. From here we must now fan out, and first to the w. Not all buildings need comment. The WALTER MOBERLY HALL is of the pre-Robertson period, blocky, free neo-Georgian, of red brick, strictly symmetrical. This is of 1954 etc. by *J. A. Pickavance*. GEOLOGY, largely of 1956 etc. and 1964 etc., is by the same. Curtain-wall front, and at the back a higher part with two monopitch roofs. CHEMISTRY, of the same dates and again by the same, except that the most recent stage (1964 etc.) is the design of *Young, Robertson & Partners*. This is one of the most successful buildings – low, with long window bands and far-projecting white canopies. At the w end a brick block with blank slit windows.

Now from the former roundabout s. The TAWNEY BUILDING, 1953 etc. by *J. A. Pickavance*, is frankly neo-Georgian, brick with a cupola. The CHANCELLOR'S BUILDING, by *Bridgewater, Shepheard & Epstein*, 1962 etc., is of three storeys, honest and neither prettified nor artificially toughened. Dark brick and glass in bands. Lecture theatre at

the back. For Barnes Hall opposite *see* below. The end along
here is the SPORTS CENTRE, also by *Bridgewater, Shepheard
& Epstein*, 1964 etc. Brick, with a hall for various sports and a
gymnasium. The hall has a clerestory and metal roof trusses

That leaves the HOUSING or residences. They are in
groups on and even off the campus. The oldest staff housing,
LARCHWOOD, 1952–3, is rather comical, just semi-detached
like on any council estate, arranged round three sides of an
oblong lawn. More recent housing differs in types, materials
and colours. The intention is to avoid any feeling of mass
accommodation. Also nothing is higher than six storeys, and
that is an exception: two to four is the rule, so that the sense of
living in landscape should always be present. The units can be
small or large. The extremes so far are BARNES HALL (1968–
70), one four-storeyed brick block with a complicated stepped
plan, and LINDSAY HALL (1963–4), in a number of small,
partly also stepped units. In the centre is a small irregularly
angular common room, white, while the rest is light brick.
Lindsay looks fine from the motorway – like a grown hill-town
far away from England. Barnes and Lindsay are both by *J. A.
Pickavance.*

It is not necessary to follow the other housing areas in detail.

8050
KIDSGROVE

ST THOMAS, The Avenue. Built in 1837 and said to be designed by *Mrs Kinnersley* of Clough Hall, Talke. Blue brick
with an embraced w tower. Lancet windows, open timber
roof. *Scott* in 1853 added the chancel with windows of geometrical tracery and a fine high chancel arch.

ST JOHN EVANGELIST (R.C.), The Avenue. By *W. Sugden &
Son*, 1891–3.

VICTORIA HALL, Liverpool Road. 1897–8 by *Wood &
Hutchings* (VCH), and quite a progressive building. Typical
of *c.*1900 are the steep pediment, the extremely short columns
and the emphasized keystones around the arch of the portal.

Close to the church, down a lane to the w, are the two entries to
the HARECASTLE CANAL TUNNELS of the Trent and
Mersey Canal, the smaller by *Brindley*, 1766–77, 2880 yds
long, the larger by *Telford*, 1824–7, 2926 yds.

(The POOL LOCK AQUEDUCT of 1829 carried the Macclesfield
Canal across the Trent and Mersey Canal.)

The entry to the HARECASTLE RAILWAY TUNNEL of 1848 is in Boathouse Lane. The tunnel is now by-passed. The main tunnel was about one mile long.

TOWER, E of the church, W of Ravenscliffe Road. Circular, of stone, with a frayed top. The date is not known, but the probability is a Georgian date.

KING'S BROMLEY

ALL SAINTS. Good Perp W tower. Perp clerestory of three-light windows. But below, the S wall is Norman – see the masonry and one small window. The S porch of course is Victorian. Much of the church is Dec, e.g. the coarse ogee-headed N doorway, the windows with Y-tracery, and the N arcade of standard elements. – PULPIT. Dated 1656, but not much is of that date. – FONT. 1664. Moulded, and with little of decoration. – SCREEN. A very unusual piece. The tracery is replaced by intertwined branches with leaves and also with human heads. – STAINED GLASS. In the vestry a jumble of late C18 glass, by *Francis Eginton*. – One chancel S window has two fine figures by *Morris & Co.* – PLATE. Silver-gilt Chalice of 1679 by *T.O.*, *T.G.*, *T.C.*, London; Paten, C17, also silver-gilt, by *SSSS*.

(KING'S BROMLEY MANOR. One four-storeyed brick tower remains; Victorian? Also a hexagonal garden house like a dovecote. DOE).

KINGSLEY

ST WERBURGH. W tower in its lower part C13. The nave is much wider. It is of 1820, by *James Trubshaw Jun.* Windows with Y-tracery. The chancel is of 1886 by *Lynam*. – STAINED GLASS. The W window with two large angels by *Morris*, 1890. – PLATE. Chalice and Paten of 1710, by *Alex Hudson*.

KINGSTONE

ST JOHN. 1860–1 by *David Brandon*. Indifferent inside, but externally dignified. NE tower, polygonal apse. Lancets and plate tracery. (The S aisle is by *Street*.*)

* Information from Paul Joyce.

KINGSWINFORD

3 m. w of Dudley

ST MARY, High Street. No certain date of building. Externally it looks Early Victorian, but the ashlar base seems Georgian. Inside the vestry (sw corner) a Norman tympanum of St Michael and the dragon.

The mound E of the church is an old slag heap. *The Beauties of England and Wales* in 1813 praises the 'elegant villas' of the 'capitalists of the glass trade'. There are indeed some good Late Georgian houses.

BROADFIELD HOUSE, Compton Drive. Brick, five bays, two and a half storeys. Porch with pairs of unfluted Ionic columns. An upper tripartite lunette window.

SOMERHILL HOUSE (now a hotel), Somerhill Road. Brick, five bays, two and a half storeys. A Venetian window in the middle, and a tripartite lunette window and a one-bay pediment over.

HOLBECHE HOUSE, 1 m. NW. Brick, the appearance C19-Elizabethan, but indeed an early C17 building. (Inside two priest holes.)

KINVER

Kinver has a nicely winding High Street and 150 ft above it, on the steep hill called Kinver Edge,* the church. You approach it by a wood, with here and there exposed red rock. There was here indeed in the Middle Ages the Royal Forest of Kinver, and there is even a house built into the rock, called HOLY AUSTIN ROCK HOUSE. It lies ½ m. NW of the church.

ST PETER. Some loose fragments remain of the predecessor of the present C14 to C15 church. Only the N aisle is Victorian (*Thomas Smith*, 1856–7). S arcade with octagonal piers and double-chamfered arches. C15 nave roof. Ogee-headed S aisle SEDILIA and PISCINA. Two-bay chancel chapels. Dec W tower. Perp E window with panel tracery, Late Perp N chapel with five-light E and W windows, the latter now inside. Late Perp S chapel. – FONT. C14, and of unusual shape: one concave-sided outline comprises base, stem, and bowl without a break. Enterprising tracery patterns. – PULPIT. 1625.

---

* Some 7½ acres of Kinver Edge have been cut off by the single bank and ditch of a PROMONTORY FORT. The defences survive in places to a height of 15 ft.

Kinver church, brass of Sir Edward Grey † 1528

Blank arches with the exclamation mark motif. – STAINED GLASS. The E window is by *Wailes*, c.1853. – PLATE. Flagon by *John Higginbotham*, London, 1750; Chalice, c.1750; two Trays by *John Darwell*, London, 1770–1. – MONUMENTS. (Mutilated Knight, mid C15. Jeavons) – Brasses (3 ft) of Sir Edward Grey † 1528, his wife and children small below as usual. Uncommonly good. – John Hodgetts † 1789. A very remarkable tablet with two urns flanked by two excessively short, excessively thick, unfluted Doric columns such as only the most revolutionary architects did in France at that moment. Heavy, massive pediment.

At the foot of Church Hill, really part of the High Street, is CHURCH HILL HOUSE, brick, of five bays and two and a half storeys with giant angle pilasters not including the half storey. Doorway without a pediment. The windows have the original glazing bars – originally obviously meaning c.1720–30. At the corner of Dark Lane the OLD GRAMMAR SCHOOL HOUSE, timber-framed, C16.

In the HIGH STREET the best houses are Nos. 17–20, C17 with a porch projection, and Nos. 28–29, six bays, with a two-bay pediment and a doorway with nice detail. Round the bend, Nos. 47–48, dated 1690 but looking older. Two canted bays, mullioned and transomed windows. Doorway bay with rusticated pilasters and nondescript pilasters on the upper floor. At the bend a SCHOOL of 1849, at the next another of 1850. Both are by *Thomas Smith*.*

At WHITTINGTON, 1 m. E, the WHITTINGTON INN, C16, timber-framed, symmetrical, with two gables and a gabled porch, and S of it WHITTINGTON HALL FARM, C18, brick and oddly townish, seven bays, two storeys, parapet.

Air photographs reveal a complex series of ROMAN MILITARY WORKS at Greensforge. The main fort has a turf rampart with two ditches, the whole measuring 550 by 450 ft. To the S lay a larger fort of a different date, surrounded by a single ditch. The forts were occupied in the middle and later C1. 1 m. to the NW lies a marching camp of about 35 acres.

KNIGHTLEY

CHRIST CHURCH. 1840–1 by *Thomas Trubshaw*. What made him design such a group of W windows, a lancet becoming a

---

* The above paragraph was written in 1971. Since then Nos. 47–48 have been demolished.

big trefoil on top, and two lancets growing ears or lugs – all these forms being glazed? Equally startling the bellcote with its excessively high and steep gable facing S not W – just to say: Watch me. The windows of 1840 are round-headed. The chancel is Gothic, more normal, and of 1882 by *Nicholas Joyce*. – FONT. This is our man of 1840 again. It is half set in the wall, the wall with the jokey windows, and the bowl (on a stiff-leaf capital) is 7½ in. across inside. – TILING. Handsome tiles on floor and E wall of the chancel. – STAINED GLASS. The E window by *Kempe*, 1900.

KNIGHTLEY GRANGE. 1860–8. Brick, free Elizabethan, asymmetrical. Arched porch and tower with a semicircular oriel above it, ending in a concave-sided spirelet.

KNUTTON

ST MARY. 1872–4 by *T. Lewis & Son*.

KNYPERSLEY see BIDDULPH and BROWN EDGE

LAPLEY

There was a Benedictine priory here, founded most probably in the late C11 or the early C12.

ALL SAINTS. High and powerful central tower, Norman below, as the arches inside show. The W arch and the blocked N arch have a single step on the simplest imposts. The E arch is now pointed and of two continuous chamfers (*c.*1300?). The tower top is Perp, with three-light bell-openings, a decorated frieze, and eight pinnacles. The nave and chancel masonry is Norman too, and there is one large Norman S window. The chancel was lengthened in the C13. Fine stepped five-light E window; SEDILIA and PISCINA. In the nave two Perp N windows. Blocked parts of arches prove former annexes. – FONT. Octagonal, Dutch, with small primitively carved scenes. Is it early C19? – SCREENS. Good chancel screen of one-light divisions with handsome tracery. The tower screen is probably a little older. – COMMUNION RAIL. Jacobean. – DOOR in the chancel. Re-set in it four panels of *c.*1535 with busts in medallions. – PLATE. Chalice, 1775, by *Charles Wright*, London; Paten, 1779–80, by *Matthew Boulton & John Fothergill*, Birmingham. – MONUMENT. Incised slab of 1500 (chancel floor).

PARK HOUSE. The house and the adjoining walls and a gatehouse with turrets are all castellated. Partly late C18, partly c.1867. (Also, a few fields away, the so-called FORT ST GEORGE. VCH)

LONGNOR HALL, 1 m. NW. A three-storey brick house dated 1726. The front is of seven bays with a top parapet and a three-bay pediment set rather ineffectually against the parapet. Quoins, doorway with Gibbs surround and pediment. Aprons below the windows.

LAWNESWOOD HOUSE see STEWPONY

LEATON HALL see BOBBINGTON

LEEK

Leek is an industrial town, but it is small enough (1971 under 20,000 inhabitants) and close enough to a fine countryside not to have suffered as the towns of the Black Country have. Silk weaving, spinning, and dyeing became the staple industries in the late C18. The time of the greatest prosperity was the C19. In architecture Leek presents the interesting case of one architect and his son almost monopolizing public and private building for the last third of the C19 into the C20. They are *William Sugden* and his son *William Larner Sugden*. William started the practice in 1849 and took William Larner into partnership in 1881. The father died in 1892, the son in 1901. They designed far more than can here be mentioned, and they designed in a variety of styles.

ST EDWARD THE CONFESSOR. A large church and impressive externally, even if confusing internally. In fact once one has been inside, one realizes outside as well how much there is that is unusual and compositionally unsatisfactory. Low, broad w tower of the C14, with a Perp top. Cusped lozenge frieze and eight pinnacles. The church was rebuilt after a fire of 1297. That dates the principal features such as the big, bold rose windows of the former transepts, based on six straight radii – a typical Dec conceit – and the cusped intersected tracery of the N aisle E window. But other features are less easily placed. The arcades inside don't look right, and they start two bays E of the W end. Originally they went that much farther, but the aisles were removed in 1556 (S) and 1593 (N). The area where the aisles had been received totally irregular fenestration. The piers were round originally and were made octagonal only in 1839. The roof of the nave, panelled and with bosses, is early C16. As for the chancel, this belongs to *Street*'s drastic restoration of 1865–7.* The s porch looks Elizabethan but is as late as 1670. The archway into the churchyard with its five pinnacles is dated 1634. – PULPIT. By *Street*. The carved statuettes by *Earp*, c.1867. – STALLS and LECTERN also *Street*. – Low stone SCREEN and iron organ SCREEN, both by *Street* too. – WEST GALLERY. 1838 – still Georgian. – STAINED GLASS. Much by *Morris & Co.*: N transept E 1902, S transept S 1907, N transept N (by *Dearle*) probably also 1907.‡ – NEEDLEWORK. Much from the School of Needlework founded in the 1870s by Thomas Wardle. – PLATE. Silver-gilt North German Chalice, C14; Swiss Chalice, 1641; two Chalices and Patens, 1777; Flagon, 1777; silver-gilt Chalice with precious stones, 1874. – MONUMENT. Brass plaque with kneeling figures to John Ashenhurst † 1597. – In the churchyard parts of two Late Saxon CROSSES, C11 no doubt. The style is close to that of the Giant's Grave at Penrith in Cumberland. The larger shaft is over 10 ft high and has a characteristic waistband.§

ALL SAINTS, Compton. 1885–7 by *Norman Shaw*. Vigorous and personal. Low central tower. Nave with very low clerestory; very broad, low porch. The chancel appears very high owing to the fall of the ground and the placing of the windows high up. Wide, broad W and E windows of nine lights, W Dec, E Perp. There is indeed no historical accuracy. The walls inside are white, the arcade bays broad. The arches of the first pair of piers are wider than the others to mark off a narthex. The central tower is not emphasized inside except by W and E cross-arches, and half-arches in the aisles. The interior conveys a happy sensation of spaciousness and placidity. The chancel decoration is by the Shaw school. *Lethaby* designed the REREDOS, and *F. Hamilton Jackson* painted it. Re-painted in 1954. – The PULPIT with its fine freely Gothic pierced work is also attributed to *Lethaby*. –

---

* The plans are signed by *J. Brealey* of Leek. He must have worked to Street's design.

‡ I owe these dates to Mr Sewter. Mr Joyce adds that the chancel windows are by *Clayton & Bell*, and Dr Robinson tells me that the glass in the N and S rose windows was designed by *Bodley* in 1903.

§ Fragments of two other crosses in the chancel and the W wall of the S porch.

So is the FONT.* – The carved chancel PANELLING is by *Gerald Horsley*, who also designed the chancel PAINTING. – That of the Lady Chapel, an originally composed Annunciation, is by him too.‡ – STAINED GLASS. Mostly by *Morris*, even in the porch. The best is S aisle E (1887). Most of it C20, i.e. after Morris's death. – Dr Gomme added in a letter that the chancel S, next to the altar, is by *Horsley*, 1891. – NEEDLEWORK. From the School of Needlework – see above.§ – PLATE. Chalice and Paten, 1569; Processional Cross, C14, called German, the staff by *Horsley* (Dr Gomme).

(Next to the church is COMPTON SCHOOL by *Robert Edgar* 1863.‖ For Edgar see also p. 254.)

ST LUKE, Queen Street. 1847–8 by *F. & H. Francis*. Big, Dec, mechanical. Chancel lengthened in 1873. – REREDOS by *J. D. Sedding*. – Very original wooden SCREEN. Attributed to *Shaw* – not an attribution to convince. – Fine ORGAN CASE, 1903. Arts and Crafts style. – STAINED GLASS. One S aisle window of 1884, obviously *Powell*. – S aisle E 1862 by *Warrington*.

ST MARY (R.C.), Compton. 1886–7 by *Albert Vicars*.¶ Large and high. Geometrical tracery. SE steeple, high-up E window. The N annexe with cross-gables looks later. Arcade piers with lush foliage capitals.

CONGREGATIONAL CHAPEL, Derby Street. By *W. Sugden* 1863. Dec style with an elaborate NW spire.

FRIENDS' MEETING HOUSE, Overton Bank. 1697. Ashlar. Little of the features of 1697 survives.

NICHOLSON INSTITUTE, Stockwell Street. 1882–4 by *W. Sugden & Son*. The building contained a school of art, a museum, and a library. It has no street frontage. From the street one sees only the tower. The design would have deserved to be presented to better advantage. Red brick, in a style inspired by T. G. Jackson, i.e. a resourceful mid C17 style.

MEMORIAL HOSPITAL, Stockwell Street. 1870 by *Sugden*. Brick, Gothic, with some polychromy. Somewhat like Waterhouse.

MARKET, Market Place. 1897.

---

* Says Dr Gomme.
‡ But Dr Gomme tells me that the painting round the altar and on the roof is by *J. Edgar Platt*.
§ Dr Gomme writes: one frontal designed by *Shaw*.
‖ Information from Dr Gomme.
¶ The cost was £12,000.

MARKET CROSS, now in the cemetery. Fluted shaft and Maltese cross head. Probably early C15; moved here in 1806.*

MOORLANDS HOSPITAL, Ashbourne Road. The former WORKHOUSE. 1838 by *Bateman & Drury* of Birmingham. Brick. The façade still Georgian. Nine bays with a three-bay pediment. Low, one-storey three-bay wings with pediment. Behind three ranges, spokewise, with the usual higher hub.

COUNTY POLICE STATION, Leonard Street. By *W. Sugden & Son*, 1891. Symmetrical, brick, of seven bays. The tourelles no doubt are meant to convey militancy. Good bold portal set in a giant arch.

PERAMBULATION. Immediately E of the parish church the VICARAGE, dated 1714, with a mullioned window and blocked windows of 1714 shape, but most windows with Late Georgian Gothic glazing bars. E of this FOXLOWE, overlooking the Market Place. Brick, five bays, two and a half storeys, nice late C18 doorcase. In the MARKET PLACE the RED LION, early C18, with two canted bay windows, and the former BLACK'S HEAD (now Woolworth's) by *Sugden*. From the S end of the Market Place E is DERBY STREET. No. 10, 1760, brick, five bays, two and a half storeys, one-bay projection with pediment. Then the ROEBUCK INN, said to have been re-erected here from a site in Shropshire.‡ The date is *c*.1626. Timber-framed, with three gables. No ornamental motifs. After that the former DISTRICT BANK, *Sugden* at his best, asymmetrical, with a pargetted gable-bay of two Ipswich windows, i.e. Shaw and Ernest George influence. The date is 1882. Back to the N end of the Market Place and on E along STOCKWELL STREET for GREYSTONES, an exceptionally fine stone house of the late C17. Symmetrical three-bay front, the fenestration 3-3-3 lights. Doorway with apsidal hood. From the E end of Stockwell Street S to the CLOCK TOWER, a real square tower, of Portland stone. 1924–5 by *Thomas Worthington & Sons* of Manchester. Back to the church and W. Mill Street descends, and at a higher level l. and r. of its start are Overton Bank with the Friends' Meeting House (*see* above) and CLERK BANK with the former GRAMMAR SCHOOL. This is of stone, of 1723, symmetrical (fenestration 3-3-3 lights), but still mullioned windows. To its l. the MAUDE INSTITUTE, brick with a Gothick doorway and a quatrefoil over. That must be

---

* Another fluted shaft of a former CROSS is in Cheadle Road, set back (DOE).

‡ The CPDD doubts the truth of the story.

c18 still. In MILL STREET itself the biggest of the silk mills WARDLE & DAVENPORT, by *Sugden*, c.1860.*

Now s of the church, i.e. along ST EDWARD STREET, the best street in Leek. No. 19 is late c18, richly but oddly decorated. Then lower down, i.e. after STRANGMAN STREET, where the WELLINGTON MILL is dated 1853 and still has the Georgian convention of the pediment. Here on the l. a three-bay house with, in the centre, an archway, two tripartite windows, and a pediment, then a house with a pretty late c18 doorway, opposite a five-bay house with a door pediment on brackets (No. 54), a stone house dated 1724 but with Early Victorian Tudor windows, a six-bay house with the door pediment on brackets (No. 64), and so, at the end, in BROAD STREET, the ASH ALMSHOUSES of 1676, restored in 1811. Rendered, nine dwellings. Seven dormers. Two-light windows. In the streets w and s of the almshouses, i.e. KING STREET and ALBION STREET, a series of typical workers' cottages, i.e. with the large top-floor windows to give the best light. These are dated 1825 and 1827. So at that time workers still worked at home. The ALBION MILLS date from c.1829. They are of three storeys and sixteen bays with a turret.‡

Four less centrally placed items: First BALL HAYE HALL, in Ball Haye Road. Late c18, of seven bays and three storeys, ashlar-faced. Doorway with unfluted Roman Doric columns and triglyph frieze. Derelict at the time of writing.§ Second, in Haregate Road HAREGATE HALL, c17, stone with mullioned windows. Third, in BUXTON ROAD is LITTLE HALES, a picturesque villa of brick and half-timber work, gabled and informal, by *W. L. Sugden*, 1880 for W. S. Brough. And fourthly in ASHBOURNE ROAD the former factory of Brough, Nicholson & Hall. The l. part of nineteen bays with a mid pediment, the r. part later.

DIEULACRES ABBEY, ¾ m. NW of the town, was a Cistercian house founded c.1150 at Poulton in Cheshire and re-founded on the new site in 1214 by Ranulph de Blundeville Earl of Chester and lord of the manor of Leek. All that remains *in situ* is the bases of two of the crossing piers of the church, clearly E.E. In addition many fragments built into the farmhouse, in

* Also in Mill Street remains of BRINDLEY'S CORN MILL, built 52. Much of the machinery survives (DOE).

‡ Miss Jerram, the Leek librarian, adds SPOUT HALL, a four-storeyed black and white house at the bottom of St Edward Street, close to the almshouses. Andrew Saint found out that it is by *Norman Shaw*, 1871.

§ Now destroyed.

outbuildings and walls. The OUTBUILDINGS of c.1820 are of stone, all Gothick, i.e. with pointed doorways and windows. One fine small stone statue of a king, mid C14. The FARM-HOUSE is timber-framed and dated 1627. The large blocked archway at the back with traceried spandrels must be considerably earlier. It no doubt used pieces from the abbey.

A little to the N the ABBEY INN, 1702, stone, with mullioned windows symmetrically arranged (3-2-3 lights). Door lintel with a pierced oval in the centre.

WESTWOOD HALL* (now Westwood High School), 1 m. W of the town. A grand house of 1850-3, by *Hadfield, Weightman & Goldie*, on an older site, for John Davenport, dilettante son of the founder of the pottery firm. A large irregular Elizabethan pile, gabled and ball-finialled, originally around two courtyards, though one has disappeared in later alterations and extensions. Apparently of one build, although one would think otherwise. The unusual and rather unsatisfactory plan surely points to John Davenport's growth of ideas as the building progressed. The S (entrance) front is reminiscent of a Cotswold manor house, but enlivened to one side by a great arched tower surmounted by a Gothic belfry. This side and the E front are faced with local red sandstone, but otherwise all is brick. Pretty leaded glazing where it has survived. The impact of the composition is reduced by the truncation of the forest of tall chimneys. The interior is disappointing, though there is a two-storey great hall and in the former dining room an exuberant Elizabethan chimneypiece dated 1852. – STABLES. Georgian and Victorian ranges. – ENTRANCE LODGE. Dated 1852, and with a giant arch. – In the grounds a charming contemporary SUMMER HOUSE.)

LEIGH

ALL SAINTS. This is the astounding masterpiece of an otherwise little-known architect: *Thomas Johnson* of Lichfield.‡ He left something of the old tower§ and rebuilt the rest. The work was complete by 1846. The church was paid for by the Bagots of Blithfield, and they spent enough to make the church absurdly large for its village. The building, all of ashlar, has

---

* The following information is provided by Mr Peter Reid.
‡ There is no justification in attributing the building to *Pugin* on arguments either of documentation or of style. He did, however, according to Mrs Stanton, design the chancel floor TILES.
§ Though what is hard to see.

a crossing tower, a chancel of three bays, transepts of two bays, and a nave with aisles of five bays. The style is Dec throughout, with flowing tracery, and the archaeological accuracy advocated by Pugin, Scott, and the Camdenians is fully achieved. The piers incidentally have a rare shape. They are cruciform with canted diagonals, or you might prefer to say square, set diagonally, and with angle fillets. The most surprising and most praiseworthy feature inside, however, is the stone rib-vaulting of chancel and tower. – (FONT. Quatrefoil; C14. Jeavons) – TILES of the chancel floor very rich. – STAINED GLASS. In the chancel SE and NE windows much old glass, e.g. a C14 Crucifixion and other C14 figures. – The E window is by *Wailes*. – In the S aisle two windows by *Gibbs* of Bedford Square (1862, 1868). – By *Morris* and *Burne Jones* the W window (1874), the aisle W windows (1890), and the S aisle E window (1913).* The finest is the great W window where the figures are placed against Morris's transparent flower quarries. – PLATE. Chalice, 1631; Paten by *S.L.*, 1717; Flagon by *Richard Beale*, 1732. – MONUMENT. Sir John Ashenhurst, alabaster, c.1520. Tomb-chest with pairs of figurines under twin canopies.

(SCHOOL and MASTER'S HOUSE. By *Street*, 1856–7, much mutilated.‡)

PARK HALL. Good iron GATES.

LEMANSLEY *see* LICHFIELD, p. 190

LEVEDALE

(SALEN. Cruck construction. VCH)

LICHFIELD

THE CATHEDRAL

INTRODUCTION

Lichfield is one of the smaller English cathedrals (371 ft), but it has two features which single it out from all others: its three spires and the Minster Pool and Stowe Pool assuring it of a picturesqueness of setting which none can emulate. Moreover

---

* I owe these dates to Mr Sewter's never-failing generosity.
‡ Mr Joyce sent me this piece of information.

LICHFIELD: THE CATHEDRAL 175

it has a Close more complete than most and more intimate than any. That to the observant visitor it is largely a Victorian cathedral may, according to the visitor, be regarded as a gain or a loss.

The history of the see starts with St Chad, Bishop of the Mercians from 669 to 672, the history of the cathedral with a building consecrated in 700. The diocese in later Anglo-Saxon times stretched from Warwickshire to the Ribble. Under the Normans, in 1075, the see was transferred to Chester. It then went to Coventry and to Coventry and Lichfield jointly. The chapter was reconstituted by Roger de Clinton in 1130. At that time much rebuilding took place or had taken place. A large apse has been excavated reaching from the central tower to about the middle of the fifth choir bay. This may have been of Clinton's time or earlier. To it, later in the C12, a narrower rectangular chapel was added. Then, *c*.1220, a new choir was begun. Its E end was at the E end of the seventh bay of the choir of today and straight-ended with an ambulatory, as at Abbey Dore, Byland, Hereford Cathedral, and Romsey. While the E part of the new choir was replaced later, as we shall see, its W part is preserved, and it is there that the visible history begins. Unfortunately we have no fixed dates at all, but the sequence must have been like this: choir, Consistory Court, and Chapel of St Chad *c*.1200–20, transepts *c*.1230–40, chapter house *c*.1240 etc., nave *c*.1260 etc., W front *c*.1280 etc., crossing tower *c*.1300, E end *c*.1310 etc., W spires *c*.1320–30. Miscellaneous Perp work followed. Of MASONS we know a *Thomas c*.1230–50, a *William*, his son, *c*.1250–65, *Thomas Wallace c*.1265–80, and then *William of Eyton c*.1320–36 and, as a consultant, *William Ramsey* from 1337.

In the Civil War the cathedral was damaged worse than any other. It was three times besieged, and the soldiery misbehaved in the building. In 1646 the spire collapsed, evidently into the choir. Restoration took place from 1661 to 1669, leading to the re-consecration in the latter year. Nearly all the Perp windows of the choir clerestory are of these years, some of the choir arches were blocked, and the spire was rebuilt. It was complete by 1666. But in the late C18 it was again necessary largely to rebuild. When Horace Walpole visited it in 1760, he wrote: 'Nothing is left in the inside of ornament.' In 1788 *James Wyatt* began restoration – his first cathedral task. He worked till 1795. He blocked up the four western choir arches, removed or altered the screen, put a glass screen in the E arch

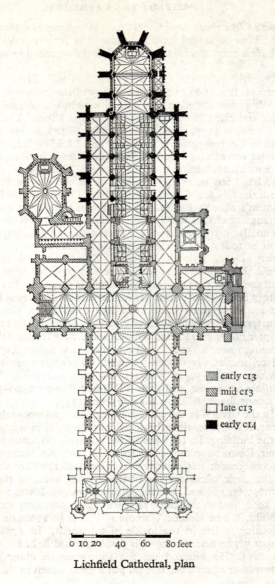

Lichfield Cathedral, plan

early c13
mid c13
late c13
early c14

0 10 20 40 60 80 feet

of the crossing, and added the two heavy buttresses outside the s transept. He also largely rebuilt the central spire. The architect on the site was *Joseph Potter Sen.* In 1842–6 *Sydney Smirke* restored further, and in 1857 *Scott* began. His restoration, continued by his son *John Oldrid Scott*, went on to 1901. Much of the cathedral as we see it today is Scott's, not only mouldings, capitals, and statues, but also most of the window tracery. The question how far it replaced accurately what had been there in the Middle Ages has never been adequately answered, and so no answer can be attempted here.*

THE EXTERIOR

There is nothing Norman remaining in Lichfield Cathedral except two faint echoes, and they are inside. Outside the story begins with the transepts, both of about 1230–40. Henry III's grant to Dean and Chapter in 1235 and 1238 to dig stone in the Royal Forest of Cannock will refer to them. Whether N came first or S is not certain, and in all stylistic considerations at Lichfield it must be remembered that the vast majority of the details is Scott's. On balance S is more likely to be a little earlier (*see* below and interior).

The NORTH TRANSEPT has a twin N portal encrusted with leaf decoration. The columns are in two tiers, attached and, in front of them, detached. In the arch are three orders of small figures in almond-shaped surrounds and three of square leaf slabs. Much dog-tooth is used too. Two niches l. and r. Above is a tier of tall, slender lancets of even length, a reconstruction of 1892, it is said, but on safe evidence. In the gable are three openings with Y-tracery. The same pattern in the w wall of the transept, blocked, l. and r. of two Perp windows. The upper N windows are large and Perp. The E side is confused by the interference of chapter house and chapter house vestibule. The buttresses of the transept are shafted. The CHAPTER HOUSE is an elongated octagon, in two storeys, the upper now the library. The windows again have Y-tracery. On top of the buttresses are tabernacles with statues. The vestibule is two-storeyed too and has groups of three stepped lancet windows to the w, Y-tracery to the N.

The SOUTH TRANSEPT has in its S wall another twin portal, also encrusted with stiff-leaf. But there are here no figure

---

* Mr G. Cobb told me that according to old photographs only the windows of the apse appear genuine.

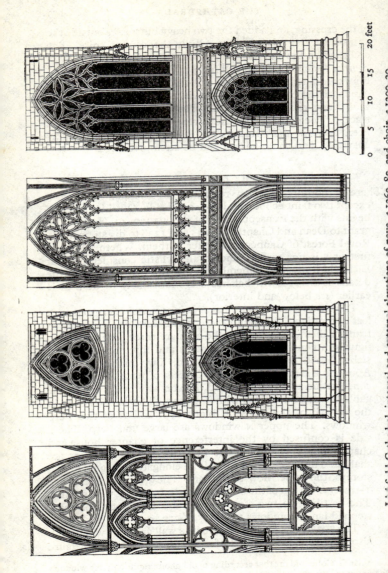

THE CATHEDRAL

panels. There is, or was, much dog-tooth again. The capitals are of the crocket type, i.e. a type a little earlier. In the spandrels two oblong framed panels, one with a shield, the other with an inscription. The buttresses are very different from those on the N side. They are square, big, and without real set-offs, uncommonly impressive and, incidentally, by *Wyatt*. L. and r. of the portal is pointed-trefoiled and gabled wall arcading. Above is a row of statues under trefoiled arches. In the gable are an elaborate rose window (restored in 1758), and trefoiled niches l. and r. and a pointed quatrefoil at the top. But the centre windows are replaced by a large, nine-light, Late Perp window with a four-centred arch. To the E is the Consistory Court (formerly sacristy) and the Chapel of the Head of St Chad, a little older than the transept. Grouped lancet windows and angle turrets, the w one shafted. The w side of the s transept has good blank arcading and above two shafted lancets in each of the two bays. The top windows are Perp, as in the N transept.

Next followed the rebuilding of the NAVE. Here both sides are the same. Three-light shafted aisle windows with geometrical tracery (trefoils in circles), but the clerestory windows in the form of spherical triangles filled with three trefoiled circles. That is a Westminster Abbey motif. The abbey was started only in 1245. So 1250 is rather too early a date for the start at Lichfield. The flying buttresses tell of stone vaulting.*

The CROSSING TOWER has shafted polygonal buttresses, and the bell stage three pairs of two-light openings and blank such openings l., r., and centre. The spire has five tiers of lucarnes and ballflowers up the edges.

Work on the nave ended with the WEST FRONT, begun probably about 1280. It is in many of its details *Scott's*,‡ but the composition is entirely that which had been illustrated by Britton in 1820. Newly designed by *Scott* are the w window and the stage above it. The Lichfield w front is not wholly satisfactory. Hardly any English C13 front is. It is a screen in the first place, a little wider than nave and aisles, and, by the tiers of statues, stressing the screen character.§ But it has two spires, and if spires are meant to aspire, these aspire too

---

* On the N side in the aisle wall is a shallow Late Perp recess with a four-centred arch and dainty foliage carving in the spandrels.

‡ On the NW tower high up are five original STATUES.

§ The STATUES are of 1876–84, replacing cement or stucco statues of 1820–2.

little. Real two-tower façades in the Continental way are York and Beverley. Lichfield, like Wells, can't make up its mind. Also, the portals are too small to join in as separate voices. The middle one is a little porch. The lowest tier of statues is between the portals, and they suffer at once, like those higher up, from the fault of standing, on brackets and under canopies indeed, but free against a smooth wall. The result over the whole façade is that all the statues seem in danger of floating on the surface. The decoration of the front is trefoils, quatrefoils, encircled cinquefoils. The tier above the portals has seated figures under trefoiled arches. The great W window is entirely *Scott*'s (of 1869). It picks up the motif of ballflower from the bell stage of the towers. The bell-openings are of only two lights, rather ungenerous. Also they don't appear central, because the angles of the whole façade are big polygonal buttresses, and they go up that high. The sides of the towers incidentally continue the screen system. The pinnacles of the towers are square, and the parapet has saltire crosses. Four tiers of lucarnes in the spires. When the spires were set up is again unknown – probably about 1325 or so. They are very noticeably lower than the central spire. Between the towers is the nave gable wall with flat pointed trefoil decoration in odd directions.

By 1325 progress had also been made on the rebuilding and lengthening of the EAST END. The LADY CHAPEL came first. All we know of dates is that Bishop Walter Langton (1296–1321) was interested in it and left money for its completion. It is as high as the chancel and it has a polygonal end, a form frequent on the Continent, but very rare in England. In the apse the windows are very tall, of three lights, and the tracery is unencircled trefoils. That also is a Westminster Abbey motif, though it became popular only in the late C13. So that is the date one would propose. It is too early, as the interior will prove. The nave of the Lady Chapel has windows of late C13 type, motifs of Y and intersection. On the buttresses two tiers of statues. In the S wall three tomb recesses with cusped and subcusped arches and ballflower, which raises the earliest likely date at once to *c*.1310. Inside there are three shallow chapels here (*see* below).

The CHOIR AISLES have windows partly Dec, partly arches upon arches, another motif of *c*.1300. Against one S buttress stands the best original STATUE in the cathedral – a female figure. In the clerestory is one window (SE) with flowing tracery; the rest is Perp of the 1660s. Arched parapet, pierced battlements, flying buttresses.

THE INTERIOR

About 1190 the rebuilding of the Norman cathedral seems to have started. It was to be a replacement of the E end, and what survives is the three W bays of the choir. This CHOIR WEST 17 PART is unmistakably dated by the conjunction of lush stiff-leaf with a few left-over Norman features, zigzag in the arch from the N aisle into the N transept, and one trumpet-scallop capital in the wall arcading of the same aisle. The rest is all E.E. and indeed looks C13 rather than late C12. The wall arcading is pointed and cusped. The piers are shafted as richly as at Wells – groups of triplets with fillets. The arches are of many fine mouldings. The aisles have plain quadripartite rib-vaulting. All above the aisles is C14, and so: *see* below. In the N aisle the easternmost wall shaft and its opposite number towards the choir 'nave' are unrestored. From the W bays of the aisles stepped lancet groups open into the transept aisles. They were originally windows. So the Norman transepts had no E aisles.

On the S side the CONSISTORY COURT and the CHAPEL OF THE HEAD OF ST CHAD. The former has a round-headed doorway with two orders of colonnettes and two bays of heavily single-chamfered rib-vaults. The vault of the chapel is not medieval, but the windows with their detached shafts are. From the chapel a handsome Dec gallery on ribbed coving opens to the aisle, no doubt for showing the relic. The entry to the gallery was originally a window. So we have another aisle window of *c.*1200–20. If the sacristy is indeed contemporaneous with the choir, then the chapel must have been an afterthought.

To the W of the Consistory Court is a small tunnel-vaulted chamber, probably originally the treasury. In the N aisle the entry to the chapter house vestibule cuts into the wall arcading. Above the entry is a shafted lancet window.

The CHAPTER HOUSE VESTIBULE has thick blank pointed-trefoiled wall arcading, blank on the E side but detached to such a degree on the W side that a row of seats results. They were for the washing of poor men's feet. The capitals of the colonnettes are original. Lancet windows in groups; stone vault in three bays with bosses. The CHAPTER HOUSE itself is approached by another double portal like those of the transepts, but less ornate. Stiff-leaf capitals, dog-tooth. In the tympanum Seated Christ in a pointed quatrefoil recess. Thick pointed trefoiled wall arcading with dog-tooth. The dean's seat in the middle of the E wall is singled out by the doubling of the colonnettes. Middle pier with ten shafts. Excellent capitals. Vault with bosses. Shafted windows. The upper storey is clearly a little later. A crowd of shafts, the motif of the Wells chapter house. Windows with deep reveals, shafted. Short vaulting shafts on figure corbels, unrestored. Above the vestibule is another room, vaulted in three bays like the vestibule.

Following the order of the exterior, the TRANSEPTS must now be described. They have an E aisle of two bays. The piers are developed from those of the choir, but differ a little and also have triple vaulting shafts from the ground. The capitals are stiff-leaf. The group of vaulting shafts is accompanied by shafts with capitals at a lower level, continued in twins with shaft-rings. Moreover the main vaulting shafts have above the abacus a Perp castellated second abacus. So there is some confusion here. The W and S side of the S transept has wall arcading, the shafts with plain moulded capitals. The upper parts belong to the Perp work of the choir and will be mentioned there. In the N transept on the E side the start from the N is two good capitals with small heads. After that all is moulded capitals now, i.e. perhaps a reduction after the lavishness of choir and S transept. In the aisle trefoiled wall arcading. One boss has four radial heads. The N lancets are shafted. On the W side is pointed-trefoiled wall arcading. The arch to the aisle also has moulded capitals as against the stiff-leaf of the corresponding S transept arch.

The CROSSING PIERS each have to the centre, i.e. set diagonally, four shafts with three rings, apart from the triples in the main directions. Many-moulded arches, and a C14 or C15 tierceron-star vault.

As externally, so internally, the NAVE is all one build, and it is so drastically restored that it seems all Victorian. The piers are still essentially of the choir and transept type, the capitals are still stiff-leaf. In the spandrels thin encircled cinquefoils cut in two by the vaulting shafts, a remarkably unclassic device at so classic a moment. Gallery of two two-light openings per bay without windows in the outer wall. Bar tracery and much dog-tooth. Vault with ridge-ribs and tiercerons. The easternmost and the two westernmost bays were re-done by *Wyatt* in plaster and remain so. The aisles have pointed cusped wall arcading with unrestored or little restored capitals and shafted windows. Vault by *Scott* with longitudinal ridge-ribs and no tiercerons. The w (tower) bay does not introduce a change of system. The s aisle entrance has to the inside one order of shafts and an extremely shallow arch.

The EAST END must, as in the exterior, be the end. The LADY CHAPEL has wall arcading with nodding ogee arches and much crocketing. Now the nodding ogee arch is early when it is before 1315, and so in spite of windows of *c.*1300 in style, the chapel cannot have been begun before 1310. So 1310–30 is perhaps the best date. Shafts for statues (designed by *Kempe*, carved by *Farmer & Brindley*, 1895) standing in the same position as e.g. in the Sainte Chapelle in Paris (which is also apsidal), a sill frieze of the upper windows with cusped zigzag, and a wooden vault with ridge-ribs and tiercerons.

On the s side three tiny chapels are attached, the first two with two bays of vaulting and a longitudinal ridge-rib. The third is more fanciful. The same scheme, but for one oblong bay only, is by four short additional ribs made to appear like four minute quadripartite rib-vaults.*

The CHOIR, in conclusion, is the most complicated part of the cathedral. Its E parts were built to link the early C13 choir to the newly built Lady Chapel. It continues topographically the work to its W but stylistically the work to its E. This could not be done without some interference with the three bays of the early C13. The junction is easy enough to see. There is no disguising the change from early C13 to early C14 foliage, especially on the (later?) N side where the capitals become bands of nobbly leaf. The piers even here, however, try to keep in a certain harmony with the old ones. However, there are of course vaulting shafts now. For the old work they were added from the floor up, but now they stand on angel brackets and carry a statue each. The statues are by *Farmer & Brindley*, 1860. Scott is supposed to have had evidence for the brackets and the statues. In the new parts the motif of the halved cinquefoils is taken over from the nave. The zigzag parapet is that of the Lady Chapel, and the vault is also derived from there. What is new and very successful is the reveals of the upper windows, which have blank quatrefoils all the way

---

* There are CRYPTS, or rather boneholes, below these chapels.

round, a motif familiar e.g. from the s transept of St Mary Redcliffe at Bristol. In the aisles the wall arcading (pointed, cusped) now has heads and foliage in the spandrels, and most of that is unrestored. One bay in the s aisle has a recess with two broad bands of nobbly leaf again all the way round. The vaults have longitudinal ridge-ribs.

It now only remains to add that the system of the upper windows is continued into the transept E walls, but without the quatrefoil framing. The transept vaults are a later renewal, whether c.1300 N and after 1350 s or both late C15 does not seem certain.

FURNISHINGS
From E to W, and N before S

LADY CHAPEL. The ALTARPIECE was carved at Oberammergau in 1895. – STAINED GLASS. Seven windows have glass brought in 1802 from Herckenrode near Hasselt by Sir Brooke Boothby (*see* below). It dates from c.1540. The style is reminiscent of *Lambert Lombard*'s. Some of the glass went to St Mary at Shrewsbury, some is in other places in Lichfield Cathedral (*see* below). – In the W bays, late C19 glass. – MONUMENT. Bishop Selwyn † 1878. In one of the S chapels. By *Nicholls*. Recumbent effigy. – The lavish WALL DECORATION by *Clayton & Bell*.

NORTH CHOIR AISLE. STAINED GLASS. Some from Herckenrode, some by *Kempe*. – MONUMENTS. Bishop Ryder † 1836. By *Chantrey*, 1841. A white kneeling figure without any setting. Chantrey liked that kind of isolation. It is a Victorian trait. – Bishop Woods † 1953. Lively bronze demi-figure praying. By *Epstein*. – Bishop Lonsdale † 1867. Recumbent alabaster effigy by *G. F. Watts*, the Gothic setting by *Scott*. Dated 1841. – Mrs Smallwood, late C17. Fine cartouche.

CHAPTER HOUSE. PAINTING. Remains of a C15 Assumption with many figures (W wall).

CHOIR. Low REREDOS and SCREEN of statues. By *Scott*, the figures by *John Birnie Philip*, 1864. – SEDILIA. The intricate canopies are largely original Perp work. – GRILLES. By *Skidmore* (*see* below). – STALLS and BISHOP'S THRONE. By *Scott*, executed by *Evans* of Ellaston. But the fronts of the middle block N and S are iron and no doubt *Skidmore*'s. – PAVEMENT. Very fine. Stone, inlaid, medallions with scenes

THE CATHEDRAL 185

from the history of the diocese, also kings and bishops. The design by *Scott*.

SOUTH CHOIR AISLE. STAINED GLASS. Some of the Herckenrode glass is here. – Also two windows by *Kempe*. – In another window fragments again from Herckenrode. – MONUMENTS. The Robinson Children, 1814 by *Chantrey*. The white marble children are asleep. Here also the sentiment begins already to turn Victorian, though the conceit of the sleeping child was taken over by Chantrey for Banks's Penelope Boothby, Brooke Boothby's daughter, at Ashbourne, of 1791. The Robinson monument is still the most popular in the cathedral. – Effigy of the type where only the bust is visible. The bust is incarcerated in the wall. – Dean Howard † 1868. White recumbent effigy by *H. H. Armstead*, dated 1872, the Gothic setting by *Scott*. – John Hutchinson † 1705. Tablet by *Edward Stanton*. – Col. Bagot † 1645 at Naseby. Purely classical tablet. – Bishop Hacket † 1670. Recumbent effigy, coloured, on a high sarcophagus. The niche for the monument is that with the bands of nobbly foliage. – Archdeacon Moore † 1876. The white recumbent effigy, dead, not asleep, by *H. H. Armstead*. Dated 1879. The design is by *Scott*. – STAINED GLASS. By *Kempe* the window above the entrance to the Chapel of the Head of St Chad and all the glass in the chapel. – The REREDOS in the chapel is also by *Kempe*.

CONSISTORY COURT. The triple SEAT must be of *c*.1670, see the panels of the back wall, the twisted columns, and the openwork panels of the front. The canopies have deliberate Gothic overtones. The seats come from the former choir stalls.

SOUTH CHOIR AISLE continued. MONUMENTS. Purbeck effigy of a bishop, *c*.1240–50, shafts and a gabled pointed-trefoiled top. Beautifully ascetic face. – Purbeck effigy of a bishop. Called Bishop Langton, but it cannot be him. He died in 1321, and the monument is of the C13, see the folds of the draperies and the stiff-leaf decoration. – John Stanley of Pipe † 1515. Defaced, alas. He is shown bareheaded and stripped to the waist – a sign of penance? The effigy is on a tomb-chest. – Major Hodson † 1858 at the storming of Lucknow. Designed by *Street* and carved by *Earp*. Totally unlike the Street one knows. Showy, restless, with chunky forms heralding today's Brutalism. Busy scenes and allegorical figures. – Archdeacon Hodson † 1855, the monument of

1860–2. Also designed by *Street*. Also with scenes of many figures. – Medallion of Erasmus Darwin; mid-C19.

NORTH TRANSEPT. STAINED GLASS. E aisle N by *Kempe*. – N lancet by *Clayton & Bell*, 1893. – MONUMENTS. Canon Lonsdale † 1907. Recumbent effigy of marble by *Farmer & Brindley*. – John Hodgson Iles † 1888. Signed *W. R. Ingram*, 1890. Recumbent effigy of stone. – Stephen Simpson † 1784. Large tablet of exquisite quality. Oval medallion with bust in relief. – William Vyse † 1770. Another large tablet – 1816 by *Samuel Hayward*. – In the NW corner Dean Heywood † 1492. Only the cadaver remains of a large monument with the effigy on an upper tier and an elaborate canopy. – General Vyse † 1825 and Mary Madan † 1827. Companion pieces. White marble with profile medallions. – Sir Charles Oakley † 1826. By *Chantrey*. Also white, also with a profile medallion. Did he then do the other two as well?

CROSSING. SCREEN. 1859–63. Designed by *Scott* and made by *Francis Skidmore* of Coventry, the figure work by *Birnie Philip*.* Iron, brass, and copper, light and transparent, of the highest craftsmanship and an ornament to any cathedral. Let Salisbury and Hereford be vandals and remove their Scott-Skidmore screens, Lichfield must hold out till High Victorianism is at last fully appreciated in its best work.

SOUTH TRANSEPT. Outside the transept is a MONUMENT with an effigy of a Civilian under a cusped arch. – In the E aisle one window with Herckenrode GLASS. – MONUMENTS. Officers and others of the 80th Regiment of Foot. 1846 by *Hollins*. In the Egyptian style. Free-standing high black base and a white sphinx on top. Large white trophy below. – Andrew Newton. By *Westmacott*, 1808. Standing monument with a group of two children l., a standing woman r., and a second leaning over the central pedestal. – Bust of Dr Johnson. By *Westmacott*, 1793 (says White). – Bust of Garrick, by *Westmacott*, 1793 (says White). – John Rawlins † 1685, good cartouche. – On the S wall three large tablets without figures: Lucy Grove † 1787, Jane Gastrell † 1798, Dean Proby † 1807. – Above STAINED GLASS of 1895 by *Kempe*.

NAVE. PULPIT. Iron, all elaborate openwork. Two staircases. By *Scott* or *Skidmore*. – LECTERN. A brass eagle. By *Hardman* of Birmingham. – FONT. Designed by *Slater* and executed by *Forsyth*, c.1862. – STAINED GLASS. The W

---

* Information given me by Mr G. P. Hives.

window is by *Clayton & Bell*, 1869. – MONUMENT. First Earl of Lichfield † 1854. Brass effigy under a canopy. Black marble slab on the floor. – WEST DOORS. Original iron scrolls, but restored.

NORTH AISLE. In the tower bay STATUE of Charles II once at the top of the gable. Attributed to *Sir William Wilson*. – STAINED GLASS. W by *Kempe*. – The westernmost N window by *Burlison & Grylls*, the next to the E by *Kempe*. – Then sixth from E again by *Burlison & Grylls*. – MONUMENTS (tower bay). Seward family † 1764, 1780, 1790. By *Bacon*. Seated mourning woman under a weeping willow. The poem is by Anna Seward and includes herself. – Lady Mary Wortley Montagu † 1789. By *Thomas Scheemakers*. Standing female figure by an urn. Run-of-the-mill. – Walmsley family † 1751, † 1785, 1786, by *William Thompson* of Birmingham. Fine tablet in several marbles. Three putto heads at the foot.

SOUTH AISLE. STAINED GLASS. The easternmost window by *Hardman*. – Next *Clayton & Bell*, then *Ward & Hughes*, then *Clayton & Bell*, under the tower *Burlison & Grylls*. – MONUMENTS. Two defaced effigies boxed in the wall, only busts and feet appearing.

PLATE. Parcel-gilt Chalice and Cover 1670.

THE CLOSE

The close was formed by Bishop Langton (licence to crenellate 1299), who built the wall and two gateways. He also created two causeways across the pool: Bird Street and Dam Street.

The Lichfield Close is closer than others, more intimate and more secluded. You can reach it along Dam Street, by the back door, as it were, but the main approach is from Beacon Street through a kind of funnel. On the l. the masonry of the former WEST GATE, on the r. NEWTON'S COLLEGE, 1800 by *Joseph Potter*, a long, even ashlar front of eleven bays, with a three-bay pediment. This three-bay centre has a rusticated ground floor with arched windows. In the centre above is an arched niche. Now turn l. At the corner some medieval masonry. No. 10 is timber-framed with oversailing upper floor. Then the VICARS' CLOSE, a pleasant backwater, reached by a narrow gangway through a house. There is lawn in the middle and a tree, and houses are timber-framed on the N and E. The w termination is a house of 1764, brick, of three widely spaced bays.*

Now the N side of the Close. First ST CHAD'S SCHOOL HOUSE, Victorian red brick, then a low C18 house with two canted bays, a higher one with a canted façade towards the cathedral and an octagonal gazebo, and so to the beautiful DEANERY, brick, of seven bays and two storeys with quoins and quoins to the pedimented three-bay centre. The staircase has twisted balusters. It is characteristic of c.1700.‡ The neighbour of the Deanery is the former BISHOP'S PALACE (St Chad's School). This is of 1687-8 and was built by *Edward Pierce*, one of Wren's best masons. It is ashlar-faced, of seven bays and two storeys, with a hipped roof and a three-bay pediment with shield and garlands. The perfectly fitting projecting wings l. and r. with their hipped roofs are an addition of 1869 – amazingly sensitively done. Inside, only one room has its original panelling and chimneypiece. The garden side has slightly projecting wings of two bays, leaving a centre of only three. Adjoining this side is a minimum-Gothic chapel, also of 1868. At the far NE corner of the garden is part of a corner tower of the medieval Close, C14, hexagonal (with an 'arched stone roof' to the lowest room; DOE). This is at the level of the moat, now a picturesquely overgrown ravine.

SELWYN HOUSE lies on its own, E of the cathedral separated from the Bishop's Palace. Trees screen the gap and allow a view of Stowe Pool. The house has a canted centre bay with the doorway set in it. It is Mid Georgian. Next the former ST MARY'S VICARAGE. The E and S walls of this are largely medieval precinct wall. At the corner a small polygonal tower. The house opposite at the NW corner of Dam Street has medieval masonry too. The one gargoyle is of course *ex situ*

---

* Miss J. Isaac of the Lichfield Joint Record Office enlarges on this as follows: Nos. 1-7 The Close mostly have Georgian façades, but there is some good timber-framing on No. 7 and at the rear of No. 6. Between Nos. 7 and 8 is the entrance to the Nether Vicarage, and by walking round here one can see traces of medieval masonry at the rear of No. 2 Vicars' Close and some good timber-framing at the rear of No. 3, with an oversailing upper floor.

No. 4 Vicars' Close (on the S side), although perhaps of little architectural merit, used to be the Vicars' Muniment Room, presumably that built in 1756. It was also originally the main entrance to their Common Hall, probably of similar date, the gable end of which fronts Beacon Street, between Darwin House and the house at the W end of Vicars' Close.

‡ Permission to build was in fact given in 1704.

THE CATHEDRAL · THE TOWN   189

The house was the Muniment Room and before that probably the C17 stable and coach house.

The S side of the Close is more varied and less rewarding. The former THEOLOGICAL COLLEGE has a doorway with Tuscan columns set against rustication, the BISHOP'S HOUSE two Early Victorian bargeboarded gables and a porch rusticated in the crazy pattern of the doorway of 1631–5 of Tutbury Castle. No. 23A is C18, Gothic, of five bays with straight-headed windows and battlements and exposed medieval masonry. One of its windows is a charming Gothick three-light job with ogee-headed lights.*

And that is the end.

THE TOWN

INTRODUCTION

Though Lichfield's history goes back to St Chad, the town is visually a Georgian town. Yet there is more left of the Middle Ages than the cathedral, some of its precincts, and St John's Hospital: for the basic street pattern is medieval,‡ the NW to SE coaching road and the parallel main streets all branching off it, and that ornament of all ornaments of Lichfield, the two pools separating the precinct from the town. The Bishop's Fish Pool extended originally far beyond the bridge to the W, and Stowe Mere NE of the cathedral was much larger too. Dam Street, as its name implies, was a causeway. The reduction to the present area of water took place only in 1855.

Lichfield was called 'a place of conversation and good company' by Defoe in 1723, and *The Beauties of England and Wales* about a hundred years later note that the houses are 'to the taste of modern times, and for the most part occupied by gentry and persons of small independent means'. It is after all Dr Johnson's town and Erasmus Darwin's town.

Lichfield had 4,842 inhabitants in 1801, 7,102 in 1851, 8,140 in 1901. It now (1971) has 22,672. So this means slow growth, but a speeding up recently.

The arrangement of the Perambulation after the churches is (A) The NW–SE axis with a few short detours, (B) and (C) the two main detours. Public Buildings are treated within the perambulations. For the Close see p. 187.

* No. 24 has medieval cellars.
‡ Mr C. C. Taylor has recently shown that Lichfield was laid out as a planned town by Bishop Roger de Clinton in the 1140s.

THE PARISH CHURCHES

St Mary. A stately Victorian building and endowed by *Street* with a steeple which holds its own against the spires of the cathedral. He did it in 1852–4. In 1868–70 *James Fowler* of Louth rebuilt the church, which was of 1717–21.* This is a competent, serious job in the Middle Pointed with four-bay arcades. Street's high tower arch goes well with it. – PLATE. All silver-gilt, a splendid collection. Chalice by *R.W.*, London, 1637; Paten by *E.G.*, London, 1671; Chalice by *E.G.*, London, 1671; Flagon by *James Wilkes*, London, 1731; Paten and Flagon by *Sleath*, 1736; Christening Bowl by *Whipham*, 1742; two Almsdishes by *John Robinson*, London, 1743.

St Chad. A fine E.E. doorway with a trefoiled opening and three orders of columns. The five-bay S arcade with octagonal piers is E.E. too, and so is the chancel – see the one S lancet. The W tower is Dec – see the arch to the nave and the W window. Dec also the chancel E window with cusped intersecting tracery. The ceiling and the brick clerestory look *c*.1800, the N aisle is externally of 1848. The arcade however seems to be Perp. – FONT. Perp, with panelled stem and shields in quatrefoils on the bowl. – PLATE. Silver-gilt Chalice and Paten, 1634; Flagon by *J.W.*, 1751; two Plates by *P. & A. Bateman*, 1798.

Christ Church, Christ Church Lane, Lemansley. 1847 by *Johnson*, the transepts etc. added in 1886–7. Early Dec style. W tower designed so as to appear Dec below but Perp above. Aisleless nave. – The roof PAINTING in the chancel is by *John D. Batten*, 1897. – REREDOS by *Bodley*, 1906. – STAINED GLASS. E and N chapel N by *Kempe*, the latter 1901.

St Michael. Fine view to the cathedral. Perp W tower with recessed spire. The body of the church seems to be E.E. – see the long lancet now in the E wall of the tower. Most of the church is of 1842–3 by *Thomas Johnson*, but the Perp E window is of *J. O. Scott*'s restoration of 1890–1. Johnson – this the church proves – was no longer satisfied with the Commissioners' convention of *c*.1820–40. To turn to serious archaeology in 1842 was quite a feat. – FONT. 1669. Octagonal with stylized fleur-de-lis and Tudor roses. – MONUMENTS. Early C13 effigy of a Civilian praying. – Louis Hayes Pett † 1849. Rectangular tablet with profile medallion. By *G. Nelson*, 1850.

* Paul Joyce tells me that *Lord Grimthorpe* claimed the design as his own

PUBLIC BUILDINGS see PERAMBULATIONS

PERAMBULATIONS

(A) The South–North Axis

This perambulation comprises St John's Street, Bird Street, and Beacon Street. Traffic being as it is, no one, except on a Sunday morning early, can take in both sides of these streets. So we will walk first the W, and then the E side.

ST JOHN STREET on the W side starts with a major monument: ST JOHN'S HOSPITAL. The hospital was probably founded by Bishop Roger de Clinton c.1140. Traces of this building are said to survive in the chapel S wall and the N wall of the chapel range. The hospital was re-founded by Bishop Smyth in 1495. In the chapel is a S lancet of C13 and a large Perp window. Perp N and E windows too. The N aisle is of 1829, but the arcade was rebuilt in 1871.* The original hall was W of the chapel. The extremely impressive E range with its eight chimneybreasts to the street looks to belong to Smyth's re-foundation. The tablet over the doorway is dated 1720. The canted bay windows to the courtyard date from 1929. In 1966–7 *Louis de Soissons* carried out a very pleasant addition (S and W ranges).

N of St John's Hospital No. 28 of c.1820 is rendered and has along the ground floor a colonnade of one plus three times two plus one fluted columns with fancy Composite capitals. No. 26 is a good early C18 house of five bays with decorated window lintels and a later porch of pairs of Tuscan columns. (A fireplace surround with giant Doric pilasters. A. Gomme) After No. 20, an early C18 house with a straight door-hood on carved brackets, the walls of the precinct of the former FRANCISCAN FRIARY appear in patches. The friary was founded c.1237, burnt in 1291, and rebuilt. Excavations have revealed much about the premises. The major remaining fragment is in FRIARY, to the W of the FRIARY SCHOOL, a stately symmetrical pile with mullioned and transomed windows, dating from 1921–8 and designed by the County Education Committee Architect, *G. C. Lowbridge*. The friars' church lay a good deal to the N, NW of the National Westminster Bank (*see* below). It had a nave and aisle, the tower in

---

* MONUMENT to the Simpson family, late C18, with a female figure by an urn

the usual position between nave and chancel, and a long chancel. To its S were two cloisters. The existing buttressed L-shaped building to the W of the school linked up with the W range along the major cloister. Further W in Friary is the CLOCK TOWER of 1863 by *Joseph Potter*, high and ambitious, and Norman (of all styles). It has a pyramid roof. Back to the school and now again N.

The corner of Friary and BIRD STREET is the NATIONAL WESTMINSTER BANK, early C19 probably and large, stuccoed, with a rusticated ground floor and to Bird Street a three-bay pediment. On the other side of the street is No. 17 Bird Street, Early Georgian, with nicely enriched window lintels and rather a wild door surround. Close to the corner of Sandford Street is No. 11 Bird Street (which has at the back a domed room with shell mosaic). Off to the W along SANDFORD STREET and QUEEN STREET for two nice doorways: No. 15 Sandford Street and No. 2 Queen Street. The SWAN HOTEL is late C18, painted, and quite big. Then in the MUSEUM GARDENS two STATUES: Edward VII, stone, by *Robert Bridgeman*, 1908, and John Smith, Commander of the 'Titanic', bronze, by *Lady Scott*, 1910. The BRIDGE should be sampled. It is a handsome design of 1816 and of course enjoys the memorable view of the Minster Pool, the dense trees and shrubs to its N, and the cathedral behind.

BEACON STREET continues from here and makes an aesthetically false start with the LIBRARY AND MUSEUM, of 1857–9 (by *Bidlake & Lovatt*), small, of yellow brick and funny,* and an aesthetically excellent second start with WEST GATE HOUSE, mid C18, stuccoed, with a doorway with pilasters and a triglyph frieze and a splendid iron gate and railings. Inside, a charming room with stucco ceiling and wall panels. The ANGEL CROFT HOTEL has a good gate and railings too and a pedimented doorway on Tuscan demi-columns. With MILLEY'S HOSPITAL this side of the S–N axis is complete. It is a C17 building of brick with stone trim and has a middle porch and mullioned windows.‡

The return journey starts a little further N with BEACON LODGE, an ashlar-faced early C19 house of three bays. No. 20 has a pretty doorway with fluted Ionic pilasters. Then the back of the house of 1764 in Vicars' Close (*see* p. 187) with Venetian side windows, and ERASMUS DARWIN'S HOUSE, high and

---

* It is in fact in Bird Street.

‡ The staff of the VCH suggests the early C16 as the original date.

1 *Scenery:* The Roaches, near Leek

2 (left) *Canals*: Tyrley (Hales), lock with canal bridge by Telford
3 (centre left) *The Potteries*: Longton (Stoke-on-Trent)
4 (below left) Wall, remains of a bath-house of the Roman town of Letocetum
5 (below) Wolverhampton, St Peter, Wolverhampton Cross, probably mid ninth century

6 (above left) Kingswinford church, tympanum, Norman
7 (left) Armitage church, font, Norman
8 (above) Gnosall church, arch between south transept and aisle, Norman and Early English

9 (left) Stafford, St Chad, nave, Norman

10 (right) Tutbury church, west front, c. 1160–70

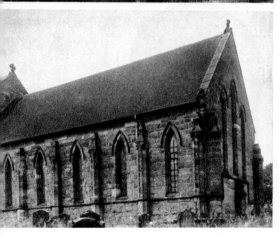

11 (left) Croxden Abbey, consecrated 1253, fragment of the west wall

12 (below left) Brewood church, chancel, early thirteenth century

13 (right) Stafford, St Mary, nave, early thirteenth century

14 (below right) Lichfield Cathedral, portal in the north transept, c. 1230–40

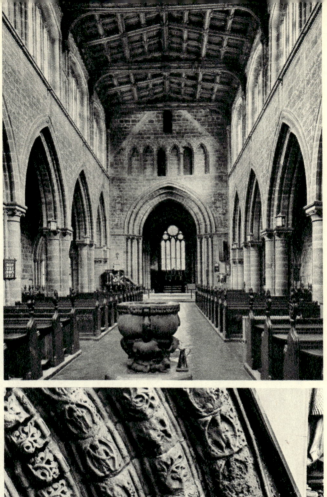

15 (left) Lichfield Cathedral, west front, begun *c.* 1280

16 (right) Lichfield Cathedral, nave, *c.* 1260–80

17 (below) Lichfield Cathedral, chancel, begun *c.* 1310

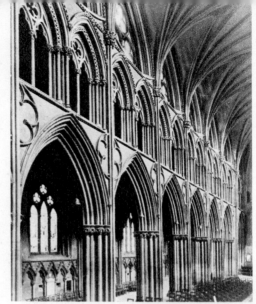

18 Swynnerton church, seated Christ, probably *c.* 1260–80
19 (above right) Lichfield Cathedral, statue outside the south choir aisle, *c.* 1310
20 (above far right) Wolverhampton, St Peter, tower, early sixteenth century
21 (right) Barton-under-Needwood church, *c.* 1533

22 (left) Elford church, monument to Sir William Smythe †1525 and his two wives
23 (above) Stowe-by-Chartley church, detail from the monument to Sir Walter Devereux †1537
24 (below) Brewood church, monument to Sir Thomas Giffard †1560 and his two wives

25 Lichfield, St John's Hospital, founded 1495
26 Stafford, High House, 1555(?)

27 Broughton Hall, 1637, restored in 1926–39
28 Balterley, Hall o' Wood, 1557(?)

29 Tixall Hall, gatehouse, *c.* 1575

30 Wootton Lodge, between 1580 and 1611

31 Caverswall Castle, perhaps by Robert or John Smythson, *c.* 1615

32 Alstonefield church, pulpit, 1637
33 (above right) Wolverhampton, St Peter, monument to Admiral Sir Richard Leveson †1605, by Hubert Le Sueur, *c.* 1634
34 (above far right) Tamworth church, monument to John Ferrers †1680 and Humphrey Ferrers †1678, commissioned from Grinling Gibbons but probably carved by Arnold Quellin; figures by C. G. Cibber
35 (right) Rugeley Old Church, detail of monument to Thomas Lauder †1670

36 Ingestre church, probably by Sir Christopher Wren, 1676
37 (above right) Little Wyrley Hall, door furniture, *c.* 1691 (*Copyright Country Life*)
38 (right) Wolverhampton, Giffard House, 1728, staircase

39 Weston-under-Lizard, Weston Park, 1671, perhaps by Lady Wilbraham
40 (above right) Oakley Hall, 1710
41 (right) Cheadle, Hales Hall, 1712

42 Lichfield, Donegal House (Guildhall), early eighteenth century

43 Tamworth, Town Hall, 1701

44 (below) Brewood, Speedwell Castle, c. 1750

45 Forton church, tower medieval, nave 1723
46 (below) Longnor church, 1780
47 (right) Wolverhampton, St John, by William Baker, 1758–76

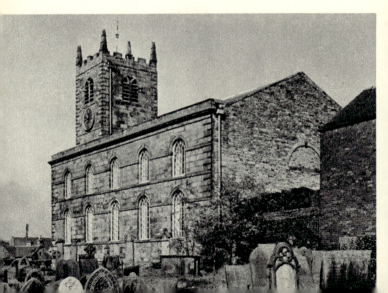

48 Shugborough, Dining Room, c. 1748, chimneypiece

49 (below) Shugborough, Red Drawing Room, by Samuel Wyatt, 1794

50 (right) Shugborough, east front, by various architects, 1693–1794

51 (centre right) Shugborough, Chinese House, completed 1747, and Chinese Bridge, 1813

52 (below right) Shugborough, Doric Temple, by James Stuart, 1760

53 (top) Shugborough, Arch of Hadrian, by James Stuart, 1761–7
54 Weston-under-Lizard, Weston Park, Temple of Diana, by James Paine, 1760s(?)

55 Enville Hall, summer house, by Sanderson Miller, 1750
56 (below) Great Barr Hall, 1777 etc.

57 Stafford, Shire Hall, by John Harvey, 1795–9
58 (below) Stoke-on-Trent, The Mount, 1803
59 (right) Rocester, Tutbury Mill, c. 1782
60 (below right) Longton (Stoke-on-Trent), Boundary Works, 1819

61 Okeover church, monument to Mary Okeover †1764 and Leak Okeover †1765, by Joseph Wilton

62 (below) Stoke-on-Trent church, monument to Josiah Wedgwood †1795 by John Flaxman

63 Trentham Park, Mausoleum, by C. Heathcote Tatham, 1807–8 (*Copyright Country Life*)

64 (below) Chillington Hall, Saloon, by Sir John Soane, 1786–9
(*Copyright Country Life*)
65 Butterton Grange, by Sir John Soane, 1816–17
66 (right) Pell Wall, by Sir John Soane, 1822–8, lodge
67 (below right) Dudley, St Thomas, by William Brooks, 1815–18

68 Walsall, St Matthew, by Francis Goodwin, 1820–1, nave ceiling

69 Bilston church, by Francis Goodwin, 1825–6

70 Uttoxeter church, nave, by Trubshaw & Johnson, 1828

71 (below Ilam church, momument to David Pike Watts, by Sir Francis Chantrey, 1831
72 (right) Lichfield, Market Place, relief on the Johnson Monument, by R. C. Lucas, 1838
73 (below right) Weston-under-Lizard church, monument to the Countess of Bradford †1842, by Peter Hollins

LISTENING TO Dr SACHEVEREL PREACHING

74 (below) Alton Towers, *c.* 1810–52
75 Alton Towers, conservatory, *c.* 1820
76 (right) Alton Towers, memorial to the fifteenth Earl of Shrewsbury, *c.* 1830

77 Trentham Park (demolished), by Sir Charles Barry, 1833–42 (*Copyright Country Life*)
78 (below) Alton Towers, chimneypiece in the Banqueting Hall, by A. W. N. Pugin, *c.* 1840–50
79 (right) Alton Castle, by A. W. N. Pugin, begun 1847
80 (below right) Cheadle, Roman Catholic church, by A. W. N. Pugin, 1841–6

81 Drayton Bassett church, monument to Sir Robert Peel †1850, by White
82 Biddulph church, monument to William and Mary Heath, by Matthew Noble, 1872

83 Lichfield Cathedral, crossing screen, by Francis Skidmore to the design of Sir George Gilbert Scott, figure work by John Birnie Philip, 1859–63

84 (left) Newcastle-under-Lyme, Holy Trinity, by James Egan, 1833–4

85 (below left) Leigh church, by Thomas Johnson, complete by 1846

86 (right) Denstone church, by G. E. Street, 1860–2

87 (below) Denstone church, by G. E. Street, 1860–2, pulpit

88 Stoke-on-Trent railway station, by H. A. Hunt, 1847–8

89 Little Aston Hall, by Edward J. Payne, 1857-9

90 Audley, houses and shops by William White, from *The Builder*, 1855

91 Burslem (Stoke-on-Trent), Wedgwood Memorial Institute, by R. Edgar and J. L. Kipling, 1863–9

92 Keele Hall, by Anthony Salvin, 1856-61

93 and 94 Hoar Cross church, by G. F. Bodley, begun 1872

95 (left) Hopwas church, by John Douglas, 1881
96 (below left) Leek, All Saints, by R. Norman Shaw, 1885–7
97 (below) Walsall, St Paul, by J. L. Pearson, 1891–3

98 (left) Burton-on-Trent, St Chad, by G. F. Bodley, designed 1903
99 (top) Stafford, Upmeads, by Edgar Wood, 1908
100 Dudley Zoo, by Tecton, 1936–7

101 Wolverhampton, St Martin, Ettingshall, by Lavender & Twentyman, 1938–9

102 Wolverhampton, St Michael, Tettenhall, west tower Perpendicular, nave by Bernard Miller after 1950

103 Keele University, chapel, by G. G. Pace, 1964–5

104 Walsall, West Midland Teacher Training College, by Richard Sheppard, Robson & Partners, 1961–4

imposing, of brick, five bays and two storeys on a high basement. Outer stairs to the door. The doorway has Tuscan columns and a pediment. One-bay crowning pediment. Venetian side windows on both main floors. The house was built between 1760 and 1784 and probably before 1777.*

Continue along BIRD STREET as before. At the corner of the Close a two-bay ashlar house that goes with Newton's buildings in the Close (*see* p. 187). MOAT HOUSE and LANGTON HOUSE have nice doorways. Nos. 20–22 has a double shop-window of the early C19. The GEORGE HOTEL is one of the best late C18 hotel buildings in the land. Nine bays, stuccoed, with a five-bay centre, rusticated below, with Ionic pilasters above. Originally the carriageway went through the middle. On the first floor in the middle is a delightful ballroom with a segmental vault and a back recess with two fluted columns. The staircase with two columns on the upper landing is original too. It is very rare for inns of the late C18 to incorporate (instead of adding) a ballroom or assembly room.

Near and at the s end of Bird Street, Market Street and Bore Street branch off. For these see Perambulations B and C.

In ST JOHN STREET No. 45 is of 1682. It was the house of the headmaster of the Grammar School. Their former building is Gothic of 1849. The headmaster's house is typical of its date, four bays, two storeys, and a hipped roof, the windows wider than in the C18. Small staircase with turned balusters, but remarkable in that it curves up and does this twice – for both upper floors. The adjoining school building is of 1901–3, by *T. Hillyer Pyke*. Finally in UPPER ST JOHN STREET, DAVIDSON HOUSE, early C19, of three bays, with a Venetian mid-window and tripartite side windows, the centre with a pediment. No. 73 has a Venetian window too.

A postscript, a little further out s. Off Borrowcop Lane is Hillside, and off HILLSIDE a footpath on the W leads to BORROWCOP HILL, on which is an C18 GAZEBO. Square, of brick, with two arches to each side, but divided by a brick cross wall. At the E end of Borrowcop Lane at the angle with TAMWORTH ROAD is QUARRY LODGE, a castellated, rendered house of 1849 with turrets.

(B) *Market Street and to its East*

In MARKET STREET No. 3 has a broad double shop-front. Nos. 11–13 are timber-framed with three gables and cusped four-

* Information from Miss Isaac.

cornered studs as the decorative motif. Nos. 15–17 has another double shop-front, the lettering the typical early C19 Egyptian. The house is of seven bays and has three doorways. So to the MARKET PLACE. Here the excellent JOHNSON MONUMENT by *Richard Cockle Lucas*, made in 1838. The reliefs show the influence of Donatello's *schiacciato* relief. They are outstandingly good. Boswell's STATUE is of bronze by *Percy Fitzgerald*, 1908. Along the S side of the square is St Mary's church. On the Market Street corner and facing the square is JOHNSON'S BIRTHPLACE, a house of 1707 with a recessed ground floor with three Tuscan columns. Rendered, and with a steep roof.

Turn N along DAM STREET to the cathedral. This is a pleasant, hardly disturbed street. Nos. 2–4 are of seven bays with a three-bay pediment. No. 8 has a pedimented doorway, and round the corner in QUONIAN'S LANE is a timber-framed house, dated 1555. No. 16 has oriels with good carved figurework. The house must be late C18. No. 18 is again timber-framed and has two gables. Then three more nice doorcases.

Turn W by the pool along MINSTER POOL WALK. MINSTER COTTAGE is Early Tudor of *c.*1830, with straight-headed windows and bargeboards to the gables. Then the back of a brick house with two tiers of Venetian windows. The front is behind Bird Street, and that is where this walk ends.

(C) Bore Street and to its East

In BORE STREET are side by side two of the best houses of Lichfield. First the TUDOR CAFÉ, early C16, timber-framed with three gables. Two overhangs. Below all closely set uprights, above herringbone, and in the gables concave-sided cusped lozenges. DONEGAL HOUSE (Guildhall) is early C18. It is of five bays and three storeys with a parapet and angle pilasters carrying one triglyph each, a doorway with Tuscan columns and a segmental pediment, and window lintels of a prettily fanciful kind. Staircase with slim turned balusters. The GUILDHALL itself is Gothic of 1846–8 (by *Potter*) and has its short end to the street. Hammerbeam roof.* Nos. 38–42 is another gabled timber-framed house.

To the N, in BREADMARKET STREET, is No. 5, with two Venetian windows. Parallel with Breadmarket Street, but E of

---

* REGALIA. Two silver-gilt Maces, 1664 and 1690; Civic Sword, 1686. – CIVIC PLATE. The Ashmole Cup, 1666 (price £23 8s. 6d.) – On the Swinfen-Broun and the Hewitt Bequests no information could be obtained. The embargo came from the insurance company.

St Mary, is the CORN EXCHANGE by *Johnson & Son*, 1849–50. Low, symmetrical, of two storeys, with an arcade of four-centred arches.

Off Bore Street to the S is the new Baker's Lane SHOPPING PRECINCT, well tucked in and well managed.

Nothing in Tamworth Street, nor in Lombard Street which branches off it, but in STOWE STREET, in the middle of new housing, a cruck cottage, and in and off STOWE HILL two major houses of *c*.1750, detached in their grounds. STOWE HOUSE is four-square, of five bays and two and a half storeys with quoins and quoins to the centre, a doorway with segmental pediment, and a staircase with twisted balusters. STOWE HILL MANSION is reached through recent bungalows. It has five bays also, and towards the town a big bow in the middle of the front. Top parapet with urns. Staircase with turned balusters. Stowe House is early, Stowe Hill mid C18.

Now return to Tamworth Street and go E along Church Street and then TRENT VALLEY ROAD. On the N side is ST MICHAEL'S HOSPITAL, the former WORKHOUSE. The oldest parts, the gatehouse and what lies immediately behind, are by *Scott & Moffatt*, 1841. George Gilbert Scott started his career in this unpromising way. It is Tudor-Gothic, brick with black brick diapers, symmetrical, with battlements on the gatehouse and otherwise gables. But there is also the Georgian cupola. Yet a little farther out is the original TRENT VALLEY STATION of 1847, by *Livock* – not today's, which is S of the road, but a building now a dwelling N of the road. Nice gabled Tudor.*

LITTLE ASTON

0000

ST PETER. A gift of the Hon. Edward Swynfen Parker-Jervis of the Hall. By *Street*, 1873–4. On its own in a leafy setting, E of the Hall. Red ashlar with a noble SW steeple. Broach-spire, windows with lancets – three E, five W, both stepped groups – and also with plate tracery. Decidedly *piquant*, if that is a term one is allowed to apply to Street, the semicircular baptistery niche with a round entrance arch. The interior also all ashlar-faced and, what with that and what with Street's unobtrusive motifs, wholly satisfying. – REREDOS, PULPIT, STALL, SEATS, ORGAN CASE, FONT, and more all by *Street*. Reredos, pulpit,

---

* Now demolished.

and font have stone mosaic. The sculptural work of the reredos is by *Earp*, of the other furnishings by *James Forsyth*.*

LITTLE ASTON HALL. The late C18 house by *James Wyatt*, called a splendid mansion in *The Beauties of England and Wales*, has been replaced by, or swallowed up in, the present mansion, also undeniably splendid, which is by *Edward J. Payne* of Birmingham and dates from 1857–9. The style is Italianate, the composition symmetrical. Front and back, i.e. entrance and garden side, are given equal regard. Two-and-a-half-storey centre of seven bays, two-storey wings of three bays. Motifs are vermiculated rustication and windows with blank shell arches, especially in the centre on the garden side. View to a lake on that side. The principal interiors must have been re-done later in the C19.

LITTLEHAY MANOR HOUSE *see* COLTON

LITTLE HAYWOOD *see* HAYWOOD

LITTLE ONN HALL *see* CHURCH EATON

LITTLETON COLLIERY *see* HUNTINGTON

LITTLE WYRLEY HALL

Little Wyrley Hall is not large, but it has an interesting architectural history, and one or two very remarkable interior features. The core of the house is timber-framed, as has been exposed inside. The date may be early C16. To this house about 1660 a long service wing was added which projects to the w. At the same time the Tudor house was faced with brick. In 1691 the Tudor house was doubled in thickness by the addition of a range of rooms along the E side. However, the feature which provides the house with its greatest charm – the divers shaped gables – are of the 1660 period only in the wing; the others were altered to match about 1820. Similarly, the small staircase with turned balusters is Early Georgian, but the delightful way in which it continues up so that the centre of the house becomes a light-well opened up to the top cupola with balconies looking into the well cannot be so early. 1820 is more likely. The best rooms of the house are on the first floor. They

---

* So Mr Joyce told me.

have excellent panelling, obviously of 1691, and door furniture 37 more ornate than one may ever see again.

LITTYWOOD see BRADLEY

LLOYD HOUSE see WOMBOURNE

LONGDON

ST JAMES. The church has a Norman S doorway with one order of colonnettes, zigzag, and a rare motif in the outer order – like linked incomplete rings. Norman also a buttress on the S side, the outline of the N doorway, and the chancel arch. This has three orders, scallop capitals, again zigzag, but here also at r. angles to the wall. Then the E.E. contributions. Early C13 a S lancet and a N lancet, late C13 the chancel with Y-traceried side windows. The E window of four lights has reticulated, i.e. Dec, tracery. The E.E. N transept is only apparently E.E. It is of 1870 (by *A. Hartshorne*). Dec the lower, Perp the upper part of the W tower. Finally of c.1500 the S chapel of two bays with its battlements and its arcade to the chancel. It was built by John Stoneywall, later Abbot of Pershore. – FONT. The bowl is Norman with diagonal reeding and a strange, very stylized top band of interlocked palmettes. The stem is a magnificent piece of mature E.E. stiff-leaf, the leaves blown horizontally. It comes from the Lichfield Cathedral nave. – STAINED GLASS. S chapel E 1906 by *Bryans*, a straight imitation of Kempe. – PLATE. Paten, 1698 by *Thomas Parr*, London; Chalice by *H.B.*, 1700. – MONUMENTS. Thomas Orme † 1716. By *E. Stanton*. Good tablet with pilasters and trophies l. and r. of them. – C. S. Foster † 1854. By *Hollins*. Sarcophagus and two child angels. – John Foster † 1860. A grandiose sarcophagus with a brass top plate.

HANCH HALL, 1¼ m. E. The house has a splendid Queen Anne front of seven bays and two storeys with a three-bay pediment. Rusticated door surround and mid-window with Gibbs surround. Entrance hall with pedimented doorways. But the range is set in a Victorian (or possibly slightly pre-Victorian) ensemble with a deep loggia with wild pillars and at the back a tower which contains the quite sumptuous staircase. And even that is not all; for in the C19 part is a room in which a timber truss is exposed which must be C15, or anyway pre-Reformation.

(BROOK COTTAGE. Timber-framed, C15–16. Decorative gable, projecting four-light window, and a timber-framed chimney-shaft. DOE)

LONGFORD HOUSE see CANNOCK

LONG LOW see WETTON

LONGNOR

ST BARTHOLOMEW. 1780. W tower with outer stair. The nave and chancel, without any separation, are of five bays and have two tiers of arched windows. However, the upper one is an addition of 1812 and made it possible for galleries to be fitted in. Only the W gallery is now there, and the ceiling makes the upper windows invisible. Venetian E window, decorated probably c.1905. – FONT. Of cauldron shape and probably basically Norman. The carved motifs are scarcely recognizable and must at least partly be re-cut. – PLATE. Chalice, c.1675 by *G.R.*; Paten, 1715 by *P.E.*

WESLEYAN CHAPEL. 1855. Three bays with a three-bay pediment.

Longnor is a market town, not a village, even if all is on a minute scale. There is a square with two townish inns and the MARKET HALL of 1873, ashlar, of three bays with the middle one raised and finished with a shaped gable.

LONGNOR HALL see LAPLEY

LONGPORT see BURSLEM, STOKE-ON-TRENT, p. 266

LONGSDON

ST CHAD. By *Gerald Horsley*, 1903–5. Norman Shaw school at its very best. Much of the inspiration must have come from Shaw's church at Leek. Horsley's W tower is a splendid piece, with its two straight-topped three-light bell-openings on each side. The spire has very low broaches and big gabled lucarnes starting right at the foot of the spire. Horsley's choice of period material was Dec, and he uses it conventionally in the nave windows. The chancel side windows, however, are placed high up, and the E window is as broad and relatively low as

Shaw's at Leek. From there also comes the treatment of the w bay inside as a narthex (see the piers demarcating it). – STAINED GLASS. The E window is by *Comper*. – EMBROIDERY. Made by the Leek School of Needlework.

DUNWOOD HALL. 1870–1 by *Robert Scrivener*. Quite a large house, especially in height. An informal composition. Gothic, with gables and a tower with pyramid roof.

LONGTON *see* STOKE-ON-TRENT, p. 259

LOWER GORNAL
2¼ m. WNW of Dudley

ST JAMES, Church Street. 1815–23, enlarged in 1836–7 by *E. Marsh*, altered in 1863 by *J. Bourne* (GR). The polygonal apse is by *T. H. Fleeming*, 1889. Stone with W tower and lancets.

RUYTON CHAPEL (Congregational), Holloway Vale and Hermit Streets. 1830.

LOWER TEAN *see* TEAN

LOXLEY

LOXLEY HALL. One would like to know about this large house. It has an eleven-bay ashlar front with a porch of four Tuscan columns and a similar entrance side with projecting three-bay wings. The details look Late Georgian, but inside is a large staircase with the twisted balusters of William and Mary style, and the house may have had its shape determined then. Moreover, the hall of the house in its position points even further back. The panelling and the paintings of the hall anyway are brought in. The panels look c.1650, the small inset pictures are Catholic, and there are in the frieze and the large overmantel any number of heraldic shields. In the frieze also the date 1607.* In the stableyard a large octagonal DOVECOTE of brick.

LOYNTON HOUSE *see* NORBURY

---

* Dr Gomme dates the front c.1795. Burke's *Seats* (1852) refers to the house as being almost rebuilt in 1817, though the hall remained unaltered.

MADELEY

ALL SAINTS. Late Norman arcade of four bays with octagonal piers, octagonal many-scalloped capitals (a rarity), and double-chamfered pointed arches. Blocked N aisle E window of the same build. The N doorway is Dec. So are the N windows, but they, like the whole exterior, are over-restored. Perp S arcade, Perp transepts, Perp N chapel (now vestry), and Perp W tower embraced by the aisles. The chancel is of 1872, by *Charles Lynam*. – FONT. With pretty Victorian foliage. – PULPIT. Jacobean, with two tiers of blank arches. The areas inside the arches filled in prettily (in 1872). – CHAPEL SCREEN. Perp, of one-light divisions. – TOWER GALLERY. 1635. Heavy balusters. – STAINED GLASS. The E window by *Clayton & Bell*, 1872. – *Kempe* glass in the S transept S and E windows. – The S aisle W window is *Morris* glass, exquisite in its placing of the three single figures and the smaller crucifix below against dense foliage. The glass was made in 1873.* – MONUMENTS. Randolph Egerton † 1522 and wife. Incised slab on a tomb-chest against which standing figurines under canopies. – John Egerton † 1518 and wife. Good brasses, the figures 22 in. long. – Sir Holland Egerton † 1730. Architectural tablet with three-quarter bust in relief.

OLD HALL, N of the church on the A road. Timber-framed, of 1647. The technique and motifs still those of the Middle Ages.

ALMSHOUSES, SW of the church. 1645. Of that date the brickwork; the porches Victorian.

SCHOOL. 1875, at the expense of Lord Crewe; enlarged 1887. Of brick, large and multiform. Separate Master's House.

OFFLEY WELL HEAD, ¼ m. S of the church. An octagonal structure with a carved back wall and spouts and basins on three sides. Attributed to the mid C19 by the DOE.

The PITHEAD BATHS of the Madeley Colliery, 1935 by *W. A. Woodland*, have recently been demolished.

MAER

ST PETER. The W tower looks Perp. It is reported to have had a date 1610. The S doorway is early Early English, with one

---

* Mr Sewter kindly told me that the St Peter is by *Morris*, St Philip and Noah by *Ford Madox Brown*, Christ by *Burne-Jones*.

order of shafts and an arch of one step and one slight chamfer – say c.1200–10. The rest is Victorian, but only a restoration, and a restoration, it seems, of a C17 building.* Only the N aisle W window is in order. It is of two arched lights, and there is a date 1614 above it. – STAINED GLASS. One window in the N aisle by *Shrigley & Hunt*. – PLATE. Chalice by *W. Bateman*, 1780. – MONUMENT. Sir John Bowyer † 1604 and wife. Recumbent effigies of stone.

MAER HALL has recently been reduced to its original Jacobean size. Wings by *Culshaw* of Liverpool and – c.1895 – by *Doyle* of Liverpool have disappeared. The street front with three gables seems to have been severely restored. More interesting the garden side, with two shaped gables and a two-storeyed porch with Ionic above Tuscan columns. Four-light windows, those in the gables of four stepped lights. The porch to the N and the columns above it are recent. – Good GATEHOUSE of the C18. Two-storeyed with a broken pediment. – GARDENS by *Mawson*. – The Doyle and Mawson work was for the Liverpool shipowner F. J. Harrison.

BERTH HILL, ½ m. NW. A univallate Iron Age hillfort crowns the top of the hill and encloses an area of some 9 acres. There is an elaborate inturned entrance on the W and a simple gap on the NE.

MAPLE HAYES
1¼ m. W of Lichfield

Late Georgian of five bays and two and a half storeys. The one-bay wings with canted bay windows were added c. 1885–90, a job very tactfully done. Erasmus Darwin laid out his botanic garden here (DOE).

MARCHINGTON

ST PETER. A charming brick church of 1742 (by *Richard Trubshaw*), reached by an avenue leading to the W tower. This has a doorway with alternating rustication, and so have the four S side windows. The top stage of the tower is octagonal and crowned by a cupola. If only the Victorians had kept away from the chancel. They rebuilt it Gothic. – PLATE.

---

* 1870 is the date of the faculty, according to Dr Robinson. The architects named are *Lewis & Son* of Newcastle-under-Lyme.

Chalice, 1658. – Also a splendid Arts and Crafts Tabernacle and Cross. – MONUMENTS. Incised slabs of a Civilian and wife (floor). – Incised slabs to Walter Vernon † 1593 and wife. On a tomb-chest are frontal figurines and elementary balusters.

MARCHINGTON HALL. Brick. This must be late C17. The front has two gables with a little balustrading between and five bays of regularly set cross-windows on the two floors.

MARCHINGTON WOODLANDS

ST JOHN. 1858–9 by *A. D. Gough* of London, an expensive church (built by Thomas Webb of Smallwood Manor in memory of his wife) and commissioned from an architect who showed this by fussy detail and touches of forced originality. The worst of these are the columns and flying buttresses on top of the broaches of the spire – or are they tabernacles? Another touch of the 'rogue' in Goodhart-Rendel's sense is the timber porch. The style of the church is late C13. Busy geometrical and sub-geometrical tracery. Nave without aisle. Chancel chapels with tripartite openings.

WOODROFFE'S, N of the church. An excellent timber-framed house on a T-plan, mostly with closely set vertical studs, but also some balusters and carved angle brackets. The date seems to be Jacobean. The front range is oblong and consists of only two rooms with a central fireplace between. Some windows have original glazing. Some decorated Jacobean panelling inside.

SMALLWOOD MANOR. By *R. W. Edis*, 1886. Large, of brick and yellow terracotta. The motifs are French and English C16. An arched porch, transomed windows, shaped gables. The whole lacks tension and indeed a clear sense of purpose.*

MARSTON

ST LEONARD. 1794 by *William Dudley*. Brick chancel, stone nave, both with arched windows. The nave masonry is re-used or simply given new features. – LECTERN. Alabaster, with an angel bust. – STAINED GLASS. Two windows by *William Pearce* of Birmingham.

---

* Dr Girouard has pointed out that the house had electricity from the start (cf. Chasetown, p. 96).

MAVESYN RIDWARE

ST NICHOLAS. Perp w tower and E.E. N aisle – see the w and one N lancet and the grouped stepped E lancets. The w lancet of course shows that the tower did not then exist. There is also a good PISCINA with a pointed-trefoiled arch of many mouldings. The nave is of 1782 and has pointed windows and a coved ceiling. Of 1782 also the polygonal apse with plaster ribs. – FONT. Norman, with one band of wavy stems and leaves. – PLATE. Flagon and Paten, 1760, by *Thomas Whipham & Charles Wright* of London; Chalice, 1761 by *Richard Gurney & Co.* of London; Tray, 1784 by *E.J.* – But the fascination of the church is the MAVESYN CHAPEL (three bays, octagonal arcade piers). Here the family monuments are assembled, and other ancestors are celebrated in a somewhat bogus way. All along the walls are alabaster panels with individual ancestors incised so as to deceive those who saw them when they were new. But when was that ?* An approximate date can perhaps be guessed from two panels brought over from Caen in 1786. There are also three small, crowded RELIEFS illustrating battles fought by Mavesyns, and they could well be late C18 too. In the centre is the tomb-chest of Sir Robert † 1403 at the battle of Shrewsbury (see the reliefs), and here again the incised image must be totally recent. It is illustrated in Shaw, the engraving being dated 1785. – Also in the chapel many other MONUMENTS. In two recesses are two Knights, one C13 with his legs not crossed, the other cross-legged. – On a second tomb-chest is the incised slab of Thomas Cawarden † 1593 and wife. – On the floor from l. to r. David Cardon † 1557 and wife, John Cardon † 1485 and wife, John Cardon † 1477, and Hugh Davenport † 1473. – HELMET, SHEATHS, and SHIELD also in the chapel.

OLD HALL, SW of the church. The present house is approached through a gatehouse range, 87 ft long and once part no doubt of a quadrangular composition. The range has a stone front for the ground floor to the outside but is otherwise timber-framed, though the timber-framing was hidden by brick probably in 1718 and is now only exposed in the centre and at the back. The gate arch is segmental and has C14 moulding details. The windows are loopholes. On the first floor a roof of tremendous timbers is exposed. The scanty details suggest the

---

* The Rev. D. G. Rogers writes that the backs of some panels have the date 1812.

C14 again. The tie-beams carry king-posts with four-way struts. The house belonged to the Mavesins (Malvoisins) till 1403, then to the Cawardens. The present house stands detached. It is of 1718, of five bays and two storeys with a hipped roof. The doorway has a bolection moulding and an open segmental pediment on brackets. The windows have aprons, and the mid-window is distinguished by a moulded surround.

RECTORY, Hill Ridware, ¾ m. NW. An early C18 brick house of five bays. The windows have aprons.

HIGH BRIDGE. Of iron, cast by the Coalbrookdale works in 1830. The span is 140 ft. The pattern of the two spandrels is not unattractive.

MAYFIELD

ST JOHN BAPTIST. Late Norman S doorway with one order of colonnettes carrying primitive capitals and complex, three-dimensional zigzags and also pellets in the arch. The S arcade is Late Norman too. Three big bays, round piers, square abaci, and multi-scalloped capitals, but also broad leaf and volute capitals. The arches have one step and one slight chamfer. The N arcade has the same arches but different capitals. They probably belong to the rebuilding of the aisle in 1854 (*F. W. Fiddian*). Good Dec chancel and good Dec S aisle windows. One would call them all late C13 rather than early C14, if it were not for the reticulation of the E window. The crenellation of the chancel is Gothick, i.e. Georgian. Perp W tower with the date 1515. Eight pinnacles. – FONT. Octagonal, Perp, dated 1514. – Excellent set of BENCHES, dated 1630 and 1633. – The PULPIT and the chancel PANELLING no doubt of the same period, but the three-sided COMMUNION RAIL looks later by a generation. The ornament is telling. – SOUTH DOOR. Perp. – PLATE. Chalice by *T.R.*, 1665.

MAYFIELD MILLS. A group of three (formerly four) mills, the oldest being the one mainly of brick, along the mill-stream, originally of three storeys. It has iron columns, iron beams, and brick vaults (cf. e.g. Tean). This mill is known as No. 1. Nos. 3 and 4 are separated by an office block, dated 1871. The owner's house is in a Late Classical style, going Italianate, and may date from the 1850s. Of the workers' housing the oldest terrace is indeed dated 1856. Doveside and Holmebank, two pedimented terraces, are dated 1871 and 1872. They are all of stone, as are the later mills.

MAYFIELD HALL, Middle Mayfield. Georgian, ashlar, of seven bays with a three-bay pediment. The STABLES entrance has a steep dome with lantern. The DOE points out an affinity with the tower of Mapleton church in Derbyshire.

OLD HALL FARMHOUSE, Middle Mayfield. Early C17, with three front gables and mullioned and transomed windows.

MEAFORD HALL see STONE

MEERBROOK

ST MATTHEW. By *Norman Shaw*, 1868 and 1873 (nave). Nave, central tower, and chancel. Three-bay nave, one-bay chancel. Some subtle touches about the buttressing of the tower. Inside, the one feature to be remembered will be the W and E arches of the tower. The character of the whole indicates inspiration from Street. Certainly Meerbrook has nothing like the originality of All Saints Leek. – PULPIT. Circular, of stone, like Street's pulpits, but carved with naturalistic fruit. – STAINED GLASS. The E window is by *Heaton, Butler & Bayne*, 1870. – The chancel has IRONWORK, ORGAN CASE, and REREDOS all of *c*.1870 (Dr Gomme). – (Embroidered ALTAR FRONTAL by *Shaw*. A. Saint)

WINDY GATES, 1½ m. NE, in a marvellous position, just below the top outcrop of the Roaches and with a view towards the Tittersworth reservoir lake. The house is dated 1634 and has Yorkshire characteristics. Symmetrical façade with two gables. Five-light transomed windows. In the gables the five lights are stepped. The porch has rude pillars and the lintel is double-stepped.

MEIR see LONGTON, STOKE-ON-TRENT, p. 261

MILFORD

MILFORD HOUSE. Georgian, rendered, of three storeys with two-storey wings. – (BATH HOUSE, near the N end of the lake. *c*.1800. Oval pool surrounded by high walls. Also a round, colonnaded SUMMER HOUSE. VCH)

MILTON see STOKE-ON-TRENT, p. 267

MILWICH

ALL SAINTS. Perp w tower. The nave of purple brick dates from 1792. Pointed windows. Short, low chancel, the E window Victorian. – (FONT. Tapering tub shape with roll-mouldings. Also blank arcading partly probably chipped off.) – PLATE. Paten of 1521 with the Lamb on a book; Chalice by *L.*, 1638; Almsdish by *John Buck* of London, 1682. – BELL. 1409 by *John of Colsale*.

Gothic VICARAGE by *H. Ward & Son* of Hanley, 1852.

MODDERSHALL

ALL SAINTS. 1903. A building of quite some charm. Nave and chancel in one, rock-faced, not high. Bell-turret not quite at the E end. Nice, low, seven-light E window.

MORETON

ST MARY. 1837–8 by *Thomas Trubshaw*. Neo-Norman, with a stunted sw tower and transepts. Remarkably long chancel. – The PARSONAGE and SCHOOL of 1839–40 are Norman too.

MOSELEY OLD HALL

3 m. NNE of Wolverhampton

The fame of the house is the stay of Charles II on his flight after the battle of Worcester. It is a timber-framed, gabled house of no regularity and was in the Victorian era encased in brick. Good C17 gatepiers, good staircase of *c.*1630 or so with turned balusters. Also several priest holes.

MOSS LEE HALL *see* IPSTONES

MOW COP

Mow Cop is half in Staffordshire and half in Cheshire. It is over 1,000 ft high. The rock (Yoredale Rocks) is the oldest in this neighbourhood, a little older than the Millstone Grit to its N and the Coal Measures further NE along the Lancashire border. The following buildings include those in Cheshire.

In Staffordshire is ST THOMAS of 1841–2 by *T. Stanley*. Thin w tower, short chancel, lancet windows and also windows of stepped lancet lights and with Y-tracery.*

---

* St Thomas is a Commissioners' church. It cost £1,665.

To the E the SCHOOL, dated 1843. Symmetrical and also lancet-Gothic.

In Cheshire is first of all the RUIN, a folly erected in 1754 as an eyecatcher for Rode Hall – a very early example of artificially creating the ruin of a castle.

Also in Cheshire is ST LUKE. 1875. Aisleless nave, polygonal apse, lancet windows, but that at the W end of the S wall cruciform.

WESLEYAN CHAPEL. 1865, yet still adhering to the Georgian tradition. Ashlar, of three bays, with arched windows.

MOXLEY see WALSALL, p. 296

MUCKLESTONE

ST MARY. A fine Dec tower, Dec even the reticulated tracery of the bell-openings. That determined *Lynam & Rickman* of Stoke-on-Trent who rebuilt the church in 1883 to choose the Dec style as well. – STAINED GLASS. The church is darkened by the constant twilight of *Kempe* windows. – PLATE. Set by *David Williams*, 1742.

FOLLY, ¾ m. SW, visible from the B-road. A brick barn, and attached to it a bogus church tower. The gash in its wall is a recent piece of vandalism. The folly no doubt is Georgian.

WILLOUGHBRIDGE LODGE, 1¼ m. NE. Placed dramatically on the top of a hill, like a castle. A stone house which ought to be better known and whose architecture ought to be investigated. A high, three-storeyed, keep-like core, embattled and provided near one corner with a higher turret crowned by an ogee cap, also of stone. Lower wings l. and r. of the W front and also behind. All mullioned windows.

(WILLOUGHBRIDGE WELLS, 2 m. NE. Warm springs were discovered in the C17. The bath house of *c.*1682 survives, square, open to the sides, and now roofless. It was built by Lord Gerrard of Gerards Bromley Hall. DOE and CL)

DEVIL'S RING AND FINGER. See Oakley Hall.

NEAR COTTON see COTTON

NEEDWOOD see NEWCHURCH and RANGEMORE

NETHERTON

1½ m. sw of Dudley

St Andrew. 1827–30 by *Thomas Lee*. Conspicuously on a hill and in the middle of an ample churchyard with old trees. The Commissioners' type, with W tower and lancets. E window and E vestries later. Inside, though the three galleries are preserved, the details are badly gothicized. The total interior effect is rather bitty.

NEWBOROUGH

All Saints. By *J. Oldrid Scott*, 1899–1901. The name would fit this proud church with its tall nave and chancel, its windows set high up, and the difference between the chancel N and S arrangements, if it were not for the S tower. Halfway up a normal elevation with stair-turret the tower changes into a long, thin, recessed, almost tubular, octagonal stage and ends in a recessed spire. This can't be Oldrid Scott. What then did happen?* – Stained Glass. The E window by Powell, 1911. – Plate. Chalice and Paten by *C.R.*, 1826.

NEWCASTLE-UNDER-LYME

There is no break at all between Newcastle and the Five, really Six, Towns. Yet Newcastle is emphatically not a Seventh, not only because it is not a pottery town, but even more because it has its own unmistakable individuality. It is for instance not a town of slummy cottages mixed with obsolete-looking factories. Yet it is essentially an industrial town. It has just over 75,000 inhabitants against Stoke's over 250,000. The name Newcastle of course refers to the royal Castle which was here but does not survive, except for a little walling adjacent to Queen Elizabeth Gardens and traces of the motte in the gardens themselves. It was built in the C12. The parish church goes back that far too, though the present building is of the 1870s. The Blackfriars established themselves at Newcastle by 1277, but of their house nothing is left. The first surviving charter was given by Henry III in 1235.

---

* The CPDD point out that an inscription on the S side of the sanctuary records indeed that the parts in question were not included in the original design.

NEWCASTLE-UNDER-LYME

ST GILES. Some but not much of the masonry of the W tower is medieval;* all the rest is by *Sir George Gilbert Scott*, 1873-6. It is a worthy parish church for a town, large and dominantly placed, varied in outline and appointed in Scott's Middle Pointed (i.e. late C13 style). The interior is unfortunately less impressive. Six bays of arcades, rather uniform. – (LECTERN. Made up from the carving of a pelican for which *Peter Meredith* was paid in 1733.) – FONT with heraldic cover given also in 1733. A square baluster. – STAINED GLASS. Mostly by *Lavers, Barraud & Westlake*. – PLATE. Chalice, 1629 by *R.C.*; Paten, 1629 by *W.S.*; silver-gilt Chalice and three Patens, inscribed 1680, by *I.K.*; silver-gilt Flagon, inscribed 1757, by *Richard Gurney & Thomas Cook*. – MONUMENTS. One sadly defaced effigy of a Civilian (?), found c.1870 in the floor of the nave of 1725. – William Kinnersley † 1788. Draped urn and objects below.

ST GEORGE, Queen Street. 1828 by *Bedford*, a Commissioners' church which cost nearly £8,000. Of stone. High W tower, aisles with tall Perp two-light windows, buttresses and pinnacles. Charming plaster rib-vault on thin quatrefoil piers.

ST PAUL, Victoria Road. By *R. Scrivener & Son*, 1905-8. In mixed Gothic styles. NW steeple with octagonal bell stage and elaborate spire. Low aisle, high clerestory windows. The aisle parapet curving up at intervals is typically 1900.

HOLY TRINITY (R.C.), London Road. 1833-4 by the Rev. *James Egan*. The reverend gentleman was not a connoisseur of the Gothic style, but he had the right ideas and created a church which one will always remember, and with an affectionate smile. The whole façade is faced with dark blue bricks, and over the whole façade tier upon tier of blank arcading is distributed. Just one window with intersecting tracery built up of bricks. The nave top is flat and embattled, the aisle tops are lower and flat and embattled. The interior is idiosyncratic too. Six bays divided by substantial shafts like vaulting shafts. But above the arcade arches are blank arches each taking in two bays and hence cut in half by the vaulting shafts. The chancel returns to the blank arcading.

EBENEZER METHODIST CHURCH, Merrial Street. 1857-8 by *Simpson* of Leeds. Brick and stone. Four bays with a pair of doorways and a pediment all across. It is still the classical tradition, carried on sedately, though with Renaissance details.

---

* Of c.1290 the Rector, Mr R. B. S. Gillman, tells me, repaired in 1841 and 1873-6 and recased in 1894.

UNITARIAN CHAPEL, just W of St Giles. 1717, the upper floor 1926. Remarkable for its age, not its architecture.

GUILDHALL, High Street. Built shortly after 1713, but much altered. Of the familiar type facing the main street with one short side. The ground floor was originally open, and the cupola and the rounded N end are of 1860–2. Giant portico of two Tuscan columns to the S, giant pilasters along the sides. Brick and stone.

MUNICIPAL BUILDINGS, Merrial Street. By *Bradshaw, Gass & Hope*. Opened in 1967. – INSIGNIA. Two Maces given in 1680; Town Crier's Staff, 1699?; Constable's Staff, 1732.

POLICE, Merrial Street. Neo-Georgian with cupola; 1936.

For domestic architecture half a dozen examples are enough. The HIGH STREET is an attractive wide street focused on the Guildhall. The W side however is gradually changing character. Behind the Guildhall the MARKET CROSS, a Roman Doric column of the C18 on medieval steps. Close to the Guildhall the former CASTLE HOTEL with two canted bays. Further N, on the other side, a giant five-bay brick house with a decorated mid-window and decorated window lintels.

In QUEEN STREET No. 6 has a doorway of unusual charm. Relief of a cherub on a lion.

In MERRIAL STREET the Conservative Club is a five-bay rendered house with a doorway with broken pediment on Tuscan columns. 1769 on a rainwater head.

NELSON PLACE was laid out early in the C19 as a centre of radiating streets. However, only one brick terrace belongs to that time.

CLAYTON HALL, Clayton Lane, 2 m. S. The development of the buildings is far from clear. The centre block has giant angle pilasters. Lantern over the centre. Also an asymmetrically placed tower *à la* Trentham. The building is rendered and probably Georgian with Italianate contributions of the 1840s.

(CHETWYND HOUSE, Northwood Lane, Clayton. Early C20, on an irregular courtyard plan, with the Voyseyesque details typical of the period – long catslide roofs, rows of small individual leaded casements, and battered chimneys with little caps. A. Gomme)

(CROSS HEATH MILL, Cross Heath. Dated 1797 on a tablet also showing a cotton bale; for the factory was originally a cotton mill. The tablet is in a pedimental gable. The building is of seventeen bays and has five storeys. Blue brick. From the start powered by a *Boulton & Watt* engine. The former

Manager's House is of before 1832 and has a pedimented doorway. The mill was built for Richard Thompson and Archer Ward.*)

SPRINGWOOD FURNACE, 3 m. NW of the town centre. One of the earliest blast furnaces in Staffordshire. Probably late C18. The brick ruin stands 40 ft high. The employees' cottages look mid C19.

The extensive ROMAN SETTLEMENT at Holditch comprised wooden and stone buildings clustering about internal roadways. No defences are known. Occupation is attested from the C1 to at least the C3.

For the ROMAN FORT at Mount Pleasant, see Chesterton.

NEWCHAPEL

ST JAMES. On top of a ridge. 1878–80 by *T. Lewis & Son*. Brick, sizeable, but without a tower. Lancet windows. – PLATE. Silver-gilt Chalice, 1716 by *Y.C.*; Paten and Plate, 1719 by *E.O.* – In the churchyard S of the E wall of the church is the GRAVE of *James Brindley*, the canal builder who died in 1772.

NEWCHURCH

CHRIST CHURCH, Needwood Forest. 1809, with alterations of 1880. Brick, W tower, tall nave windows, and a short chancel. That much is 1809; the tracery e.g. is c.1880.‡ – PLATE. Flagon by *P. & A. Bateman*, 1791; Chalice, Paten, and Almsdish, 1809 by *P. & W. Bateman*; Chalice and Paten, 1826.

NEEDWOOD SCHOOL. See Rangemore.

NEW CROSS see WOLVERHAMPTON, p. 321

NEWTOWN

CHURCH. 1837. Nave and chancel in one. Just two side windows. They are in rusticated surrounds. Venetian E window. Nice lettering of the date panel.

METHODIST CHAPEL. 1821. Window l., window r., doorway in the middle.

NORBURY

ST PETER. Although what strikes the eye first is the Georgian brick tower, what remains in one's memory is the unity of a

---

* The building has recently been demolished.
‡ Faculty 1878 (Dr Robinson).

c14 church, of wide nave and long chancel, all done to one plan between *c.*1300 and *c.*1350. The tower may be by *William Baker*, 1759. It is solid, of three stages, with clasping buttresses, corner pinnacles, and pointed windows. The nave has two-light windows with enriched intersected tracery. The chancel has tall windows with flowing tracery. The E window is too good to be true. It was designed by Miss *C. S. Burne* in 1873. All windows have hood-moulds on head-stops, some even (unfunctionally) inside. SEDILIA and PISCINA also with heads. The amplitude of the nave is helped much by the trussed-rafter roof of wagon type. The same kind of roof in the chancel. The amplitude of the nave on the other hand suffers painfully from the interference of the organ. – FONT. A baluster; 1738. – PULPIT. With Elizabethan or Jacobean blank arches. – COMMUNION RAIL. Jacobean; of flat openwork balusters. – PLATE. Chalice and Paten by *W.S.*, 1676. – MONUMENTS. On the N side of the chancel is the effigy of a cross-legged Knight, no doubt the donor of the church (Ralph Butcher † *c.*1310 or Ralph Butcher † 1342?).* He lies in a tomb recess with buttress shafts, a cusped arch, and a crocketed gable. Some cusps are heads, and the spandrels of the cusps have figures too, of not very high quality. – Defaced effigy of a Knight, late c14 (chancel). – Effigy of a Lady, late c14 (chancel N). – Effigy of a Lady, early c15 (chancel S). – Brass of Lady Hawys Botiller, late c14. A 4 ft figure, restored, very fine. – Charles Skrymsher † 1708. Large architectural tablet.

(LOYNTON HOUSE, ¾ m. NW. Late c18 to early c19. Five-bay front. Doorway with columns and pediment. DOE)

(Two road tunnels under the CANAL, which is carried here by an immense embankment (CPDD). Also, S of Norbury, a long series of LOCKS.)

NORTON CANES

ST JAMES. The walls of a church of 1832 by *Thomas Johnson* were re-used in the rebuilding of 1888 by *Osborn & Reading*. W tower with big coarse pinnacles looking rather 1832 than 1888. The fenestration of the church now is two-light Perp. – PLATE. Chalice 1696; Paten c17; Paten *c.*1710.

NORTON-IN-THE-MOORS see STOKE-ON-TRENT, p. 267

* S. A. Jeavons's date is *c.*1290.

Norbury church, brass of Lady Hawys Botiller, late fourteenth century

OAKAMOOR

HOLY TRINITY. 1832 by *J.P. Pritchett* of York. Built on falling ground so that there is a substantial lower church or church hall. The upper church has – an unusual feature – three-light straight-headed Perp windows. The E window is of four lights under a four-centred arch. W tower. Open traceried roof. – MONUMENT. John Horatio Cotterill † 1833. By *Hinchcliffe*. With a kneeling woman by a jar.

BOLTON MEMORIAL CHAPEL (Free Church). By *Edward F.C. Clarke* of London, 1878. Towerless, with geometrical tracery. – STAINED GLASS. The E window 1878, evidently by *Powell*.

The Boltons were the local manufacturers. Their copper-works still exist. One brother lived at LIGHTOAKES, a charming house with many bargeboarded gables and an attached glasshouse, the other at MOOR COURT, a neo-Jacobean house with shaped gables.

OAKLEY HALL

A date tablet says 1710. That fits the splendid façade. It is of eleven bays, with ample stone dressings. For instance the whole of the three middle bays is ashlar-faced. The centre has giant end pilasters from the ground up. The two end bays l. and r. project a little and have quoins of even length. All

Oakley Hall, 1710

windows have moulded surrounds. The stress on the doorway is by a segmental pediment on brackets, the stress on the mid-window by garlands and bottom volutes. The present pediment is of the early C20. The pediment that had been was in its curvaceous, fancy shape much more fitting.* The best rooms inside are of c.1800, except for the staircase, whose turned balusters suit 1710 well.

(To the w a well preserved ICE HOUSE. A. Gomme)

DEVIL'S RING AND FINGER. These two stones, 6 ft high, have been incorporated into the wall on the w side of the park. One has a large hole, 20 in. in diameter, cut in it. The stones may represent the remains of a megalithic tomb.

OCKER HILL see WEST BROMWICH, p. 304

OKEOVER

OKEOVER HALL. The result of a complicated architectural history is this: The house is of three ranges round a courtyard open to the N. The w wing is Georgian, the E wing was Georgian, and its N wall is still original and identical with that of the w wing. The s wing and the rest of the E wing are by *Marshall Sisson*, 1953–60, and a remarkably good job it is, given that one accepts the necessity to add neo-Georgian to real Georgian (which one must be permitted to deny). The w wing consists of two parts which must differ in date. Leak Okeover began rebuilding his Elizabethan or Jacobean house in 1745, to a design by *Joseph Sanderson*. The main part of the w wing is conservative for that date. Brick, of nine bays and two storeys, with a handsomely carved three-bay pediment. Windows with moulded surrounds. To the l., without an effort at conformity, is a bigger and higher one-bay block, the start for the central (s) range which Leak Okeover never built. It has a canted bay window on the ground floor to the w and a large upper Venetian window which reaches up into a high attic decorated with pilasters. To the s the ground floor has blank rusticated arches. If the nine bays were designed in 1745, this block looks 1755 or 1760. That date would go with the STABLES, a separate nine-bay range much more classical than the nine-bay dwelling range. The stables are also of brick, but have widely spaced windows and a centre with a three-bay pediment on Doric pilasters over three large rusticated arches. As for the interior of the house, the finest rooms are the Drawing Room and the staircase. The Drawing Room has a coved ceiling with stucco of the 1730–40 type culminating in a large

---

* A new curved pediment has recently been substituted.

roundel with two mythological figures. There are plaster ceilings also in an adjoining room and in one – very Rococo – on the first floor. The staircase has an excellent wrought-iron rail by *Robert Bakewell*, the Derby smith, who supplied it in 1748. *Bakewell* worked for Okeover in 1736–49 and was paid £451, a substantial sum. He was followed after his death by *Benjamin Yates*, who received between 1756 and 1759 about £170. The most ornate of the GATES is that of the inner entrance between piers with alternating rustication and vases on top. This is more likely to be by Yates than Bakewell. The outer entrance piers carry obelisks. More gates in the Bakewell style between the house and the church.

In the garden to the E, the NECESSARY HOUSE, i.e. a lavatory (and rather distant for such a purpose). Arched entry with alternating rustication, two niches l. and r., and a broken pediment. In the garden to the N the TEMPLE OF POMONA, 1747–8, a similar composition but the side bays with Palladian half-pediments. Inside the white marble STATUE of a young woman with a rose-bud on her bosom. She is called 'The Dawn of Love' and is by *Giuseppe Borgonzoli*.

ALL SAINTS. The church stands only some thirty yards from the house and is so neat that one may well take it for a Victorian estate church. But it is not; it is Dec, and the flowing tracery of the E window and the Y-tracery and two-light reticulated tracery in other places are genuine. The church has a W tower, and nave and chancel are now (restoration by *Scott*, 1856–8) under one roof. – FONT. Ornate Victorian. – SCREEN and STALLS. With elaborate and enjoyable carving. Designed by *Scott*. – STAINED GLASS. In the chancel window original C14 figures and fragments. – Nave SE by *Warrington*, 1857. – PLATE. Tankard, 1649; silver-gilt Chalice by *A.M.*, 1666; Tankard by *Richard Green*, 1726. – MONUMENTS. Brass to Humphrey Okeover † 1538. Palimpsest of a wife of William Lord Zouch, c.1447. The figures are 39½ in. long. – Leak and Mary Okeover † 1765 and 1764. By *Wilton*, and of exquisite beauty. An angel stands by an urn extinguishing a torch. On the base of the urn double-profile portraits.

OLD SPRINGS HALL *see* HALES

ONECOTE

ST LUKE. 1753–5. W tower, nave with arched windows, short, low chancel with plain Venetian E window. – PULPIT with tester, of the same time. – COMMANDMENT BOARD. A large panel with the painted figures of Moses, Aaron, and Joshua. Signed *J. Woolf* pinxit – *W. Brown* sculpsit, and dated 1755. Was it then all copied from an engraving, complete with the signatures?

ORGREAVE HALL see ALREWAS

OULTON

ST JOHN EVANGELIST. 1874 by *R. Scrivener & Son* (GR). N aisle 1894–5. Rock-faced, with bellcote. The lancet windows in the chancel are shafted. – PLATE. Paten by *William Trayes*, 1812.

ST MARY'S ABBEY (R.C.). By *E.W. Pugin*, 1854. He was only nineteen but acted as his late father's successor. The large, dignified chapel is indeed in style more like A.W.N. Pugin than like the later E.W. Five bays, the side windows high up. Lower chancel. Very large W and E windows. The style is Dec. Good panelled and painted chancel ceiling. – Excellent iron SCREEN. – The range attached to the (ritual) E end is no doubt also Pugin's. Chapter house, sacristy, and presbytery are of 1892 (Kelly).

OULTON LOCKS see NORBURY

PALFREY see WALSALL, p. 296

PARK HALL HOTEL see SEDGLEY

PATSHULL

ST MARY. The church is in the grounds of the Hall and was built, like the Hall, for John Astley. It is by *Gibbs*, as is the Hall, and was consecrated in 1743. Ashlar with a W tower – the cupola of course Victorian – and sides of five bays, with arched windows. A three-bay pedimented projection in the middle. In it a Tuscan porch. Venetian E window. The N side was pushed out in 1874, and internally an arcade was inserted (*W.C. Banks*). The interior is simple otherwise, with a coved ceiling. – The SCREEN is of 1893 (by *Banks*).* – FONT. Baluster type;

---

* It is of wrought iron, gilded. The Rev. G. C. Firth points out that wrought iron was used also for the door grille, the tower window, and the churchyard gates.

probably c.1743. – COMMUNION RAIL. With twisted balusters. – PLATE. Silver-gilt Chalice and Flagon, 1725 by *Paul de Lamerie*; Paten, 1726 by *Peter Ley*, also silver-gilt. – MONUMENTS. Sir John Astley † 1532. Alabaster couple and small figures, mostly couples, on the tomb-chest. – Sir Richard Astley † 1687. A very large composition not entirely in order. Standing figure, two seated wives below him, and between them a relief with the deceased on horseback and a group of horsemen. Top with ornamental motifs. – Lord Pigot † 1795 and Sir Robert Pigot † 1796, both by *P.F.Chance* and both with a standing female figure by an urn. – In the churchyard a STATUE said to come from Sandwell Hall (*see* p. 303).

PATSHULL HALL. By *Gibbs*, c.1750. Large and too little known. It is badly in need also of clearing up its architectural history and determining what inside belongs to what dates. Splendid approach: gatepiers, a first forecourt with two pedimented gateways l. and r., a wide gatehouse of five bays with giant angle pilasters also to the angles of the centre. Pedimented archway with paired Tuscan columns. Fancy attic, and in the centre a cupola. In niches two Civil War soldiers. Finally a second forecourt with five-bay buildings with central arches l. and r., and so to the façade. It is big but a little disappointing. Seven bays with a three-bay pediment. Angle towers, the fenestration differing in levels from that of the centre. Both these tower blocks and the wings beyond them have the appearance of later alterations or additions (maybe in more than one stage) and must be viewed with caution.* The porch is certainly Victorian; the fine original doorway is inside. One enters and has, again axially arranged, two splendid Gibbs rooms: the entrance hall with pilasters and a coved ceiling, and the white Salon with rich wall panels and a ceiling with a central wreath. There may have been a shallow dome there. The chimneypiece in the entrance hall has two atlantes. As the two rooms are set transversely to the front wall, they represent an exceptional depth for the house. Many of the rooms, *en enfilade* along the front, have original chimneypieces and original Rococo stucco. The balusters of the principal staircase are thin and twisted.

The garden front is raised in its importance by a terrace and spectacular stairways owing to the fall of the land. Also

* The further w wing is of 1882. Designs of 1754 by *William Baker* for a parlour and library are recorded.

the front itself is for the same reason one basement storey higher than the entrance side.

Once again, this description is inadequate, as research on the house was not available.

PATTINGHAM

ST CHAD. The church has a beautiful E.E. chancel with lancet windows and chamfered buttresses. The E wall has two lancets and a mid-buttress. SEDILIA and PISCINA with trefoil arches. The S arcade, though restored out of recognition, is supposed also to represent E.E. work. Earlier still is the N arcade. Two bays, round piers, round minimum capitals, single-step round arches – i.e. Late Norman. The W tower was built into the church in the C14. The arches to E, N, and S have continuous chamfers. The spire dates from the restoration by *Scott* and is quite spectacular. It has angle pinnacles, and a second set of inner pinnacles attached to the spire. The fenestration of the church is all the restorer's. An exception is the S doorway with continuous mouldings. – FONT. Octagonal, small, fluted, and with minimum leaf decoration. Probably of c.1660. – REREDOS. By *J. Oldrid Scott*, Scott's son, 1890. With mosaic work. – STAINED GLASS. N aisle NW by *Kempe & Tower*, N aisle W by *Kempe* (CPDD). – PLATE. Chalice and Paten by *John Dingle*, London, 1663–4. – In the churchyard, CROSS with the complete shaft. – Also a baluster SUNDIAL. – Against the church S wall an angel BUST from the Houses of Parliament, the work of Barry and Pugin's years.

VICARAGE. Georgian, brick, five bays, three storeys, giant angle pilasters.

PEATSWOOD HALL *see* HALES

PELL WALL*
s of Market Drayton

Built in 1822–8 by *Soane* for a friend, Purney Sillitoe. The builder was *John Carline* of Shrewsbury. Stone. The entrance front is of three bays only, with giant pilaster strips decorated by a simple incised line pattern in the typical Soane way. The porch is not original; there was a recessed loggia instead with

---
* Now in Shropshire.

columns, an architrave, and an open segmental arch. The long sides of the house are irregular. Interesting, unexpected treatment of the dormers.

The LODGE is one of Soane's most fanciful designs – a triangle with canted corners (or a hexagon) and oblong projections from the canted corners. The projections have entrances and windows with depressed pointed arches and rise above the rest in heavy attics.

PELSALL

ST MICHAEL. 1843–4 by *George E. Hamilton*, a Commissioners' church. Lancets and two feigned transepts, in fact porch and vestry. The tower is of 1875, the chancel of 1889 by *Fleeming*. – The REREDOS of 1843–4 is now on the N wall.

LITTLE WYRLEY HALL, 1¾ m. NNW. See p. 196.

PENKHULL see STOKE-ON-TRENT, p. 263

PENKRIDGE

ST MICHAEL. The strange thing about Penkridge church is that it possesses complete unity inside and out, although the story of the exterior and the interior are two completely different stories. Nor is the impression one of a unity of the interior and a different unity of the exterior. The two merge visually though not at all historically. Historically the interior comes first: the chancel arcades of four bays with round piers and round abaci and arches with one hollow chamfer and one roll with fillet, and the nave arcades of four much wider bays with the same elements. The bases of the piers alone show that the chancel came before the nave – say *c.*1225 versus *c.*1250. The nave arches incidentally have a plain instead of a hollow chamfer. Traces of one lancet window at the E end of the N aisle. The C13 roof-line is also still recognizable inside. As for the exterior, the W tower is Dec below (see the large doorway with continuous sunk quadrant mouldings) and Perp above (see the bell-openings). Eight top pinnacles. The tower is buttressed into the nave. C14 also the lower storey of the two-storeyed S porch and the florid E window. The rest of the external features is Late Perp, but as the tall two-light chancel windows have cusped Y-tracery, even if with a transom, and the transomed N and S aisle windows two pointed-trefoiled lights and a trefoil over, they go perfectly with the C13 interior. The nagging doubt even remains (in spite of the verdict of the VCH) that the window-heads are re-used C13 material. The chancel arch was raised by 8 ft in the restoration of 1881. The best view of the church is from the E with all the parts, all embattled, appearing at once.

FONT. Octagonal, with tapering sides. Dated 1668, and the ornament is indeed extremely simplified and also geometricized, as is typical of fonts of the 1660s. The most prominent motif is a fleur-de-lis. – SCREENS. The majestic iron screen between nave and chancel is Dutch. It comes from Cape Town and has the date 1778. – A dainty Perp screen of one-light divisions is between chancel and S chapel. – STALLS. Late C15. Some original carving of the fronts, and also six MISERICORDS. They are decorated with foliage. – STAINED GLASS. Nothing special. The E window (1864) and three S aisle windows by *Ward & Hughes*. Two of them are dated 1889 and 1890 (CPDD). – S aisle also one *Lavers & Barraud* and one *A.J. Dix*. – A second *Dix* in the N aisle. – Also in the N aisle one *Nicholson*. – PLATE. Paten by *J.H.S.*, 1802. – MONUMENTS. Sir Edward Littleton (of Pillaton Hall) † 1558 and two wives. Of alabaster. Recumbent effigies. Excellent portraits. Against the tomb-chest standing figurines. Twisted colonnettes. Black-letter inscription. – Sir Edward † 1574 and wife. Also recumbent effigies, also standing figurines. Baluster colonnettes and still black letter. – Sir Edward † 1610 and wife and Sir Edward † 1629 and wife. Large, standing, two-tier monument. Recumbent couples on both, and below both their kneeling children l. and r. are black columns below, obelisks above. In the S aisle is a round-headed recess in which an incised slab to Richard Littleton † 1518 and wife. – Against the N chapel wall a charming incised slab of kneeling figures of the children of some effigies. The date must be *c.*1630–40.

The two most interesting houses of Penkridge are close to the church.

OLD DEANERY, N of the church. Stone centre and timber-framed wings. In the centre doorway and a low six-light window. On the upper floor, not in line, low five-light window. The centre may be of *c.*1600.

WHITE HART, E of the church, on the A-road. Timber-framed with three gables. Herringbone timbers on the first floor, concave-sided lozenges in the gables.

A three-bay brick COTTAGE E of the church has the date 1740 and is Georgian in type.

In School Square SCHOOL HOUSE, brick, three bays, with pointed doorway and windows. 1818 by *Joseph Potter*.

CUTTLESTONE BRIDGE, ½ m. SW. C18; five segmental arches, cutwaters continued to the top as a kind of stumps of pilaster strips.

A large ROMAN FORT (26½ acres) of two main periods lay at Kinvaston Hall Farm. Its ramparts have been ploughed down to extinction, but the double ditches are revealed by air photographs. The fort probably dates from the time of the earliest ingress of Roman troops into this area, i.e. the mid C1.

Part of the Roman settlement of PENNOCRUCIUM lay in this parish (*see* Brewood).

PENSNETT

2 m. WSW of Dudley

ST MARK, High Street. 1846–9 by *J. M. Derick*. A large, serious, decidedly High Victorian building. It cost £6,700. Small ashlar, with transept and an unfortunately incomplete tower. Mainly lancet windows. Round piers, high nave with clerestory, high chancel. – STAINED GLASS. The E window probably of *c.*1850.

PILLATON

PILLATON HALL. Remains of the large late C15 brick mansion of the Littletons. The range which survives has the gatehouse and the chapel. There was a large courtyard, and the hall range was no doubt the end range. Of that we have only the stone base of a fireplace. Of the rest a brick cliff exists of the E range and a whole chimney of the W range. The GATEHOUSE has four rounded angle turrets and an archway with four-centred head. To its l. and r. are mullioned and transomed windows, probably Jacobean. The CHAPEL is of stone and was largely rebuilt in 1488. It has a S doorway and long windows of two lights with a transom. – FONT. Half an octagonal Perp bowl with blank arches. – SCULPTURE. A small seated figure of a saint, carved of wood and according to its style of the late C13. There is no reason to assume that it is foreign, though English wooden sculpture of the C13 is extremely rare.

PIPE PLACE *see* WALL

PIPE RIDWARE

ST JAMES. 1840, with a chancel of 1899 by *J. Oldrid Scott*. A neo-Norman front with a bellcote on top, but lancet windows along the sides. The chancel is externally of no interest; internally it is separated from the nave by a stepped triple arcade. – FONT. Norman, of cauldron shape with two bands of decoration, a small chain motif and large loops. – CANDLE-HOLDERS. On the pews; Victorian. – PLATE. Elizabethan Chalice.

THE POTTERIES *see* STOKE-ON-TRENT

PRESTWOOD
Near Stewpony

(PRESTWOOD HOUSE. Later C16, remodelled Gothic in the early C19. The grounds were landscaped by *Repton* in 1790.)

PYE GREEN *see* CANNOCK CHASE

QUARNFORD *see* FLASH

QUARRY BANK *see* BRIERLEY HILL

QUIXHILL

ENTRANCE TO ALTON TOWERS (former). Two lodges with Tuscan columns *in antis* carrying pediments too wide for the columns. The pediments are set against a heavy attic. Between the widely spaced lodges is a monumental free-standing arch. It has Tuscan columns set in a curious way.

RANGEMORE

ALL SAINTS. By *Butterfield*, 1866–7, at the expense of Michael Thomas Bass, and with none of the familiar Butterfield features or quirks. Also changed in character, not so much by the s aisle of 1884–6 (though it has clustered piers of polished Purbeck marble), as by *Bodley*'s chancel of 1895. The work of 1884–6 and 1895 was paid for by Michael Arthur Bass, first Lord Burton and son of Michael Thomas. It makes the church a Bodley rather than a Butterfield experience. Butterfield's are the w steeple with broach-spire and the plate tracery of the N windows. Bodley made his chancel rich, as the money was ample. On the E wall a composition of three lights with three angel figures under. Inside, the walls are canted towards the E wall, and there is more statuary. – Characteristic *Bodley* also the REREDOS, the PAINTING of nave and chancel roofs, and the black and white marble FLOORING.

M. T. Bass also paid for the SCHOOL, built in 1873, and Lord Burton for the CLUB, built c.1887. The latter is probably by *Edis*.

BYRKLEY LODGE, 1¼ m. E, was Lord Burton's brother's house. This was also by *Edis*, and has been pulled down. The style as known from an illustration tallies with that of the club, and again the club and the surviving NORTH LODGE, dated 1887, go well together. Lord Burton's own house was Rangemore Hall, now

NEEDWOOD SCHOOL, ½ m. SW. Again largely by *Edis*. A small Georgian house was sweepingly enlarged in 1879 and again in 1900. (The stables are dated 1895, and there is a large brick-lined ICE HOUSE, 18 ft deep and approached by a long tunnel.)

EAST LODGE, 1 m. N. Georgian, of five bays, ashlar. Porch of two pairs of Tuscan columns. Heavy Grecian pedimental features to the windows.

RANTON

ALL SAINTS. A C13 church with a brick chancel of 1753. The stone part is E.E. – see the three w lancets, the middle one placed higher than the others, the s doorway with one order of colonnettes, and the N doorway with a depressed arch and one continuous roll-moulding. Perp windows. – PLATE. Chalice by *I.G.*, 1640.

RANTON ABBEY was a house of Augustinian canons founded from Haughmond c.1150. The principal survival is the powerful w tower of the C15. Two-light bell-openings and a saltire frieze. The doorway has a decorated hood-mould, the window above five lights. The high arch to the former nave has embattled capitals. In the arch are four windows one above the other, a sign that the tower was used as a dwelling. (A portion of the nave s wall also survives. It has a Norman doorway with a continuous roll-moulding.) The big house called Ranton Abbey, a house of c.1820 and now ruinous, lies immediately E and SE of the tower. This is the reason why the abbey church and its surroundings have never been excavated. Only of the E end footings have been found.

(VICARAGE FARMHOUSE, 1 m. E. Timber-framed with closely set verticals. Inside some decorative Jacobean panelling. NMR)

REAPS MOOR

ST JOHN. 1842. An odd arrangement. The church is on the upper floor, reached by an outer staircase. The parish room (former school?) is below, and a house is attached to the end under the same roof (cf. Hollinsclough).

ROCESTER

Rocester had an Augustinian ABBEY founded *c.*1146 by Richard Bacon, nephew of the Earl of Chester. The earthworks indicate the site but seem to be post-medieval.*

ST MICHAEL. The unbuttressed W tower with a recessed spire looks very fresh in its masonry and has C13 features. It is original though much restored. The spire belongs to the rebuilding by *Ewan Christian* in 1870–2 (CPDD). It is externally a remarkably quiet design. Inside are short polished marble columns with naturalistic capitals. The chancel is elaborate internally. – STAINED GLASS. Old fragments in the S aisle W windows. – The E window is by *de Morgan*, who according to the D.N.B. gave up stained glass in 1872 to specialize in the making of the lustre tiles for which (and his late novels) he is now famous. – PLATE. Elizabethan Chalice. – In the churchyard the best preserved CHURCHYARD CROSS of Staffordshire. Steps, base, complete shaft and fragmentary top. The shaft has dog-tooth enrichment on two sides. So the cross will be as early as the C13.

TUTBURY MILL. The long E range towards the river was built by Richard Arkwright *c.*1782 as a cotton mill. It is of four storeys, and twenty-four bays long by only two bays. There are no structural elements of interest inside. Large later additions behind.

FACTORY OF MESSRS J. C. BAMFORD. Nearly two hundred years later – and what a difference! The new factory is low, immensely long, and wholly windowless. All lighting is striplighting. Also, while the old building imposed itself on

---

* The opinion is that of the staff of the VCH.

the landscape, the new creates landscape. Two lakes have so far been made – by means of the product of the factory, which is excavators.

BANKS FARMHOUSE, ½ m. w. A folly or gazebo, but of some size. Focused, it seems, on Woodseat. Red brick, L-shaped, of two storeys, with, at the outer angle, a three-storeyed tower, five sides of an octagon. Quoins of projecting brick courses, similar projecting brickwork round the windows. That is something designers about 1670 liked. The tower has a vertical oval too, another motif favoured at that moment. But the windows are segment-headed, which one does not expect before 1700. Is this the work of a man then who had grown old at the time of Anne?

WOODSEAT, ¼ m. further s. Late C18; now in ruins.

A ROMAN FORT lies in the area about the church and Abbey Fields at the E end of the town. It was founded c. A.D. 70/5 and abandoned in the period 120–50. Little is known of its internal arrangements. After 200 another system of defences was constructed on the same site and, at least partially, on the same line. This work of 9 acres may have been military or civilian.

ROLLESTON

ST MARY. Basically this is a Norman church – see the two nave doorways and a chancel N window. The s doorway has one order of colonnettes with scalloped capitals and a roll-moulding. The N doorway is now inside, surrounded by the later work. The s porch and the adjoining room are late C13. The plain Y-tracery is characteristic. Dec N and s aisles, only starting a good deal further E than usual, leaving half the nave aisleless. Two bays, octagonal piers, double-chamfered arches. Windows with reticulated tracery, also cusped intersected, also one straight-headed with an odd combination of trefoils and lozenges over – odd, but not unique in Staffordshire. The W tower must have been started c.1300. Later recessed spire. Good N chapel: 1892 by *Sir Arthur Blomfield* (CPDD). – STAINED GLASS. Chancel E, chancel s, s aisle w by *Kempe*. – MONUMENTS. Bishop Sherburne of Chichester † 1536. Recumbent effigy let into a wall niche like a coffin but in such a way that a stone hides the middle of the figure, which is in fact not carved (cf. Elford). The hiding block has dainty Early Renaissance decoration. – Thomas Caldwell † 1554 and wife and children. Made c.1600. Three kneeling figures, the middle one frontal, and two more above. – Sir Edward Moseley † 1638. Standing monument. Recumbent effigy, strapwork on the back wall, top obelisks. – Several incised slabs. – Oswald Mosley † 1789, with a standing female figure. – Sir Tonman Mosley † 1891. Elaborate Gothic tablet. – Sir Oswald Mosley † 1915. Neo-Georgian. – In the churchyard large Anglo-Saxon CROSS HEAD, of the wheel type. Assigned to the mid C9. It comes from Tatenhill.

ROLLESTON HALL, the house of the Mosleys, built in 1871, has been pulled down.

SCHOOL, SW of the church. Diapered brickwork. 1638 or 1640.

ALMSHOUSES. Prettily placed by a bank. 1712. Single-storeyed range of brick, with quoins and a broken pediment.

SECONDARY SCHOOL, Station Road. By *Yorke, Rosenberg & Mardall*. Not in the clean, crisp, preferably white and black manner for which this firm is famous. The plan is of many rectangles of different sizes projecting from a spine. The boldest are assembly hall and gymnasium, one to the N, the other to the S. Brick and copper-sheathed roofs.

RUDYARD

9050

The making of the lake was authorized in 1797 as a reservoir to feed the Caldon Canal.

RUDYARD HALL. A C17 stone house with a symmetrical front. Two storeys. Windows without transom in the rhythm of 2-3-2 lights. The plan of the house is T-shaped. Also a BARN with mullioned windows and good GATEPIERS.

CLIFFE PARK HALL, on the W bank of the lake. Built for a Wedgwood. Ashlar, Gothic, of *c*.1830, with small angle turrets, small upright windows, and battlements. To the lake symmetrical front with a bow. To the S vaulted porte-cochère. On the opposite side a gatehouse motif flanked by turrets. Staircase with iron rail. Gothic archway to the former stables.

RUGELEY

0010

ST AUGUSTINE (old church). What remains is this: the Dec W tower, the E.E. four-bay N arcade, and chancel and N chapel. The arcade is not of a piece. The E bay is earlier C13 than the W bays. The latter have quatrefoil piers with fillets. The piers between chancel and chapel date the chapel, whose handsome

E window is Victorian. The chancel itself has, apart from windows of c.1300, one lancet, dating it to the time of the tower. – STAINED GLASS. In the lancet some original glass. – Chancel E by *Kempe*. – MONUMENTS. Brass of 1566 (30 in. figures), still entirely in the medieval tradition. – Thomas Lauder † 1670. Large tablet, at the foot his corpse in a winding-sheet, as if it were a hammock. – (In the churchyard Edward and Emma Hollinghurst † 1696. In their winding-sheets. Jeavons)

ST AUGUSTINE (new church). 1822–3 by *Underwood*. Remarkable for its date. A large church with Perp features, even if the mouldings of the tracery are elementary. The intersecting motifs of the big W tower are curious too. Thin piers rounded with four shafts. Galleries. The whole E end is of 1905–6 by *Pearson*. – STAINED GLASS. Chancel E and N chapel by *Kempe*. – PLATE. Silver-gilt set of 1855 by *Francis Skidmore* of Coventry (cf. Lichfield Cathedral, p. 186).

In the town hardly anything requires notice. The only prominent item is the POWER STATION (opened in 1963). In the Market Square the rather miserable MARKET HALL and TOWN HALL, brick, Gothic, of 1878–9.* Opposite a nice house, now NATIONAL WESTMINSTER BANK: doorway with pilasters and segmental pediment, enriched window above. Along into LOWER BROOK STREET for an early C19 house (pairs of upper fluted giant Ionic pilasters, wreaths above the former entrances). In HORSE FAIR No. 30 is Georgian (four bays with angle pilasters). In WOLSELEY ROAD No. 9 has a charming doorway with an open curly pediment perhaps not *in situ*. A little farther out in PENKRIDGE BANK ROAD is STONE HOUSE, derelict at the time of writing (Jacobean,‡ with some mullioned windows).

The best place in the town is however HERON STREET, where the Catholic church and the Catholic convent meet.

ST JOSEPH AND ST ETHELREDA (R.C.). By *Charles Hansom*, 1849–50, with a crazy steeple made to look crazier by having lost one turret. High spire. It is quite a large church. – STAINED GLASS. The E window is by *Pugin*.

ST ANTHONY'S CONVENT (R.C.). This was originally a villa – Heron Court. It was built in 1851 and is big, of brick, in the Elizabethan style, and picturesquely composed.

---

* By *W. Tadman Foulkes*, according to the CPDD.
‡ But the DOE dates the house early C16.

RUSHALL see WALSALL, p. 295

RUSHTON SPENCER 9060

St Lawrence. This is a dear little church, all on its own in the fields and architecturally hard to take seriously. It has a funny weatherboarded bell-turret whose saddleback roof sits transversely, and it has two outsize dormers (of 1842) in the roof. Features for dating are the plainly mullioned windows and others whose lights are arched. The C17, rather early, is what suggests itself. However, above the E window is the date 1690, and a small S doorway has the date 1713. So it may all be the extreme retard of provincial masons. But masons were not responsible for the building in an earlier state; for inside it reveals itself as a timber-framed structure. The posts now separating a narrow N aisle from the nave were originally the framing. Two splendid trusses with tie-beams remain, one of them carrying the WEST GALLERY. The parapet is of flat balusters. – FAMILY PEW at the E end of the N aisle. – PULPIT. Later C17. With detached colonnettes. – PLATE. Silver-gilt Paten, 1709; Chalice by *James Smith*, 1727.

SALT 9020

St James. What Goodhart-Rendel called rogue architecture is usually connected with the High Victorian style of the 1860s. Here however is architectural roguery in 1840–2. The church is by *Thomas Trubshaw*, built at the expense of Lord Talbot. On approaching from the E you see at once what you have to expect. An exaggeratedly steep bellcote, an exaggeratedly large rose window with a complicated star pattern, two single lancets l. and r., and a mysterious buttress-like bulge at the foot. The S porch is again exaggeratedly large and steep, and the W lancets have fancy tracery. Moreover, the nave has to the N five relatively normal windows, but to the S just one of seven lights. Go in and you will see that of the roof-trusses standing on corbelled-out columns two are placed so as to divide the seven lights into 1 + 5 + 1. You will also see that the chancel arch is tripartite and – with a pang – that the single E lancets have disappeared. They light minimal vestries. – In the N vestry is a RELIEF of Christ and the Evangelists, just heads, not even busts. – The SCREEN is of *c.*1893 and was made for Alton parish church (CPDD). – PLATE. Chalice, 1690.

VICARAGE. Gabled, and with pretty bargeboards.

SANDFIELDS

PUMPING STATION. 1858 by *E. Adams*, but according to the CPDD only the extension of 1873 remains. Brick in the Rundbogenstil. (Fine iron interior. NMR)

SANDON

ALL SAINTS. The botched w front shows at once that something unusual must have happened. The explanation given is indeed that the Perp sw tower was set into the existing s and w walls. They would be the walls of a church represented by the present s aisle. In the C13 this received a narrow N aisle. Then, shortly after, i.e. about 1300, the present chancel was built as the chancel for a new church, and a new nave was duly put up for which the former nave became the s aisle. This nave in its turn in the early C14 was given a short N aisle. The windows indeed have flowing tracery in that aisle. However in the s aisle the same type of late C13 windows is used as in the chancel; Y-tracery, intersected tracery, also three-stepped lancet lights. Excellent arch-braced roofs – that of the chancel of massive timbers, that of the nave thin and probably post-Reformation. The N aisle in 1851 was ornately remodelled inside to serve as the family chapel of the Earls of Harrowby. – FONT. It is so primitive that at first one may think of Early Norman. In fact it is dated 1669, and the four angle figures are just extremely rustic. – SCREEN. Some Perp tracery etc. re-used in the chancel panelling. – REREDOS. Three pedimented mid C17 panels. – PULPIT. Of the same time,* with blank arches. Fine tester. – BENCHES also of the same time, flat-topped and with panels and the exclamation-mark motif. – In the chancel similar panels used for FAMILY PEWS. – COMMUNION RAIL. Jacobean type. – PAINTING. On the chancel N wall a feigned window and l. and r. the family tree of Samson Erdeswick (*see* below). – STAINED GLASS. A small early C14 fragment in the w window. – Heraldic glass of the early C17 in the E window. – The w window is by *Wailes*; date of death commemorated 1845. – PLATE. Elizabethan Chalice; Salver, 1771 by *Richard Rugg*; Chalice, 1829 by *F.C.* – MONUMENTS. Four incised

---

* The altar table is dated 1644.

slabs to members of the Erdeswick family, all probably made *c.*1600. – Samson Erdeswick, the antiquary, † 1603. Made in 1601. Large standing monument with recumbent effigy between two big columns. Against the back wall two wives kneeling in profile. Heavy superstructure. – George Digby † 1675. Standing white marble monument without effigy.

SANDON PARK. By *William Burn*, 1852, for the second Earl of Harrowby. The previous house was destroyed by fire in 1848. A scheme by *Cubitt* for rebuilding was rejected. Two storeys, of ashlar, Jacobean in style. Entrance (N) side of nine bays with in the centre a porte-cochère and two turrets and l. and r. of the centre shaped gables. At the l. corner a turret. The opposite (S) side of the house is flat and monotonous, again with shaped gables. Bits of strapwork above the windows. The short E side is more dramatic. The W side is the lower 'private wing', with a separate entrance from the N. The oddest feature of the house is the quoin stones like clasps of leather. The state rooms of the house have Jacobean ceilings. Fine composition of the entrance hall with a series of columns to the l. to the hall, to the r. to the staircase. The staircase is big and opulent, starting in one flight and returning in two. The style is Jacobean too.

(CONSERVATORY. 1864 by *Stevens & Robinson*. Joined to the house by a curved link. Splendidly evocative Victorian interior.)

ICE HOUSE. By the drive.

TOWER TOP. The Italianate top of the tower of *Barry*'s Trentham Park has been transferred to Sandon. It has the openings of three arched lights which are typical of the second quarter of the C19.

PERCEVAL SHRINE. To the murdered Prime Minister. An alcove in the hillside. Four-centred arch to the opening. The date is of course *c.*1812.

PITT COLUMN, further away. 1806. Doric. An urn on the top.

(HOME FARM. 1777–80s. An axial layout of house and farm buildings. Chaste neo-classical, in fine ashlar, with low-pitched roofs. The house has a canted front and Doric colonnades. An exceptionally fine example of a Georgian model farm. It is by *Samuel Wyatt* (Harrowby MSS). EH)

(Estate buildings in the VILLAGE by *Sir E. Guy Dawber*, *c.*1905. The group includes cottages, the Dog and Doublet Inn, and the Village Club, in a picturesque Arts and Crafts manner.

The neo-Jacobean entrance lodges appear to be part of the same scheme. EH)

STATION. 1849. The porte-cochère for the Earl is worth noting.

SEDGLEY

3 m. NW of Dudley

ALL SAINTS, Vicar Street. 1826–9 by *Thomas Lee* at the expense of the first Earl of Dudley. Of Commissioners' type* and very impressive. Tooled ashlar. S – not W – tower with recessed spire and many pinnacles. Nave and aisles; internally no chancel. The galleries have been taken out. Long two-light windows with geometrical tracery along the aisles. The same type, but of five lights, E and W. Perp piers. Plaster tierceron-vault.

ST CHAD AND ALL SAINTS (R.C.), Catholic Lane, ¼ m. SSE of the former. 1823 – which is a remarkably early date for so ambitious a Catholic church. Who was the architect? Ashlar, with lancets and an oblong tower over the chancel. Inside, the chancel has a charming plaster tierceron-vault, still rather Rococo or Gothick compared with that of All Saints.

CONGREGATIONAL CHURCH, Bilston Street. Gothic. By *Bidlake & Lovatt*, 1856–7.

BEACON TOWER, 1½ m. NE. Early C19; brick, a thin article, dwarfed moreover by some recent steel beacons l. and r.

PARK HALL HOTEL, not really inside Sedgley or indeed the Dudley area. 1¾ m. N of All Saints. It looks late C17, but may be a very conservative C18 design. Brick, of five bays and three storeys. In the middle a frontispiece of three tiers, with attached columns, Tuscan, Ionic, Corinthian. Above the doorway a steep open triangular one. The carvings of the frieze above the doorway look positively Jacobean. Long, low two-storeyed wings to l. and r.

SEIGHFORD

ST CHAD. The exterior does not prepare for the interior. C17 brick tower, but the Gothick details and the flat embracing buttresses and stone pinnacles are of 1748.‡ Brick S wall. The chancel alone seems stone. Go round and you see that the N

---

* Listed as a Commissioners' church by Dr Port. It cost £10,784.

‡ Information from the Rev. D. H. Evans, who also raised other questions.

side is all stone and medieval. The fenestration is Perp; only the priest's doorway may be C13. But, inside, the N arcade of two bays plus one bay is Norman (round piers, square multi-scalloped capitals, single-step arches). One might call that 1150, but the W respond has a waterleaf capital. So anything earlier than 1170 must be excluded. Norman also is the chancel arch. One order of shafts, and in the arch one step and one roll. Outer moulding with fifty-two circles. The N chapel W respond is E.E.; does that date the chapel? – FONT. Small, octagonal, with shields. Probably c.1660. – PULPIT. Jacobean, with two tiers of blank arches. – COMMUNION RAIL. Jacobean. – SQUIRE'S PEW. 1748. – STAINED GLASS, chancel S. C15 figures and fragments. – MONUMENTS. William Bowyer † 1593 and wife. Alabaster effigies. Tomb-chest with statuettes and elementary balusters, also twisted. – Francis Eld, 1777. Large obelisk; no figures. – In the churchyard two prominent memorials – one classical with an urn, the other Gothic with a spire.

SEIGHFORD HALL, ½ m. NW. Timber-framed. Late C16 core with three gables. Large Late Victorian additions. (Inside, an Elizabethan overmantel with two caryatids.) Separate is a brick tower to look like a church tower. The little building was a gamekeeper's cottage. The coach house has openings with segmental arches.

CLANFORD HALL, ¾ m. SW. Timber-framed hall with a three-storeyed porch of brick. One ornamental motif is crosswise-placed balusters – centripetal, but leaving the bull's-eye white.

SHARESHILL

ST LUKE. A handsome Georgian brick church with a Perp stone W tower. The tower has a frieze of saltire crosses below the battlements,* the church round-headed windows with pilasters. The most interesting motifs are the S porch, semi-circular with two pairs of Tuscan columns, and the apse with a Venetian window and inside a triple-arched screen to isolate it from the nave. The apse has a pretty shell demi-vault, the nave a coved ceiling. The parapet is opened over each window into a stretch of balustrade. The church was built c.1742. – Much of the original FURNISHINGS is preserved: WEST GALLERY, BOX PEWS, PULPIT, and COMMUNION RAIL (alternating

* According to the Rev. E. Downing the tower base is C15 and the upper part of the tower C16 – probably c.1562.

turned and twisted balusters). – PLATE. Chalice of 1562; Patens of *c.*1570 and 1608; Flagon and Cover of 1759–60 by *Thomas Whipham & Charles Wright.* – MONUMENT. The two isolated alabaster effigies of Sir Humphrey Swynnerton † 1562 and his wife. The tomb-chest has gone.

PARSONAGE. 1845, rural Tudor.

SHARPECLIFFE HALL *see* IPSTONES

SHEEN

ST LUKE. Rebuilding of the church began in 1850 to the design of *C. W. Burleigh* of Leeds, and it seems at first from outside a building of no special interest. As it happened, however, A. J. B. Beresford Hope was patron of the living, and Beresford Hope was rich, Anglo-Catholic, a friend of the Cambridge Camden Society, and the man essentially responsible for the building and furnishing of All Saints Margaret Street in London. The founders of the Cambridge Camden Society, as everyone knows, were Mason Neale and Benjamin Webb, and the architect of All Saints, as also everyone knows, was Butterfield. So Beresford Hope gave the living to Webb and engaged *Butterfield* to complete the church. How much and what Butterfield actually did is guess-work, but it can be assumed that the recessed pyramid roof of the W tower and the crosses on the roofs are his, and there can be no doubt that the idea of steep stone tunnel-vaults with closely set transverse arches or ribs for chancel and vestry were his too. Nor did Beresford Hope and Butterfield stop at the church, as we shall see presently. – CANDLESTICKS. By *Butterfield.* – STAINED GLASS. All the glass is by *O'Connor*, 1854 (TK). – MONUMENTS. Almost totally defaced effigy (of a priest?) in the churchyard E of the church. – Also in the churchyard the shrine-like memorial to the Crichton family; probably of the 1850s. – Inside, memorial tablet to Beresford Hope, who died in 1887. – Tablet to Lady Mildred Beresford Hope † 1881 with a medallion portrait.

SCHOOL. By *Burleigh*, 1851.

PARSONAGE. By *Butterfield*, 1852, and if anyone wants an example of how Butterfield dealt with a parsonage of some size, here it is, with his broad chimneystacks with set-offs, his half-hipped roofs, his polygonal staircase attachment with a steep roof and stone steps inside. On the garden side is a bay window, canted below but, by means of massive corbelling, square above. Windows have pointed-trefoiled lights. It is all personal and forceful, but what one would dearly love to know is this: Would even the most enthusiastic young Victorian fan choose to live in this house with the same unhesitating delight with which the young of a generation before would have moved into a Georgian house of the same size?

SHENSTONE

ST JOHN. 1852–3 by *John Gibson* of London. Surprisingly grand, and in its dark stone somewhat forbidding. Nave and aisles, a powerful N tower N of the N aisle, and an outer S chapel S of the S aisle. Large W rose window. Style of *c.*1300. – FONT. C14, octagonal, with pointed quatrefoils. – PLATE. Paten, 1701 by *William Fawdery*, London; Chalice, Flagon, and Plate, 1768 by *John Payne*, London.

Of the predecessor church the W tower, the W wall of the N vestry, and a length of the S wall with an E.E. doorway remain just NW of the church. The tower arch has characteristic E.E. responds. The S doorway originally had two orders of colonnettes. Excavations have shown that there were transepts, S E.E., N C14.

SHENSTONE HALL, ½ m. NE. To the road a Jacobean forecourt and a façade with mullioned windows and three gables. The gables were made Gothick at the time when the other side of the house received a complete Gothick dress. Delightful porch of clustered shafts, ornate motifs behind, quatrefoils in the three gables. Charming, lightly Gothic entrance hall.

SHENSTONE COURT, ½ m. S, has been pulled down. The LODGE must be of *c.*1840 and has a canted bay between two porches or verandas of two Ionic columns.

(VIEWPOINT, St John's Hill. By *A. J. Seal & Partners.* Built *c.*1939–40 and decidedly modern for its date, at least in English terms, i.e. brick, with a flat roof, horizontal windows, and a rounded corner with the windows sweeping round.)

SHOBNALL see BURTON-ON-TRENT, pp. 87, 90

SHORT HEATH see WALSALL, p. 295

SHUGBOROUGH

For picturesque grounds and garden furnishings few houses in England can compete with Shugborough. The approach from the Milford Lodges is an experience which will never be forgotten.

The MILFORD LODGES are square with a pyramid roof and on the main sides pairs of columns *in antis*.* Simple, but refined gates. The lodges at once introduce the best architect to work at Shugborough: *Samuel Wyatt*, busy here in 1790 and 1806.

The next building is the STAFFORD WOOD LODGE, polygonal, with a Tuscan porch. So into woodland *in statu naturali*. Deep below is the RAILWAY TUNNEL ENTRANCE by *Livock* (1847), with a round arch, turrets, and battlements.

Now the more serious park ornaments begin to come into sight. First the LANTERN OF DIOGENES, really the Choragic Monument of Lysikrates. This was erected in 1764–71 in conjunction with the activity of *James Stuart*, Athenian Stuart, at Shugborough. James Stuart and Nicholas Revett, on behalf of the Society of Dilettanti of which Thomas Anson, the then owner of Shugborough, was a foundation member, had gone to Athens in 1748 to draw and publish the principal buildings. They returned in 1755. Volume one of the *Antiquities of Athens* came out in 1762, volume two in 1789, volume three in 1795. The Lantern of Demosthenes was illustrated in volume one. As recently restored incidentally the Shugborough copy has the top bowl, the tripod, and the dolphins of fibre-glass. The bowl was originally of *Wedgwood*'s Black Basalt ware.

On the hill-top is the ARCH OF HADRIAN, also illustrated in the *Antiquities*, but in volume three. This is a large and very Baroque affair, as ancient Roman architecture goes, with a superstructure; transparent and breaking forward and backward. Set into that structure are a naval trophy on a pedestal and l. and r. sarcophagi and the busts of Admiral Lord Anson and Lady Anson carved by *Peter Scheemakers*. So this monument, erected by Athenian Stuart in 1761–7, commemorates the admiral's circumnavigation of 1740–4 and his naval career. He was First Lord of the Admiralty from 1751. Thomas Anson, the owner of Shugborough, was his elder brother. Lord Anson died in 1762. Near the arch is the TOWER

* The LICHFIELD LODGES further E are of the same design. They were removed to the present site *c*.1845. (Information given me by Mr F. B. Stitt, the County Archivist. He also made some other improvements.) At the time of writing that drive is closed.

OF THE WINDS, another replica (*Antiquities*, volume one). It was built *c.*1765.* The appearance is familiar – octagonal, and two-storeyed. But it never had the reliefs of the original. Instead it has, on opposite sides, two Corinthian porches with pediments and in addition a bustle containing the staircase. (Fine coffered ceiling in the upper room.)

By the time the Tower of the Winds is reached, the HOUSE has come into full view. It looks all of a piece but betrays in fact on close examination a complicated building history. The centre is of 1693 etc., the wings and the links connecting them with the centre of *c.*1748.‡ But the links were one-storeyed then. They were heightened, probably by Athenian *Stuart* and after 1768. Then, in 1794, *Samuel Wyatt* added the eight-column giant portico, a fine climax, and in 1803–6 at the back the awkwardly projecting Saloon, former Dining Room, with its shallow convex front, and the Drawing Room at the NW corner with the rooms corresponding with it at the SW corner. The columns of the portico are of wood faced with small slabs of slate – an odd idea§ – and have *Coade* stone capitals. The links are clumsy, the three-bay wings with their big bows and their domes a successful accompaniment of the centre. This is of three storeys, the wings are of two. The motif of the bow is reiterated on the S side, but here – and this is Wyatt's charming conceit – it is an ellipse inside and holds a two-flight staircase.

Elliptical also is *Wyatt*'s Entrance Hall. With its detached yellow scagliola columns it makes an exquisite start. The casts of sculpture in the Capitoline Museum were made in 1765 for the house. Straight on one reaches at once the Saloon, former Dining Room. This also has detached yellow columns, six each along the long walls.‖ Of the other rooms, to the N of the Entrance Hall is the Bust Parlour with a Rococo chimney-piece with bearded faces. This is of *c.*1748. The NE corner is the present Dining Room of *c.*1748 with a coved ceiling decorated by *Vassali* with Rococo plasterwork and a replica of Reni's 'Aurora'. Painted architectural fantasies against the walls. They are by *Nicholas Thomas Dall*, a Dane, working in

---

* The village of Shugborough was here. It was gradually removed from the 1750s to the early C19.
‡ Attributed to *Thomas Wright*.
§ Is it unique?
‖ The windows in this wing of the house were drastically altered early in the C20 (information from Mr Stitt).

England.* In the NW corner is the Red Drawing Room of 1794. Here the ceiling is coved too, but the stucco decoration is Adamish. The staircase has a discreet metal handrail of *c.*1794. The upper decoration is recent. The Library, S of the Entrance Hall, is in two parts, connected by a screen of columns and a three-centred arch. The N part is within the C17 house, the S part within the link of *c.*1748, and 1748 is the date of the decoration of the room. Rococo ceilings by *Vassali*, one with a Fama, the other a Minerva. Finally the Verandah Room, whose Rococo ceiling was transferred from the Chinese House (on which *see* below). On the first floor the chief attraction is the Bird Room behind the centre of the portico. It has its back part separated from the rest by two brown columns. Adamish stucco ceiling.

It now only remains to note those outbuildings and garden buildings which have not been taken in *en route*.

STABLES, S of the house. 1765. Eleven bays. The end bays have a giant blank arch and a Venetian window over. In the middle is a giant archway with pediment and cupola.

N of the house, in the garden, as against the park, first the RUIN, across the terrace to the W. This dates from *c.*1748 and was formerly much more substantial.

DORIC TEMPLE. Six-column portico, the temple itself open to the portico, i.e. really an alcove. The Grecian Doric dignity is only skin-deep. After that of Hagley the Shugborough temple – like that of Hagley by *Stuart* – is the earliest monument of the Greek Revival in any country and any place.

CHINESE HOUSE. Completed in 1747. Chippendale trellis in the windows. Delightful Chinoiserie woodwork inside.

CHINESE BRIDGE. 1813. Of cast iron.

MONUMENT TO A CAT. A pet either of Thomas Anson or of the Admiral. Urn on a high base, the whole *c.*20 ft high.

SHEPHERD'S MONUMENT. Very fancy rusticated columns carry a triglyph frieze and Italian-type battlements or cresting and frame a rocky arch The relief of 'Et in Arcadia ego' is by *Scheemakers*. It is a copy after Poussin and of outstanding sculptural quality. The initials have remained mysterious.

This leaves as extras the following two:

RAILWAY BRIDGE, ¾ m. E of the tunnel (by the present camping site). Rusticated arch, two pairs of unfluted Ionic

---

* However, a visitor in 1748 wrote that they were painted in Bologna, which was indeed the centre of that kind of painting in Italy.

columns, and a top eminence for a shield of arms and supporters. Fine rising retaining walls.

TRENT LODGE, near the Essex Bridge (*see* Haywood, p. 144). 1859. Single-storey, Italianate.

SILVERDALE

ST LUKE. 1853 by *R. Armstrong*.

SINAI PARK *see* BRANSTON

SLINDON

ST CHAD. By *Basil Champneys*, 1894, for J. C. Salt, of the banking family. A little gem of a Late Victorian church. Champneys knew his Gothic, but he carried his knowledge lightly. The general impression is of the past, but the detail is individual. There is a low crossing tower for instance, but the framed panels on its walls are Champneys. The windows are Dec, but the tracery has personal deviations, and there is no precedent for the window splays at the E end projecting diagonally. Very unassuming interior, yet the crossing space and the very short chancel are rib-vaulted. Pretty sedilia. – STAINED GLASS. Several *Kempe* windows, c.1900.

SMALLTHORNE *see* STOKE-ON-TRENT, p. 267

SMALLWOOD MANOR *see* MARCHINGTON WOODLANDS

SOMERFORD
1 m. E of Brewood

SOMERFORD HALL. Mid C18, of seven bays in the rhythm 1-5-1, rendered. Low one-bay wings with arched windows under broken pediments. Moulded window surrounds.

SOMERFORD GRANGE, in the hamlet. An eyecatcher for the Hall and a companion piece to Speedwell Castle at Brewood, though a little less ornate. Brick, Gothick, three-storeyed, with two canted bay windows and battlements. Pointed windows and keyed-in round windows. It is really a façade set in front of a normal house.

SPRINGFIELDS *see* STOKE-ON-TRENT, p. 265

SPRINGWOOD FURNACE *see*
NEWCASTLE-UNDER-LYME

9020

STAFFORD

INTRODUCTION

Stafford is an ancient town. The site was fortified by Ethelfleda in 913. A royal Norman castle was built in 1070, the baronial castle, of which something still exists, about 1350. King John's charter dates from 1206 and may not be the first. The Greyfriars had settled by 1274, the Austin Friars in 1344. The establishment of friars' houses is always an indication of urban importance in the Middle Ages. Nothing of their premises has survived. The wool and cloth trade prospered in the later Middle Ages. From the late C18 onwards shoemaking was the chief industry; now it is engineering (English Electric Co., *c.*6,000 employees). Stafford had 3,900 inhabitants in 1801, 14,000 in 1901, 60,000 in 1961.

Visually Stafford is, next to Lichfield, the most attractive town in Staffordshire. Architecturally Stafford is exceptionally lucky in its public buildings: the Shire Hall is as excellent for 1795 as the Borough Hall for High Victorian Gothic and the County Buildings for Edwardian Baroque (even if pre-Edwardian).

In the following pages Inner will be divided from Outer Stafford. Inner Stafford is the area within the former town walls with an extension to the Station. Outer Stafford is all the rest, including the castle and the priory.

INNER STAFFORD

CHURCHES

ST MARY. W of St Mary in 1954 the foundations were found of the Late Anglo-Saxon church of St Bertelin, the local saint. It consisted of a nave and a narrower chancel. That was all. St Mary is a very large church and was indeed collegiate in the Middle Ages. It is placed, as such buildings in towns should be, away from the noise of main traffic. It is an impressive building, and it would no doubt be less so, if it had not been thoroughly restored by *George Gilbert Scott* in 1841–4. It was the first of his numberless restorations, and is of course not what we today – after nearly a hundred years of the pleading for preservation rather than restoration by William Morris and his disciples – could possibly approve of. An attempt is made in the following paragraphs to distinguish between original or facsimile features and Victorian features.

As one approaches the church from the E, one finds the scene set for the particular mixture of E.E. and early Scott which characterizes the exterior. Three windows under three gables, the mid one – chancel E – the most ambitious. All three have lancet elements. All three were Perp when Scott arrived. As for the N chancel aisle, Scott had an original window *in situ* which he could match. The tracery is of diagonally placed quatrefoils. Work here is considerably later (1871). The N transept for lack of money was left alone by Scott. It has a fine N doorway with thick leaf capitals and in the arch fleurons and ballflowers. So that will be *c*.1310–20. The large upper window is in character still *c*.1300, but has some ogees. Also the transept has a Perp clerestory, whereas in the chancel and S transept Scott removed the clerestory. On the S side the chancel aisle has much that is Scott's. He did the SE turret and the two SW windows replacing what had been Perp. But one of the two SE windows is original later C13 (geometrical tracery) and the other is Scott's copy of it. The S transept has impressively tall lancet windows. They are entirely Scott's except for the W window, which is original. This is where Scott derives authority from for his lancets. In the nave Scott seems to have left things alone. The S aisle has Dec windows with triangular heads, and only the S porch and S doorway are Scott. The N aisle has Perp windows under segmental arches, but there is one steep trustworthy E.E. doorway with continuous chamfers. The clerestory is Perp. As for the W front, it has an E.E. portal with moulded capitals and a window with three foiled arches – no doubt an alteration of the late C13. The upper parts of the famous octagonal crossing tower are original Perp work, twin two-light openings in the main directions, battlements and pinnacles. The spire fell into the chancel in 1594, and that caused all the havoc in the first place.

The interior even more than the exterior impresses by size. Nave and aisles are divided by arcades of five bays. The date of the arcades is clearly the early C13. The majority of the piers are square with four demi-shafts, but one pair has thin diagonal shafts instead of the corners of the square. This is the only pair too with fillets. The capitals of the piers are of crocket type, all by Scott, who had, however, some evidence. The original capitals had been largely cut away when galleries were inserted in the late C17 and early C18. Crossing arches with many shafts and crockets, all rebuilt by Scott. Two small windows set in four blind arches above the crossing W arch and below the original roof-line. Chancel arcades of five bays, the quatrefoil piers of a type no longer E.E., i.e. with deep continuous hollows between the filleted foils. The arch into the S transept from the aisle has moulded capitals, its opposite number (N) bossy foliage. The arch into the S transept from the S chapel has stiff-leaf trails of an unusual kind. But whether they are Scott's restoration or Scott's invention could only be decided if sufficiently detailed records existed. The two interesting pieces of blank arcading in the N wall of the N transept can be trusted. Scott would not have designed something like that. Two lights with gables instead of arches and under one steep super-gable.

FURNISHINGS. FONT. Norman and under Italian influence. Quatrefoil, with an inscription on the rim and four primitive figures in the re-entrant angles. On the foot lions, crouching figures, and the continuation of the inscription. The inscription reads as follows, starting on the NE side: 'Tu de Jerusalem ror ... alem Me faciens talem tam pulchrum tam specialem' (Thou bearest from Jerusalem the divine fount, endowing me with beauty and grace). Starting on the SE side: 'Discretus non es si non fugis ecce leones' (You are not wise if you don't flee from the lions). – ORGAN. The case is of 1790. – STAINED GLASS. The W window is by *Gerente*, extremely good in the effort to revive the true C13 character. – N transept E by *Kempe*. – N aisle W commemorating a death in 1846. By *Hardman* to *Pugin*'s design.* – PLATE. Paten Cover, 1622, London, by *R.S.* – MONUMENTS. Two in the N transept. Sir Edward Aston † 1568 and wife. Recumbent effigies. Against the tomb-chest figurines and twisted colonnettes. On the wall above panel with shield. – Barbara Clifford † 1786 by *John Francis Moore*. Large relief with a sarcophagus under a flat arch, the whole placed under a Gothick gable – picking up the motif of the blank arcading on the N wall. –

* Information given me by Dr D. B. Robinson.

In the S transept Humphrey Hodgetts † 1730. Large architectural tablet.

Close to the church ST MARY'S SCHOOL, 1856 by *Scott*.
ST CHAD, Greengate Street. Norman, but with a Perp crossing tower with a lozenge frieze below the battlements. Restoration started under *Ward* in 1854 and was completed by *Scott*, who in 1873–4 built the W front entirely. He also donated the statue of St Chad. When restoration started, the Norman nave arcades were blocked. So were the Norman chancel windows. The aisles and the S transept had disappeared. Already in 1650 the church was called ruinous. What we have now of Norman work is this. Four-bay nave, strong round piers, round multi-scalloped capitals, one-step arches. To the E the arches have zigzag. One W pier has pellets in the abacus. The clerestory is Norman too. Crossing arches with two demi-shafts. The W arch has two orders of beakhead and sumptuous zigzag. In the chancel is large blank arcading of intersecting arches. The aisle walls date only from 1874–5 and 1880, the N transept from 1886. – FONT. Can this barbaric bowl really be of the 1850s? Such ferocious masks seem unlike anything High Victorian piety would have tolerated.* – FONT COVER. A high, slender octagonal tower by *Sir Charles Nicholson*.
ST THOMAS, South Street. 1862–4 by *W. Culshaw* of Liverpool.
WESLEYAN CHAPEL, Chapel Street. 1863–4 by *Hayley & Son*, and very remarkable indeed for being a basilican building, i.e. in the Early Christian tradition. These brick basilicas are a rare conceit before the 1880s. This one has a rather unfortunate tower.

PUBLIC BUILDINGS

SHIRE HALL, Market Place. By *John Harvey*, 1795–9. An outstanding building by a little-known architect. Sparing in the motifs, crisp in the execution, and beautifully proportioned. Nine bays, two storeys, ashlar facing. Rusticated ground floor. In the centre upper Roman Doric columns carrying a pediment (carved by *Rossi*). The side to Market Street has three large windows, tripartite under blank arches. Inside a fine, spacious entrance hall with a segmental vault and galleries or loggias on the upper floor with unfluted Ionic columns – paired in the back wall.‡ The Shire Hall connects with the JUDGE'S

---

* Yet the CPDD has evidence that the font is indeed of 1856.
‡ In one of the two courts BUST of Judge Talfourd by *J. G. Lough*, 1855.

House of c.1800, ashlar, of three bays, and the County Buildings have their main entrance in a short range which continues with only slight changes the system of the Judge's House.

COUNTY BUILDINGS, Martin Street. By *H. T. Hare*, 1893–5. The building is unmonumentally, but picturesquely, placed – the extreme foreshortening suits it. Brick with generous stone dressings, especially round portal and windows. Baroque with gusto, an unpedantic Baroque which admits Arts and Crafts motifs. Asymmetrical front with the biggest window – a Venetian one – in the r. end bay. Behind this is the Council Chamber with another Venetian window at the back and a shallow dome. The size of the chamber is 42 by 42 ft. In four niches four allegorical figures by *W. Aumonier*. The stucco decoration by *F. E. E. Schenck*. Fine progress up the long staircase and along a corridor to the Council Chamber. Only, alas, the entrance is not axial with the staircase as e.g. in Hare's Oxford Town Hall. Another interesting room is the Library (of 1900) with wooden columns in the four corners. Hare liked cupolas, and the Council Buildings have one characteristic of him.

Also in Martin Street is a small extension to the County Buildings, the Superintendent's House, two-storeyed, free Tudor, and dated 1893.

BOROUGH HALL, Eastgate Street. 1875–7 by *Henry Ward*. As Gothic as Harvey was classical and Hare Baroque. Nine bays, rusticated ground floor, high upper windows, the centre a big gable with beneath a window of four lights with plate tracery.

WILLIAM SALT LIBRARY, Eastgate Street. *See* Perambulation.

POST OFFICE, Greengate Street. *See* Perambulation.

STATION. 1961–2 by *W. R. Headley*, Architect Midland Region. One of the best of the new stations in medium-sized towns.

ROYAL BRINE BATHS, Greengate Street. 1892. 'Planned and constructed by Mr *W. Blackshaw*, Borough Surveyor. The exterior was designed gratuitously by Councillor *Wormal*' (inscription *ex situ*). This explains the rampant ignorance of the tower with the big gash.

PERAMBULATION

We start in the MARKET SQUARE. The building of LLOYDS BANK is said to be of c.1795. It was originally the bank of

Stevenson, Salt & Co.* It seems designed to harmonize with
the Shire Hall. Adjacent to it, the OLD WILLIAM SALT
LIBRARY, previously the Old Bank House, looks mid C19
with its handsome foliage frieze. It is ashlar-faced too.

In GREENGATE STREET (the ALEXANDRA HOTEL, now
demolished, had an excellent entrance hall and a staircase
with twisted balusters. NMR). Opposite, HIGH HOUSE is the
only monumental timber-framed house in Stafford. It is dated
1555, the numerals not being original. The date indeed seems
too early for these cusped quatrefoils and ogee braces. Four
equal gables, ornate mid-oriel. Overhangs on brackets. It is
truly a high house. Alas, it is over-restored. The r. hand
annexe to the SWAN HOTEL has a length of Jacobean staircase
with unusual openwork balusters with stunted capitals. (The
DOE reports a vaulted stone cellar beneath.) Off in TIPPING
STREET No. 15 has a Tuscan porch. Back into Greengate
Street. On the E side an Early Georgian five-bay brick house
with aprons to the windows and a decorated mid-window. The
ground floor is one Victorian shop-front with plenty of
incised ornament: 1850s or 1860s.

Down MILL STREET to see the spacious NOEL'S ALMS-
HOUSES of c.1660. Stone, round three sides of an oblong space.
Six dwellings either side of the chapel. This has a big, simple
ogee gable and beneath a shield etc., again with a small ogee
gable. The dwellings have dormers.

Back again into Greengate Street for No. 23 (E) with a pretty
doorcase with fluted pilasters. The end here is the POST
OFFICE, the most ambitious private house in Stafford. It was
originally CHETWYND HOUSE. Brick and stone with
two projecting wings. Their front has angle giant pilasters and
moulded window surrounds. Recessed centre of five bays.
Doorway with moulded surround and segmental pediment.
The house looks Queen Anne, but is said to have been built in
the 1740s. Fine iron gates to close the forecourt.

From here one can walk along South Walls to reach the far end of
EASTGATE STREET, on which one can return to the centre.
The first thing that will be noticed is a piece of walling. This is
part of the EASTGATE *ex situ*. It is all that is left of the gates of
Stafford. No. 28 has two two-storeyed bows and a Tuscan

---

* The Stevenson family founded the bank and it retained the name of
Stevenson, Salt & Co. until joining with Lloyds. The Salt family were cousins
of the Stevensons. They entered the bank fairly late in its history but
acquired control when the Stevenson members died.

doorway with pediment. The WILLIAM SALT LIBRARY is housed in a handsome house of six bays erected *c.*1730–5.* Elegant (later ?) doorcase with broken pediment. More such doorcases on the other side of the street, Nos. 76 and 77. Then the former CHIEF CONSTABLE'S OFFICE, more splendid than the others: seven bays, pedimented Tuscan doorway, staircase with twisted balusters.

That is enough for the inner perambulation. A postscript may be appended, but for a very optional extension. VICTORIA ROAD was made in 1865–6, and that is also the date of the STATION HOTEL by *Robert Griffiths*, which no reassessment of Victorian architecture will turn into a good building.‡ Behind, in TENTER BANKS, the WINDMILL, built in 1796 with stones from the Elizabethan predecessor of the Shire Hall.

OUTER STAFFORD

An attempt is made at grouping according to directions, starting N and going on clockwise.

NORTH

CHRIST CHURCH, Foregate Street. Yellow brick. 1837–9 by *G. E. Hamilton*. His church had transepts, a flattish apse, and a clumsy w tower. The aisles with arcades at least as clumsy are by *T. W. Goodward*, 1863. The tripartite entry to the apse also by him.

MASONIC LODGE (former METHODIST CHAPEL), Gaol Road. 1848. Three bays with giant Doric pilasters and pediment. Grecian doorway.

FRIENDS' MEETING HOUSE, Foregate Street. 1730. An oblong brick house. Nothing much need be added. (Inside, the panelling, also of the gallery and the elders' gallery, is original. So is the staircase and the overseers' bench.)

FERNLEIGH HOSPITAL, Marston Road. The former WORKHOUSE, 1837–8 by *Thomas Trubshaw*. Brick, an exceptionally elaborate layout. The centre two-storeyed with deliberately heavy, elementary stone dressings. Courtyards l. and r. closed by walls. Wings ending in pavilions with temple roofs and, besides normal, also lunette windows.

GENERAL HOSPITAL, Foregate Street. Built in 1766–71 to the design of *Benjamin Wyatt Sen*. Seven bays and two and a half

---

* The date comes from a find of which Mr Stitt told me.
‡ It has recently been pulled down.

storeys and lower two-storey wings of three bays with pediments across.* The very long front is of 1892–7 by *Sir Aston Webb*. It has Queen Anne windows. Portal with big semicircular hood on short columns – typical 1900.

ST GEORGE'S HOSPITAL, approached from the s end of Gaol Road. Vast premises. The centre 1814–18. Three and a half storeys. Brick. Porch of pairs of Tuscan columns on the first floor reached by outer stairs. Frontage of thirty-one bays. At the back the chapel with lancet windows and also a monstrous boiler house, like a keep, with round-headed windows.

H.M. GAOL, Gaol Road. The centre is of 1793. *The Beauties of England and Wales* in 1813 call it extensive. More enlargements in 1832–3. In the middle of the centre a deliberately elementary Venetian window of stone. On the roof two groups of chimneystacks and a cupola.

In COMMON ROAD the factory of Messrs EVODE with excellent additions of 1961–2 by *Ove Arup & Partners*. Two buildings, steel-framing and brick, very crisp, very Miesian.

EAST

STAFFORD PRIORY, or Priory of St Thomas Becket, St Thomas' Farm, at the s end of Blackheath Lane. The priory was founded c.1174 for Augustinian Canons. It was from the beginning dedicated to Becket and is one of the earliest foundations under his name. Not much survives, and what does survive does not tell much. Of the church one sees a stretch of the N transept N wall, 39 ft long, now on the N side of the garden. In it is a C13 respond with a capital, and this belonged to the arch into an E chapel. The S range of the cloister can also be recognized. It stands to the height of the first floor. The refectory was here (as usual), and the thickening of the wall represents the substructure of the reading pulpit. The w side of the house probably coincides with the w wall of the church. (In the house are some columns, not *in situ*.) The house itself is late C17, of seven bays and two storeys, with cross-windows. The doorway has carved brackets, the staircase twisted balusters. The service range with mullioned and also circular windows appears C17 too, but the masonry is pre-Reformation.

ST JOHN, Weston Road. Designed by *Sir Charles Nicholson* in 1928, but only the chancel with annexes built. Brick outside,

---

* Much of this, I am told, has survived.

ashlar inside. Gothic, but only lightly. Arches into the side rooms continuous and totally unmoulded. E window of five stepped lights with round heads.

COTON HILL HOSPITAL, Weston Road. Built for private mental patients in 1850–4. The design by *Fulljames & Waller*. Large block of brick and stone with projecting wings, symmetrical, many-gabled, Tudor. Also a pair of low embattled towers.

SOUTH EAST

ST PAUL, Lichfield Road. 1844 by *Henry Ward*, the steeple 1887 by *Griffiths*. The original church is of Commissioners' type, with transepts and hammerbeam roofs.

HOLY TRINITY, Baswich Lane. Medieval W tower with C18 top and Norman chancel arch, the responds with capitals in a muddle. Red brick nave and chancel of 1740. Arched windows, doorway with heavy intermittent rustication. Circular window over. Two recent transeptal brick attachments; good externally, but certain fitments seem to have disappeared. – C18 WEST GALLERY, elevated FAMILY PEW, three-decker PULPIT, and COMMUNION RAIL (twisted balusters). – PLATE. Cup and Paten, 1798; Almsdish, 1809 by *Paul Storr*. – MONUMENT. Brian Fowler and wife, 1587. Tomb-chest with shields and four tapering square balusters.

ST LEONARD'S PRIMARY SCHOOL, Lichfield Road. 1904 by *H. Sandy*. Brick and yellow terracotta with cupola and other paraphernalia characteristic of those years.

LOCKUP. Square, of stone, vaulted inside. Next to the White Lion, Lichfield Road.

Also in Lichfield Road is a house once called FOREBRIDGE VILLA which became the nucleus of ST JOSEPH'S CONVENT (R.C.). It is of five bays, stuccoed, and has a one-storey portico of four stubby Tuscan columns with pediment.*

Much farther out in the Lichfield Road, off Radford Bank, in RADFORD RISE, is SHAWMS, 1905 by *T. Sandy*, a substantial house in the Voysey style, roughcast with the window surrounds totally unmoulded. Voysey's influence was great, all over England.

SOUTH

BAPTIST CHAPEL, The Green. 1895 by *Harper*. In the free Perp style favoured by the Nonconformists at the time. Brick.

* The larger building to the r., containing also the chapel, is by *E. Bower Norris*. Built in 1931–2.

Curious spire, entirely openwork, and without any decorative enrichments.

BOROUGH LIBRARY, Lichfield and Newport Roads. 1914–15 by *Briggs, Wolstenholme & Thornely*. Two storeys looking like one, and a big attic. Semicircular porch.

SOUTH WEST AND WEST

ST MARY CASTLECHURCH, Newport Road. Perp w tower, the church itself by *Scott & Moffatt*, 1844–5. Norman style, but the lower chancel with lancets, a nice historicist touch. N aisle 1898 by *John Oldrid Scott*, using his father's old Norman N windows. The piers he made Norman too. – SCULPTURE. Large mysterious slab with close abstract decoration, mysterious as to date (Anglo-Saxon? Norman?) as well as function (lintel? cross shaft? hogback? altar?).

ST AUSTIN (R.C.), Wolverhampton Road. The original church was built in 1791, behind the Presbytery, and this (three bays, brick, doorway with broken pediment) indeed looks 1791. The church was extended to the E *c*.1815–17, and the extension shows from the road (rendered, with lancet). But the present church, much larger of course, is of 1861–2, and, at least internally, unmistakable *E. W. Pugin*. Brick-built with stone dressings. Awkward façade with one stunted tower. Geometrical tracery. Four plus two narrow bays, wide apse. Short columns of polished granite, with E. W. Pugin's typical capitals, simple in the extreme and totally neglectful of any period precedent. Awkward roof with scissor bracing. – STAINED GLASS. In the w window Flemish C16 figures and many fragments. – The E windows evidently by *Hardman*.

CASTLE. The first castle of Stafford stood by the river Sow, at the N end of Tenter Banks (*see* above, p. 246). The castle whose remains survive was built by Ralph de Stafford (licence to crenellate 1348) on the site of a Norman motte and bailey castle. It was of the type of Dudley and of Nunney in Somerset: an oblong block with four (polygonal) corner towers. However, what we see now is no more than a partial reconstruction. In 1643 orders were given for the demolition of the castle. The reconstruction was undertaken *c*.1817 by Sir George Jerningham (later Lord Stafford) with a view to creating a Gothick-looking mansion. Only two towers were completed, but the large rooms were made habitable. Lancet windows of two lights, gallery along the long walls, *c*.8 ft up. Elevated dais end. Much of this incomplete rebuilding has now been demolished; only the shell of the ground floor remains.

KING EDWARD'S GRAMMAR SCHOOL, Newport Road. Brick. Gothic of 1862 plus additions, especially the polygonal chapel of 1928.

More individual houses here than in the other directions. Opposite the Grammar School, lying back, THE MOUNT, c.1820 with a porch of two pairs of Greek Doric columns. The house is of three bays, stuccoed. At the S end of Rowley Avenue in its grounds is ROWLEY HALL, c.1817 by *William Keen*. Ashlar. Seven bays, three of them a bow with six detached unfluted Ionic columns. Round the corner a colonnade of such columns. On the estate, in LAWN ROAD, a terrace of High Victorian brick houses, atrocious without a doubt, remarkable without a doubt. Farther out in the NEWPORT ROAD is UPMEADS by *Edgar Wood*, 1908, one of the most interesting houses of that date in the whole of England. The name refers to a view across lawns and fields now spoiled by housing. The building is of brick with much stone, and strictly cubic, even to the extent of having a flat roof. Only on the entrance side the centre is caved in. Mullioned windows, totally unmoulded. The garden side has different fenestration l. from r. of the centre. The house, although far from large and internally indeed decidedly *petit*, is axially planned, with a groin-vaulted passage from the entrance to the hall, which goes through both storeys and is groin-vaulted too. Another such passage on the upper floor leads to a hall balcony. A cross corridor on the upper floor has two skylights. This and the whole exterior will no doubt be mis-dated by twenty years by any but the connoisseur.* Formal gardens S and W of the house.

BURTON HALL, at the S end of Burton Manor Road, just past the Motorway. By *E. W. Pugin*, completed in 1855. Red brick, with blue and yellow brick enrichment. Gothic, gabled, with windows with pointed-trefoiled lights, as Pugin's father had used them in domestic designs. Original staircase with a lot of stop-chamfering. Several ceilings and chimneypieces.

STANDON

ALL SAINTS. The W end of the church is somewhat complicated. Most of the masonry of the W wall of nave and N aisle

* Mr J. H. G. Archer refers to 'the free eclectic spirit of the detailing', and also draws attention to the original marble fireplaces.

is Norman. It was the W wall of a church whose N doorway (with one order of colonnettes) is still *in situ*. The C14 W tower set on only part of the front made adjustments necessary inside. The tower has an arch to the E and another to the N, both of two continuous chamfers. E.E. N arcade and much higher S arcade ending against the tower in a half-arch, as the tower was built after the arcade. The chancel in the best lancet style is possibly by *Scott*, who restored the church (White: 'rebuilt') in 1846–7 and removed most of the other windows as well. But the clerestory windows are genuine Perp. – MONUMENTS. Brass of the C15; only two arms of a cross remain (floor, by the pulpit). – Incised slab to Francis Ross † 1500 (vestry). – Nicholas Hyde † 1526, only the upper half and lower quarter (chancel N).

STANDON HALL, now a hospital, is by *J. Francis Doyle* of Liverpool, 1910. It is large and varied, of red sandstone, L-shaped and Elizabethan, with mullioned and transomed windows. One arm of the L contains the services. This is three-storeyed. The main range is of two storeys, but they are considerably higher.

STANSHOPE HALL *see* ALSTONEFIELD

STANSMORE HALL *see* DILHORNE

STANTON

ST MARY. 1846–7 by *W. Evans* of Manchester. Nave and lower chancel; lancets; bellcote.

STATFOLD

CHURCH. A chapel, and probably pulled about. The features now are a plain Late Norman W doorway, a Dec S doorway, windows of the C13 (two tiny ones in the nave), the C14 (chancel), the C16 or C17 (chancel E end) and 1906 (nave). Two Dec tomb recesses in the chancel, and in them two MONUMENTS, two ladies holding their hearts in their hands. Both are second half of the C14, S probably *c*.1370, N *c*.1390. Also a large architectural tablet to Francis and Frances Wolferstan, 1676. – FONT. Plain, with one frieze of scallops. Inscription round the rim: Nascentes morimur. Finisque ab origine pendet. The pedestal is C14, the inscription C17. – PULPIT. Plain; C18. – PLATE. Silver-gilt Chalice and Paten,

1676 by *I.W.*, London. – STAINED GLASS. In the E window small continental panels of the C17 and C18. – Medieval Bishop in a S window.

STATFOLD HALL. The core is Elizabethan. A former dovecote had a date 1571. The thin polygonal tower at the back is dated 1671. The E and W bay windows were added in 1777, the E and S wings in 1817–19. The N wing was demolished in 1937. Inside, a fine staircase with a brass and iron railing. The room has an oval skylight.*

STEWPONY

A LOCK of the Staffordshire and Worcester Canal.

A little to the W STOURTON CASTLE, brick, with a very Gothic lodge and a symmetrical façade. Wings with shaped gables, centre with a rendered castellated tower.

LAWNESWOOD HOUSE. A pretty house (with a short tower) and a prettier lodge. The house is of *c.*1840–50, Italianate, stuccoed.

STOKE see STOKE-ON-TRENT, p. 261

STOKE-ON-TRENT

INTRODUCTION

The Five Towns are an urban tragedy. Here is the national seat of an industry, here is the fourteenth largest city in England, and what is it? Five towns – or, to be correct, six – and on the whole mean towns hopelessly interconnected now by factories, by streets of slummy cottages, by better suburban areas. There is no centre to the whole, not even an attempt at one, and there are not even in all six towns real local centres.

Yet a long tradition there is; only one does not see it. In 1953 at Sneyd Green two kilns of *c.*1300 were found, and in the manor court rolls of Tunstall in the C14 several men are called Le Potter and Le Thrower. Early in the C17 the Adams family produced pottery, and the first potter of the Wedgwood family was born in 1617. The family made utilitarian wares and they worked in villages. The trade remained largely

---

* Information supplied to the CPDD by Major F. C. P. Wolferstan.

domestic until the mid C18. The turn came with Josiah Wedgwood. His Etruria factory, opened in 1769, was the first large factory, and he maintained a London showroom. He was also instrumental in getting the Trent and Mersey Canal built to make transport of his products easier. The canal was designed by *Brindley* and completed in 1777. Pottery factories still exist, if not as old as this, at least of the early C19. The offices face the streets, and in the yard behind were the kilns. But the kilns are disappearing rapidly, which is visually a great loss; for their odd shapes were the one distinguishing feature of the Five Towns and used to determine their character – kilns bottle-shaped, kilns conical, kilns like chimneys with swollen bases. They have a way of turning up in views with parish churches and town halls as their neighbours. As for the surviving offices and warehouses, some are quite handsome, and they will here be recorded. The DOE has not so far done that adequately. The six towns are sorely under-listed.*

The churches of the six towns are interesting too. There is a recurring pattern of no medieval survivals, of quite sizeable C18 parish churches (Burslem, Hanley, Longton), of second parishes with churches of the Commissioners' type, and of a multitude of Victorian churches. There is also a multitude of Nonconformist chapels, and too few of them are recorded in the gazetteer.

The six towns were united into one County Borough in 1910. That might have helped, but it didn't. In 1925 the whole became the City of Stoke-on-Trent. That might have helped, but it didn't either. Now the population is (1971) *c.*265,000, and Stoke is England's fourteenth city.

In the following pages the six towns will be treated individually, and they will be arranged alphabetically. Each town will be divided in an inner, walking, and an outer, driving, area. For the driver the directions from the centre are added to the addresses.

BURSLEM

Burslem is the only one of the six towns which has a centre. It may not be up to much, but it is undeniably a centre, even in spite of the fact that the parish church is outside it.

* It is hoped that the Gladstone Works, Uttoxeter Road, Longton, will be opened in 1974 as a museum of the pottery industry, with exhibition rooms and demonstrations of pottery processes.

INNER BURSLEM

ST JOHN BAPTIST, Cross Hill. At the time of writing in scandalously undignified surroundings. Short Late Perp w tower. The rest of 1717, except for the chancel, which is of 1788. Brick nave of six bays, apse with Venetian window on the curve. Inside there is a w gallery, but the side galleries inserted in 1878–80 were demolished *c.*1930. – (SCULPTURE. Two terracotta plaques by *Enoch Wood* (1759–1840), one modelled when he was fifteen, the other when he was eighteen. Enoch Wood was also a manufacturer and became one of the leading figures in the town.) – PLATE. Flagon by *C.A.*, 1718; Chalice by *T.F.*, 1723; Paten by *B.P.*, 1724.

ST JOSEPH (R.C.), Hall Street. 1925–7 by *J. S. Brocklesby*. Of brick, Romanesque, with one square and one smaller round w tower (ritually w). Basilican interior, three bays to one super bay. Flat ceiling; apse. The apse has a PAINTING of Christ Pantokrator by *Moira Forsyth*.

ST PAUL, Church Square. A large Commissioners' church, designed by *Lewis Vulliamy* and built in 1828–31. It cost over £10,000, and is placed, as such churches so often are, outside the old centre. Big w tower, nave and aisles, large Perp three-light windows, buttresses, battlements. The galleries inside have been removed.*

CENTRAL METHODIST MISSION, Swan Square. 1969–71 by *Hulme, Upright & Partners*.

Now the TOWN CENTRE. It consists of Fountain Place, Market Place, Queen Street, Wedgwood Street, Chapel Bank, and Swan Square. The visitor will find it hard to work out which is which; they run into one another.

The PUBLIC BUILDINGS are these:

OLD TOWN HALL. 1852–7 by *G. T. Robinson* of Leamington. With giant pilasters and a portico to the w of clustered giant columns. Baroque top. Impressive entrance hall and staircase.

TOWN HALL, Wedgwood Street. 1911 by *Russell & Cooper* of London. Classical, with pairs of giant columns *in antis*.

91 WEDGWOOD MEMORIAL INSTITUTE, Queen Street. 1863–9 by *R. Edgar* and *J. L. Kipling*. Brick with much terracotta. Eleven bays, two storeys. Pointed windows, the upper ones blank and filled by reliefs of the Months of the Year (by

---

* The church is to be demolished.

M. H. Blanchard according to Gunnis, by *Rowland Morris* according to the VCH).

SCHOOL OF ART, Queen Street. 1905–7 by *A. R. Wood*. Brick and yellow terracotta. Symmetrical, of three bays. Large upper studio windows.

BURSLEM SUNDAY SCHOOL, Westport Road, N of Fountain Place. Built as the HILLTOP METHODIST CHURCH in 1836–7 by *Samuel Parch*. Very monumental for a chapel of that date. Five bays, upper ground level and gallery level. On the upper ground level eight Tuscan columns. Top pediment.

PUBLIC PARK. By *Mawson*. Opened 1894. EH)

Of PRIVATE BUILDINGS in this centre less than half a dozen require comment. Next to the Sunday School is the WADE HEATH POTTERY, one of the best of the pottery offices and warehouses. It is dated 1814. Canted corner with archway. Venetian window and pediment with a plaque. At the corner of Fountain Place there is another such arrangement on the diagonal, less well preserved (MAINWARING ORGANISATION). In the centre of the centre the LEOPARD INN, S of the Old Town Hall, with two three-storeyed bows, the three parts of each bow separated by columns. At the corner of Wedgwood Street and Chapel Bank the MIDLAND BANK, a former private house, and the best in Burslem. It has a date 1751 and the initials of Thomas and John Wedgwood.* Five bays, two and a half storeys with a one-bay pediment and a porch of Tuscan columns carrying a triglyph frieze and a pediment.

OUTER BURSLEM

CHRIST CHURCH, Church Terrace, Cobridge (S). 1838–40 by *L. G. Hales*, a local brass-founder. New chancel 1899. Yellow brick. W tower with lancet bell-openings. Lancets and buttresses along the sides.

ST JOSEPH (R.C.), Waterloo Road and Grange Street (S). 1937 by *E. Bower Norris*.

BETHEL METHODIST CHAPEL, Waterloo Road (S). 1824. Stuccoed. Five bays, three-bay pediment, arched windows. Are the wings part of the design?

BROWNHILLS HIGH SCHOOL FOR GIRLS. 1927–9 by *S. B. Ashworth* and *W. H. Reynolds*, incorporating a house of 1782 altered in 1830.

---

* So I was told by the staff of the VCH.

In WATERLOO ROAD (s), which was made in 1817, is THE
AMERICAN, a public house with one bow exactly like the two
of the Leopard. Opposite the WASHINGTON WORKS, of the
1830s, a façade with slight breaks forward and backward.*
Further s in Waterloo Road detached houses for the better
classes, Late Classical and also gabled.

Two more noteworthy factories: PRICE'S TEAPOT WORKS in
Longport (w) has two pediments over the end bays, and at
W. MOORCROFT's factory in Sandbach Road, Cobridge, is a
preserved and accessible kiln in full working order.

And one more former private house: PORTLAND HOUSE (w) in
Newcastle Street (College of Art), of three bays with Venetian
and tripartite lunette windows, so wide and heavy that the
date 1832 is no surprise.

FENTON

INNER FENTON

ALBERT SQUARE is the centre, lopsided, as two sides are grand,
the other two mean.

CHRIST CHURCH, the *magnum opus* of *Charles Lynam* of Stoke –
magnum, however, only in size. Built in 1890–1, the tower in
1899. Red brick, with a high w tower with a yet higher stair-
turret. Long nave with clerestory, long chancel. The clerestory
has twice as many windows as the lower parts have bays. Exposed brick interior, open timber roof.

TOWN HALL. 1888–9 by *R. Scrivener & Son* of Hanley. Brick,
symmetrical, Gothic – but with a number of little originalities
which help to relieve the portliness of the building.

Behind the town hall is the MAGISTRATES' COURT, same
architect, same date, but William-and-Mary style.

Next to this the LIBRARY, 1905–7 by *F. R. Lawson*.

At the corner of CITY ROAD the former ATHENAEUM, now a
bank. Five bays, nicely Italianate. 1853 by *Ward & Son* of
Hanley.

OUTER FENTON

ST MICHAEL, Victoria Road (N). 1887 by *Lewis & Son*.

The rest is pottery matters.

In CITY ROAD at its E end a factory of nine bays with the usual
central archway, the Venetian window over, and the broken

* Now demolished.

top pediment. N of King Street, by Park Lane, two of the by now rare bottle-shaped KILNS growing out of the roof of a building. In King Street also the former FOLEY POTTERIES. Two ranges with the same central motifs. One of eight bays, the other symmetrical of thirteen. Opposite Foley works, housing, c.1830 or 1840, classical in character.

HANLEY

Hanley is the most townish of the six towns. It has much new building, much new shopping, and quite a number of busy streets. But it has no civic centre. The parish church is at the time of writing in a desert, and the town hall is in a place where one would not expect it.

INNER HANLEY

ST JOHN, Town Road. 1788–90, the polygonal apse of 1872 (by *W. Palmer*). The predecessor building of 1738 was built partly at the expense of John Bourne. The site had been given by John Adams. Brick, with a W tower and a six-bay nave with arched window. In the four end bays, W and E, pedimented doorways with Tuscan columns. – PLATE. Chalice, 1750 by *Peter Archambo & Peter Meure*; Flagon, 1788 by *Thomas Wynne*; Paten, 1788 by *Robert Jones*.

BETHESDA CHAPEL, Albion Street. 1819, but the façade of 1859. Of five bays; rendered. Ornate Italianate. Porch of eight columns, large Venetian window. Round the corner in Bethesda Street the SCHOOL to the chapel. Also rendered, but classical in style. It carries the dates 1819 and 1836.

TOWN HALL, Albion Street. By *Robert Scrivener*, 1869. Built as the QUEEN'S HOTEL. Brick and stone, symmetrical, with French pavilion roofs. In front of the Town Hall the WAR MEMORIAL, 1921–2 by *Harold Brownsword*.*

MUSEUM AND ART GALLERY, Broad Street. 1954 by *J. R. Piggott*, the City Architect.

LIBRARY, Bethesda Street. 1968–70 by *J. W. Plant*, the present City Architect. A sensible job.

(LIBRARY (former), Pall Mall. On the l. the former British School and Art School, 1818, with a remarkable attic storey of

---

* Just below the Town Hall, in JOHN STREET, is a terrace of houses dated 1807, the oldest surviving buildings in the centre, says the VCH, though Dr Gomme refers to an C18 five-bay house with pedimented doorway in CANNON STREET. At the time of going to press the terrace is being destroyed.

1880. On the r. the former Mechanics' Institution, 1859–61 by *Robert Scrivener*, now deprived of its Ionic top storey. A. Gomme, VCH)

POST OFFICE, Tontine Street. Complete in 1906. Design by *John Rutherford* of the Office of Works. Monumental, classical, ashlar-faced.

MARKET HALL, Tontine Street. 1831. A severely classical front, single-storeyed, with a centre which once probably had a cupola and two pedimented end pavilions. Tuscan columns.

MARKET, Market Square. 1849. Eight-bay palazzo, a quiet, dignified façade.

OUTER HANLEY

ALL SAINTS, Leek Road (SE). By *Gerald Horsley*, 1910–13. Brick, without a tower. The S aisle has not yet been built. Clerestory and aisle windows differ, not only in pattern, but also in style – i.e. 1910 carried its antiquarian learning lightly. Picturesque NE vestry. An open-air pulpit on the W wall of the nave. Impressively high interior with boldly wide chancel arch. Nice openings from chancel to N chapel.

ST JUDE, College Road (SW). 1898–1901 by *R. Scrivener & Son*. Large, of brick, without a tower, but with façade turrets. Polygonal S baptistery.

ST LUKE, St Luke Street (ESE). 1852-4 by *H. Ward & Son*.

ST MARK, Snow Hill (S). Another of the large Commissioners' churches built about 1830 outside the centres of the growing pottery towns. 1831-3 by *J. Oates*. W tower with thin, steep doorway and large lancet bell-openings. Nave with lancets, thin buttresses, and battlements. The church cost nearly £10,000. The polygonal chancel is by *Scrivener*, 1868. Interior with galleries. – REREDOS. Three large terracotta reliefs by *George Tinworth*, 1896.

ST MATTHEW, Etruria (W). 1848–9 by *H. Ward & Son*, a Commissioners' church. Only partly remaining.

HOLY TRINITY, Lower Mayer Street (NE). 1848–9 by *J. Trubshaw*. Yet another Commissioners' church (price £2,714). N steeple with broach-spire. Paired lancets, short chancel.

(HANLEY PARK (S). Opened in 1894. *Mawson*'s first public park. PAVILION by *Dan Gibson*. EH)

The one expedition any cultural traveller will wish to make is to ETRURIA, Josiah Wedgwood's works built here in 1769. The trip will turn out a bitter disappointment. The Wedgwood warehouses along the canal and the Wedgwood kilns have all been pulled down by the present owners of the area in the sixties. The only remaining building by the canal is a ROUNDHOUSE of brick with a brick dome. Only Josiah Wedgwood's own house survives, even if extended and internally altered. ETRURIA HALL now belongs to the Shelton Iron and Steel Works. The house was designed by *Joseph Pickford* and completed in 1770, is of five bays and two storeys, and has to the s a three-bay pediment and three just a little enriched windows. The two wings were added during the owner's lifetime. From his house he could look across landscape to the canal, inspired by him, and the works, built by him. Now that view is all desolation.

One postscript: Behind BROAD STREET (SW) to the NW and accessible from MORLEY STREET is a building for MASON'S IRONSTONE CHINA, datable by style to *c*.1815. It is a full twenty-five bays long, of two storeys, with a three-bay pediment and a Venetian window beneath it. In the end elevation also a Venetian window.

LONGTON

Longton has – to date, for the time being – preserved more of the Georgian or Georgian-type pottery offices and warehouses and more of the kilns than the other towns in the Potteries.

INNER LONGTON

Here is urban pride and a sense of civic dignity! The town hall faces the railway, and the railway cuts off the parish church from the town hall.

ST JOHN BAPTIST, King Street. The first building, in 1761, was paid for by John Bourne, the present one dates from 1792–5. Brick, with an embraced w tower. w doorway with Tuscan demi-columns. A circular window over. Doorway and window are under one giant blank arch. The nave is five bays long; pointed windows in two tiers, galleries inside. Transepts and chancel 1827–8.

Behind the church the CHURCH SCHOOL of 1822. Symmetrical, of one storey, with two steeply pointed, tall doorways, side by side and under one gable in the middle.

TOWN HALL, Times Square. Times Square was first laid out in 1789. The first town hall was built here in 1844. The present building is of 1863 by *Burrill*. Ashlar, of thirteen bays, classical in style. The centre has a three-bay porte-cochère and giant upper Ionic columns carrying a pediment. Pediments also over the angle bays. The less stressed parts have only blank windows on the main floor. The s extension is of 1912–13 by *J. H. Beckett*. The MARKET HALL is behind.

Immediately s of the market hall is the BENNETT PRECINCT, a new shopping centre, by *Ian Fraser & Associates*, opened in 1965, and architecturally the best of the Five Towns.

Of POTTERY STRUCTURES the following are near. In KING STREET, the road that leads without a break into Fenton, the PHOENIX WORKS, dated 1881 but still with the Georgian motif of the tripartite mid-window – only now it is no longer Venetian and the mullions are – blatantly Victorianly – stop-chamfered. Then the BOUNDARY WORKS, dated 1819, and one of the best. Seventeen bays, with a five-bay centre raised to two and a half storeys. Archway, Venetian window, tripartite window, gable. In CAROLINE STREET a conical kiln, i.e. an example of the oldest type (Caroline Pottery). In SUTHERLAND ROAD the AYNSLEY POTTERY, dated 1861 – and yet still entirely the Georgian type. Fifteen bays, the centre the usual archway, one Venetian window, but a tripartite window above it, because the building now is of three, no longer of two floors. N of Aynsley's two bottle KILNS have so far saved their lives. Opposite Aynsley's are the SYDNEY WORKS of 1879, and they are not under the Georgian spell any longer. The motifs of the central frontispiece are vaguely Italian and entirely Victorian. In CHADWICK STREET another two bottle kilns (Salisbury China Co.). In EDENSOR ROAD (Electra Porcelain Company) two conical KILNS, and in GREEN DOCK STREET the QUEEN ANNE WORKS, late c19. It still has an echo of the Georgian frontispiece, but it is now three stepped arched lights on the first and the same on the second floor. Also the materials are now red brick, yellow brick, and yellow stone.

OUTER LONGTON

HOLY EVANGELISTS, Belgrave Road (SE). 1847 by *George Gilbert Scott* at the expense of the Duke of Sutherland (cf Trentham). The N aisle 1891–2 by *John Lewis*. Not a masterpiece. Middle Pointed with a s aisle with small one-light windows. No tower. – PLATE. Chalice of 1781 by *William Bell*.

ST JAMES THE LESS, Uttoxeter Road (SE). 1832–4 by *T. John-*

son. A large Commissioners' church which cost over £10,000. W tower, chancel and nave in one, six bays, clerestory. Short chancel and polygonal apse. – STAINED GLASS. The E window by *Capronnier*, 1874. – MONUMENT. John Carey † 1843. By *Baily*. The usual kneeling, mourning female by an urn, but unusually well done.

N of the church a bottle KILN.

ST MARY AND ST CHAD, Anchor Road (NE). 1898 by *J. M. Brooks*, completed by *J. S. Adkins*. The baptistery an addition of 1910. A large brick building without a tower. Nave and chancel under one big roof. Small cupola at the W end of the chancel. Small lancets, except for the groups of four W and three E lancets. The brickwork is exposed inside. Tall, impressive chancel arch.

HOLY TRINITY, Uttoxeter Road and Box Lane, Meir. 1890–1.

RESURRECTION, Belgrave Road (s). The church is an architectural mystery. It is of red brick, very loudly diapered, and it has a polygonal apse with cross-gables, another motif that strikes one as rather demonstrative. Even more so is the interior, which is of yellow brick with red brick bands and has piers continuing into single-chamfered arches. Yet the literature says: Consecrated 1853, designed by *George Gilbert Scott*, enlarged 1873 by *Lynam* (GR only), the chancel enlarged 1903 by *J. H. Beckett*. Nothing of all this seems to make sense.*

CONGREGATIONAL CHURCH, Drubbery Lane and Trentham Road. 1969 by *Thomas Lovatt*. Dark brick, with a pyramid roof.

SUTHERLAND INSTITUTE AND FREE LIBRARY, The Strand (s). 1897–9 by *Wood & Hutchings*. Red brick and yellow terracotta. Symmetrical. Across the centre above the ground floor a frieze of terracotta relief illustrating the pottery industry. This is of 1908–9.

STOKE

Although Stoke has the grandest town hall of the six towns and remains of the medieval parish church, it has no civic centre. Leave the place where town hall and parish church are seen together, and you are at once, visually, in a small town.

---

* Though the polychromy is consistent with that at Scott's church at Crewe Green in Cheshire of 1857–8 (EH).

INNER STOKE

ST PETER AD VINCULA. In the garden to the S are the picturesquely displayed remains of the medieval parish church. Piers, responds, and arches of the C13 were re-erected in 1887 by *Lynam*. Two responds are meant to indicate the length of the N aisle, two half-arches look like flying buttresses. The new church is of the Commissioners' type and was built in 1826–9 to designs of *Trubshaw & Johnson*. W tower, five bays of long three-light Perp windows, chancel of two bays with a five-light E window. Battlements and pinnacles. Three galleries inside. – REREDOS. Marble scenes; 1888. – SCULPTURE. Small C17 ivory Crucifix, called Spanish (pulpit). – STAINED GLASS. The E window by *David Evans*, referred to in 1830. – PLATE. Two Flagons, 1809 by *Peter & William Bateman*. – MONUMENTS. Here are the monuments of three members of the greatest pottery families. Josiah Wedgwood † 1795 by *Flaxman*. Brilliant portrait, three-quarter view, in a medallion. – Josiah Spode II † 1827. Kneeling, mourning female figure. – John Bourne † 1835. Large, melodramatic angel. By *Behnes*. – Also by *Behnes* John Tomlinson † 1839 with a frontal bust on top. – John Chappel Woodhouse † 1832. Profile bust.

N of the church is BROOK STREET, a terrace of various neo-Jacobean houses of yellow brick. It is of before 1830, and thus remarkably early.

TOWN HALL. By *Henry Ward*, begun in 1834, but the wings completed only *c*.1842 (N) and after 1850 (S). Originally the centre was built for a market. It was converted into the Council Chamber etc. in 1888. The King's Hall was added behind in 1910–11 (*T. Wallis & J. A. Bowater*). Nineteen bays' frontage ashlar. The centre has a giant upper portico of unfluted Ionic columns and a big, heavy attic piled on top. The angles have three-bay pedimented pavilions.

STATION AND NORTH STAFFORD HOTEL. The finest piece of Victorian axial planning in the county. Begun in 1847 by *H. A. Hunt* of London.* The square between the two buildings is called WINTON SQUARE and has the STATUE of Wedgwood by *Edward Davis*, 1863. The buildings are of brick with black brick diapers, Elizabethan to Jacobean in style. Windows with mullions and transoms; shaped gables. The hotel (opened in 1849) is more compact (E-plan), the station (opened in 1848) spreads out more. On the first floor of the station, the eight

---

* The name of the architect was conveyed to me by the CPDD.

light double-transomed window lights the former Board Room of the North Staffordshire Railway Company. The window includes the arched Ipswich motif. Tuscan colonnade on the ground floor, now glazed. A similar composition, but less lavish, is on the other side of the rails. To the l. and r. of the hotel former staff housing. ½ m. s of the station is the ROUNDHOUSE, large but purely utilitarian. It is reached from City Road (*see* also below).

Also within walking distance are the following:

To the s, in London Road, PUBLIC HEALTH DEPARTMENT (former SCHOOL OF SCIENCE AND ART), 1858–60 by *James Murray*. Seven bays, Gothic, of brick with much terracotta. LIBRARY, next door. 1877–8 by *Charles Lynam*. The windows of the upper ground floor are circular.

Opposite are MINTON'S large premises, 1950–2. The STATUE is of C. Minton Campbell, Herbert Minton's nephew (1887 by *Thomas Brock*).

To the E off City Road the roundhouse, and, adjoining it, WHIELDON'S GROVE (actually in Fenton). This was Thomas Whieldon's, the potter's house. Five bays and two storeys; mid C18. Late in the C18 a N wing was added, and the doorway of this wing is now reset, next to the old house. It has Ionic columns and a broken pediment.

OUTER STOKE

ALL SAINTS, London Road, Boothen (s). 1887–8 by *Lynam & Rickman*.

(ST JOHN, Newcastle Road, Trent Vale (SW). 1909 by *A. R. Piercy*. The s aisle the former nave of a church of 1843–5.)

(Surrounding the church is the leafy garden suburb of the Sutton Dwellings Trust. 1926–9. Friendly neo-Georgian cottages in pairs and short terraces. A. Gomme)

OUR LADY OF THE ANGELS (R.C.), Hartshill Road (NW). Part of a CONVENT. By *Charles Hansom*, 1857. Yellow brick and red brick stripes. Gothic, in the style of 1300. The church is large, and broadly, even rudely, treated. No tower. Attached to the E end is the present Presbytery. This and half the frontage belong to 1857. The size of the convent was increased and a new chancel built by *A. E. Purdie* in 1884–5. The frontage as it now is still represents Hansom's style. It is wholly informal.

ST THOMAS, Rothwell Street, Penkhull (SW). By *Scott & Moffatt*, 1843. Built at the expense of the Rev. Thomas Webb

Minton. w tower with broach-spire. Transepts and a short chancel. Open timber roof. The style is Middle Pointed. The aisles are by *E. P. Warren*, 1892 – nothing special. Nor is Scott's work, compared with what he achieved at Holy Trinity.

The surroundings of the church have recently totally changed. They are now pretty modern (even *moderne*) terraces. A little further s, in and off VALLEY ROAD, a garden estate of 1910–14, by *W. S. Stewart* – ninety-five houses in all.

HOLY TRINITY, Hartshill Road (NW). Built at the expense of Herbert Minton to the design of *George Gilbert Scott* in 1842, i.e. an early work. And, thanks to Minton's attitude, also a large work. It is entirely Camdenian, or rather Puginian, i.e. it appears with the claim to be genuine Middle Pointed. W steeple, windows with geometrical tracery. The chancel incidentally was given its apsidal end only about the 1860s or 1870s. The date of the plaster rib-vault is not recorded. It obviously cannot be Scott's. It need hardly be said that glazed *Minton* tiles are copiously used inside, especially for the dado zone.

Scott also did the SCHOOL behind and the PARSONAGE to the w, and again Herbert Minton paid. The school is quite large and an interesting design. The parsonage has been totally altered.

Again built with Minton money is the long and varied group of Gothic brick houses with black brick diapering more or less opposite the church. They must be of before 1858.

CITY GENERAL HOSPITAL, Newcastle Road (W). Started as the WORKHOUSE in 1832. Among the oldest buildings surviving is one of fifteen bays, dated 1842 and called Parish Hospital. This and a range duplicating it have pedimented gables on the end bays and the middle bay and in the middle bay a window of three-arched lights such as they are characteristic of the 1840s. The twenty-one-bay, much more monumental, Elizabethan range is of course later.

BLIND AND DEAF SCHOOL, Greatbatch Avenue (W). The school centre is THE MOUNT, the house built in 1803 by Josiah Spode II. Seven bays, two storeys, brick, but in the middle a big bow of ashlar with attached giant unfluted Roman Doric columns. Pretty staircase and a circular skylight and an iron handrail with balusters and trellis panels. – Handsome LODGE with a portico of four Tuscan columns and a pediment.

BRITISH CERAMIC RESEARCH ASSOCIATION, Queen's Road (W). 1947–50 by *Wood, Goldstraw & Yorath*. Symmetrical, neo-Georgian, but with a giant portico of thin pillars and a cupola inspired by Tengbom and altogether the Sweden of before 1930.

A postscript for THE VILLAS, a cul-de-sac off the London Road (S). They are all Italianate and boast the short towers so typical of the Italianate of the 1840s.

(Just under 1 m. SW at TRENT VALE is THE WOODLANDS, a five-bay Georgian house with a one-bay pediment. It stands behind Nos. 149–163 NEWCASTLE ROAD.)

(SPRINGFIELDS HOTEL, Newcastle Road, Springfields (W). A mid C18 house of five bays. Small pediment. Doorcase with Corinthian pilasters. A. Gomme)

TUNSTALL

INNER TUNSTALL

CHRIST CHURCH. 1830–1. By *F. Bedford*. Another big Commissioners' church (cost £3,146) outside the town centre proper. W tower with pinnacles and spire; embraced. Nave of three wide bays with pairs of lancet windows. The transepts and chancel are of 1885–6 by *A. R. Wood*.

SACRED HEART (R.C.), Queen's Avenue. 1925–30 by *J. S. Brocklesby*, completed by Father *P. J. Ryan*. Large and eager to impress. Romanesque, with three low domes and an apse. The aisles separated from the domed nave by clusters of four shafts with shaft-rings. One big, square W tower and one smaller round one with a conical roof.

TOWN HALL, Tower Square. 1883–5 by *A. R. Wood*. Nine bays, brick, in a sort of Italian, ill-defined. In Tower Square is the CLOCK TOWER of 1893.

MARKET, The Boulevard. 1857–8 by *G. T. Robinson*.

QUEEN VICTORIA JUBILEE BUILDING, The Boulevard. 1889 and 1898 by *A. R. Wood*. Large, red brick, indifferent.

In VICTORIA PARK close to the Jubilee Building and the Catholic church is a CLOCK TOWER; very acceptable. Its date is 1907.

The centre of Tunstall has no more than one really urban street.

OUTER TUNSTALL

ST JOHN, High Street, Goldenhill (N). 1840–1 by *Stanley* of Shelton. Brick, Norman, with a W tower with spire. Single, tall, shafted, round-headed lancets. Lombard friezes, but triangular instead of arched. Very short, narrow chancel. Open timber roof.

ST MARY, Hammond Street (SW). 1858–9 by *J. W. & J. Hay* of Liverpool. Not like most of their other work. Brick, with a NE steeple. Big lancets.

Next door the uncommonly excellent SCHOOL. Five bays, brick and Gothic, the style used, however – as Webb did – as ground-work only. No frills, nothing picturesque – just a functional front.

CENTRAL METHODIST CHAPEL, Calver Street, close to St Mary. 1822, enlarged 1832, but the showy façade of 1860. Ashlar, of five bays, with a three-bay pediment and a big three-bay segmental porch.

WESTCLIFFE INSTITUTION, Turnhurst Road (NE). The former WORKHOUSE. The core is of 1838–9. To this belongs the yellow brick range in Tudor Gothic. Many additions.

Former GREENFIELD POTTERY, Furlong Road (NE). The old building, dated 1818, stands at r. angles to the street. It is of two storeys and has a pediment.

STOKE VILLAGES

ABBEY HULTON

HULTON ABBEY, of which nothing is now visible above ground, was a Cistercian house founded in 1223. (Recent excavations have uncovered much masonry.)

BLURTON

ST BARTHOLOMEW. Small, with a bell-turret. The core of the building is of 1626 – see the three-light mullioned windows. The church is however altered. It was restored and enlarged by *Lynam* in 1867. – PLATE. Elizabethan Chalice and Paten.

BUCKNALL

(ST MARY. 1854–6 by *Ward & Son* of Hanley. E.E. CPDD)

HANFORD

ST MATTHIAS. 1868 by *C. Lynam*. Small, with a thin square SW tower accessible by an outer stair. Black brick columns and exposed red brick otherwise. An enterprising job. The chancel, thickly ornate, is by *Rushworth*, 1862, and indeed more High Victorian in character than Lynam's work.

MILTON

ST PHILIP AND ST JAMES. 1865. Recently two bays were added at the w end, and a HALL.

METHODIST CHURCH. 1862 by *George B. Ford*. Really repulsive. The mystery is that this was designed as fitting and accepted as such. Gothic.

NORTON-IN-THE-MOORS

ST BARTHOLOMEW. On the top of a hill with views to the E towards the Peak – nature, and yet factories and Stoke housing as well. 1737–8 by *Richard Trubshaw*. The E half by *J. H. Beckett*, 1914. Brick, with a W tower. The W doorway has a rusticated surround of alternating sizes of the blocks. Ball finials. The original building probably had just three bays and a short chancel. Square piers and low, flat ceilings. Beckett added transepts and a new chancel. – PLATE. Two Plates by *I.P.*, 1737; Flagon by *Richard Gurney & Co.*, 1747; Chalice, *c.*1747.

SMALLTHORNE

FORD GREEN HALL, by the railway crossing. Now a museum. A lovely, timber-framed house with a two-bay Georgian addition. The timberwork is mostly closely set verticals, but higher up also concave-sided lozenges. The gables are plain white now. – Square brick DOVECOTE.

STONE

Stone in the Middle Ages possessed an Augustinian Priory. It was founded *c.*1135. Some walling remains in ABBEY STREET, and in the house called THE PRIORY in LICHFIELD STREET a rib-vaulted undercroft of four or more bays (single-chamfered ribs). Also architectural fragments in the garden, including part of a large pier of quatrefoil section with hollows between the foils – probably early C14.

ST MICHAEL. 1753–8 by *William Robinson* of the Board of Works, *William Baker* supervising. A remarkably early piece of Gothic Revival, and entirely matter-of-fact in the sense of Georgian Enlightenment, without any Rococo frills. Square W tower embraced, the embracing parts flat-topped with battlements. Windows along the sides in two tiers. All the windows with Y-tracery. Battlements on the nave too. The chancel unfortunately made Perp in 1887. Inside, two galleries, wooden supports and frieze all right, the parapet probably Victorian. – FONT. Of the baluster type. – ORGAN and PULPIT by *Sir Charles Nicholson*. – Original BOX PEWS. – The large PAINTING of the Archangel Michael is by *Beechey*. – PLATE. Paten, 1703 by *R.*; Flagon, 1757 by *Francis Crump*; two Almsdishes, 1762 by *T. Whipham & C. Wright*; two Chalices, 1767 by *M.* – MONUMENTS. Under the tower defaced effigies of a Lady and a Civilian (?); C13. Probably from the abbey. – In the churchyard two Elizabethan or Jacobean effigies, members of the Crompton family. Date of death 1606. – Admiral St Vincent † 1823. The tablet by *Whitelaw*, the bust on top and perhaps the naval trophy by *Chantrey*. – In the churchyard the St Vincent MAUSOLEUM, strictly classical, with a raised pedimented centre and lower rusticated windowless side pieces. The mausoleum was designed by *Robinson* and built by *Baker*. If this is correct, it is of course a Jervis, not a St Vincent, mausoleum.

CHRIST CHURCH, Radford Street. Brick, with an ill-organized W front. Freely Dec motifs. The nave is of 1899–1900 (by *Lynam*), the chancel and apse of 1885 (by *W. Hawky Lloyd*). The nave interior is much more satisfactory than the exterior, with neat capitals. The clerestory curiously has plain mullioned windows, as if it were an Elizabethan addition to a Dec church.

IMMACULATE CONCEPTION AND ST DOMINIC (R.C.), Margaret Street. A large, towerless building, spacious inside, with nave and aisles and transepts. The style is late C13. Instead of a W rose a big spherical triangle. The same shape in small for the clerestory windows. The nave is by *Charles Hansom*, 1852–4, the E part by *G. Blount*, 1861–3. His is the effective S chapel (ritually S). – MONUMENT to Archbishop Ullathorne, 1889 by *J. S. Hansom*. Tomb-chest with recumbent effigy.

The attached CONVENT is of brick, with a symmetrical gabled front. The S side is of 1852–3 by *J. A. & Charles Hansom*, the W side 1856–8 by *Charles Hansom*, the S side 1861–3 by *Gilbert Blount*. In the garden of the convent is, quite on its own, the CHAPEL OF ST ANNE. This little brick building of nave and chancel is by *A. W. N. Pugin*, 1852–3. Poor Pugin, nearly always what he dreamt to be rich, dignified, elevating, turned out to be mean – for lack of money. There is really about this chapel not a feature one could set down except that the windows have pointed-trefoiled tops.

CONGREGATIONAL CHAPEL, Granville Terrace. 1870–1 by *Bidlake*. Late C13 style with a NW steeple.

TRENT HOSPITAL, Crown Street. The former WORKHOUSE. Built in 1792–3 as a copy of part of the Romford Workhouse of 1787. Enlarged in 1838–9. Of 1792–3 two storeys of the H-shaped centre, of 1838–9 the heightening plus two-storey wings, gatehouse, infirmary (since added to), etc. Plain brick. Some windows of 1838–9 have arched lights *à la* Loudon.

STATION. 1848 by *H. A. Hunt*. Brick, with shaped gables; symmetrical.

In the HIGH STREET a few houses worth a line or two, the best of course the CROWN HOTEL by *Henry Holland*, 1778. Two bows and a porch, with unfluted Ionic columns between. Also JOULES'S BREWERY OFFICES, with two bows only on the ground floor. Porch with Tuscan columns. One or two more nice doorcases on the same side of the street.

MEAFORD HALL, 1½ m. NW. Two buildings side by side. They are by *Burn & McVicar Anderson*, 1874–7. One of the two was only a conversion, and the shell-hood of a door is genuine early C18. The new house is not large. Garden front of five bays, not entirely symmetrical. A little strapwork enrichment, and a French dormer over the middle. The entrance side is a freer composition. Inside, staircase with thick iron handrail.

BURY BANK, 1 m. N of Darlaston Hall. A small Iron Age hill-fort marked by a badly weathered and eroded bank and ditch enclosing some 3 acres. Single inturned entrance on the NW.

STONNALL

ST PETER. 1822, the chancel by *Joseph Potter*, 1843. The difference between Commissioners' and Camdenian criteria is evident. Early the small castellated W tower and the nave with Y-tracery, late the long chancel, ashlar inside as well as outside and in the style of c.1300.

STOURTON CASTLE *see* STEWPONY

STOWE-BY-CHARTLEY

ST JOHN. Norman basically – see the chancel S window and the shallow chancel S buttress, and see both nave doorways (scallop capitals, zigzag in the arches), but don't see the chancel arch, which is totally C19, even if it represents what was there before. The broad, short W tower is probably Dec –

see the w doorway with sunk-quadrant moulding and the low, wide arch to the nave with two continuous chamfers. Dec also several windows. The N aisle is by *Habershon & Pite*, 1875. – PLATE. Set of 1722 by *Thomas Farrar*. – MONUMENTS. Sir Walter Devereux † 1537 and two wives. Against the tombchest pairs of figurines and characteristic Early Renaissance decoration: little balusters, shallow S-curves instead of ogees, etc. – William La Touche Congreve † 1916 and Sir Walter Norris Congreve † 1927. Tablets by *Lutyens*,* in his late, Wren-to-Georgian style. His own is the use of different materials and colours.

INGLENOOK COTTAGE. A pretty thatched cottage with eyebrow dormers.

STRAMSHALL

ST MICHAEL. 1850–2 by *Thomas Fradgley* of Uttoxeter. Nave and chancel and a sw turret. Steep roof, lancets, grouped and internally shafted at the w and E ends.

STRETTON

2 m. N of Burton-on-Trent

ST MARY. 1895–7 by *Micklethwaite & Somers Clarke*. Built at the expense of John Gretton of Bass, Ratcliff & Gretton, the Burton brewers. Large, and with powerful and quite original canted tower. Instead of a transept the organ chamber s, two-storeyed vestries N. Short chancel with the E window high up. Nave and aisles; clerestory. The features are Dec. – (STAINED GLASS. The E window was designed by *Sir William Richmond*.)

DOVE CLIFFE, 1 m. NNE. Late Georgian, of brick, five bays and two storeys; pedimented doorway with columns set in front of rustication. Low-pitched roof.

STRETTON

3 m. sw of Penkridge

ST JOHN. Norman chancel with three small windows, but the E window has reticulated tracery. The priest's doorway with the typical slight continuous chamfer. Nave and transepts 1860. – COMMUNION RAIL. Jacobean or a little later. – STAINED GLASS. Bits in the E window.

* Information from Mr Nicholas Taylor.

STRETTON HALL. Early C18, of brick, seven bays and three storeys (the topmost added *c.*1860; VCH), with a segmental pediment. Quoins of even length. Moulded window surrounds. On the entrance side a Victorian porte-cochère with rusticated piers. The windows above have their Early Georgian Gibbs surrounds. Inside a very fine staircase, the intermediate landing on two twisted columns, the upper flight secured by chains. To each tread one turned and one twisted, charmingly detailed baluster. Carved tread-ends.

AQUEDUCT. Of iron, inscribed by *Telford*, 1832. It carries the Shropshire Union Canal across Watling Street.

A ROMAN FORT lay on Watling Street at Stretton Mill. Its dimensions were *c.* 470 ft by 450 ft, and it possessed a single ditch on its SE side, double ditches on the other three. An annexe lay on the SE side. A second fort, of a different but unknown date, was on the same site. Both forts are undated, but both are likely to belong to the middle and later decades of the C1 A.D.

SWINFEN HALL

The old house stands close to, and is part of, a prison. It was built in 1755 (date on a later stone tablet) by *Benjamin Wyatt*, father of James. It is a house still in the Smith of Warwick tradition, brick with ample stone dressings, a seven-bay front of two-and-a-half storeys, the half-storey above the main cornice and perhaps later. Top balustrade. Giant Ionic pilasters at the angles and the angles of the centre. Doorway with Tuscan columns, triglyph frieze, and pediment. The garden (E) side has recent terraces and a recent single-storey bow. And what is the date of the S quadrant? Does it represent a Palladian link to a wing? As it is it merges with big Edwardian additions (a date 1913 is inscribed), especially a wing as large as the house, with a big Music Room and other big rooms. Much of their decoration is strict imitation of the sumptuous mid C18 work in the house itself, and so one is left in doubt as to how much of that work may not also be imitation. Grand entrance hall with a back gallery on fluted Ionic columns. Pedimented doorways. Chimneypiece with an open early top. Fine large staircase with three slim turned balusters to the tread and carved tread-ends. Many stucco ceilings and several chimneypieces. Also wood panelling and wooden window surrounds with volutes at the foot. Much more ought to be found out about the house.

(FREEFORD HALL. Early C19. Five-bay front, two-storeyed porch. DOE)

SWYNNERTON

ST MARY. Norman W doorway in the tower, probably re-set, and more elaborate Norman W doorway in the tower E, rather the W doorway to the church until the tower was built than a normal tower arch. The outer doorway has one order of colonnettes and shallow zigzag, the inner also has one order but in the arch prominent beakheads and a hood-mould with pellets. E.E. chancel with late geometrical tracery and a tomb recess with a cusped arch. The chancel arch has shafts with shaft-rings. The chancel S windows are now internal, but the S chapel must have been built soon after.* Windows with Y-tracery, but the E window reticulated, i.e. early C14. The SEDILIA and PISCINA of the chapel are defaced. W of this chapel and separated by a solid wall, the S aisle end is another chapel: Perp, of two bays, embattled. The nave arcades of standard elements are E.E. A half arch divides the Perp chapel from the rest of the aisle. – SCREEN. Perp, of one-light divisions, with charming, dainty tracery. – STATUE. A seated Christ, 7 ft high, and of a quality worthy of Westminster Abbey or Lincoln Cathedral. Where may it come from? The style is that of 1260–80, with the facial features a little feline (Reims is the origin), and the close drapery folds and the belt are unmistakable indices of date. – STAINED GLASS. The E window by *Powell*, 1864, designed by *Sedding*. Very remarkable, bold in colour and bold in the stylization of the figures in the scenes represented. Inspired probably by Burne-Jones's glass for Powell's of the pre-Morris years. – PLATE. Chalice, Paten, and Dish, 1820 by *William Bateman*. – MONUMENT. Cross-legged Knight, early C14.‡

(QUEENSWOOD, the former Rectory, E of the church. 1760 by *Charles Cope Trubshaw*. Five bays, two storeys, pedimented doorcase.)

SWYNNERTON HALL. By *Francis Smith* of Warwick for Thomas Fitzherbert. The date, according to Dr Gomme, is 1725–9.

* The Rev. D. Leck tells me that the chapel is supposed to be the original church.
‡ S. A. Jeavons dates the monument to the mid C13 instead.

A richly detailed ashlar house of nine bays and two and a half storeys, the half-storey above the main cornice. The centre is of three bays with giant Tuscan pilasters each carrying one triglyph. The angles of the whole façade have quoins of even length. The windows have moulded surrounds, and those of the ground floor are pedimented. The doorway has rustication, Ionic columns, and a bolection frieze. The doorway in the five-bay side round the corner dates probably from the time of *James Trubshaw*'s major alterations inside, i.e. *c*. 1810. The principal result of these alterations is the great hall in its present form, two-storeyed with, in front of the back wall, Tuscan columns below, Ionic columns above. The main staircase is spacious and has a discreet iron balustrade. It goes through to the top of the house.

OUR LADY OF THE ASSUMPTION (R.C.), next to the Hall. 1868–9 by *Gilbert Blount*. Very lavishly detailed inside, with luscious naturalistic capitals to the columns of the S (ritually S) arcade and W gallery. L. of the chancel an arcade of three narrow bays, r. of two. The chapel has to the outer, public, side a bellcote N of the W (all ritually) window. The style is the Middle Pointed, i.e. the later C13.

WATER TOWER, ½ m. N. Probably of the 1890s, though it looks older. A monumental square tower of yellow and red brick with giant arches supporting the tank.

HATTON PUMPING STATION, 1¾ m. NW. 1890, 1898, etc. A group of buildings of yellow and red brick, in an extremely antiquated round-arch style, almost as if they were of the 1850s. The climax is of course the chimney, but the climax but one is the central building with an Italianate tower on one corner. (Interior with Corinthian columns.)

SWYTHAMLEY PARK

The old house was burnt in 1813. The CHAPEL is of 1905, rock-faced, with a rose window with plate tracery.*

TALKE

ST MARTIN. A brick church of 1794 with four arched windows to the S and an apse with a window on the curve. The bell-turret is Victorian. So is the big transept (*c*.1850).

---

* Information kindly supplied by Sir Philip Brocklehurst.

A house opposite has two two-storeyed bow windows with columns instead of mullions (cf. Burslem, pp. 255 and 256).

ST SAVIOUR. 1879 by *F. W. Hunt* of London. Demolished in 1971. It is a great pity; for the church was inventive, and, though quite large, decidedly human in scale and detail. It was of timber and roughcast. There was variety of outline, and the three very large gabled dormers in the roof to allow light to stream in were a very happy idea.

In the NEWCASTLE ROAD are two early C19 LODGES to the former Clough Hall.

In FIRST AVENUE at its very E end a funny little COTTAGE ORNÉ of one storey and three bays with a wooden veranda.

HARECASTLE FARM, ¼ m. SE, off the A road, is a remarkable Jacobean stone house, with a symmetrical front. The centre is recessed, and here, in spite of the symmetry, the position of the hall is still marked. The door is not in the middle but pushed to the l. and the window pushed to the r., whereas the window above the hall window resumes a centre position. The windows are mostly of five lights transomed.*

TAMWORTH

The first mention of Tamworth refers to 781, when Offa, King of Mercia, signed a document in his palace at Tamworth. King Alfred's daughter Ethelfleda fortified Tamworth (in timber) in 913. After the Conquest the area was given to Robert de Marmion. It went to the Frevilles in 1294, the Ferrerses in 1423, and finally the Townshends in 1751. Much medieval history is still visible in the castle and the parish church. Defoe in 1723 called Tamworth 'a small but very handsome market town'. No one would say that now. Inhabitants 1971 over 40,000.

ST EDITHA. This is one of the largest parish churches of Staffordshire (*c*.190 ft long) and one of the most interesting. It is well placed away from the clanging traffic and yet connected with the day-to-day life of the town by one of the new shopping developments. The architectural history of the church has unfortunately never been fully unravelled. The building is dominated by its powerful W tower, and there are nave and aisles, transepts, and a number of E end annexes, the SE ones Victorian. Most of what one at once takes in is Dec, but nearly all is also restored to a degree which removes the difference

---

* Dr Gomme drew my attention to this house.

between new and old. What ought to be found out is where restorers re-did what had been there, and where they invented. *Scott*, following *Ferrey*, worked in the fifties, *Butterfield* in 1871.

Architecturally it is, in these circumstances, more profitable to start examination inside than outside. The first surprise is the evidence of a former crossing tower. The evidence is vestigially Late Anglo-Saxon and more obviously Late Norman. The one indication of Saxon origin is that the outer angles of the crossing tower project into the aisles and chancel aisles. Norman crossing towers are exactly the width of nave and chancel. The slight enlargement is to be found e.g. in Late Saxon Stow in Lincolnshire and Sherborne in Dorset. The Saxon existence of a church at Tamworth is indeed known, in the C8 and again after the Danish sack of 874. The church was made collegiate somewhat later. Back to the crossing. The N and S crossing arches are evidently Norman. The Norman E and W arches have been swept away. But the crossing is by no means all that is left of Norman work. The chancel S wall is largely Norman masonry, and there are a plain doorway, an extremely shafted window next to it, and shafted buttresses visible in the S vestry and the N chapel. So the Norman church probably went as far E as it does now. Masonry also proved that it went exactly as far W as now (S aisle, NW corner). The E.E. contribution is minimal – just the N porch with its plain rib-vault. The N aisle windows with geometrical tracery would go with that, but can they be trusted? Or can the chancel E window with its geometrical tracery? Hardly.*

In 1345 a fire occurred, and most of the church is Dec of after that misfortune. Rebuilding was due to Baldwin de Witney, dean, who died in 1369. To enumerate: Dec are the S aisle windows (cusped intersected tracery), the N doorway, the chancel N side with three cusped and subcusped tomb recesses and with windows above them which are now internal, the large blocked S transept window now also internal, and the N transept W and E arches. Dec also the nave arcades, which have quatrefoil piers with fillets and thinner shafts in the diagonals. The arches are finely moulded. Below part of the S aisle is a CRYPT of four bays with single-chamfered ribs – also Dec, but probably (Clapham) pre-fire. The W tower is Perp,

---

* Mr Pace calls it 'renewed' and 'peculiar'.

but its doorway an addition by *Champneys*. The twin two-light bell-openings look older than Perp. Big, heavy pinnacles. The tower has at its SW angle a most remarkable spiral stair. It is a double-spiral, i.e. two spiral stairs starting on opposite sides and never meeting. It is the conceit best known in Leonardo da Vinci's drawing and at the château of Chambord, but also existing at Much Wenlock and Pontefract. Perp also is the clerestory of three-light windows – in the chancel with crocketed niches between them – and so are the nave and chancel roofs, the specially rich S aisle roof, and of course the N chapel. – FONT. By *Scott*, 1854. – Stem of another font and other Perp fragments (S aisle E). – REREDOS. By *Scott*; the statues by *Birnie Philip*; 1852. The mosaic panels are by *Salviati* and date from 1887. – SCREEN. Of wrought iron. C18; elegant but modest. – STAINED GLASS. Some old bits in the vestry E window. – The E window by *Wailes*, 1870. – Much by *Morris*, and the older windows wonderfully perfect, i.e. the three in the chancel clerestory, 1873, designed by *Ford Madox Brown*, and the N chapel E window designed by *Burne-Jones*, 1874. Later Morris glass in the same chapel. – In the aisles *Holiday*: also much by *Powell*. Again the earlier (S, 1881–6) much better than the later (N, 1917–18). – PLATE. Chalice, 1671, by *W.G.*, London; Chalice, 1672?, by *R.C.R.S.*; Paten, 1683, by *D.B.*, London; two Flagons, 1768, by *W. & J. Priest*, London. – MONUMENTS. Of the time of the building of the church, i.e. about the middle to end of the C14, and all badly mauled. Two of the three effigies in the recesses in the chancel: a Lady and a couple, probably Sir Baldwin Freville † 1400 and his wife. – Also C14 an Ecclesiastic in the N chapel (probably Baldwin de Witney † 1369). – The third monument in the recesses is Sir John Ferrers † 1512 and wife. Alabaster effigies with small figures under tiny canopies. – In the N transept a late C15 Knight also badly preserved. – John Ferrers and his son Humphrey † 1680 and † 1678. Two decidedly Baroque kneeling figures, similar to those at Withyham in Sussex of 1677. They are by *Cibber*; the Ferrers tomb was commissioned from *Grinling Gibbons* but probably carved by *Arnold Quellin* (cf. the Rustat Monument in Jesus College, Cambridge). The two figures kneel l. and r. of a big base, with the inscription on. Above cherubs, garlands, a sarcophagus and an urn. – John Horner † 1769 (N aisle). Weeping putto holding the portrait medallion. – John Clarke † 1818. Kneeling mourning woman by a sarcophagus. – Elizabeth C. Blood

† 1899, yet entirely Georgian in conception. Kneeling woman below a weeping willow.

ST JOHN (R.C.), St John Street. 1829, but mostly 1954–6 by *Morris, Smith & Partners* of Birmingham.

CHAPEL OF ST JAMES (Spittal), Wigginton Road. The chapel of a hospital founded in the C13. A small, plain building with a plain Late Norman N doorway and a patched-up E.E. S doorway. The E window is Perp (much restored); the W lancets are C20.

UNITARIAN CHAPEL. See Perambulation.

THE CASTLE. The palace of 781 has been mentioned. If anything of this or of Ethelfleda's of 913 survives it is earthworks only. The earliest visible evidence is the herringbone masonry just below the present entrance, i.e. to the E of the irregularly shaped Norman shell-keep, which now as then dominates the approach from the S across the river Tame. The herringbone walling is late C11, the shell-keep C12. Incorporated in the shell on the E side is a keep-like tower with angle buttresses but no ancient windows. The main entrance is a small later medieval doorway l. of the tower. A postern exists on the N side. The attractive thing about Tamworth Castle is the way in which the space inside the shell has been gradually filled up with mixed structures, the main one being the Hall. This, facing you as you pass through the principal entrance, is in its present form Jacobean, the time when the Ferrers family held the castle. The Marquess Townshend in 1786 faced the side of the shell to the S with ashlar and gothicized its Jacobean transomed windows. The gables and two one-storeyed bay windows also went. Buck in 1729 shows them still. What is Jacobean of the exterior of the shell is the Warder's House l. of the keep-tower. There is here a wooden chimneypiece with tapering pilasters and shields in blank arches. Two more sumptuous chimneypieces are in two upper rooms S of the Hall and are probably a little later than Jacobean. The Hall itself has large mullioned and transomed windows to the courtyard – really a glass wall – and inside doorcases in the style Sir John Summerson calls Artisan Mannerism, i.e. the style preceding Wren's. The tricky details are typical of *c.*1660. The chimneypiece with an open curly pediment looks twenty years later. More doorcases of *c.*1662 in other places. The old Kitchen was on the r. of the Hall; so the two rooms with the chimneypieces, called the State Drawing Room and the Oak Room, are in a solar position. The State Drawing Room is panelled and has a frieze of heraldic shields. The chimneypiece has decorated columns and an overmantel mostly of nicely detailed panels. The Oak Room has a heraldic frieze too and a more ornate overmantel with caryatids in addition to panels. Of the C17 also is the staircase projection on the r. of the Hall. The LODGE to the castle estate is of 1810.

TOWN HALL, Market Street. 1701. (Paid for by Thomas Guy of Guy's Hospital.) A charming little building of stone and brick. Two-bay front, five-bay side. Open arches on Tuscan columns below. To the w two arched windows, a pediment, and a cupola. – INSIGNIA. Two Maces, later C17; Loving Cup, 1711–12 by *Humphrey Payne*, London. – In front of the building STATUE of Sir Robert Peel, 1853 by *Matthew Noble*.

MUNICIPAL OFFICES. See Perambulation.

ASSEMBLY ROOMS. 1889. Looking like a large, utilitarian Nonconformist chapel. Brick and stone. Five bays and more along the sides. Arched windows; big, three-bay segmental pediment.

PERAMBULATION. How is one to walk? Tamworth has done a lot of rebuilding after the Second World War, including two new shopping areas. What they should not have done is to put up six big blocks of flats, fifteen storeys high. They are visually fatal and functionally, in a town of this size, unnecessary. As for earlier buildings, they have never been up to much, and now they are lost among the new. It is enough to name the following: At the corner of Hollowway and Market Street is the CASTLE HOTEL, brick, with a Tuscan porch. To Market Street Ionic pilasters on the ground floor. In Market Street the NATIONAL WESTMINSTER BANK, by *John Gibson*, 1864. This is the best Victorian building in the town, of ashlar, Latest Classical, symmetrical, chaste in the details, but with the French pavilion roofs fashionable in the sixties.* In COLESHILL the UNITARIAN CHAPEL of 1724, and one Georgian five-bay house with a Tuscan porch; rendered. In GUNGATE, GUY'S ALMSHOUSES, 1913, a handsome front with a steep gable and a cupola, and friendly houses behind. In CHURCH STREET the MUNICIPAL OFFICES, a former private house, C18, five bays, rendered, with giant angle pilasters. In LICHFIELD STREET the former PEEL SCHOOL, 1850 by *Sydney Smirke*. The houses in Lichfield Street are dwarfed by the high blocks already condemned. No. 19 is of brick chequer and has three wide bays. MOAT HOUSE, back

* Demolished since.

from the street on the s side, is said to be dated 1572. It is of brick, symmetrical, with slightly projecting wings. The windows are sashed, and in the wings is an upper Venetian window. The most prominent feature is five stepped gables. Good staircase with flat openwork balusters. In the garden a one-bay C18 garden house with a pyramid roof (NMR). Also in Lichfield Street the MANOR HOUSE, of seven bays, with a recessed window and a hipped roof. No. 93 has a pedimented doorway (so have two others here) and a stucco-rusticated bow. But the best house is out to the SE, immediately behind the RAILWAY VIADUCT (nineteen arches; 1837-9). It is BOLE HALL in Amington Road. Early Georgian, of three bays, with a rusticated door surround and a segmental pediment above the door. Giant angle pilasters too.

TATENHILL

ST MICHAEL. A sizeable church, and one of visual unity. The impression is Perp, but the walls must be E.E., as there is an E.E. s doorway with three orders of columns and a finely moulded arch with fillets and also a single E.E. priest's doorway. But the W tower is Perp, the nave has large, four-light Late Perp windows with a transom (the lights have uncusped rounded arches!), and the chancel has large, slightly earlier Perp transomed four-light windows with panel tracery. – *Bodley* restored the church in 1890, and his are the REREDOS, the STALLS, the PULPIT, and the black and white marble FLOORING. – (FONT. Later C13 base with shafts with bases and capitals. Jeavons) – STAINED GLASS. The E window by *Ward & Hughes*, 1882; bad. – PLATE. Chalice of 1800 by *Paul, Ann, & William Bateman*. – MONUMENT. The wife and two daughters of Henry Griffiths. Mrs Griffiths died in 1641. Kneeling figure of a child, and below a baby in a drawer as it were. Two elementary columns, on top three elementary putti – all very rustic.

OLD RECTORY. A fine Early Georgian brick house. Five bays, two storeys, the doorway with fluted Doric pilasters, the window above with volutes at its foot.

TEAN

CHRIST CHURCH, Upper Tean. 1843 by *Johnson* of Lichfield. With lancets, a bellcote, and a short chancel. Poor hammerbeam roof.

Providence Chapel. 1822. Three bays with a pediment across.

Wesleyan Chapel. 1843. Three-bay pediment, arched windows.

Tean Hall Mills, Upper Tean. The tradition is that in 1747 John and Nathaniel Philips brought over a Dutchman to instruct local carpenters in the building of looms. The looms were first mainly in cottages, and on the present site was the manager's house, 'loom-houses', and warehouses. The manager's house is in two halves. The E half is an early C18 extension of two storeys, with stone angle pilasters and aprons to the windows. The W half is a timber-framed house of 1613, asymmetrical, with diagonal struts and concave-sided lozenges. The earlier parts of the mill frontage are of three storeys and eleven bays, asymmetrical, with a two-bay pediment and a cupola, the latter containing a bell dated 1833. In 1823 a four-storeyed building, twenty-seven bays long and four bays wide, was added at r. angles to exploit the advantages of steam-power. Yet later, in 1885, the road frontage was completed by a four-storey building of eight bays and a two-bay pediment.

Terraces of weavers' cottages in several locations at Upper Tean. Specially remarkable the octagonal privies behind Nos. 1 and 3 New Road and Nos. 4, 6, 8, 10, and 12 Old Road.*

Heath House, Lower Tean. Built for John Burton Philips in 1836 to the design of *Thomas Johnson* of Lichfield. The Philips family owned the Tean Hall Mills, as we have seen, and as for Johnson, he was an architect of local repute and a good one. Heath House is his domestic *chef d'œuvre*. It is in the Tudor style just then very fashionable, and it is freely and well composed and solidly built of roughly chiselled ashlar. The windows are mostly of the cross type and uncommonly slim. Gables are steep and of an odd mixture of straight and shaped. Both the entrance side, with porte-cochère and tower, and the garden side, with two canted bay windows, are symmetrical, but the longest front, to the N, is not. However, its length does not represent extensive state rooms. It is for more than half its length the service wing. Spacious staircase starting in one flight and returning in two. Many ceilings with plaster ribs.

Fine classical orangery of 1831 by *Thomas Trubshaw*. Five bays with pilasters and for the central bays slightly recessed columns.

---

* Mr Sherlock drew my attention to these.

About ½ m. NE is a TEMPLE. Classical, with a stone dome and incorporating the eight unfluted Ionic columns of the veranda of the house preceding the present one.

LODGES. SW Tudor, NE classical, probably of 1816, NW Late Classical and more original than NE.

TEDDESLEY HAY

9010

(TEDDESLEY HALL has been demolished, but various LODGES are still about. The VCH lists them.)

TETTENHALL see WOLVERHAMPTON, pp. 324–6

THORPE CONSTANTINE

2000

ST CONSTANTINE. An estate church, though the W tower with its recessed spire seems to be medieval. Nave and lower chancel of 1883. Windows with cusped Y-tracery. The chancel interior a little richer than that of the nave. The architect was *J. Oldrid Scott*.*

THORPE HALL. A five-bay centre and three-bay wings, all rendered. The centre is actually a house of 1651 and had three shaped gables. It also had the three tiers of pilaster strips which it still has. The wings are of 1800 (N) and 1812 (S) by *Thomas Gardner* of Derby. On the garden side there are shallow bows instead of wings. Delightful staircase, balustrading of iron, and a fine, discreet Adamish ceiling in the drawing room.

THOR'S CAVE see WETTON

THROWLEY

1050

THROWLEY HALL. Close by the imposing ruin of an early C16 house. The early C16 seems more likely than the accepted date 1603. The place has never been recorded, and some research would be welcome. All the surviving windows have uncusped four-centred heads to the lights, a Henry VIII type. Broad three-storeyed tower. A large bay window known from illustrations‡ has collapsed.

Among the outbuildings of Throwley Hall one has seven bays of two-light mullioned windows on two floors and is known as THROWLEY BARRACKS.

---

* I owe the name to Dr D. B. Robinson.
‡ Still in Garner & Stratton's volumes.

TIPTON

2½ m. w of West Bromwich

ST MARTIN, Lower Church Lane. 1795–7 by *J. Keyte* of Kidderminster, but the w apsidal attachment and the chancel of 1874–6 (by *A. P. Brevitt*). Restoration 1963. Chancel and w attachment are of exposed brick. The rest is rendered. Sides with arched windows set in blank arches on pilasters. Three galleries, thin iron supports.

Opposite the w end the huge modern GAS WORKS.

SACRED HEART (R.C.), Victoria Road. 1940 by *Sandy & Norris*. Brick, blocky w front, long, paired, arched side windows. Low passage aisles.

ST PAUL, Owen Street. 1837–8 by *Robert Ebbles*. Brick, with a w tower and lancets.

ST MATTHEW, Dudley Road. 1876 by *J. H. Gibbons*. Brick, with a SE tower and small lancets.

LIBRARY, Victoria Road. 1905–6 by *George H. Wenyon*. Quite a spectacular building compared with what else Tipton has to offer. Brick and very yellow terracotta, with an asymmetrically placed tower. The motifs are Elizabethan, Baroque, and Arts and Crafts.

The OBELISK in the park to the N is a First World War Memorial.

TITTENSOR

ST LUKE. 1880–1 by *Roberts* of Trentham (CPDD). Walling irregularly mixed of stone and brick. NE tower whose top stage is timber-framed. The w side has a timber-framed gable and one straight-topped six-light window under. Goodhart-Rendel writes: 'Roberts must have been an amateur or an engineer or something – his detail is babyish. A weak brick nave and chancel design with half-timber gables and a N tower with a half-timbered clock stage under a conical capping. Something awful has happened to the w window which is straight-headed under a tiebeam outside, with an enormous blank tympanum inside – the whole thing looks like a Boulton & Paul ready-made.'

TIXALL

ST JOHN. 1849 by *Wyatt & Brandon* for the Hon. J. C. Talbot. Nave with bellcote and chancel. Low N aisle. Small windows with pointed-trefoiled heads.

TIXALL HALL. The house does not survive, but the GATE-
HOUSE, built c.1575 for Sir Walter Aston, may well be called
the most ambitious gatehouse in the county. Sampson
Erdeswick in 1598 went further and called it 'one of the
finest pieces of work made of late times that I have seen in
all these countries'. Three bays and three storeys and four
polygonal angle turrets with ogee caps. The windows are of
four lights and transomed, and they are framed by pairs of
columns, Roman Doric below, then Ionic, then Corinthian.
The spandrels of the archway have soldiers on one side,
winged females on the other. Above the archway the windows
become shallowly canted bays. It is all a relentless grid, and
the fact that it is now roofless reinforces the sense of a dark
grid and light interstices.

STABLES. Early C19. A magnificent composition, semicircular and single-storeyed, with three higher pavilions, the
middle one with a three-bay Tudor-Gothic porch. The other
pavilions are at the ends. The composition continues axially
behind.

TIXALL COTTAGE, 200 yds W of the church, has very fine big
C18 urns.

BOTTLE LODGE, on the road, a little further NE. Octagonal, with
a big ogee roof. Is this c.1575 too?

OBELISK. At the main crossing of the village, also a milestone.
Dated 1776.

ROTUNDA of Tuscan columns, really an octagon, open and with
a dome. Recently transferred from Ingestre. Mid C18.

(HOLDIFORD BRIDGE. Ashlar, of three segmental arches, probably c.1805. DOE)

(AQUEDUCT, W of the bridge. Four segmental arches. Probably
c.1770. CPDD)

TRENTHAM PARK

It is the principle of *The Buildings of England* not to describe
buildings which have been demolished. Trentham Park must
make an exception, not only because it was a house which was
spectacular and had a spectacular following, but even more
because its remains are extensive enough for any visitor to ask
at once after their context. The house, whose bulk was demolished in 1910–12, was initially built where an Augustinian
priory had been founded c.1150 and been dissolved probably
in 1537. The property was bought by James Leveson in 1540.
The house with which the following description is to deal was

built in 1833–42 by *Sir Charles Barry*, the architect of the Houses of Parliament, and it was in its own way architecturally as important as the Houses of Parliament. The client was the second Duke of Sutherland, of the Leveson-Gower family. How the Levesons got together with the Gowers, how titles (including Marquess of Stafford) were accumulated, is too complicated to be explained here. It is sufficient to say that the second Marquess of Stafford married the greatest of British heiresses, the Countess of Sutherland, and was himself created Duke of Sutherland. The second Duke was his son. He inherited in 1833 and at once began to make plans for a conversion and vast enlargement of the house existing on the site. This was designed by *Francis Smith* and built in the early C18 'after the model of the Queen's Palace in St James's Park', i.e. Buckingham House (as *The Beauties of England and Wales* rightly states). It was enlarged from nine to fifteen bays by *Capability Brown* and *Holland* in 1768–78. It faced a large LAKE proposed by Capability Brown in 1759. That lake, altered when the mansion was built, was of impressive size and fortunately still exists. It sets the scale not only of the house but also of the vast PARTERRE by *W. A. Nesfield* connecting house and lake. The pattern of the parterre was originally more complex than it is now.

77 The HOUSE was in the Italianate style, sub-species Italian Villa, though its scale was palatial and not at all villaesque. However, villa as against *palazzo* was the term to indicate a house of informal composition with an asymmetrically placed tower. The type was created on a small scale by Nash at Cronkhill about 1802. Wyatville raised it to the grandest scale in the N wing of Chatsworth. This was started in 1820. Trentham came next, and Trentham formed the pattern for Prince Albert's Osborne, and on the strength of that august fane for other mansions in Britain and even in Germany.

The GRAND ENTRANCE was from the W, a semicircle between two five-bay wings and a porte-cochère in front of the centre of the semicircle. All this still stands. The porte-cochère is more ornate than anything of the rest. It has complex columns alternately blocked and a heavy attic similarly treated and with thickly carved coats of arms. The semicircle and the wings are one-storeyed with arched openings and unfluted Ionic columns. This motif Barry took over from *Charles Heathcote Tatham*'s Orangery built c.1808. This is in fact the r. wing of the two just referred to.

Behind rose the house, with a façade symmetrical to the forecourt within the semicircle. But the symmetry was not continued, and here no doubt was a flaw in the planning, disappointing in an architect who, in the Houses of Parliament, proved himself a master in planning. The reason was that Barry had to use the C18 house. Its s front towards the lake became his s front; its fifteen bays, divided by giant pilasters into five units of three, were entirely kept and only lightly remodelled in the interest of greater evenness. Behind this s front were Barry's three state rooms, and behind them was irregularity, the grand staircase, some small rooms, and the splendid TOWER whose top is now in the grounds of Sandon Park (*see* p. 231). The tower is purposely asymmetrical from the s but symmetrical from the w. It was built in the 1840s. Its open three-bay arcading at the top is inspired by Wyatville's tower added to Chatsworth in the 1820s. s of the tower and E of the s front a wing projected to the s to match Tatham's orangery, and then, further E, followed yet another range, nine bays long, with two tiers of superimposed columns *à la* Inigo Jones's Banqueting House. Yet further E and N is the STABLEYARD with riding school, a sculpture gallery on the upper floor, and a CLOCK TOWER. This group was designed only in 1840 and built from 1841 to *c.*1850. It represents a different style, less faithfully Italianate, freer indeed, but also more severe with its long band of windows separated by low Doric pillars. Only the tower is the typical villa piece.

By the end of 1841 the Duke had spent £123,000 on Trentham Park.

Of minor buildings the following need a reference.

On the w side of the parterre is a large three-bay LOGGIA.

The main entrance has two LODGES by *Tatham* and GATEPIERS large enough to have a small room inside.

1¼ m. s of the house is the MONUMENT to the first Duke, erected in 1836. It is a plain column on a drum pediment and carries a colossal bronze statue. Designer *Winks*, sculptor *Chantrey* (VCH).

ST MARY AND ALL SAINTS. By *Barry*, 1844. Large and uniform outside, with nave and chancel in one. E.E. porch, but Perp window, and inside Late Norman arcades of four bays. They are a puzzle. The round shafts are medieval and most probably come from the priory church. The capitals with their flat leaves and crockets also are too authentic not to be copies of something existing on the spot. They indicate *c.*1180–90. –

REREDOS. The PAINTING of the Entombment is by *William Hilton*, c.1810–20. L. and r. Commandment Boards. – SCREENS. Jacobean with balusters (1633) and imitation-Jacobean. – WEST GALLERY. Georgian. – STAINED GLASS. s chapel s by *Willement*. – PLATE. Silver-gilt Chalice, Jacobean; Chalice and Paten by *R.W.*, 1637; Flagon by *R.F.*, 1670; Paten by *F.B.*, 1834. – MONUMENTS. In the N aisle fragment of the effigy of a Knight dated by Jeavons c.1215. – Most of the monuments are in the s chapel: Large alabaster tablet to Sir Richard and Lady Leveson-Gower † 1559 and 1591. Against the back wall, brasses, kneeling. – Statue of the first Duke of Sutherland, 1838 by *Chantrey*. – Recumbent effigy of the Duchess † 1868. By *Noble*. – A. S. Leveson-Gower † 1874. By *Noble*. Bust in an alabaster surround. – Florence Chaplin † 1881. Medallion of a young woman, rather French. – Eldest son of the third Duke † 1888. Bust of a boy by *Noble* – In the s aisle fourth Duke of Sutherland, by *Tinworth*, 1917. Small terracotta relief of Christ in the house of Simon the Leper.

MAUSOLEUM, across the A road, opposite the main gates. The isolation is a shame; for the building is so overpowering that it needs a good deal of elbow room. It has one door and, at the back, one window. There are also four small top windows. The material is all ashlar. The walls have a strong batter, and indeed (just as the architects do it today) canting is done everywhere. The middle part rises above the rest. Inside that is not marked. The plan there is a Greek cross with tunnel-vaulted arms. The origin of a design so cyclopean, and so ruthless, is the most radical French architecture of the Boullée–Ledoux period. The architect was indeed *Charles Heathcote Tatham*, who had spent three years in Rome in the 1790s, at a time when the *pensionnaires* of the Académie de France in Rome were intoxicated with the ideas of Piranesi and Boullée. The mausoleum was built in 1807–8.

TRENT VALE *see* STOKE-ON-TRENT, pp. 263, 265

TRYSULL

ALL SAINTS. Norman a small re-set arch outside the N aisle. Of c.1300 the N aisle windows and also probably the arcades, N with round, s with octagonal piers. The bays are not in line with the windows nor the N bays with the s. No chancel arch. Early C14 s aisle E window and a little later the more ambitious chancel E window with flowing tracery. The tower is medieval – Dec or Perp. Two splendid Perp roof trusses in the nave with four raking queenposts and trefoils. – FONT. Perp, octagonal, with quatrefoils. – PULPIT. Jacobean, with one tier of blank arches and arabesque panels over.* – SCREEN. Late Perp, with Flamboyant pierced panels. – SCULPTURE. Small bust of a bishop under a pointed trefoiled arch – C13. – STAINED GLASS. In the E window two fine small late C14 figures. The rest of this window by *D. Evans* of Shrewsbury, 1844. – Of 1856 and 1857 the chancel side windows and the S aisle E window. – PLATE. Chalice by *T.F.*, 1628; Chalice, Paten, Bread Plate by *P.Y.* of London, 1637; Almsdish, 1718; Flagon by *John Robinson*, 1756.

RED HOUSE, W of the church. Georgian, of three bays. Brick with Venetian windows.

(TRYSULL MILL. 1854. Brick, six bays. The iron mill wheel survives. DOE)

TUNSTALL *see* STOKE-ON-TRENT, p. 265

TUTBURY

TUTBURY CASTLE lies splendidly 100 ft above the plain, NW of the town and S of the river Dove. It goes back to the late C11, when it belonged to Henry de Ferrers. From the Ferrers family, in 1265, it passed to the Earls of Lancaster, and it still belongs to the Duchy now. The oldest parts surviving are the chapel of the C12 and the NE gateway of the early C14. The rest is C15 and later. The castle is most usefully described topographically, i.e. as visitors see it. The entrance is through the S wall of the former KING'S LODGING, built in 1631–5 with odd details. The window surrounds have stones laid alternately vertically and horizontally. Doorway with coarse pilasters and pediment. This range is on the site of the former hall. Beyond it to the W is the motte, and on it, instead of the medieval shell keep, a much smaller round FOLLY KEEP of after 1760. To the E of the range of 1631–5 is the SOUTH TOWER, built in 1442–50. It consists of two towers side by side with a staircase projection between them towards the bailey. The ground floors were intended to be vaulted, but in

---

* Made up from parts of a three-decker. Information from the Rev. J. H. Urwin.

the end were not. The springers indicate a tunnel-vault in the w part, a rib-vault in the E part. Doorways lead into both rooms. Upper windows. Following the curtain wall to the NE one passes the remains of a small tower and then arrives at the NORTH TOWER. This was built in the 1450s. It is similar to the small tower. The ground floor here has a pointed tunnel-vault. No more buildings follow until the NE GATEWAY is reached. Its inner parts are of the early C14 – see the remaining window tracery. The outer towers are again C15. Freestanding in the bailey are the remains of the Norman CHAPEL. (The Norman chapels of Ludlow Castle and Pontefract Castle are free-standing too.) It is a plain building of nave and narrower chancel. The W portal had one order of colonnettes.

ST MARY. The church lies elevated above the town, yet not as high as the castle. It formed part of a priory founded by Henry de Ferrers probably in the 1080s and colonized from St Pierre-sur-Dives in Normandy. Of the monastic quarters nothing survives, and the church does not survive in its entirety. It originally had an apse, succeeded by a larger choir and also transepts and a crossing tower. The missing parts were replaced by *Street* in 1866. He provided a chancel and apse. The chancel opens to the nave by a very wide pointed arch. One should begin however with what is left of nave and aisles. The system of the piers changes, but the style does not change. One would call it early C12. The E piers are round, the W piers are an odd elongated quatrefoil shape. The capitals have scallops, not as large as before 1100 nor as small as in the late C12. The arcades have two big rolls. Twin vaulting shafts rise but are cut off, as the full height is not preserved. The present clerestory was a gallery, as the shafting indicates. The W front ended operations. This is so lavish that it must be as late as *c.*1160–70. Externally first there is a W doorway of seven orders, the capitals highly fanciful, with beasts and figures, the arch with beakhead and also radiating motifs. The outermost order incidentally represents the earliest use of alabaster in England. In the S tower, whose upper parts are Dec to Perp, are a W window and a S window, both originally simply part of the S aisle. Above the W doorway is a window also with a decorated surround including beakhead and l. and r. intersecting arches with zigzag. In the gable three round windows with zigzag. The S aisle doorway is Norman too, with three orders of colonnettes and again with figured capitals. The lintel shows a boar hunt. The aisle otherwise is Perp. The N aisle is an odd conceit of 1820–2 by *Joseph B. H. Bennett*: stepped lancet lights under a round arch and with two transoms. Inside, the W doorway and the S doorway have zigzag surrounds, and the W wall has intersecting arches also inside. The S aisle W parts have Norman responds. The tower is supported in the S aisle by a shallow, flying-buttress-like Dec arch. – REREDOS, PULPIT, STALLS, FONT, etc., by *Street*, 1867–8.* – PLATE. Chalice, 1706 by *John Downes* of London. – MONUMENT. George Robinson † 1837. By *Joseph Hall* of Derby. Standing Grecian figure by a broken column.

At the foot of Castle Hill in Duke Street close to the start of the High Street is CROFT HOUSE, Georgian, of three wide bays. Doorway with pediment. The middle window is a little enriched. In the HIGH STREET the DOG AND PARTRIDGE is a timber-framed house with closely set uprights and an oversailing upper floor. No. 6 opposite has a very pretty 'Venetian' doorway. Several more Georgian doorways follow, and the TUTBURY INSTITUTE of three bays with a three-bay pediment. This was built as a Methodist Chapel. With the bend in the street looser building begins (Lower High Street) and is introduced by a detached Georgian house of three bays with a pedimented doorway.

(FAULD WORKS. By *B. Hickman*. Good.)

TYRLEY see HALES

UPPER GORNAL
2¼ m. NW of Dudley

ST PETER, Kent Street. 1840–1 by *R. Ebbles*. A Commissioners' church. It cost £2,353. Stone, towerless, with lancet windows. The front has two polygonal turrets *à la* King's College Chapel. Short, low chancel. Open timber roof. – PLATE. Two Chalices by *Patrick Robinson*, 1764.

UPPER PENN see WOLVERHAMPTON, p. 323

UPPER TEAN see TEAN

* I thank Mr Joyce for this addition.

UTTOXETER

ST MARY. Early C14 tower with a recessed spire. The nave of 1828 (by *Trubshaw & Johnson*). Long two-light windows with one reticulation unit at the top. Battlements and angle pinnacles. The chancel is in its present form of 1877. The nave has thin octagonal piers and two galleries. – PLATE. Paten, 1696 by *I.A.*; Chalice, 1704 by *W.A.*; Chalice, 1716 by *Stephen Coleman*; Flagon, 1751. – MONUMENTS. Recumbent alabaster effigy of a Lady; early C16. – (Thomas Kinnersley and wife, *c.*1500. Remains of an alabaster tomb. The chest has baluster-pilasters. Against it kneeling figures. Incised lid. Jeavons) – Edward Smith † 1753. Purely architectural, with corroded Rococo ornament at the foot. – Thomas Keelinge † 1804. Woman kneeling by an altar.

ST MARY (R.C.), Balance Street. 1839 by *Pugin*, but almost totally altered by aisles, a narthex, and changes in the chancel. The w rose window and the sedilia are Pugin's.

CONGREGATIONAL CHURCH, Carter Street. 1827–8. Brick, three bays, with pediment. Arched windows in two tiers. Entrance with Tuscan columns *in antis*.

METHODIST CHURCH, High Street. 1812. Brick, three bays with pediment. Arched upper windows. Doorway with Tuscan columns and pediment.

FRIENDS' MEETING HOUSE, Carter Street. The late C17 meeting house, with gallery, lies behind a plain brick cottage.

TOWN HALL, High Street. 1853–4 by *Thomas Fradgley*. Latest Classical, with a recessed centre and two pedimented wings.

Uttoxeter has not got much shape. The centre is the two adjoining squares, both irregular. In one the Gothic MARKET CROSS of *c.*1922, in the other the classical WEIGHING MACHINE of 1854 by *Thomas Fradgley*, with four pediments and a stone dome. In four or five streets are worthwhile houses, the best in CHURCH STREET. The COUNTY COURT OFFICES have a pretty Gothick doorway with a pointed arch, pointed-trefoil-cusped. The MANOR HOUSE is of five bays and two and a half storeys with a three-bay pediment with three urns. Doorway with Tuscan columns and a metope frieze. Farther on JERVIS HOUSE with two canted bay windows and a doorway with Tuscan columns. Belonging to ALLEYNE'S GRAMMAR SCHOOL (buildings of 1858 etc.) is the Georgian Headmaster's House of five bays.

In BALANCE STREET three Georgian brick houses of interest, the POLICE and Nos. 38 and 53. LEIGHTON TERRACE (Nos. 35–41) must be of *c*.1850: Latest Classical.

In CARTER STREET are the WHITE HART HOTEL with a porch across the pavement and a group of three timber-framed cottages (Nos. 32–36).

In the HIGH STREET the imposing but much pulled-about UTTOXETER HOUSE, high, rendered, with three dormers with finials. (Also No. 72, THE OLD BANK HOUSE, formerly with datestone 1798. Red brick, three storeys, five bays. Good plain Tuscan doorcase with engaged columns. DOE)

Along the road to Derby the county border runs across the DOVE BRIDGE, an impressive structure of two pointed C14 and two later (1691?) round arches. Heavy cutwaters.

(CRAKEMARSH HALL, 2 m. N. A compact two-storeyed stucco villa of *c*.1820. The front is of three bays with a Tuscan porch of four columns; the sides have polygonal bays the full height of the house. At the back a long range culminating in a further polygon was added later in the century. All very quiet and modest; and the surprise is to find that the house seems to have been built (or possibly rebuilt) round a sumptuous C17 staircase: surely a very unusual thing to do in the early C19; but the evidence of the screen of two pairs of disproportionately squat Ionic columns under one flight seems conclusive. The staircase, which occupies the whole of the entrance hall, has lavish openwork panels of acanthus foliage set between big square newels decorated with fruit and carrying urns of flowers. The carving, vigorous as it is, is somewhat rough and ready, and suggests a local imitation of Edward Pearce's great staircase at Sudbury, a few miles to the s. Behind the hall is a high passage with segmental plaster vault with broad moulded ribs. The rest of the interiors is chastely Victorian, but a few older bits and pieces survive, including one bolection-moulded marble fireplace and the back staircase with simple turned balusters – both early C18. Stable block with a tower over the archway.*)

WALL

ST JOHN. Consecrated in 1843, but in 1839 *Scott & Moffatt*, i.e. young George Gilbert Scott, invited tenders. Is the church theirs, then? Dark stone, aisleless, with a short chancel and a

---

* This entry was written by Dr Andor Gomme.

thin w steeple. Straight-headed two-light windows, except for the E window, which has Perp panel tracery. – Brass and iron LECTERN with a statuette. – STAINED GLASS. One s window by *Kempe & Tower*.

ALDERSHAWE, ½ m. N. Designed by *Samuel Luxton* and built in the 1890s. Brick, with half-timbered gables.

(PIPE PLACE, on the A 461. About 1700. Five bays, two storeys, hipped roof. Segment-headed cross-windows; doorway with pediment on brackets.)

The Roman site of LETOCETUM on Watling Street went through a complicated history. A series of forts began with a large work dating from the reign of Claudius. Overlying this are the remains of three smaller forts in timber, dating from the period 60–75. A much later work is a small stone-walled enclosure standing astride Watling Street: this dates from the C4. Immediately to the N of the modern village are the remains of a compact bath-house, attached to a dwelling which may have been a *mansio* or resting place for official travellers.

WALSALL

Walsall, with in 1971 nearly 185,000 inhabitants, though a medieval town (charters earlier C13 and 1309), is a mess, and the plentiful and highly creditable recent new building has not removed the chaos of the centre. Yet it has done something to the one place worth doing something about, the approach to the parish church, which stands splendidly on a hill. The approach is now through a new pedestrian shopping (and market) square and by an underpass to the High Street, which runs straight up the hill.

ST MATTHEW. 1820–1 by *Francis Goodwin*, who encased the walls of the medieval nave (hence the irregular plan) and retained the Perp chancel with an arched passage below the E bay. Only one (blocked) window is original. The chancel was drastically restored by *Ewan Christian* in 1877–80. The church is ashlar-faced. Wide sw and NW transept-like chapels. S tower with recessed spire largely rebuilt in 1951. Goodwin's window tracery is of iron. Thin Perp arcade piers of iron, three galleries, flat ceiling delightfully decorated in a still Georgian Gothick tradition, with fans and pendants. Beneath the three w bays of the chancel is a CRYPT. This is in two parts. The outer (E) part has an ashlar tunnel-vault of the C15. The lower courses of the walls could even be C14. The inner (W) crypt has a blocked opening to the outer part which seems to be Norman. There are in that wall also two lancet windows of the C13, proof that this was an outer wall. The vault has slender ribs of the C13 or C14 and a C15 doorway to a newel staircase. – FONT. Perp, with shields held by angels. – LECTERN. A stone surface on a panelled corbel in the chancel N wall. – STALLS. C15, with eighteen MISERICORDS, the largest set in the county. Among representations e.g. a Miller(?) carrying a sack (N), a Pelican (N), a man playing an instrument (N), a man with a club (N), several beasts, a Centaur (S), several masks (S). – STAINED GLASS. The W window of c.1850 or earlier, the E window by *Burlison & Grylls*, c.1880. – PLATE. Two Chalices and two Flagons, London, 1636; Flagon by *Benjamin Traherne*, 1698; Paten, 1698. – (MONUMENT. Sir Roger Hillary † 1399 (in the S aisle). Recumbent effigy, battered.)

Opposite the S side of the church the MEMORIAL GARDENS by *G. A. Jellicoe*, 1950–1. Brick walls in the neo-Georgian fashion, but a pavilion at the corner with vertical fins.

ST MARY (R.C.), Vicarage Walk. 1825–7 by *Joseph Ireland*. Grecian with pedimented W and E ends with giant Doric pilasters, the E end totally windowless. Its composition was repeated in 1833 smaller on the l. of the E end for the Presbytery, a father and son effect. Wide aisleless interior, tall, straight-headed windows, beautiful shallow coffered tunnel-vault. The E wall has fluted, attached Ionic columns in five bays.

Just S of this the VICARAGE WALK BAPTIST CHURCH, 1879, Italianate and also pedimented, with the same father and son motif, here for the School.

(ST MICHAEL, Caldmore. 1870–1 by *J. R. Veall*. Red sandstone, E.E. style, nave and aisles, apsidal chancel. VCH)

ST PAUL, St Paul's Close. By *Pearson*, 1891–3. Large, Dec in style, with transepts and an apse. The porch tower was never built. Wide and high interior, tall piers, canted roof. The transepts have differing end windows, the chancel has differing two-bay chapels.

ST PETER, Stafford Street. 1841 by *Isaac Highway*. Brick, lancets, W tower with polygonal buttresses.

COUNCIL HOUSE, with adjoining buildings, Lichfield Street and Leicester Street. The Council House is by *J. S. Gibson*, 1905, proudly Baroque. Ashlar, symmetrical, with a high tower, its motifs reminiscent of Greek Thomson. Big portal with sculpture. It could all do with more viewing space.* The LIBRARY is by *Gibson* too, 1905–6. It has a recent addition containing the ART GALLERY. Rough concrete, with few windows. By *A. T. Parrott*, the Borough Architect, 1965. In Leicester Street the COUNTY COURT, built privately and used for the Walsall Literary and Philosophical Society. 1831, with a Greek Doric temple front. Also in Leicester Street the TOWN HALL, 1902–5, also by *J. S. Gibson*. A Baroque façade *à la* Rickards. At the back grey brick with arched windows.

Former LIBRARY, Goodall Street. 1859 by *Nichols & Morgan*. Tripartite windows and pedimented centre.

GUILDHALL, High Street. 1867 by *G. B. Nichols*. Not large, but weighty in scale, Italianate, of two high storeys.

Former SCIENCE AND ART INSTITUTE, Bradford Place. Brick, Gothic, symmetrical. 1888 by *G. Dunn* and *W. Hipkiss*.

TECHNICAL COLLEGE, Duncalfe Street and St Paul's Street. 1947–61 by *Hickton, Madeley & Salt*.

(STATION. The building of 1849 survives. It is in Station Street.‡)

Just a few buildings to be looked for. In DIGBETH the ARCADE of 1895–7 by *Jonathan Ellis*, T-shaped, with a glass tunnel-vault. At the s end of STAFFORD STREET another new shopping centre. It is called TOWNEND SQUARE and is by *Ardin & Brookes & Partners*, of 1968–70. In BRADFORD STREET a fifteen-bay stucco composition with centre portico and angle pavilions.

In CALDMORE GREEN, the WHITE HART is a substantial Jacobean brick house with shaped gables ending in semicircles and with two canted bays. Low mullioned windows. Not a symmetrical composition. In WEST BROMWICH STREET the TRUSTEE SAVINGS BANK has recently put up a handsome little building. Rectangular giant surrounds for the five two-storeyed bays, continued as a two-bay screen on the l. By *Hickton, Madeley & Partners*.

OUTER WALSALL

For Willenhall *see* p. 312.

NORTH

ALL SAINTS, High Street, Bloxwich. About 1791–4, but gothicized, altered otherwise, and provided with a new chancel

---

* INSIGNIA. Two Maces, 1627–8, London-made; by *F*
‡ Information given me by the staff of the VCH.

and a w tower with pyramid roof and stumpy pinnacles in 1875–7 by *Davis & Middleton*. Brick, lancets, plate and geometrical tracery. Interior with galleries, the piers with thin details like those of St James and St John at Dudley.

(ST ANDREW, Birchills Street. 1884–7 by *J. E. K. Cutts*. Large, with clerestory. Brick, and much exposed brick inside. Lancets. No structural division between nave and chancel. EH)

(CHRIST CHURCH, Blakenall Heath. 1865–72 by *Naden*. Limestone; E.E. style. VCH)

ST PETER (R.C.), High Street. 1869 by *Bricknall & Donovan*. GR also refers to *E. Kirby*. His and no doubt a good deal later must be the façade with the two short towers and the Kirby kind of brick treatment. The rest can be 1869. Short round piers, plain Romanesque capitals, polygonal apse.

HOLY TRINITY, Coltham Street, Short Heath. 1854–5 by *W. Horton*. A Commissioners' church.

T. P. RILEY SCHOOL, Lichfield Road, an excellent comprehensive school by *Richard Sheppard, Robson & Partners*, 1956–61.

NORTH EAST

ST MARK, Butts Road. 1871. – (In the church a reredos with a sculptured PANEL from St Mary Wolverhampton. It is Flemish and represents the Crucifixion.)

ST MICHAEL, Leigh Road, Rushall. 1856 by *James Cranston*. Aisleless, with a nearly isolated sw tower. The church was lengthened and the (ignorantly or naughtily detailed) spire added in 1867–8. Transepts and a short chancel. – FONT. C13, round, with vertical strips of dog-tooth. – WALL PAINTINGS. Large angels in the transepts. By *Reginald Frampton*, 1905–6.

Next to the church is RUSHALL HALL, with a C15 gatehouse and extensive curtain walling. The gatehouse is a rough structure with segmental arches to the gateway and a tunnel-vault inside. It was originally two-storeyed. (The walling shows remains of fireplaces.)

MELLISH ROAD METHODIST CHURCH. Ashlar, free Gothic, with a steeple and Arts and Crafts details. Good. By *Hickton & Farmer*, 1910.

SOUTH EAST AND SOUTH

ST GABRIEL, Walstead Road, Fullbrook. By *Lavender & Twentyman*, 1939.

(ST MARY AND ALL SAINTS, Palfrey. 1901–2 by *J. E. K. & J. P. Cutts*. Red brick; Tudor style. VCH)

WEST MIDLAND TEACHER TRAINING COLLEGE, Broadway and Gorway Road. For 300 residential and 150 day students. By *Richard Sheppard, Robson & Partners*, 1961–4. Their finest building in the county, formally composed, yet not at all tight. Four ranges round a central court in which rises the square teaching block. The teaching block is exactly in the middle, but the courtyard is sunk asymmetrically. Three of the outer ranges hang together, the fourth (N) is isolated. This houses dining hall, assembly hall, library, lecture theatre, etc. At the back, to the N, the gymnasium is attached. The range is tripartite, parts one and two being similar but not identical, part three being different. The other three ranges are occupied by the study-bedrooms. They are far from identical. The S range has less depth than the others, and W is longer than E. Also S is one even block; W and E are divided into small blocks (twelve rooms with service core per block) with connecting links. The teaching block in the middle stands on heavy retracted supports. It seems to me a mistake that the S side of the block is symmetrical at first sight, but indeed not quite. The chequer arrangement of the matchstick mullions in such a composition strikes me as whimsy. The block is largely glass, but with windowless concrete bays. The concrete exposes the shuttering rawly – a touch of toughness whose introduction one can well understand.

SOUTH WEST

In the DARLASTON area three churches and nothing else of note.

ST LAWRENCE, Church Street, the parish church. By *A. P. Brevitt*, 1871–2. The exterior – W tower with recessed spire and plate tracery – does not prepare for the interior, though windows in tiers, representing galleries at a time when galleries were taboo, and ashlar with some brick decoration may be a warning. The church indeed has galleries, and the piers are of cast iron and carry two tiers of capitals of unprecedented and very summary shape. – PLATE. Two Cups, 1804 by *P., A., & W. Bateman*; Almsdish, 1807 by *P. & W. Bateman*; two Goblets, 1810 by *Crispin Fuller*; Jug, 1823 by *John Bridge* of London. – In the churchyard STATUE (Mother and Child) in the Gill style. By *Thomas Wright*, 1958.

ALL SAINTS, Holyhead Road, Moxley. 1850–1 by *W. Horton*, a

Commissioners' church. Aisleless with a NW steeple. Pairs of lancets nicely shafted inside with the shafts detached.

ALL SAINTS, Walsall Street, Darlaston. By *Lavender, Twentyman & Percy*, 1951–2. It replaces a church by *Street* (1871–2) which was destroyed by a landmine (P. Joyce).

ST GEORGE, The Green. 1851–2 or thereabouts, by *T. Johnson*. At the N end of THE GREEN a STATUE of St George. By *Thomas Wright*, 1959.

WEST

This includes Willenhall, for which *see* p. 312.

EMMANUEL, Queen Elizabeth Avenue, Bentley. By *Lavender, Twentyman & Percy*, 1956. More accommodating and much prettier than their pre-war work.

ST JOHN, Pleck Road. 1857–8 by *Griffin & Weller*.

MANOR HOSPITAL, Pleck Road. The former WORKHOUSE. This was built in 1838–42 and is in the form of two connected crosses at the N end (corner of Moat Road). Many later additions.

FRANK F. HARRISON SCHOOL, Leamore Lane. 1966 by *Austin Parrott*, the Borough Architect.

WALSALL WOOD

ST JOHN. 1837 by *Highway* and 1886 and 1895. What is Early, what Late Victorian is obvious enough. The S aisle and chancel of 1895 are by *H. E. Lavender*. Surprisingly retrograde for 1886 and 1895 are the cast-iron columns and thin, flat leaf capitals. The W tower of 1837 is decidedly lean, the chancel, again in spite of its date, still short.

WALTON HALL *see* CHEBSEY

WALTON-ON-THE-HILL

ST THOMAS. 1842 by *Thomas Trubshaw*. Brick, with lancets, nave, transepts, short chancel, and N tower with recessed spire. – STAINED GLASS. S transept S *Kempe*, 1888. – MONUMENTS. In the churchyard a big Gothic memorial to members of the Byrd Levett family, 1882. – Richard Byrd Levett † 1917.

He fell in the war. Recumbent effigy by *R. Bridgman & Sons*, the canopy and the war memorial chapel by *Cecil Hare*, 1919.

WARSLOW

ST LAURENCE. Nave with arched windows, unbuttressed tower. The church was built in 1820, the chancel added in 1908 by *Lynam & Sons*. (Inside, a W gallery and a family pew.) – Two-decker PULPIT and tester. – BOX PEWS. – STAINED GLASS. By *Morris & Co.* several, but as late as 1909, 1910, 1920, and 1923.

A village of enjoyable stone houses of Peak District character.

WATERFALL

ST JAMES AND ST BARTHOLOMEW. 1792 the W tower and the nave with its arched windows. The chancel rebuilt in 1890, but with the use of old masonry. And the chancel arch is indeed Norman, even if over-renewed. It has zigzag, and in the hoodmould saltire crosses. The S doorway has a Norman arch too, placed above a doorway with classical surround. It looks curious. – FONT. Small; C17. – SCREEN. Jacobean, with balusters. – COMMUNION RAIL. Late C17. – PLATE. Paten with engraved Lamb, *c.*1500; Elizabethan Chalice.

WATERHOUSES

LEE HOUSE. Mid Georgian. Three bays, two and a half storeys. Quoins. Doorway with rusticated surround and pediment.

WEDGWOOD MONUMENT *see* AUDLEY

WEDNESBURY

2¼ m. NW of West Bromwich

ST BARTHOLOMEW, Church Hill. A prominent and an interesting church. That it is medieval is proved by the C14 tower arch and a yet earlier re-set slightly chamfered arch in the N aisle. The latter looks *c.*1200. But the impression of the church is half early C19, half late C19. The nave and the N transept are indeed of *c.*1827, the E end and the S transept of 1890 by *Basil Champneys*. The windows of c.1827 are of three lights with cusped intersected tracery and have transoms. Champneys is resolutely Perp, following in this and in the use of a polygonal apse (*à la* Lichfield) what had already been there in the early C19. The W tower has a recessed spire. Interior of five bays with tall octagonal piers, clearly c.1827. Painted decoration in the chancel. – PULPIT. 1611. The usual blank arches, and above these arabesque panels. – LECTERN. A wooden C14 or C15 cock. – PAINTING. Former altarpiece by *Jean Jouvenet*, 1698; big. – STAINED GLASS. Sixteen windows by *Kempe*, the dates commemorated from 1889 to 1910. – PLATE. Chalice and Paten Cover by *R.D.*, 1622, London; Sweet Dish by *C.P.*, 1642, London; Set of 1829 by *J. E. Terry & Co.*, London. – MONUMENTS. In the N aisle Richard Parkes † 1618 and wife. Alabaster effigies, she with a widow's hood. Against the tomb-chest small figures and some nice ribbon-work. – Thomas Parkes † 1602. Relief tablet with two kneeling figures facing one another (chancel S). – Seated female figure by an urn with the profile medallion of the deceased. By *Peter Hollins* (chancel N). – Samuel Allison † 1817. Angel by a sarcophagus. Also by *Hollins* (N aisle). – Rev. Isaac Clarkson † 1860. Portrait bust, *Hollins* again (S aisle).

ST JAMES, St James's Street. 1847–8 by *W. Horton*, a Commissioners' church. Aisleless, with a short W tower and lancet windows. The chancel is of 1857 by *Griffin & Weller*, the apse of 1865.

ST JOHN, Lower High Street. 1845–6 by *Dawkes & Hamilton*. Lancets and a NW tower with a spire slightly odd in outline. Aisles, clerestory, chancel with high chancel arch.

ST MARY (R.C.), Church Hill, N of the parish church. 1873–4 by *Gilbert Blount*. Brick, with a thin NW steeple. The red brick has some black brick decoration. Lancet windows, polygonal apse with windows with plate tracery. Octagonal piers. – The PRESBYTERY is probably same architect same date.

TOWN HALL, Holyhead Road. 1872, but the façade 1913 by *Scott & Clark*. No interest. Next to it the funny ART GALLERY, 1890–1 by *Wood & Kendrick*.

In the Market Place CLOCK TOWER of 1911 by *G. W. D. Joynson*. Square, brick, with a Baroque stone top.

In Walsall Street the LIBRARY, 1908 by *Crouch, Butler & Savage*, the best secular building of Wednesbury.

Next to it the MEMORIAL GARDENS. In the back wall set piece with Roman Doric columns and a pediment: 1926 by *Bateman* of Birmingham.

WEDNESFIELD
2 m. NE of Wolverhampton

ST THOMAS. 1751, but burnt in 1902 and rebuilt by *F. T. Beck* in 1903. He totally replaced the chancel of 1842–3 by *Wyatt & Brandon*. The rest must be facsimile, and apparently a good deal of the exterior may have been kept. Brick with a W tower. Its pedimented doorway and the two tiers of aisle windows all have Gibbs surrounds. The tower has a top balustrade. The interior is Beck's. Three galleries. – PLATE. Chalice of 1752 by *John Priest* of London; Paten and Flagon of 1753 by *Richard Gurney & Co.* of London.

COTTAGE HOMES, Amos Lane. An interesting venture of the Board of Guardians. On an area of twenty acres *George H. Stanger* in 1889–90 provided accommodation for pauper children not in a big barracks but in houses of moderate size. Unfortunately the layout is only partly preserved.

WEEFORD

ST MARY. 1802. The bell-turret bay and the chancel Victorian. Aisleless, but with transepts. The nave windows are (strangely enough) segment-headed, the S transept window is large and pointed. – In it STAINED GLASS brought in 1803 from the chapel of the Duke of Orleans near Paris. It is in the Netherlandish Mannerism of the later C16.

BLACKBROOK FARMHOUSE, ½ m. SW, on the A446. Early Georgian, five bays, segment-headed windows and doorway. *James Wyatt* was born here in 1746.

WERGS HALL see CODSALL

WERRINGTON

WINDMILL, on the A road. A brick tower provided with battlements. The mill existed in 1820.

ASH HALL, Ash Bank. Also on the A road. Built shortly after 1841 for Job Meigh, an earthenware manufacturer. Tudor with shaped gables. Symmetrical entrance side with a deep porch. Lower wing round the corner also symmetrical and also with shaped gables.

WEST BROMWICH

Tipton, *see* p. 282.
Wednesbury, *see* p. 298.
West Bromwich has at least a wide and long High Street to give it some identity, though the parish church and the best building are quite far away from the centre.

INNER WEST BROMWICH

CHRIST CHURCH, High Street. 1821–9 by *Goodwin*. High W tower with a prettily decorated portal (two busts). Three-light Perp window with iron tracery. Short chancel. Three galleries. Ribbed ceiling of low pitch.

ST MICHAEL (R.C.), High Street. 1876–7 by *Dunn & Hansom*. Steeple 1911. Red brick and small lancets.

GOOD SHEPHERD WITH ST JOHN, Lyttleton Street. 1967–8 by *John Madin*. Dark brick, a complex composition with a handsomely screened front garden.

The church belongs to the LYNG ESTATE, a good combination of high and low elements. It was designed by *A. Philip*, the Chief Borough Architect, and built in 1962–9.

TOWN HALL, High Street. 1874–5 by *Alexander & Henman*. Quite large, of brick, asymmetrical, Gothic – the motifs no longer of High Victorian assertiveness.

LIBRARY, next to the Town Hall. 1906–7 by *Stephen J. Holliday*. Brick and stone, with giant fluted Ionic columns and a one-bay pediment. Not large, but monumental.

(New TOWN HALL and LIBRARY in the HIGH STREET between New Street and Bull Street in the new SANDWELL SHOPPING CENTRE by the *John Madin Design Group*.)

FARLEY CLOCK TOWER, Carters Green. 1897 by *Edward Pincher*. Square, brick, with an openwork cupola. The style is called in the opening brochure 'the Gothic Renaissance style'.

MUSEUM (Oak House), Oak Road. A spectacular, if not large, timber-framed, gabled house of the C16. Closely set uprights, the main windows slightly projecting on brackets, upper overhang. The porch introduces ogee struts. The curious tower with two gables is no doubt later. Does it belong to the time in the late C16 and early C17 when a large part of the house was encased in brick? One end gable is stepped, the gables at the back are shaped. Also early C17 the staircase with flat pierced balusters. The handsome upper arrangements of the entrance hall belong to the restoration by *Wood & Kendrick*, 1898. – STOCKS displayed behind the house.

(HILL HOUSE, Dagger Lane. Though partly derelict at the time of writing, this has been identified by the VCH as a timber-framed building of the earlier C16 with brick additions of the C17–19.)

OUTER WEST BROMWICH

Clockwise, starting with the parish church, i.e. NE, and ending with N.

NORTH EAST

ALL SAINTS, All Saints Street. The W tower is C14 and C15. The medieval church lay to its E. In 1872 *Somers Clarke* made that space the S aisle of a new nave. The nave is long, the chancel short, the fenestration late C13, and the quality of the whole alas not high. – FONT. Large, octagonal, with shields in quatrefoils. – Architectural FRAGMENTS in the tower; Norman. – CHEST. Carved out of one tree trunk. – STAINED GLASS by *Powell* (designed by *Wooldridge*). The angels (chancel S) are the best. Also chancel N and also the W window. 1872–3. – MONUMENTS. Two alabaster effigies, an Elizabethan Lady and a Man of c.1650, now united on one tomb-chest. She is probably Anne Whorwood † 1599, he Field Whorwood † 1658.

S of the church is CHURCHFIELD SCHOOL, by *Richard Sheppard & Partners*, 1956–7. A large comprehensive school, but split up into houses, each for 180 children. Two houses form one building and have a common dining hall. The buildings are of prefabricated parts.

ANNUNCIATION, Yew Tree Estate, 2 m. NE of the parish church. 1956–8 by *Hickton, Madeley & Stanley Thomas Salt*.

MENZIES HIGH SCHOOL, Clarke's Lane, ½ m. W of the parish church. By *Richard Sheppard, Robson & Partners*, 1962–3. A number of separate oblong blocks. They are two 'houses', assembly hall, gymnasiums, and laboratories.

GROVE VALE SCHOOLS, Grove Vale, 1½ m. ENE of the parish church. By *H. T. Cadbury-Brown*, 1962–4. A group of irregularly shaped units. Brick and timber.

HALLAM HOSPITAL, Hallam Street. Started life as the WORKHOUSE in 1851. The building is of brick and Gothic.

The present gatehouse could belong to that date. Many additions.

MANOR HOUSE, Hall Green. The sensation of the discovery of the West Bromwich Manor House is still unforgotten. Here was a dreary, derelict old house on the point of being demolished. Then the local council began an investigation advised by the architect *W. Maurice Jones* of Worcester, and in 1953 the existence of the hitherto hidden medieval building was confirmed. Restoration was the decision. It was done enthusiastically by the architect *James A. Roberts* of Birmingham. He started in 1957, and in 1960 Ansell's Brewery took over the premises, adapting them for the use of a pub and restaurant. The result is the renovation of a C14 and C16 manor house more eloquent than most. The moat was dug out again and is filled with water. A timber-framed Elizabethan gatehouse receives the visitor. It has an overhang, closely set studs, and on the upper floor the familiar concave-sided lozenges. One enters a small courtyard and faces the doorway into the great hall. This dates from the early C14 (built for William de Marnham?) and has its fine roof reinstated. The supports are base crucks with shafts carrying capitals of typical early C14 mouldings. The hall also has its dais with a canopy of honour (cf. e.g. Rufford Old Hall in North Lancashire) and its screens passage. The screen is a spere truss (cf. Lancashire too). Two small ogee-headed doors lead to the service quarters. There are also two doors at the high-table end. Here is an ample rectangular (later) bay window as well. Two wings project to the courtyard. Both date from the C15. The r. (N) one has the solar, also with an open roof, and E of it the chapel with a five-light E window, the lights having ogee heads. On the W side (to the moat) the wings also project a little, and one has an ogee-headed doorway. SW of this wing is a separate range, which originally contained the kitchen.

SOUTH EAST

HOLY TRINITY, Trinity Street. 1840–1 by *J. W. Dawkes* of Cheltenham. Red brick. Lancet windows, short chancel, W tower with polygonal buttresses and pinnacles.

SANDWELL HALL. All that remains is the GATEWAY, now right in the motorway roundabout. A massive piece with perfectly plain entrance and exit arches, a tunnel-vault inside, and pediments. It could be by *William Smith*, as the staff of the

VCH has recently discovered that Smith rebuilt Sandwell Hall in 1703–c.1712.

WEST AND NORTH WEST

ST PETER, Whitehall Road, Greets Green. 1857–8 by *T. Johnson & Son* of Lichfield. Large, and better than the run of the Victorian mill. Cream-coloured stone. Features of c.1300. W tower, wide nave, arcades of octagonal piers with correct arches of c.1300.

ST MARK, St Mark's Road, Ocker Hill. 1849 by *Hamilton & Saunders*. Of dark blue bricks – which is unusual. Plate tracery; no tower.

NORTH

ST JAMES, Hill Top. 1839–41 by *Ebbles*. The façade is very odd, because c.1890 it was made asymmetrical by the building of a SW tower. As Ebbles's church had a façade of the Royal Chapel type, i.e. with two high pinnacles l. and r. of the large mid-window, there is a clash between the tower and the r. pinnacle. Inside all is clear. Wide nave, alas deprived of its galleries, and short low chancel. Lancet side windows.

WESTON

ST ANDREW. The church has one of the finest E.E. towers in the county, broad and sturdy, with broad clasping buttresses, single lancets below, and on the bell stage lancets richly shafted and framed by blank shafted lancets. The arch to the tower is wide and triple-chamfered, and the responds have capitals with crockets on big flat single leaves. All that indicates the beginning of the C13. The arcades and the chancel arch are a little later. The piers are quatrefoil, the arches moulded. But externally, apart from the tower and in spite of the arcades, all is Victorian: the N aisle by *Scott* 1860, the S aisle by *Butterfield* 1872. Butterfield also did the clerestory, and the mildly polychromatic geometrical decoration up on that level gives him away. For the chancel and the narrow chancel aisles with their curious piers we have no name and no date. Genuinely C13 seems to be the pointed-trefoiled arch now part of the S porch.* – FONT. Copied from old fragments.

---

* Mr John Burke suggests that the chancel windows ought to be mentioned. They are C14 or C15, but not *in situ*.

It has a broad top band of stylized stiff-leaf. – STAINED GLASS. The E window evidently by *Gibbs*, Butterfield's favourite. – BELLS. Two of *c*.1400; among the oldest in the county. – PLATE. Paten, probably of the C15, with the Hand of God; Set of 1824 by *John Bridge* of London.

ABBEYLANDS, opposite the church. Symmetrical Jacobean front, freer entrance side with an oriel window. By *G. G. Scott*, 1858.

WESTON HALL, ½ m. w. Monumental Jacobean stone house of three storeys plus the gables. There are four, the inner ones narrower and steeper. On the two main floors the windows have transoms. The porch is Victorian.

WESTON-UNDER-LIZARD

WESTON PARK. Weston Park is a large, square brick house, eleven by nine bays and three storeys high, its three ranges originally enclosing a courtyard open to the N. It was built by Sir Thomas and Lady Wilbraham in 1671, *Lady Wilbraham* being credited with the design. The S front is most characteristic of 1671. The l. and r. two bays have big broken segmental pediments, the middle bay is stone-faced. Doorway with garlands and some stress on the window over it. Top balustrade. The E side was made the entrance side in 1865 and given its porch. The pediment however is original. So Weston Park is an exceptionally early effort in the classical style. The W side is altered more drastically by the addition of the large canted dining-room bay window. In 1762 the estate passed on to the Bridgemans, later Earls of Bradford of the second creation.

The ORANGERY to the W, with its arched windows, is of 1865. The STABLES, dated 1688, are eleven bays long with a three-bay pediment and a pedimented doorway. They lie to the E and are linked with the house by a wing of 1865.

The entrance hall has on the r. a screen of two Roman Doric columns. The staircase has a spectacular wrought-iron railing of 1899. Fine chimneypiece with rams in the Tapestry Room. The former entrance hall, now Drawing Room, has two apses with attached Ionic columns, and that arrangement looks *c*.1770 or so. Tripartite arrangement of Corinthian columns in the Library, former Dining Room. The present Dining Room is of 1865, but has recently been remodelled.

N of the stables the FARM BUILDINGS. Round three sides

of a courtyard and including an immense brick barn, with angle towers. Described by Christopher Hussey as 'one of the noblest architectural products of the agricultural "revolution" worked by the great landowners of the late eighteenth century'.

Weston Park has a remarkable number of ornamental buildings in the park, the finest being the TEMPLE OF DIANA, by *James Paine*. It has an orangery front with three bays of glazed arcading, the columns carrying fluted capitals, and two narrow bays with niches l. and r. The ceiling inside has penetrations, an elliptical centre, and delicate plasterwork. Wall paintings by *G. B. I. Colombe*. Behind and attached lies a more solid structure with a central circular tea room, and a façade with a canted middle bay terminating in a dome. The side pieces there have Palladio's typical half-pediments. Adjoining the tea room is an octagonal music room.

Other structures in the grounds are the ROMAN BRIDGE by *Paine* with two erections like sentry-boxes, the SWISS COTTAGE beyond the bridge, with a wooden trellis veranda, the MAUSOLEUM of 1870, in a Beaux-Arts Grecian with a portico of two pairs of Tuscan columns, an OBELISK of moderate size, and a medievalizing Victorian square TOWER with a polygonal turret. There are also BOATHOUSES, and vases and urns in suitable places.

ST ANDREW. The church also was an enterprise of *Lady Wilbraham*, and adjoins the house on the NW. It was built in 1700–1. Only the E wall with a three-light C14 window over the W tower remained. It is unbuttressed and called Perp but looks post-Reformation. The church itself has keyed-in arched windows, pilasters between them, and a bolection frieze. In 1876–7 *Ewan Christian* added a family chapel and a vestry and made them Norman to go with the existing round arches. The coved wooden ceiling is also of these years. – (FONT. Designed by *Street*, who restored the church in 1869–70.*) – PULPIT of c.1701, beautifully carved, especially the tester. On the body of the pulpit compositions of corn-ears. – COMMUNION RAIL. Wrought iron, early C18. Very fine. Of course *Bakewell*'s name has been put forward. – Some NORMAN STONES in the tower S wall. – STAINED GLASS. The E window is by *Hardman*, 1876, using parts of original figures and ornament of the C14. – Also, in a N window, the ubiquitous Netherlandish panels of the C17. – In the family

---

* Information from Mr Joyce.

chapel one window by *Kempe*, c.1895. – PLATE. Chalice by *William Keatt*, 1693; Paten 1797 by *William Sumner*, London. – Many MONUMENTS, beginning with two cross-legged oaken Knights (chancel). The back tablets no doubt provided by Lady Wilbraham. – She also set up the several tablets to ancestors in ornamental surrounds. They are of c.1671 and were made by *William Wilson*. They are more traditional than the two back tablets referred to and also than her own memorial and its companion piece in the chancel E wall. She died in 1705. These two are large, standing pieces with open segmental pediments. – In the family chapel Countess of Bradford † 1897 by *J. Taylor*. Small recess with a white reclining figure and kneeling angels l. and r. – Earl of Bradford † 1825. Putto with torch. By *Hollins*. – Countess of Bradford † 1842 also by *Hollins*. Larger. She lies asleep, but angels carry her body up. Gunnis called it his finest work. – Earl of Bradford † 1800 by *Rossi*. With a seated girl. – More architectural tablets in the nave.

WESTWOOD HALL *see* LEEK

WETLEY ROCKS

ST JOHN. 1833–4, i.e. W tower, nave and aisles, thin octagonal piers, windows with Y-tracery. The chancel 1901 by *J. Beardmore* (GR).

WETLEY ABBEY. Called 'recently built' in 1836. It looks as if an older house was enlarged in a resolutely Gothic taste. Cruciform. All the detail is heavy – mouldings, crockets, and the like. The use of the pediment ill fits these Gothic features. To emphasize the reference to the name Abbey the cross and the mitre are used as decoration. One would like to know more about the house.

WETTON

ST MARGARET. The W tower is unbuttressed, and the enormous quoin stones suggest an early date. Perp top. The body of the church was rebuilt in 1820. Pointed windows with Y-tracery or (E) intersecting tracery. But, though the windows try to be Gothic, the quoins are classical.

THOR'S CAVE, ½ m. SW, overlooking the E bank of the river Manifold. This visually impressive cave has produced evidence of Iron Age and Romano-British occupation extending over several centuries.

LONG LOW CAIRNS, 1¼ m. SE. These two round cairns are unique in that they are linked by an apparently contemporary stone bank. The larger N cairn is still 75 ft in diameter and 8 ft high. It covered a massive, closed stone chamber containing thirteen inhumation burials and three leaf-shaped flint arrowheads. The site presumably belongs to the Late Neolithic period (*c.* 2000 B.C.).

At Borough Fields lay a ROMANO-BRITISH SETTLEMENT of some size, although no individual plans of buildings were recorded in the original excavation of 1845–64. The finds indicate occupation in the C3 and C4 at least.

WHEATON ASTON

ST MARY. 1857 by *Bidlake & Lovatt*, the chancel by *C. Lynam*, 1893. Nave, N aisle, NW turret with spire. Transeptal S extension. Late geometrical tracery. – STAINED GLASS. E window by *Kempe*.

PRIMITIVE METHODIST CHAPEL. 1856, and still basically Georgian. Front with a round-headed window, and, instead of a pediment, a big semicircular pedimental gable.

WHISTON

ST MILDRED. 1910 by *J. H. Beckett*. A very attractive little church. Nave and chancel in one, deep roof so that the low windows touch the eaves. The buttresses reach up higher than the eaves. Broad E window of five lights in a free Perp. Three pointed stone arches cross the interior space.

WHITEHOUGH see IPSTONES

WHITMORE

ST MARY AND ALL SAINTS. Timber-framed bell-turret, and one gable timber-framed. A length of S and a length of N walling are Norman. Nave and chancel in one. The features are of 1676 and/or 1880. – PLATE. Set of 1761 by *F.W.*; Paten of 1766 by *W.T.*

The great attraction of the church and of Whitmore is the setting, the houses of the village and the avenue which connects churchyard and Hall. They are separated only by a ha-ha.

WHITMORE HALL. A timber-framed house, now all encased, and with a s front towards the church of 1676. Nine bays, two storeys, of brick. The mid-window and the corresponding windows of bays two and eight are decorated. Top balustrade. The doorway is a paramount example of what Sir John Summerson calls Artisan Mannerism, i.e. the non-courtly style of 1650–60. The porch is of 1847, but the frieze of naval trophies inside it matches the style of the doorway perfectly. On the w side two blank ovals placed vertically; this is a sign of c. 1660–70 too. Mid Georgian entrance hall with two fine Corinthian columns.

The STABLES, probably of c.1620–30, are as rewarding as the house. The fenestration of the three-bay front is symmetrical, and inside the boxes are perfectly preserved, with rustic columns of wood and wooden arches with big globular pendants. The arches repeat against the back wall.

WHITTINGTON
Near Lichfield

ST GILES. The tower largely medieval, the spire no doubt later, the nave of brick and the ashlar bays embracing the tower of 1761. Long nave, windows with Y-tracery, chancel of 1881 (by *Ewan Christian*). – PULPIT. 1671,* with a tester. The stem is a twisted baluster. – STAINED GLASS. A chancel s window has four much restored C15 figures. – Smaller piece in a N window. – PLATE. Paten, 1697 by *Harry Green* of London; silver-gilt Chalice, 1737 by *George Smith* of London. – Many TABLETS.

WHITTINGTON HALL. Largely of 1891, e.g. the side with the tower, but on the garden side a C17 two-stage stone porch. Round entrance arch between columns, a mullioned and transomed window over. Also a genuine C17 garden gateway and two gatepiers dated 1673.

WHITTINGTON *see* KINVER

---

* I owe the date to the Rev. P. D. Brothwell, who also says that the pulpit was originally in Lichfield Cathedral.

WIGGINTON

St Leonard. 1777, the chancel by *Joyce* of Burton, 1861–2. Brick nave with three arched windows. Square turret supported inside impressively on two Tuscan columns. The N aisle with its two iron posts instead of an arcade is of 1830. The chancel is faced in crazy paving. – FONT. Victorian; very odd.

(Wigginton Lodge, 1¼ m. sw. Early C19. Two storeys, stuccoed, with canopied veranda. EH)

WIGHTWICK
3 m. w of Wolverhampton

Wightwick Manor. A *tour de force* of *Edward Ould* (of *Grayson & Ould*), built for Theodore Mander in two campaigns, 1887 and 1893. The result is an extensive house of great variety, eminently picturesque and externally quite conventional. The principal feature is timber-framing. The older part uses in addition much hard, bright Ruabon brick, and much tile-hanging, the newer essentially timber-framing only. On the long s, i.e. garden, side, the two stages can at once be distinguished, l. 1887, r. and round the corner to the E 1893.* The entrance group on the N is of course 1887.

The interior also has variety and picturesqueness. The sequence of rooms always surprises. It culminates in the Great Parlour, really Great Hall, of 1893, which goes through the two storeys.

It is difficult to say more than this without yielding to the temptation of doing what *The Buildings of England* must not do, i.e. to discuss a collection, not the fitments and fixtures of a house. For Sir Geoffrey and Lady Mander, inspired by W. G. Constable, decided in 1935 that the house and its contents, including work by *Morris* and by *Kempe*, should be preserved as a period piece, and the collection has since been augmented by much else of the Pre-Raphaelite and Morris schools. *Kempe* co-operated in the work both of 1887 and of 1893. By him the STAINED GLASS in the Entrance Hall, allegorical figures, dated 1888. Earlier still, and indeed remarkably early, i.e. of *c.*1875, the glass in the Drawing Room. In the bay window of the same room Kempe glass from

---

* Mr Hubbard says that only at Hill Bank in Cheshire was Ould so pure.

Kempe's own house, Old Place, Lindfield.* The imitation-Jacobean plaster ceiling is by *L. A. Shuffrey*. The chimneypiece is Italian, of the C16. The beautiful green and white tiles inside are by *de Morgan*, and other tiles by him are in other rooms.

The Entrance Hall has an irregular shape and links up by two arches with a large passage which held the staircase, until this was transferred to the later part of the house. Off the passage is the Library, once Dining Room. The *Morris* glass here and in other rooms and the many Morris wallpapers and the pieces of furniture were all brought in later, as were the carved cupboards which came from Swinburne's (i.e. Theodore Watts Dunton's) house, The Pines, Putney. Some *Morris* textiles, however, were bought for the house when it was built. Such are those in the Drawing Room (silk and wool) and the Honeysuckle Room (chintz).

The Great Parlour or Great Hall has as *Kempe*'s work the decoration of the panelled roof, the plaster frieze below, inspired by Hardwick Hall and deliberately naive, and the gesso decoration of the overmantel in the inglenook. The glass in the nine-light bay was again made for the house, i.e. is of 1893. The two brass chandeliers of traditional shape are by *W. A. S. Benson*. In the Billiard Room the charming tiles are very early *Morris*. The plaster ceilings here and in the Dining Room are again by *Shuffrey*, again imitation-Jacobean.

The GARDEN was planned by *Alfred Parsons*, but the terrace is an addition of *T. H. Mawson*. In it some fragments from the Houses of Parliament obtained after the bombing in the Second World War.

The LODGE and the BARN adjoining it are parts of the old Manor House of Wightwick. They date from the late C16 or early C17, but have been restored almost out of existence (by *Ould*). Only the brickwork of the barn is in order. Ould's windows are of red terracotta.

E of Wightwick Manor in MOUNT ROAD is THE MOUNT, the house of Charles Benjamin Mander, cousin of Theodore and Charles Benjamin's son, also partly by *Ould*, also the result of growth. It was built *c.* 1870 and enlarged in 1891 and 1908. Brick and stone dressings, asymmetrical, with a two-storeyed great hall and a two-storeyed entrance hall. Both have neo-Jacobean plaster ceilings. W of the Mount is WIGHTWICK

---

* More glass from Old Place in the Oak Room.

COURT, brick, big and Jacobean, with a tower. The lodge is in Bridgnorth Road.

CHRIST CHURCH, Church Road. *See* Outer Wolverhampton, p. 325.

WILLENHALL

3 m. W of Walsall

ST GILES, Walsall Street. 1866–7 by *W. D. Griffin*. With a NW tower projecting to the W. Geometrical tracery.

ST ANNE, Ann Street, Spring Bank. 1856–8 by *H. Jeavons*, an amateur. A curious exterior, as if the plan were two-naved. In fact it is nave and chancel and a wide N aisle; only the chancel is much narrower than the nave.

ST STEPHEN, Wolverhampton Street. 1853–4 by *Griffin*.

Willenhall's centre is the Market Place. But it is not really a centre.

There is just one valuable Georgian house: DALE HOUSE, at the N end of Bilston Street. Five bays and a free Adamish doorcase.

WILLOUGHBRIDGE see MUCKLESTONE

WILNECOTE*

HOLY TRINITY. 1821, of sooty stone. Five bays; no separate chancel. Tall windows with Y-tracery, the entry in the middle of the S side. Starved W turret. Wide nave. – PLATE. Chalice and Paten of 1636.

WILNECOTE HALL, ¼ m. SE of the church, S of Watling Street. Brick with stone dressings. Three bays divided by thin giant pilasters, each of them carrying a bit of a bulgy entablature. Steep centre pediment. Probably early C18.

WINDY GATES see MEERBROOK

WINSHILL see BURTON-ON-TRENT, p. 88

THE WODEHOUSE see WOMBOURNE

WOLSELEY BRIDGE see COLWICH

* Formerly in Warwickshire.

WOLSTANTON

ST MARGARET. The N steeple is Dec. The church is by *Ward & Son*, the chancel by *Salvin*. The date is 1859–60, the style E.E. to Dec. Ornate asymmetrical w front. – FONT. Very High Victorian. – MONUMENTS. Sir William Sneyd † 1571 and wife. Recumbent effigies. Tuscan columns and a segmental arch. Big strapwork on top. Against the tomb-chest, bolt upright, five sons and six daughters. – Cartouche for William Sneyd † 1689. – John Sneyd † 1710. Urn in an architectural surround with looped-up curtains. Two putti l. and r. Good quality.

Opposite the church the SCHOOL, 1871 by *Brooks*, an outstandingly original design, with the even rhythm of small two-light casement windows divided by a detached shaft with shaft-ring, and the master's house at the end of the falling lane more domestic. *Brooks* also made extensive additions to the PARSONAGE. Some tile-hanging and a half-hip, i.e. very up-to-the-minute.

ST ANDREW, Port Hill. 1886 by *A. R. Wood*. The s aisle 1897.

METHODIST CHURCH, High Street. 1894–5 by *Wood & Hutchings*. Brick and stone, in the characteristic free Perp of the Nonconformists about 1900.

METHODIST CHURCH, Bradwell Lane. 1966 by *Hulme & Upright*. Of engineering bricks with slit windows. Good. The Hall is of 1959 by *Hollins, Jones & Oldacre*.

(BRADWELL HALL FARM. Inside some wood-carving and a stucco overmantel.)

MORETON HOUSE, s of the parish church. Dated 1743. Brick, five bays and two and a half storeys. The first-floor windows segment-headed. Top parapet.

WOLVERHAMPTON

INTRODUCTION

Wolverhampton appears first in a charter of 895 and under its full name in 1078. The cross by the parish church is indeed Anglo-Saxon, and the church itself at least medieval. The trade of the town was originally wool, but became iron and tinplate in the C18. Lord Torrington, scathing as usual, called Wolverhampton (in 1792) 'large, black, swelling with commerce', the *Beauties of England and Wales* a generation later stressed the 'many handsome seats'. Both statements contain truth, but both are no longer the whole truth. Wolverhampton is no longer all that black, and many of the seats have disappeared. If a number of seats remain all the same, that is largely due to the fact that the town is now a County Borough including a number of formerly independent towns and villages. The population of the County Borough is 265,000.

For Bilston *see* p. 70, for Moseley Old Hall p. 206, for Wednesfield, p. 300, for Wightwick p. 310.

INNER WOLVERHAMPTON

The boundaries are the Inner Ring Road, E to the Station, and roughly S, back to the Ring Road.

CHURCHES

ST PETER. The proud parish church of a prosperous town, prosperous in the Middle Ages when the church was collegiate, prosperous when all was over-restored in 1852–65 (by *Ewan Christian*). From 1479 to 1846 the church was a Royal Peculiar united with Windsor. Red sandstone with a crossing tower. Well placed close to, but above, the town centre, both the commercial and the administrative. The long aisleless chancel and the polygonal apse are entirely by *Christian*, in the style of the late C13. It replaced a chancel of 1682–4. The crossing is of the late C13, see the bases and capitals of the responds and the triple-chamfered arches. Again of that date or a little later the s transept, see the fine five-light E window and the PISCINA in the S wall. The N transept is Late Perp; so is the crossing tower itself. The former has bold panelling inside and an unusual arch to the N aisle, with continuous mouldings, the latter panelling outside, panelled battlements, and pinnacles. In the S transept wall are three Perp upper two-light windows, straight-headed with transoms. They continue identical along the nave clerestory, two to the bay. There are five bays. The nave was rebuilt *c.*1450–80. The arcades have octagonal piers. The arch from s aisle to s transept goes with them. Two-storeyed s porch, largely Victorian, the upper floor entirely, the lower only gone over. W front by *Christian*.

FURNISHINGS. PULPIT. Perp, of stone, panelled. Remains of colour. Stone staircase with, at its foot, a large seated lion. – LECTERN. Said to come from Halesowen Abbey. – FONT. Perp, stone, with statuettes and interesting bowl dated 1660. It has stylized motifs – leaf, a bell, a sun. – SCREEN. In the s

CHURCHES 315

transept Perp screen, inspired by the burnt screen of Tettenhall church. – STALLS. Perp, twelve from Lilleshall Abbey, taken to Wolverhampton in 1546. – WEST GALLERY. 1610. – PAINTING. Virgin and standing donors, now S transept. Large, by *Liefrinck*. – Also a painted record of benefaction to a charity school. It must be later than 1773 and includes two charity children. – STAINED GLASS. In the chancel side windows small medallions etc., Netherlandish and German. – The W window is of 1854. – S aisle windows by *Kempe*. – By *Powell* the window by the font and the westernmost N aisle window. – PLATE. Chalice, 1697 by *Winans* of London; Chalice, 1702 by *Matthew Cooper* of London (originally at Cottam); two Sets, 1722 by *William Lukin* of London; Almsdish, 1822 by *Garrard* of London. – MONUMENTS. John Leveson † 1575 (S transept). Alabaster couple on an alabaster tomb-chest with small figurines and twisted colonnettes. – Thomas Lane † 1585 (N transept). Alabaster couple on an alabaster tomb-chest with small figures and some minimum Renaissance motifs. – Admiral Sir Richard Leveson † 1605, but made c.1634 (S transept). By *Le Sueur*, who was promised £300 for the monument. Bronze. All that remains is the standing effigy and two loose cherubs. – Col. John Lane † 1667 (N transept). Attributed to *Jasper Latham*. Standing wall-monument, black and buff; on the base a large relief of trophies. The top is an open scrolly pediment. – South African War Memorial, 1902 (N aisle). Interesting in that historicism had, by then, reached the imitation of late C17 cartouches.

Outside the church the famous Anglo-Saxon WOLVERHAMPTON CROSS, probably of the mid C9. Mighty round shaft, 14 ft high. The decoration is in zones, the lowest continued downward in pendant triangles. The rather wild acanthus ornament betrays Carolingian inspiration. – WAR MEMORIAL. By *C. T. Armstrong*, 1922.

ST GEORGE, Bilston Road. 1828–30 by *James Morgan*, a Commissioners' church. It cost £10,268. Classical, of ashlar, with an embraced W steeple. Grand portal with coupled Tuscan demi-columns. Also aisle W entrances. Arched windows, but the E window Venetian. The interior has its galleries, but is much changed. Only the W half is still as in 1830. – SCREEN. 1897 by *F. T. Beck*. – REREDOS. 1906–7.

ST JOHN, St John's Square. 1758–76 by *William Baker*, or the builder *Roger Eykyn*. Ashlar. Fine W tower, the bell stage octagonal and crowned by a spire. Portal with intermittently blocked columns. The side windows in two tiers, all in Gibbs surrounds. At the E end is a blank Venetian window. Interior with three galleries on short square pillars carrying upper columns. The aisles are groin-vaulted, the nave has a segmental tunnel-vault. Short chancel. – The REREDOS and chancel PANELLING are of 1899. – ORGAN. By *Renatus Harris*, from the Temple Church in London; *c*.1682. – PAINTING. Deposition by *Joseph Barney*, late C18. – PLATE. Set by *Whipham & Wright*, 1760. – Good GATEPIERS to the precinct.

ST MARY AND ST JOHN (R.C.), Snow Hill. 1851–5 by *Charles Hansom*, enlarged E end by the same 1879–80. Brick, towerless. Geometrical tracery. Nave and aisles, transepts, polygonal apse. – STAINED GLASS. In the apse probably by *Hardman*.

ST PATRICK (R.C.), Westbury Street. 1866–7 by *E. W. Pugin*. Towerless, of brick. Style of *c*.1300. Nave and aisles, polygonal apse. Typical E. W. Pugin arcade capitals.

ST PETER AND ST PAUL (R.C.), North Street, behind and attached to Giffard House (*see* p. 319). One of the finest churches of Wolverhampton. 1825–7 by *Joseph Ireland*, but the domed altar space and the beautiful domed S transept with four fluted Ionic corner columns 1901 by *Edward Goldie*. The nave has no aisles. High up lunette windows with penetrations into the tunnel-vault. Stuccoed exterior with pilaster pairs in accentuated places. – PAINTING. Christ appearing to Thomas. By *Barney*, late C18.

HOUSE OF MERCY (R.C.), St John's Square. A Georgian corner house (*see* p. 318), but in George Street an ashlared Gothic brick range and behind an added aisleless chapel with a polygonal apse. Both by *E. W. Pugin*, 1860.

QUEEN STREET CONGREGATIONAL CHURCH. 1863–6 by *G. Bidlake*. Grand, of ashlar, with a corner steeple. Free Italian, but in the long side to Princess Street with its two tiers of triple arched windows remarkably independent.*

METHODIST CHAPEL, Darlington Street. 1900–1 by *Arthur Marshall*. A free English Early Georgian but with a hemispherical copper dome and two façade turrets. A very uncommon kind of design for the purpose.

---

* The church has been pulled down – Wolverhampton's loss.

PUBLIC BUILDINGS

TOWN HALL, Market Square. 1869–71 by *E. Bates*. Large, symmetrical, of fifteen bays, with French roofs. – INSIGNIA. Silver-gilt Mace, given to St Mawes in Cornwall in 1822.

CIVIC HALL, next to the former. By *Lyons & Israel*, 1936–8. With an eight-column loggia, the columns very thin and octagonal, inspired by Tengbom's Stockholm Concert Hall of 1920–6.

COUNTY COURT, Queen Street. *See* p. 319.

STATION. 1964–7 by *R. L. Moorcroft* (Architect to the Midland Region). Also, at the corner of Railway Street and Horseley Fields the original station ticket-office of 1849. Grey brick, high, simply Italianate, symmetrical, with orders of columns and two square turrets.

COLLEGE OF TECHNOLOGY, N of St Peter. 1926 by *P. Woodcock*, the then County Architect. Additions of 1933, and the forties and sixties. Large, symmetrical, brick, with a stone frontispiece. (In the Board Room PANELLING from the late C17 Deanery of St Peter which was on this site.)

POLYTECHNIC DEPARTMENT OF ART AND DESIGN, in the Ring Road, N of St Peter. By *Diamond, Redfern & Partners*, 1968–9. Concrete. A block of eight storeys, quite straightforward. The window surrounds are canted in the four corners.

LIBRARY, Garrick Street and Bilston Street. By *E. T. Hare*, 1900–2. A delightful little building of brick and yellow terracotta with an angle entrance loggia and a cupola or turret.

MARKET HALL, N of St Peter. 1902–3 by *J. W. Bradley*, the then Borough Engineer. Brick and yellow terracotta. A pretty building.

RETAIL MARKET, Salop Street and School Street. By *A. G. E. Chapman*, Deputy Borough Architect. Recent. Partly covered, partly open-air. Also a restaurant and an underground car park.

MUSEUM AND ART GALLERY, Lichfield Street and St Peter's Close. 1883–5 by *Chatwin* of Birmingham. Original, and functional. Italianate, with several frontispieces with columns, the principal holding the porch of pairs of pink granite columns. The characteristic motif is that only the ground floor has windows. The galleries above have skylights, and so the walls allow for long relief panels illustrative of the purpose of the building. They are by *Boulton* of Cheltenham.

PERAMBULATION

The centre of Wolverhampton is too intricate for easy perambulating, and the streets contain too little of significance to form into a consecutive whole. So an alphabetical list is preferred. Those who require guidance for a true perambulation can go as follows: from the Station Lichfield Street to Queen Square, then N (Lich Gates), W (Darlington Street), and off N for North Street, and N farther W again for Waterloo Road. Again from Queen Square S Victoria Street and SW Dudley Road with detours. E through King Street, farther S, E through Queen Street, and finally S (Market Street), Bilston Street and Garrick Street.

BILSTON STREET. The THEATRE ROYAL (now Bingo) was built *c*.1879. 'Jolly' is the word.

DUDLEY STREET. LLOYDS BANK is of 1878, but was then only half its present size. It is of three and a half storeys, Italianate, sparing in motifs and of high quality.

GARRICK STREET. The WULFRUN SHOPPING CENTRE, by *Bernard Engle & Partners*, is a southern continuation of the Mander Centre (*see* Queen Square). The centre is a circular piazza, with façades of vertical fins above the shops. The centre faces to the S on Cleveland Street.

GEORGE STREET. It leads straight to the E end of St John and has late C18 brick terraces with nice doorways on both sides. The N corner to St John's Square (House of Mercy) is a little more ambitious (cf. p. 316). The doorway with columns is in the square.

KING STREET. Minor Georgian houses.

LICHFIELD STREET. From the Station W. First the GRAND THEATRE, 1893–4 by *C. J. Phipps*, brick, with a five-bay upper loggia of arcading. The interior is quite splendid. Then at the corner of Princess Square the ROYAL LONDON MUTUAL INSURANCE, 1900–2 by *Essex, Nicol & Goodman*, ashlar, English Baroque, with cupola. After that the Museum and then the large and varied Gothic BARCLAYS BANK, by *Thomas Henry Fleeming*, *c*.1876 and later.

LICH GATES. From Queen Square to St Peter. An eight-bay brick house, with rusticated pilasters. Dated 1726. Spoiled by the shop-front.

NORTH STREET. With the enlargement of the Market Square North Street has lost its sense and the two only important houses, two of the best in Wolverhampton, stand lonely and moreover grotesquely divided one from the other by the Inner Ring Road. First GIFFARD HOUSE, dated 1728 and very characteristically Early Georgian. Five bays and two and a half storeys. Brick, with all windows segment-headed. Good iron gates and excellent staircase with three thin twisted balusters to each tread. In the upper reaches intricate stair provisions. The Catholic church is built right into the house.

Then the MOLINEUX HOTEL. The façade to the Ring Road is of c.1740-50. Five bays, three storeys, characteristic ensemble. Shortly after, a new front was made at the back and an extension built to the N. This has two Venetian windows and they are sumptuously appointed, belonging to a room with a Rococo plaster ceiling and also plaster wall panels. The staircase belongs to the earlier date. It has three thin twisted balusters to the tread. A Georgian s wing and a Victorian turret complete the loose composition.

QUEEN SQUARE. For Barclays Bank see Lichfield Street. In the square equestrian STATUE of Prince Albert, 1866 by *T. Thorneycroft*. In the square also an entry to the MANDER CENTRE, 1968-70 by *James Roberts*. Shops are on two levels. The vertical accent is Mander House of ten storeys; quite simple. The centre also borders on Victoria Street and links up with the Wulfrun Centre (see Garrick Street).

QUEEN STREET. The best street of Wolverhampton. Watch the s side. From the station first the former MECHANICS' INSTITUTE and ATHENAEUM (Army Recruiting Centre), stuccoed, of five bays, with two entrances and a raised centre. It was built in 1835. Then Nos. 44-45, brick, with doorcases with broken pediments on columns. After that No. 46, the former DISPENSARY, built in 1826. Seven bays, stuccoed, with upper Greek Doric demi-columns. No pediment. Nos. 47-49 are like Nos. 44-45. The COUNTY COURT dates from 1813 and was given its upper floor in 1829 by *Vulliamy*. It was built as a Library and Assembly Room. It is of seven bays, stuccoed, and has two Tuscan porches. In the centre a two-storeyed pedimented portico, Tuscan below, unfluted Ionic above. Finally No. 56 is again like Nos. 44-45.

VICTORIA STREET. At the corner of St John's Street the only worthwhile timber-framed house of inner Wolverhampton. The date is C15 or early C16. Typical closely set verticals.

WATERLOO ROAD. On both sides still some stuccoed terraces of c.1840-50.

OUTER WOLVERHAMPTON

Only very few of the outer districts and areas of Wolverhampton have a character of their own. Therefore only Bilston and Wednesfield are treated separately, see p. 70 and p. 300 respectively. The rest is arranged by directions, clockwise – with one more exception: Wightwick Manor, which for other reasons is taken on its own – see p. 310.

NORTH

CHRIST CHURCH, Waterloo Road. 1867 by *E. Banks*. Big rock-faced, red sandstone. The tower not built. The style is c.1300. Good chancel. – PAINTINGS on the chancel walls 1903 by *J. Edie Read* and *Wyndham Hughes*. – MONUMENT Pretty repoussé Arts and Crafts panel to Edward Glover † 1894 (chancel arch).

ST MARY, Bushbury. Ashlar, with a W tower. Medieval but over-restored. Much of the masonry is in order, but nearly all features are Victorian. The Perp tower W window is to be trusted, and probably the chancel side windows with cusped intersected tracery. Anyway, the chancel SEDILIA with ogee heads and the EASTER SEPULCHRE niche are original Dec. The nave arcades are of five bays with octagonal piers and double-chamfered arches. – FONT. Late Norman, of drum shape, but the large palmettes alternatingly upright and reversed and the leaves of the base look early C16. – STAINED GLASS. Two small early C14 figures in a chancel S window. – E window by *Charles Winston* (TK). Is it the present one? – PLATE. Coffin Paten of the C14; Elizabethan Chalice; Paten by *Joseph Stokes* of London, 1701; Flagon by *John Le Sage* of London, 1740. – MONUMENTS. In the Easter Sepulchre defaced effigy of a Priest; C14. – Many tablets, especially John Goughe † 1665. – Also incised slabs (chancel, SE corner) badly preserved. – (In the churchyard* part of a circular Saxon CROSS.)

BUSHBURY HALL is close to the church, the five-bay Georgian type, rendered. Also close to the church (Sandy Lane) new SWIMMING BATH, by *A. Chapman*, the Borough Architect 1964–6.

(CROWN BUILDINGS, Birch Street. 1970–2 by *Norman & Dawbarn*.)

---

* So Mr Rix communicated to me.

RACECOURSE, Dunstall. The date of the two old grandstands of identical design seems unrecorded. They are of brick and have at their backs two tiers of arched windows and between the windows pilaster strips.

FALLINGS PARK is an early garden suburb. It covers quite a large area and was laid out by *Thomas Adams, Pepler & Blow* in 1907. The plan is formal, with a central circle surrounded by an almond shape, two ovals N and S of it, and radiating streets. It looks ornamental on paper but is not noticed visually as one walks around. Moreover, the architecture is not at all enterprising. Small public buildings face the central circle.

Adjoining is OLD FALLINGS HALL, now ST CHAD'S COLLEGE. It was the owner of this house who started the garden suburb. The house is early C18, of five bays and two storeys, with a hipped roof and angle pilasters with lush Corinthian capitals. The mid-window has garlands and, at the foot, volutes. Panelled hall, the staircase with three quite substantial twisted balusters to the tread.

NORTH EAST

For WEDNESFIELD see p. 300.

ST BARNABAS, Wednesfield Road. 1892–3 by *T. H. Fleeming*. Brick, towerless, with lancet windows.

Near by in WEDNESFIELD ROAD is some of the best recent HOUSING. It is of 1963 etc. by *A. Chapman*. One large group at HEATH TOWN (Woden Road to Tudor Road and Grosvenor Street to Deans Road), the other at NEW CROSS. High white slabs, lower ranges plum brick. Pedestrian streets at upper levels.

ST STEPHEN, Hilton Street. 1907–9 by *F. T. Beck*. Brick and red terracotta. No tower. Free Gothic features, e.g. an interesting clerestory. Octagonal piers carrying giant arches which include the clerestory. The arcade arches are segmental and of brick exposed. No separate chancel.

HOLY TRINITY, Church Street, Heath Town. By *E. Banks*, 1850–2. Large, of ashlar, Dec details.

NEW CROSS HOSPITAL, Wednesfield Road. Started life in 1903 as a WORKHOUSE. Several of the original buildings are still used. They are by *Arthur Marshall*. Good recent buildings by *George, Trew, Dunn*. Also the POSTGRADUATE MEDICAL SCHOOL by *Mason & Richards*, two-storeyed, irregularly canted. When completed the hospital will have 2250 beds.

EAST

(EAST PARK. 1895–6 by *Thomas H. Mawson*. At the W end an ENTRANCE LODGE by Mawson's partner *Dan Gibson*, though not up to the standard of his Lake District houses. There is a central avenue and balustraded terrace, but plans for a bandstand etc. were not executed. The E end is informal and closely planted. CLOCK TOWER dated 1896. EH)

SOUTH EAST

For BILSTON *see* p. 70.

ALL SAINTS, Steelhouse Lane. 1877–9 by *T. T. Smith & G. F. Roper*, the chancel by *F. T. Beck*, 1892–3. – (REREDOS by *Sir Charles Nicholson*; PAINTINGS on either side by *A. K. Nicholson*.)

ST MARTIN, King Street, Bradley. 1866–8 by *Bidlake*. An impressive building with a high SE steeple, the spire with exceptionally high broaches, and with a high, steep nave roof. The windows have geometrical tracery. Wide nave with round piers with Early French Gothic capitals. The E bay is treated transeptally outside. Short polygonal chancel. – STAINED GLASS. The E windows in beautiful deep colours are by *Gardner* of St Helens (TK).

ST MARTIN, Dixon Street, Ettingshall. By *Lavender & Twentyman*, 1938–9. Brick, impressively blocky. Broad W tower, low blocks l. and r. of it. Nave with long, round-arched windows. Low passage aisles. The arcade piers without capitals. 1939 is just a little late for all this; if it were of 1933, it would be remarkable – at least in England. The St Martin against the tower is by *Donald Potter*.

SOUTH

ST LUKE, Upper Villiers Street. 1860–1 by *G. T. Robinson* of Leamington. He evidently could be what Goodhart-Rendel called a rogue architect. The church is furiously unruly. Red brick with yellow and black brick. SW steeple with a highly fanciful spire. Windows with plate tracery. But the clerestory windows are spherical triangles filled with roundels. Polygonal chancel. Inside, the piers are of iron, thin and doubled –

ROYAL WOLVERHAMPTON SCHOOL, Penn Road. The former Royal Orphanage. 1853 etc. by *Joseph Manning*, the wings added in 1863, the Headmaster's House in 1885. The centre is a long, symmetrical brick and stone range with shaped gables and a tower in the middle. The chapel is of 1894–5 by *Beck* (and has *Kempe* stained glass). Additions early C20.

longitudinally, not transversely. Who in the name of reason would do that?

SOUTH WEST

ST BARTHOLOMEW, Church Hill and Vicarage Road, Upper Penn. A *mixtum compositum*, including a blocked N window which may just be Norman, two bays of the N arcade which are C13 (octagonal piers) and the bays further w which are Perp, a charming brick w tower of 1765* with such typical Gothick details as ogee gables and quatrefoils, the brick NW annexe dated 1826, the w half of the s side with lancet windows, which is of 1845 (by *W. Evans*), and the whole ashlar-faced E end in the style of 1300 which is of 1871–2 by *Paley* of Lancaster, whose brother was the incumbent then. – FONT. Perp, octagonal, with panelled base and panelled short stem. – PLATE. Set of 1796 by *W. Sutton* of London. – MONUMENT. John Marsh, 1802 by *Flaxman*. High and slender tablet with a standing mourning woman beneath the profile medallion of the deceased. – Mrs Bradley † 1817. By *J. Stephens*. Kneeling woman with an anchor. – In the churchyard circular base and part of the circular shaft of a Saxon CROSS (cf. St Peter, p. 315).

PENN HALL,‡ w of the church in Vicarage Road. From the outside the house now appears completely of the early C18, but internal evidence shows a C17 house encased within later walls. There is indeed a largely unaltered C17 wing to the r. of the main block, simple, of two storeys, brick, which was clearly used as a servants' wing in the C18 and may always have been such. The main house has a s front six bays wide with its entrance in the fifth bay from the l. Here there is a round-headed doorway under a broken segmental pediment surmounted by an Art Nouveau sundial. The bay containing the entrance projects from the façade and has a triangular pediment above with a cartouche of arms. The garden front

---

* The Rev. A. R. Gaskell corrects: the tower is C15, encased in brick in 1765.

‡ The following description is by Andor Gomme.

(w) is more orthodox – seven bays, with a central doorway with triangular pediment. Rainwater heads are dated 1787, a date which may apply to alterations including an oriel window on the N side. The house is irregular inside, suggesting an original L-shape now blocked into a square. There is some rather crude C17 plasterwork in the hall and (more interesting) in one first-floor room (including figures in the corners of the coving), which also has C17 panelling. Otherwise the interior is all C18 and later. Of note are: the staircase, with twisted balusters on a continuous string and top lighting with a circular light surrounded by heavy plaster carving of fruit and flowers – of a late C17 type, yet no doubt like the staircase and the house of c.1720–30. The dining room has more heavy fruit and flower decoration of the same type as that on the staircase ceiling. It has a mid C18 fireplace and overdoors. In fact *Baker* worked for the owner of Penn Hall between 1748 and 1758. There are a number of unusual doors upstairs, consisting of one very large panel over four small ones. – BARN, dated 1779, with ogee blank arches. – Two SUMMER HOUSES, one pedimented, early C18, the other octagonal, early C19 Gothick, in ruins.

ST CHAD, Owen Street. 1907–8 by *F. T. Beck*. Brick and red terracotta. No tower. Free Gothic treatment.

ST MICHAEL (R.C.), Coalway Road, Bradmore. 1965–8 by *Desmond Williams*. A spacious circular body of dark brick, with twin slit windows and raised light shafts with monopitch roof. They throw light into the church, whose ceiling otherwise is hidden by a suspended, folded canopy with a low dome. The interior, though circular, has semicircular seating. The tower is a largely detached object. – Abstract bronze REREDOS by *Robert Brumby*, 1968.

CEMETERY, Jeffcock Road. 1847–51. (Near the S end the MONUMENT to G. B. Thorneycroft, 1853, a cast-iron obelisk on a circular base surrounded by weeping cherubs.)

WEST AND NORTH WEST

For WIGHTWICK *see* p. 310.

ST ANDREW, Coleman Street. 1965–7 by *Twentyman, Percy & Partners*. Blocky, of brick, and convincing. – (STAINED GLASS. The W window by *John Piper*, executed by *Patrick Reyntiens*.)

CHRIST CHURCH, Church Road, Tettenhall. 1865–6 by

Bateman & Corser. Rock-faced with cross-gables, a polygonal apse, and no tower. Geometrical tracery. Wide nave. – Some STAINED GLASS by *Kempe*.

ST JUDE, Tettenhall Road. 1867–9 by *Bidlake*. Rock-faced, with a SW steeple and geometrical tracery.

ST MARK, Chapel Ash, really inner Wolverhampton, if it were not for the Ring Road. 1848–9 by *C. W. Orford*. A Commissioners' church. It cost £4,850. W steeple with low broaches. Nave and aisles. Lancet windows. Polygonal apse. Thin piers, quatrefoil and octagonal alternatingly. Steep timber roof.

ST MICHAEL, Church Road, Tettenhall. The Tettenhall parish church. This was a major medieval church, but it was almost totally destroyed by fire in 1950. Of what remained the W tower is Perp, the vaulted S porch by *A. E. Street* of 1882–3. The church was rebuilt by *Bernard Miller*, and it needed a good deal of courage to design these cross-gabled aisle windows traceried throughout in totally unmedieval forms. They are halfway between Lethaby and Mr Pace. The E window, while also non-period, is not quite so daring. But the arcades and the cross-gabled aisles are. The piers are round and excessively short and have leaf capitals again not sanctioned by any style of the past, and the aisle roof is odd too. – FONT. Drum-shaped and decorated with mosaic. By *G. Mayer Marton*.

UKRAINIAN (former WELSH PRESBYTERIAN) CHURCH, Bath Road. 1892–3. Red brick. Nave and chancel in one; apse. Small lancets; no tower.

TECHNICAL TEACHERS' COLLEGE, Compton Road. By *Twentyman, Percy & Partners*, 1962–9. Spacious, pleasant, and without any need for a vertical accent.

WULFRUN COLLEGE OF FURTHER EDUCATION, Clark Road. By *A. G. E. Chapman*, the Borough Architect, 1959–67. A five-storey curtain-wall block and an extension with large prefabricated panels.

UPLANDS JUNIOR SCHOOL, Finchfield Hill. 1969–70; by *Chapman* too.

GRAMMAR SCHOOL, Compton Road. 1875 by *Giles & Gough*. Brick; Early Tudor style, with a central gatehouse, the hall of eight bays to the l., a shorter wing to the r. Behind a big building *à la* William and Mary. This houses the library. It is by the then County Education Committee Architect, *G. C. Lowbridge*, and dates from 1930.

EYE INFIRMARY, Compton Road. 1887–8 by *T. H. Fleeming*. Elizabethan with a mid-tower.

(WEST PARK. 1879–81 by *R. H. Vertegans*. An effective and largely informal layout with a lake. Original GATES and RAILINGS remain. CLOCK TOWER, 1883, and a later CONSERVATORY by *Dan Gibson*. – STATUE of Charles Pelham Villiers, 1878 by *Theed*. EH)

COMPTON HALL dates from *c.*1840–50, rendered, modest in size, and still Latest Classical in its conventions. *William Morris* designed the last of his wallpapers for this house and called it Compton.

There are two areas of decided character in this part of Wolverhampton: Wightwick and Tettenhall. Wightwick (including Mount Road) for reasons of Wightwick Manor has an entry of its own (*see* p. 310); for Tettenhall the area is Wood Road and to the E, to the church.

In Wood Road is TETTENHALL TOWERS, large, stuccoed, and rather dull, Late Georgian, and in 1866 altered and endowed with the two polygonal towers. They still have Latest Classical details. Originally they ended in balustrades, as the lodge still does. Tettenhall Towers is now part of TETTENHALL COLLEGE. The main buildings of this are in College Row, brick, Gothic, by *Bidlake*, 1865. Again further E ROCK HOUSE, Old Hill, a five-bay brick house with a pedimented doorway with Gothic surround. To the E of this the handsome UPPER GREEN.

Finally, to return into the centre, a Late Georgian terrace, Nos. 24 and 26–32 TETTENHALL ROAD. Pedimented doorcases.

WOMBOURNE

ST BENEDICT BISCOP.* The W tower C14–15, red below but the spire grey. It has attached pinnacles. Most of the body of the church is by *Street*, 1862–7. Typically decorated S porch and S aisle E window. The tracery of the aisle windows differs N from S. – FONT, PULPIT, STALLS, low SCREEN, etc., by *Street*. – SCULPTURE. Excellent small Italian early C16 relief. – STAINED GLASS. Much *Kempe*, in the chancel *Clayton & Bell* (P. Joyce). – Also by them S aisle E, 1881 (P. Joyce). – PLATE. Chalice and Paten, 1553 (Oman: *c.*1570); repoussé

---

* A unique dedication in England, says the Rev. J. D. D. Porter.

Dish, Portuguese (?), c.1606; Chalice, Paten, Bread Plate, by *P.Y.*, 1637; silver-gilt Set by *Henry Nutting*, London, 1812. – MONUMENT. Richard Bayley Marsh, 1820 by *Chantrey*. Large tablet with a seated woman by an urn. Profile medallion on the pedestal.

THE WODEHOUSE, ¼ m. NE. An interesting house, of which one would like to know more. Jacobean-looking façade on the E pattern, the wings with fanciful shaped gables. More such gables in a less formal arrangement round the corner. The r. projecting wing is continued by a CHAPEL, and this was decorated by *C. R. Ashbee*, c.1896–8. By *Ashbee* also the sundial on the porch, the gables, the parapet with inscription, the wrought-iron weather-vanes, and the former Billiard Room in the NE corner (timber-framed). Additions to the E front 1912 by *H. E. Lavender*.* – Good STABLES, brick, Georgian, with central pediment and cupola.

LLOYD HOUSE, 1 m. NE. A fine late C18 house of ashlar, formerly larger than it is now. Façade of nine bays, the centre a bow with two detached unfluted Ionic giant columns. The bow belongs to the former entrance hall, and an apsed brick wall corresponds to it.

THE BRATCH, ¾ m. NW. A canal lock and octagonal lock-keeper's office or look-out. The canal is the Staffordshire and Worcestershire. Opposite, the WATERWORKS, dated 1895, red brick, with a kind of keep, sporting tourelles.

WOOD EATON HALL *see* CHURCH EATON

WOODLANE

ST FRANCIS DE SALES (R.C.). 1795, enlarged 1834. Built on to the three-bay Presbytery. Brick, small, with transepts, a short chancel, obelisk pinnacles, Y tracery. Is the E window with its elaborate, historically totally incorrect tracery of 1834?

WOOTTON LODGE

Lodge is French *loge*, and the *loge* in a theatre is English box. We speak of a shooting box, and that is what lodge (among other things) meant. Another name is standing, and German *Stand* is where you watch stag-hunts. Such standings, and

---

* I owe all these details to Alan Crawford.

often lodges as well, are in elevated, exposed positions. So is Wootton Lodge; only it is far too monumental to be described in such utilitarian terms.

It was built by Sir Richard Fleetwood before 1611 for heraldic and after 1580 for stylistic reasons. It is a compact building of calm perfection – a basement for kitchen and services, an elevated ground floor, and two upper half-floors. Windows are large and even, but walls are not reduced to the extent they are at Hardwick. They are of four lights and have one transom on the ground floor, two on the upper floors. The façade is simple in plan: five bays only, but wide bays. The centre bay is a rectangular projection with the portal set in. This has coupled fluted Ionic columns and coupled obelisks on top of them. The end bays are canted projections of two plus three plus two lights set some distance away from the angles. The façade is topped by a balustrade. Round the corners, again some distance in, is on each side an ample bow window of three plus three lights. After that the Elizabethan or Jacobean work ceases. The house was badly damaged in the Civil War, no doubt in these back quarters. Inside little of old work survives – one subsidiary staircase and one room with Queen Anne panelling – but recently some Early Victorian Tudor-Gothic items worth noting have been imported: the (re-arranged) staircase and some chimneypieces from Osmaston Manor in Derbyshire (1846–9 by *Stevens*).*

Wootton Lodge is one of a group of houses by *Robert Smythson* or close to him in style. Characteristic features are half-basements, 'more window than wall', and the relentless grid of mullions and transoms. For these qualities one ought to compare with Worksop (no longer extant), Wollaton, and Hardwick of the early eighties, 1580–8, and 1590–7 respectively. For high compactness the nearest parallels are Barlborough in Derbyshire of 1584–5, Heath Hall in the West Riding of 1585, and Gawthorpe in Lancashire of c.1600–5. Finally for bow windows Burton Agnes in the East Riding of 1601–10 is a good example, and, moreover, Burton Agnes was built by a cousin of Sir Richard Fleetwood.

At the back of the house are a formal pool and a summer house with a pyramid roof. They are of about 1700. There is also some recent extension – not as happy as the equally recent large-scale landscaping. This, done by the new owner,

---

* There are also three Early Victorian statues from Alton Towers.

Mr Bamford, is prodigious. He manufactures excavators (at Rocester; *see* p. 225) and demonstrates here (as at Rocester) to what good use his excavators can be put. He has created a lake and terraces and rockeries of large boulders. His scale goes with the self-confidence of the mansion.

WORDSLEY

8080

3½ m. SW of Dudley

HOLY TRINITY, High Street. 1829–30 by *Lewis Vulliamy*, but the E window in the short chancel is of 1857. Tall piers, clerestory, flat ceiling, galleries. The side windows of two lights, long, with tracery of *c*.1300. – REREDOS. Rich Victorian Gothic; 1891. – PLATE. Set of 1831 by *Clowes & Co.* of Birmingham.

SCHOOL, by the church. 1836. Also by *Vulliamy*.* Brick, with stepped end-gables. Six-bay front with mid-gable and two dormers.

In STREAM ROAD a glass-making brick cone to remind one that here is the centre of the English glass trade – Stourbridge, Brierley Hill, etc.

WORDSLEY HOSPITAL, the former WORKHOUSE. The centre building with two shaped gables and a mid-tower; *c*.1900.

WRINEHILL

7040

THE SUMMERHOUSE. A swagger three-bay brick façade a little above the road. Three bays only, but with giant pilasters and a pediment across. The pediment may not be in the original state, as it contains a window with strips of rustication l. and r. Doorway with segmental pediment, segment-headed window. The date may be *c*.1710.

WROTTESLEY HALL

8000

The house dates from 1696 but does not now appear in that form. It was of three storeys throughout, but after a fire was adjusted to a one-and-a-half storey centre and one-storey wings. The pediment with garlands and a shield is the original one and hence appears a little overbearing.

---

* So Dr Robinson told me.

WYCHNOR

St Leonard. Nearly all Dec, see the straight-headed two-light windows, the doorway with a continuous fleuron frieze, the lower part of the SW tower, and the chancel side windows with their interesting tracery with trefoils developing into saltire crosses. The chancel E window is probably by *Ferrey*. Also Dec the chancel arch with three continuous chamfers and the S arcade with its quatrefoil piers. Only the E arch of the tower awkwardly set into the arcade is much earlier – probably of c.1200. Unmoulded pointed arch on very simple imposts. The tower top is of brick, late C16 or C17. – FONT. Large, octagonal, Perp, with shields in pointed quatrefoils. – STAINED GLASS. Old bits in the chancel N and less S and E. – PLATE. Paten, 1697 by *Thomas Farr*, London; Chalice, 1741 by *John Gould*.

Wychnor Hall. A composite building of which one would like to know more. The main range is of seven bays and three storeys with a recessed centre. Porch of four Tuscan columns. To the r. of this range a higher two-bay block with quoins of even length. In the main range staircase with twisted balusters.

Wychnor Bridges Farmhouse, ⅜ m. E. A substantial seven-bay brick house with a canted bay as its centre. The ground floor of this bay is treated as the porch and has four Tuscan columns.

YOXALL

St Peter. Mostly by *Woodyer*, 1865–8; but the S doorway is of c.1200 (leaf capital, moulded, round arch), the five-bay arcades are Dec, and the W tower is Perp but has also been assigned to the C17. A nice Woodyer touch is the chancel S window, filled nearly completely by reticulation. – SCREEN under the tower arch. Little is ancient. What is dates probably from the second quarter of the C16 (cf. Hamstall Ridware). – STAINED GLASS. W by *Wailes*. – PLATE. Chalice by *J.F.*, London, 1571; Flagon by *Samuel Wheat*, London, 1757. – MONUMENTS. Alabaster monument to Humphrey Welles † 1565 and wife. Tomb-chest with shields and twisted colonnettes. The inscription is still in black letter. – Admiral

Meynell † 1865. White recumbent effigy, four short pillars in front carrying a canopy. By *Baron Marochetti*.

THE ROOKERY, ¼ m. s, on the A-road. A five-bay brick house of three storeys with a pedimented doorcase.

(YOXALL GRANGE. Timber-framing and brick with two Dutch gables on the front. DOE)

GLOSSARY

ABACUS: flat slab on the top of a capital (q.v.).

ABUTMENT: solid masonry placed to resist the lateral pressure of a vault.

ACANTHUS: plant with thick fleshy and scalloped leaves used as part of the decoration of a Corinthian capital (q.v.) and in some types of leaf carving.

ACHIEVEMENT OF ARMS: in heraldry, a complete display of armorial bearings.

ACROTERION: foliage-carved block on the end or top of a classical pediment.

ADDORSED: two human figures, animals, or birds, etc., placed symmetrically so that they turn their backs to each other.

AEDICULE, AEDICULA: framing of a window or door by columns and a pediment (q.v.).

AFFRONTED: two human figures, animals, or birds, etc., placed symmetrically so that they face each other.

AGGER: Latin term for the built-up foundations of Roman roads; also sometimes applied to the banks of hill-forts or other earthworks.

AMBULATORY: semicircular or polygonal aisle enclosing an apse (q.v.).

ANNULET: see Shaft-ring.

ANSE DE PANIER: see Arch, Basket.

ANTEPENDIUM: covering of the front of an altar, usually by textiles or metalwork.

ANTIS, IN: see Portico.

APSE: vaulted semicircular or polygonal end of a chancel or a chapel.

ARABESQUE: light and fanciful surface decoration using combinations of flowing lines, tendrils, etc., interspersed with vases, animals, etc.

ARCADE: range of arches supported on piers or columns, free-standing: or, BLIND ARCADE, the same attached to a wall.

ARCH: round-headed, i.e. semicircular; pointed, i.e. consisting of two curves, each drawn from one centre, and meeting in a point at the top; segmental, i.e. in the form of a segment;

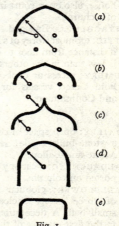

Fig. 1

pointed; four-centred (a Late Medieval form), see Fig. 1(a); Tudor (also a Late Medieval form), *see* Fig. 1(*b*); Ogee (introduced *c.*1300 and specially popular in the C14), *see* Fig. 1(*c*); Stilted, *see* Fig. 1(*d*); Basket, with lintel connected to the jambs by concave quadrant curves, *see* Fig. 1(*e*) for one example; Diaphragm, a transverse arch with solid spandrels carrying not a vault but a principal beam of a timber roof.

ARCHITRAVE: lowest of the three main parts of the entablature (q.v.) of an order (q.v.) (*see* Fig. 12).

ARCHIVOLT: under-surface of an arch (also called Soffit).

ARRIS: sharp edge at the meeting of two surfaces.

ASHLAR: masonry of large blocks wrought to even faces and square edges.

ATLANTES: male counterparts of caryatids (q.v.).

ATRIUM: inner court of a Roman house, also open court in front of a church.

ATTACHED: *see* Engaged.

ATTIC: topmost storey of a house, if distance from floor to ceiling is less than in the others.

AUMBRY: recess or cupboard to hold sacred vessels for Mass and Communion.

BAILEY: open space or court of a stone-built castle; *see* also Motte-and-Bailey.

BALDACCHINO: canopy supported on columns.

BALLFLOWER: globular flower of three petals enclosing a small ball. A decoration used in the first quarter of the C14.

BALUSTER: small pillar or column of fanciful outline.

BALUSTRADE: series of balusters supporting a handrail or coping (q.v.).

BARBICAN: outwork defending the entrance to a castle.

BARGEBOARDS: projecting decorated boards placed against the incline of the gable of a building and hiding the horizontal roof timbers.

BARROW: *see* Bell, Bowl, Disc, Long, *and* Pond Barrow.

BASILICA: in medieval architecture an aisled church with a clerestory.

BASKET ARCH: *see* Arch (Fig. 1e).

BASTION: projection at the angle of a fortification.

BATTER: inclined face of a wall.

BATTLEMENT: parapet with a series of indentations or embrasures with raised portions or merlons between (also called Crenellation).

BAYS: internal compartments of a building; each divided from the other not by solid walls but by divisions only marked in the side walls (columns, pilasters, etc.) or the ceiling (beams, etc.). Also external divisions of a building by fenestration.

BAY-WINDOW: angular or curved projection of a house front with ample fenestration. If curved, also called bow-window: if on an upper floor only, also called oriel or oriel window.

BEAKER FOLK: Late New Stone Age warrior invaders from the Continent who buried their dead in round barrows and introduced the first metal tools and weapons to Britain.

BEAKHEAD: Norman ornamental motif consisting of a row of bird or beast heads with beaks biting usually into a roll moulding.

GLOSSARY

BELFRY: turret on a roof to hang bells in.

BELGAE: Aristocratic warrior bands who settled in Britain in two main waves in the C I B.C. In Britain their culture is termed Iron Age C.

BELL BARROW: Early Bronze Age round barrow in which the mound is separated from its encircling ditch by a flat platform or berm (q.v.).

BELLCOTE: framework on a roof to hang bells from.

BERM: level area separating ditch from bank on a hill-fort or barrow.

BILLET FRIEZE: Norman ornamental motif made up of short raised rectangles placed at regular intervals.

BIVALLATE: Of a hill-fort: defended by two concentric banks and ditches.

BLOCK CAPITAL: Romanesque capital cut from a cube by having the lower angles rounded off to the circular shaft below (also called Cushion Capital) (Fig. 2).

Fig. 2

BOND, ENGLISH or FLEMISH: see Brickwork.

BOSS: knob or projection usually placed to cover the intersection of ribs in a vault.

BOWL BARROW: round barrow surrounded by a quarry ditch. Introduced in Late Neolithic times, the form continued until the Saxon period.

BOW-WINDOW: see Bay-Window.

BOX: A small country house, e.g. a shooting box. A convenient term to describe a compact minor dwelling, e.g. a rectory.

BOX PEW: pew with a high wooden enclosure.

BRACES: see Roof.

BRACKET: small supporting piece of stone, etc., to carry a projecting horizontal.

BRESSUMER: beam in a timber-framed building to support the, usually projecting, superstructure.

BRICKWORK: *Header:* brick laid so that the end only appears on the face of the wall. *Stretcher:* brick laid so that the side only appears on the face of the wall. *English Bond:* method of laying bricks so that alternate courses or layers on the face of the wall are composed of headers or stretchers only (Fig. 3*a*). *Flemish Bond:* method of laying

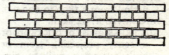
(*a*)

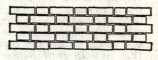
(*b*)
Fig. 3

bricks so that alternate headers and stretchers appear in each course on the face of the wall (Fig. 3*b*).

BROACH: see Spire.

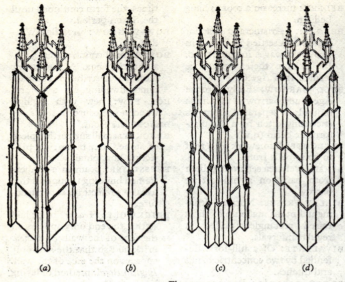

Fig. 4

BROKEN PEDIMENT: *see* Pediment.

BRONZE AGE: In Britain, the period from *c.*1800 to 600 B.C.

BUCRANIUM: ox skull.

BUTTRESS: mass of brickwork or masonry projecting from or built against a wall to give additional strength. *Angle Buttresses:* two meeting at an angle of 90° at the angle of a building (Fig. 4*a*). *Clasping Buttress:* one which encases the angle (Fig. 4*d*). *Diagonal Buttress:* one placed against the right angle formed by two walls, and more or less equiangular with both (Fig. 4*b*). *Flying Buttress:* arch or half arch transmitting the thrust of a vault or roof from the upper part of a wall to an outer support or buttress. *Setback Buttress:* angle buttress set slightly back from the angle (Fig. 4*c*).

CABLE MOULDING: Norman moulding imitating a twisted cord.

CAIRN: a mound of stones usually covering a burial.

CAMBER: slight rise or upward curve of an otherwise horizontal structure.

CAMPANILE: isolated bell tower.

CANOPY: projection or hood over an altar, pulpit, niche, statue, etc.

CAP: in a windmill the crowning feature.

CAPITAL: head or top part of a column.

GLOSSARY

CARTOUCHE: tablet with an ornate frame, usually enclosing an inscription.

CARYATID: whole female figure supporting an entablature or other similar member. *Termini Caryatids:* female busts or demi-figures or three-quarter figures supporting an entablature or other similar member and placed at the top of termini pilasters (q.v.). Cf. Atlantes.

CASTELLATED: decorated with battlements.

CELURE: panelled and adorned part of a wagon-roof above the rood or the altar.

CENSER: vessel for the burning of incense.

CENTERING: wooden framework used in arch and vault construction and removed when the mortar has set.

CHALICE: cup used in the Communion service or at Mass. *See also* Recusant Chalice.

CHAMBERED TOMB: burial mound of the New Stone Age having a stone-built chamber and entrance passage covered by an earthen barrow or stone cairn. The form was introduced to Britain from the Mediterranean.

CHAMFER: surface made by cutting across the square angle of a stone block, piece of wood, etc., usually at an angle of 45° to the other two surfaces.

CHANCEL: that part of the E end of a church in which the altar is placed, usually applied to the whole continuation of the nave E of the crossing.

CHANCEL ARCH: arch at the W end of the chancel.

CHANTRY CHAPEL: chapel attached to, or inside, a church, endowed for the saying of Masses for the soul of the founder or some other individual.

CHEVET: French term for the E end of a church (chancel, ambulatory, and radiating chapels).

CHEVRON: Norman moulding forming a zigzag.

CHOIR: that part of the church where divine service is sung.

CIBORIUM: a baldacchino.

CINQUEFOIL: *see* Foil.

CIST: stone-lined or slab-built grave. First appears in Late Neolithic times. It continued to be used in the Early Christian period.

CLAPPER BRIDGE: bridge made of large slabs of stone, some built up to make rough piers and other longer ones laid on top to make the roadway.

CLASSIC: here used to mean the moment of highest achievement of a style.

CLASSICAL: here used as the term for Greek and Roman architecture and any subsequent styles inspired by it.

CLERESTORY: upper storey of the nave walls of a church, pierced by windows.

COADE STONE: artificial (cast) stone made in the late C18 and the early C19 by Coade and Sealy in London.

COB: walling material made of mixed clay and straw.

COFFERING: decorating a ceiling with sunk square or polygonal ornamental panels.

COLLAR-BEAM: *see* Roof.

COLONNADE: range of columns.

COLONNETTE: small column.

COLUMNA ROSTRATA: column decorated with carved prows of ships to celebrate a naval victory.

COMPOSITE: *see* Order.

CONSOLE: bracket (q.v.) with a compound curved outline.

COPING: capping or covering to a wall.

CORBEL: block of stone projecting from a wall, supporting some feature on its horizontal top surface.

CORBEL TABLE: series of corbels, occurring just below the roof eaves externally or internally, often seen in Norman buildings.

CORINTHIAN: *see* Order.

CORNICE: in classical architecture the top section of the entablature (q.v.). Also for a projecting decorative feature along the top of a wall, arch, etc.

CORRIDOR VILLA: *see* Villa.

COUNTERSCARP BANK: small bank on the down-hill or outer side of a hill-fort ditch.

COURTYARD VILLA: *see* Villa.

COVE, COVING: concave undersurface in the nature of a hollow moulding but on a larger scale.

COVER PATEN: cover to a Communion cup, suitable for use as a paten or plate for the consecrated bread.

CRADLE ROOF: *see* Wagon roof.

CRENELLATION: *see* Battlement.

CREST, CRESTING: ornamental finish along the top of a screen, etc.

CRINKLE-CRANKLE WALL: undulating wall.

CROCKET, CROCKETING: decorative features placed on the sloping sides of spires, pinnacles, gables, etc., in Gothic architecture, carved in various leaf shapes and placed at regular intervals.

CROCKET CAPITAL: *see* Fig. 5. An Early Gothic form.

CROMLECH: word of Celtic origin still occasionally used of single free-standing stones ascribed to the Neolithic or Bronze Age periods.

Fig. 5

CROSSING: space at the intersection of nave, chancel, and transepts.

CROSS-WINDOWS: windows with one mullion and one transom.

CRUCK: big curved beam supporting both walls and roof of a cottage.

CRYPT: underground room usually below the E end of a church.

CUPOLA: small polygonal or circular domed turret crowning a roof.

CURTAIN WALL: connecting wall between the towers of a castle.

CUSHION CAPITAL: *see* Block Capital.

CUSP: projecting point between the foils in a foiled Gothic arch.

DADO: decorative covering of the lower part of a wall.

DAGGER: tracery motif of the Dec style. It is a lancet shape rounded or pointed at the head, pointed at the foot, and cusped inside (*see* Fig. 6).

GLOSSARY

Fig. 6

DAIS: raised platform at one end of a room.

DEC ('DECORATED'): historical division of English Gothic architecture covering the period from c.1290 to c.1350.

DEMI-COLUMNS: columns half sunk into a wall.

DIAPER WORK: surface decoration composed of square or lozenge shapes.

DIAPHRAGM ARCH: see Arch.

DISC BARROW: Bronze Age round barrow with inconspicuous central mound surrounded by bank and ditch.

DOGTOOTH: typical E.E. ornament consisting of a series of four-cornered stars placed diagonally and raised pyramidally (Fig. 7).

Fig. 7

DOMICAL VAULT: see Vault.

DONJON: see Keep.

DORIC: see Order.

DORMER (WINDOW): window placed vertically in the sloping plane of a roof.

DRIPSTONE: see Hood-mould.

DRUM: circular or polygonal vertical wall of a dome or cupola.

E.E. ('EARLY ENGLISH'): historical division of English Gothic architecture roughly covering the C13.

EASTER SEPULCHRE: recess with tomb-chest, usually in the wall of a chancel, the tomb-chest to receive an effigy of Christ for Easter celebrations.

EAVES: underpart of a sloping roof overhanging a wall.

EAVES CORNICE: cornice below the eaves of a roof.

ECHINUS: Convex or projecting moulding supporting the abacus of a Greek Doric capital, sometimes bearing an egg and dart pattern.

EMBATTLED: see Battlement.

EMBRASURE: small opening in the wall or parapet of a fortified building, usually splayed on the inside.

ENCAUSTIC TILES: earthenware glazed and decorated tiles used for paving.

ENGAGED COLUMNS: columns attached to, or partly sunk into, a wall.

ENGLISH BOND: see Brickwork.

ENTABLATURE: in classical architecture the whole of the horizontal members above a column (that is architrave, frieze, and cornice) (see Fig. 12).

ENTASIS: very slight convex deviation from a straight line; used on Greek columns and sometimes on spires to prevent an optical illusion of concavity.

ENTRESOL: see Mezzanine.

EPITAPH: hanging wall monument.

ESCUTCHEON: shield for armorial bearings.

EXEDRA: the apsidal end of a room. See Apse.

FAN-VAULT: see Vault.

FERETORY: place behind the

high altar where the chief shrine of a church is kept.

FESTOON: carved garland of flowers and fruit suspended at both ends.

FILLET: narrow flat band running down a shaft or along a roll moulding.

FINIAL: top of a canopy, gable, pinnacle.

FLAGON: vessel for the wine used in the Communion service.

FLAMBOYANT: properly the latest phase of French Gothic architecture where the window tracery takes on wavy undulating lines.

FLÈCHE: slender wooden spire on the centre of a roof (also called Spirelet).

FLEMISH BOND: see Brickwork.

FLEURON: decorative carved flower or leaf.

FLUSHWORK: decorative use of flint in conjunction with dressed stone so as to form patterns: tracery, initials, etc.

FLUTING: vertical channelling in the shaft of a column.

FLYING BUTTRESS: see Buttress.

FOIL: lobe formed by the cusping (q.v.) of a circle or an arch. Trefoil, quatrefoil, cinquefoil, multifoil, express the number of leaf shapes to be seen.

FOLIATED: carved with leaf shapes.

FOSSE: ditch.

FOUR-CENTRED ARCH: see Arch.

FRATER: refectory or dining hall of a monastery.

FRESCO: wall painting on wet plaster.

FRIEZE: middle division of a classical entablature (q.v.) (*see* Fig. 12).

FRONTAL: covering for the front of an altar.

GABLE: *Dutch gable:* A gable with curved sides crowned by a pediment, characteristic of *c*.1630-50 (Fig. 8*a*). *Shaped gable:* A gable with multi-curved sides characteristic of *c*.1600-50 (Fig. 8*b*).

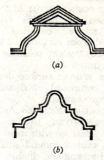

Fig. 8

GADROONED: enriched with a series of convex ridges, the opposite of fluting.

GALILEE: chapel or vestibule usually at the W end of a church enclosing the porch. Also called Narthex (q.v.).

GALLERY: in church architecture upper storey above an aisle, opened in arches to the nave. Also called Tribune and often erroneously called Triforium (q.v.).

GALLERY GRAVE: chambered tomb (q.v.) in which there is little or no differentiation between the entrance passage and the actual burial chamber(s).

GARDEROBE: lavatory or privy in a medieval building.

GARGOYLE: water spout projecting from the parapet of a wall or tower; carved into a human or animal shape.

GAZEBO: lookout tower or raised

summer house in a picturesque garden.

'GEOMETRICAL': *see* Tracery.

'GIBBS SURROUND': of a doorway or window. An c18 motif consisting of a surround with alternating larger and smaller blocks of stone, quoin-wise, or intermittent large blocks, sometimes with a narrow raised band connecting them up the verticals and along the face of the arch (Fig. 9).

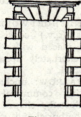

Fig. 9

GROIN: sharp edge at the meeting of two cells of a cross-vault.

GROIN-VAULT: *see* Vault.

GROTESQUE: fanciful ornamental decoration: *see also* Arabesque.

HAGIOSCOPE: *see* Squint.

HALF-TIMBERING: *see* Timber-Framing.

HALL CHURCH: church in which nave and aisles are of equal height or approximately so.

HAMMERBEAM: *see* Roof.

HANAP: large metal cup, generally made for domestic use, standing on an elaborate base and stem; with a very ornate cover frequently crowned with a little steeple.

HEADERS: *see* Brickwork.

HERRINGBONE WORK: brick, stone, or tile construction where the component blocks are laid diagonally instead of flat. Alternate courses lie in opposing directions to make a zigzag pattern up the face of the wall.

HEXASTYLE: having six detached columns.

HILL-FORT: Iron Age earthwork enclosed by a ditch and bank system; in the later part of the period the defences multiplied in size and complexity. They vary from about an acre to over 30 acres in area, and are usually built with careful regard to natural elevations or promontories.

HIPPED ROOF: *see* Roof.

HOOD-MOULD: projecting moulding above an arch or a lintel to throw off water (also called Dripstone or Label).

ICONOGRAPHY: the science of the subject matter of works of the visual arts.

IMPOST: bracket in a wall, usually formed of mouldings, on which the ends of an arch rest.

INDENT: shape chiselled out in a stone slab to receive a brass.

INGLENOOK: bench or seat built in beside a fireplace, sometimes covered by the chimneybreast, occasionally lit by small windows on each side of the fire.

INTERCOLUMNIATION: the space between columns.

IONIC: *see* Order (Fig. 12).

IRON AGE: in Britain the period from *c.* 600 B.C. to the coming of the Romans. The term is also used for those un-Romanized native communities which survived until the Saxon incursions.

JAMB: straight side of an archway, doorway, or window.

KEEL MOULDING: moulding whose outline is in section like that of the keel of a ship.
KEEP: massive tower of a Norman castle.
KEYSTONE: middle stone in an arch or a rib-vault.
KING-POST: see Roof (Fig. 14).
KNEELER: horizontal decorative projection at the base of a gable.
KNOP: a knob-like thickening in the stem of a chalice.

LABEL: see Hood-mould.
LABEL STOP: ornamental boss at the end of a hood-mould (q.v.).
LACED WINDOWS: windows pulled visually together by strips, usually in brick of a different colour, which continue vertically the lines of the vertical parts of the window surrounds. The motif is typical of c. 1720.
LANCET WINDOW: slender pointed-arched window.
LANTERN: in architecture, a small circular or polygonal turret with windows all round crowning a roof (see Cupola) or a dome.
LANTERN CROSS: churchyard cross with lantern-shaped top usually with sculptured representations on the sides of the top.

LEAN-TO ROOF: roof with one slope only, built against a higher wall.
LESENE or PILASTER STRIP: pilaster without base or capital.
LIERNE: see Vault (Fig. 21).
LINENFOLD: Tudor panelling ornamented with a conventional representation of a piece of linen laid in vertical folds. The piece is repeated in each panel.
LINTEL: horizontal beam or stone bridging an opening.
LOGGIA: recessed colonnade (q.v.).
LONG AND SHORT WORK: Saxon quoins (q.v.) consisting of stones placed with the long sides alternately upright and horizontal.
LONG BARROW: unchambered Neolithic communal burial mound, wedge-shaped in plan, with the burial and occasional other structures massed at the broader end, from which the mound itself tapers in height; quarry ditches flank the mound.
LOUVRE: opening, often with lantern (q.v.) over, in the roof of a room to let the smoke from a central hearth escape.
LOWER PALAEOLITHIC: see Palaeolithic.
LOZENGE: diamond shape.
LUCARNE: small opening to let light in.
LUNETTE: tympanum (q.v.) or semicircular opening.
LYCH GATE: wooden gate structure with a roof and open sides placed at the entrance to a churchyard to provide space for the reception of a coffin. The word *lych* is Saxon and means a corpse.

LYNCHET: long terraced strip of soil accumulating on the downward side of prehistoric and medieval fields due to soil creep from continuous ploughing along the contours.

MACHICOLATION: projecting gallery on brackets constructed on the outside of castle towers or walls. The gallery has holes in the floor to drop missiles through.

MAJOLICA: ornamented glazed earthenware.

MANSARD: see Roof.

MATHEMATICAL TILES: Small facing tiles the size of brick headers, applied to timber-framed walls to make them appear brick-built.

MEGALITHIC TOMB: stone-built burial chamber of the New Stone Age covered by an earth or stone mound. The form was introduced to Britain from the Mediterranean area.

MERLON: see Battlement.

MESOLITHIC: 'Middle Stone' Age; the post-glacial period of hunting and fishing communities dating in Britain from c. 8000 B.C. to the arrival of Neolithic communities, with which they must have considerably overlapped.

METOPE: in classical architecture of the Doric order (q.v.) the space in the frieze between the triglyphs (Fig. 12).

MEZZANINE: low storey placed between two higher ones.

MISERERE: see Misericord.

MISERICORD: bracket placed on the underside of a hinged choir stall seat which, when turned up, provided the occupant of the seat with a support during long periods of standing (also called Miserere).

MODILLION: small bracket of which large numbers (modillion frieze) are often placed below a cornice (q.v.) in classical architecture.

MOTTE: steep mound forming the main feature of C11 and C12 castles.

MOTTE-AND-BAILEY: post-Roman and Norman defence system consisting of an earthen mound (the motte) topped with a wooden tower eccentrically placed within a bailey (q.v.), with enclosure ditch and palisade, and with the rare addition of an internal bank.

MOUCHETTE: tracery motif in curvilinear tracery, a curved dagger (q.v.), specially popular in the early C14 (Fig. 10).

Fig. 10

MULLIONS: vertical posts or uprights dividing a window into 'lights'.

MULTIVALLATE: Of a hill-fort: defended by three or more concentric banks and ditches.

MUNTIN: post as a rule moulded and part of a screen.

NAIL-HEAD: E.E. ornamental motif, consisting of small pyramids regularly repeated (Fig. 11).

Fig. 11

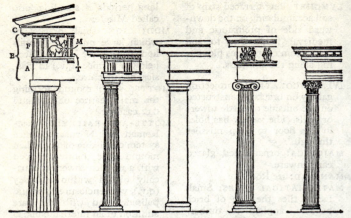

Fig. 12. Orders of Columns (Greek Doric, Roman Doric, Tuscan Doric, Ionic, Corinthian) E, Entablature; C, Cornice; F, Frieze; A, Architrave; M, Metope; T, Triglyph.

NARTHEX: enclosed vestibule or covered porch at the main entrance to a church (*see* Galilee).

NEOLITHIC: 'New Stone' Age, dating in Britain from the appearance from the Continent of the first settled farming communities *c*. 3500 B.C. until the introduction of the Bronze Age.

NEWEL: central post in a circular or winding staircase; also the principal post when a flight of stairs meets a landing.

NOOK-SHAFT: shaft set in the angle of a pier or respond or wall, or the angle of the jamb of a window or doorway.

NUTMEG MOULDING: consisting of a chain of tiny triangles placed obliquely.

OBELISK: lofty pillar of square section tapering at the top and ending pyramidally.

OGEE: *see* Arch (Fig. 1c).

ORATORY: small private chapel in a house.

ORDER: (1) *of a doorway or window:* series of concentric steps receding towards the opening; (2) *in classical architecture:* column with base, shaft, capital, and entablature (q.v.) according to one of the following styles: Greek Doric, Roman Doric, Tuscan Doric, Ionic, Corinthian, Composite. The established details are very elaborate, and some specialist architectural work should be consulted for further guidance (*see* Fig. 12).

ORIEL: *see* Bay-Window.

OVERHANG: projection of the upper storey of a house.

OVERSAILING COURSES: series of stone or brick courses, each one projecting beyond the one below it.

OVOLO: convex moulding.

PALAEOLITHIC: 'Old Stone' Age; the first period of human culture, commencing in the

Ice Age and immediately prior to the Mesolithic; the Lower Palaeolithic is the older phase, the Upper Palaeolithic the later.

PALIMPSEST: (1) *of a brass:* where a metal plate has been re-used by turning over and engraving on the back; (2) *of a wall painting:* where one overlaps and partly obscures an earlier one.

PALLADIAN: architecture following the ideas and principles of Andrea Palladio, 1518–80.

PANTILE: tile of curved S-shaped section.

PARAPET: low wall placed to protect any spot where there is a sudden drop, for example on a bridge, quay, hillside, housetop, etc.

PARGETTING: plaster work with patterns and ornaments either in relief or engraved on it.

PARVIS: term wrongly applied to a room over a church porch. These rooms were often used as a schoolroom or as a store room.

PATEN: plate to hold the bread at Communion or Mass.

PATERA: small flat circular or oval ornament in classical architecture.

PEDIMENT: low-pitched gable used in classical, Renaissance, and neo-classical architecture above a portico and above doors, windows, etc. It may be straight-sided or curved segmentally. *Broken Pediment:* one where the centre portion of the base is left open. *Open Pediment:* one where the centre portion of the sloping sides is left out.

PENDANT: boss (q.v.) elongated so that it seems to hang down.

PENDENTIF: concave triangular spandrel used to lead from the angle of two walls to the base of a circular dome. It is constructed as part of the hemisphere over a diameter the size of the diagonal of the basic square (Fig. 13).

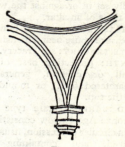

Fig. 13

PERP (PERPENDICULAR): historical division of English Gothic architecture covering the period from *c.*1335–50 to *c.*1530.

PIANO NOBILE: principal storey of a house with the reception rooms; usually the first floor.

PIAZZA: open space surrounded by buildings; in C17 and C18 England sometimes used to mean a long colonnade or loggia.

PIER: strong, solid support, frequently square in section or of composite section (compound pier).

PIETRA DURA: ornamental or scenic inlay by means of thin slabs of stone.

PILASTER: shallow pier attached to a wall. *Termini Pilasters:* pilasters with sides tapering downwards.

PILLAR PISCINA: free-standing piscina on a pillar.

GLOSSARY

PINNACLE: ornamental form crowning a spire, tower, buttress, etc., usually of steep pyramidal, conical, or some similar shape.

PISCINA: basin for washing the Communion or Mass vessels, provided with a drain. Generally set in or against the wall to the S of an altar.

PLAISANCE: summer-house, pleasure house near a mansion.

PLATE TRACERY: see Tracery.

PLINTH: projecting base of a wall or column, generally chamfered (q.v.) or moulded at the top.

POND BARROW: rare type of Bronze Age barrow consisting of a circular depression, usually paved, and containing a number of cremation burials.

POPPYHEAD: ornament of leaf and flower type used to decorate the tops of bench- or stall-ends.

PORTCULLIS: gate constructed to rise and fall in vertical grooves; used in gateways of castles.

PORTE COCHÈRE: porch large enough to admit wheeled vehicles.

PORTICO: centre-piece of a house or a church with classical detached or attached columns and a pediment. A portico is called *prostyle* or *in antis* according to whether it projects from or recedes into a building. In a portico *in antis* the columns range with the side walls.

POSTERN: small gateway at the back of a building.

PREDELLA: in an altarpiece the horizontal strip below the main representation, often used for a number of subsidiary representations in a row.

PRESBYTERY: the part of the church lying E of the choir. It is the part where the altar is placed.

PRINCIPAL: see Roof (Fig. 14).

PRIORY: monastic house whose head is a prior or prioress, not an abbot or abbess.

PROSTYLE: with free-standing columns in a row.

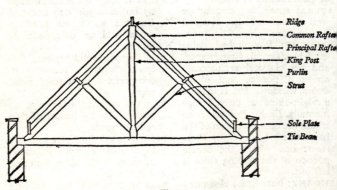

Fig. 14

PULPITUM: stone screen in a major church provided to shut off the choir from the nave and also as a backing for the return choir stalls.

PULVINATED FRIEZE: frieze with a bold convex moulding.

PURLIN: see Roof (Figs. 14, 15).

PUTHOLE or PUTLOCK HOLE: putlocks are the short horizontal timbers on which during construction the boards of scaffolding rest. Putholes or putlock holes are the holes in the wall for putlocks, which often are not filled in after construction is complete.

PUTTO: small naked boy.

QUADRANGLE: inner courtyard in a large building.

QUARRY: in stained-glass work, a small diamond- or square-shaped piece of glass set diagonally.

QUATREFOIL: see Foil.

QUEEN-POSTS: see Roof (Fig. 15).

QUOINS: dressed stones at the angles of a building. Sometimes all the stones are of the same size; more often they are alternately large and small.

RADIATING CHAPELS: chapels projecting radially from an ambulatory or an apse.

RAFTER: see Roof.

RAMPART: stone wall or wall of earth surrounding a castle, fortress, or fortified city.

RAMPART-WALK: path along the inner face of a rampart.

REBATE: continuous rectangular notch cut on an edge.

REBUS: pun, a play on words. The literal translation and illustration of a name for artistic and heraldic purposes (Belton = bell, tun).

RECUSANT CHALICE: chalice made after the Reformation and before Catholic Emancipation for Roman Catholic use.

REEDING: decoration with parallel convex mouldings touching one another.

REFECTORY: dining hall; see Frater.

RENDERING: plastering of an outer wall.

REPOUSSÉ: decoration of metal work by relief designs, formed by beating the metal from the back.

REREDOS: structure behind and above an altar.

RESPOND: half-pier bonded into a wall and carrying one end of an arch.

RETABLE: altarpiece, a picture or piece of carving, standing behind and attached to an altar.

RETICULATION: see Tracery (Fig. 20e).

REVEAL: that part of a jamb (q.v.) which lies between the glass or door and the outer surface of the wall.

RIB-VAULT: see Vault.

ROCOCO: latest phase of the Baroque style, current in most Continental countries between c.1720 and c.1760.

ROLL MOULDING: moulding of semicircular or more than semicircular section.

ROMANESQUE: that style in architecture which was current in the C11 and C12 and preceded the Gothic style (in England often called Norman). (Some scholars extend the use of the term Romanesque back to the C10 or C9.)

GLOSSARY

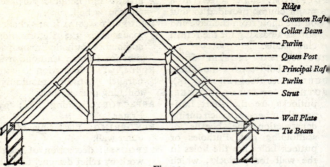

Fig. 15

ROMANO-BRITISH: A somewhat vague term applied to the period and cultural features of Britain affected by the Roman occupation of the C1–5 A.D.

ROOD: cross or crucifix.

ROOD LOFT: singing gallery on the top of the rood screen, often supported by a coving.

ROOD SCREEN: *see* Screen.

ROOD STAIRS: stairs to give access to the rood loft.

ROOF: *Single-framed:* if consisting entirely of transverse members (such as rafters with or without braces, collars, tie beams, king-posts or queen posts, etc.) not tied together longitudinally. *Double-framed:* if longitudinal members (such as a ridge beam and purlins) are employed. As a rule in such cases the rafters are divided into stronger principals and weaker subsidiary rafters. *Hipped:* roof with sloped instead of vertical ends. *Mansard:* roof with a double slope, the

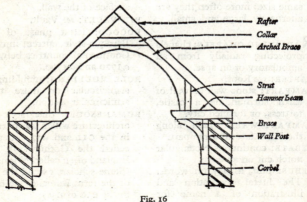

Fig. 16

lower slope being larger and steeper than the upper. *Saddleback:* tower roof shaped like an ordinary gabled timber roof. The following members have special names: *Rafter:* roof-timber sloping up from the wall plate to the ridge. *Principal:* principal rafter, usually corresponding to the main bay divisions of the nave or chancel below. *Wall Plate:* timber laid longitudinally on the top of a wall. *Purlin:* longitudinal member laid parallel with wall plate and ridge beam some way up the slope of the roof. *Tie-beam:* beam connecting the two slopes of a roof across at its foot, usually at the height of the wall plate, to prevent the roof from spreading. *Collar-beam:* tie-beam applied higher up the slope of the roof. *Strut:* upright timber connecting the tie-beam with the rafter above it. *King-post:* upright timber connecting a tie-beam and collar-beam with the ridge beam. *Queen-posts:* two struts placed symmetrically on a tie-beam or collar-beam. *Braces:* inclined timbers inserted to strengthen others. Usually braces connect a collar-beam with the rafters below or a tie-beam with the wall below. Braces can be straight or curved (also called arched). *Hammer-beam:* beam projecting at right angles, usually from the top of a wall, to carry arched braces or struts and arched braces. (*See* Figs. 14, 15, 16.)

ROSE WINDOW (or WHEEL WINDOW): circular window with patterned tracery arranged to radiate from the centre.

ROTUNDA: building circular in plan.

RUBBLE: building stones, not square or hewn, nor laid in regular courses.

RUSTICATION: *rock-faced* if the surfaces of large blocks of ashlar stone are left rough like rock; *smooth* if the ashlar blocks are smooth and separated by V-joints; *banded* if the separation by V-joints applies only to the horizontals.

SADDLEBACK: see Roof.

SALTIRE CROSS: equal-limbed cross placed diagonally.

SANCTUARY: (1) area around the main altar of a church (*see* Presbytery); (2) sacred site consisting of wood or stone uprights enclosed by a circular bank and ditch. Beginning in the Neolithic, they were elaborated in the succeeding Bronze Age. The best known examples are Stonehenge and Avebury.

SARCOPHAGUS: elaborately carved coffin.

SCAGLIOLA: material composed of cement and colouring matter to imitate marble.

SCALLOPED CAPITAL: development of the block capital (q.v.) in which the single semi-circular surface is elaborated into a series of truncated cones (Fig. 17).

Fig. 17

- **SCARP**: artificial cutting away of the ground to form a steep slope.
- **SCREEN**: *Parclose screen*: screen separating a chapel from the rest of a church. *Rood screen*: screen below the rood (q.v.), usually at the W end of a chancel.
- **SCREENS PASSAGE**: passage between the entrances to kitchen, buttery, etc., and the screen behind which lies the hall of a medieval house.
- **SEDILIA**: seats for the priests (usually three) on the S side of the chancel of a church.
- **SEGMENTAL ARCH**: see Arch.
- **SET-OFF**: see Weathering.
- **SEXPARTITE**: see Vault.
- **SGRAFFITO**: pattern incised into plaster so as to expose a dark surface underneath.
- **SHAFT-RING**: motif of the C12 and C13 consisting of a ring round a circular pier or a shaft attached to a pier.
- **SHEILA-NA-GIG**: fertility figure, usually with legs wide open.
- **SILL**: lower horizontal part of the frame of a window.
- **SLATEHANGING**: the covering of walls by overlapping rows of slates, on a timber substructure.
- **SOFFIT**: underside of an arch, lintel, etc.
- **SOLAR**: upper living-room of a medieval house.
- **SOPRAPORTE**: painting above the door of a room, usual in the C17 and C18.
- **SOUNDING BOARD**: horizontal board or canopy over a pulpit. Also called Tester.
- **SPANDREL**: triangular surface between one side of an arch, the horizontal drawn from its apex, and the vertical drawn from its springer; also the surface between two arches.
- **SPERE-TRUSS**: roof truss on two free-standing posts to mask the division between screens passage and hall. The screen itself, where a spere-truss exists, was originally movable.
- **SPIRE**: tall pyramidal or conical pointed erection often built on top of a tower, turret, etc. *Broach Spire*: a broach is a sloping half-pyramid of masonry or wood introduced at the base of each of the four oblique faces of a tapering octagonal spire with the object of effecting the transition from the square to the octagon. The *splayed foot spire* is a variation of the broach form found principally in the south-eastern counties. In this form the four cardinal faces are splayed out near their base, to cover the corners, while the oblique (or intermediate) faces taper away to a point. *Needle Spire*: thin spire rising from the centre of a tower roof, well inside the parapet.
- **SPIRELET**: see Flèche.
- **SPLAY**: chamfer, usually of the jamb of a window.
- **SPRINGING**: level at which an arch rises from its supports.
- **SQUINCH**: arch or system of concentric arches thrown across the angle between two walls to support a superstructure, for example a dome (Fig. 18).
- **SQUINT**: a hole cut in a wall or through a pier to allow a view of the main altar of a church from places whence it could not otherwise be seen (also called Hagioscope).

GLOSSARY

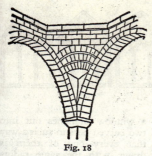

Fig. 18

STALL: carved seat, one of a row, made of wood or stone.

STAUNCHION: upright iron or steel member.

STEEPLE: the tower of a church together with a spire, cupola, etc.

STIFF-LEAF: E.E. type of foliage of many-lobed shapes (Fig. 19).

Fig. 19

STILTED: see Arch.

STOREY-POSTS: the principal posts of a timber-framed wall.

STOUP: vessel for the reception of holy water, usually placed near a door.

STRAINER ARCH: arch inserted across a room to prevent the walls from leaning.

STRAPWORK: C16 decoration consisting of interlaced bands, and forms similar to fretwork or cut and bent leather.

STRETCHER: see Brickwork.

STRING COURSE: projecting horizontal band or moulding set in the surface of a wall.

STRUT: see Roof.

STUCCO: plaster work.

STUDS: the subsidiary vertical timber members of a timber-framed wall.

SWAG: festoon formed by a carved piece of cloth suspended from both ends.

TABERNACLE: richly ornamented niche or free-standing canopy. Usually contains the Holy Sacrament.

TARSIA: inlay in various woods.

TAZZA: shallow bowl on a foot.

TERMINAL FIGURES (TERMS, TERMINI): upper part of a human figure growing out of a pier, pilaster, etc., which tapers towards the base. *See also* Caryatid, Pilaster.

TERRACOTTA: burnt clay, unglazed.

TESSELLATED PAVEMENT: mosaic flooring, particularly Roman, consisting of small 'tesserae' or cubes of glass, stone, or brick.

TESSERAE: see Tessellated Pavement.

TESTER: see Sounding Board.

TETRASTYLE: having four detached columns.

THREE-DECKER PULPIT: pulpit with Clerk's Stall below and Reading Desk below the Clerk's Stall.

TIE-BEAM: see Roof (Figs. 14, 15).

TIERCERON: see Vault (Fig. 21).

TILEHANGING: see Slatehanging.

TIMBER-FRAMING: method of construction where walls are built of timber framework with the spaces filled in by plaster

GLOSSARY

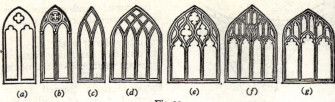

(a) (b) (c) (d) (e) (f) (g)

Fig. 20

or brickwork. Sometimes the timber is covered over with plaster or boarding laid horizontally.

TOMB-CHEST: chest-shaped stone coffin, the most usual medieval form of funeral monument.

TOUCH: soft black marble quarried near Tournai.

TOURELLE: turret corbelled out from the wall.

TRACERY: intersecting ribwork in the upper part of a window, or used decoratively in blank arches, on vaults, etc. *Plate tracery:* see Fig. 20(a). Early form of tracery where decoratively shaped openings are cut through the solid stone infilling in a window head. *Bar tracery:* a form introduced into England c.1250. Intersecting ribwork made up of slender shafts, continuing the lines of the mullions of windows up to a decorative mesh in the head of the window. *Geometrical tracery:* see Fig. 20(b). Tracery characteristic of c. 1250–1310 consisting chiefly of circles or foiled circles. *Y-tracery:* see Fig. 20(c). Tracery consisting of a mullion which branches into two forming a Y shape; typical of c. 1300. *Intersecting tracery:* see Fig. 20(d). Tracery in which each mullion of a window branches out into two curved bars in such a way that every one of them is drawn with the same radius from a different centre. The result is that every light of the window is a lancet and every two, three, four, etc., lights together form a pointed arch. This treatment also is typical of c. 1300. *Reticulated tracery:* see Fig. 20(e). Tracery typical of the early C14 consisting entirely of circles drawn at top and bottom into ogee shapes so that a net-like appearance results. *Panel tracery:* see Fig. 20(f) and (g). Perp tracery, which is formed of upright straight-sided panels above lights of a window.

TRANSEPT: transverse portion of a cross-shaped church.

TRANSOM: horizontal bar across the openings of a window.

TRANSVERSE ARCH: see Vault.

TRIBUNE: see Gallery.

TRICIPUT, SIGNUM TRICIPUT: sign of the Trinity expressed by three faces belonging to one head.

TRIFORIUM: arcaded wall passage or blank arcading facing the nave at the height of the aisle roof and below the clerestory (q.v.) windows. (See Gallery.)

TRIGLYPHS: blocks with vertical

GLOSSARY

grooves separating the metopes (q.v.) in the Doric frieze (Fig. 12).

TROPHY: sculptured group of arms or armour, used as a memorial of victory.

TRUMEAU: stone mullion (q.v.) supporting the tympanum (q.v.) of a wide doorway.

TUMULUS: see Barrow.

TURRET: very small tower, round or polygonal in plan.

TUSCAN: see Order.

TYMPANUM: space between the lintel of a doorway and the arch above it.

UNDERCROFT: vaulted room, sometimes underground, below a church or chapel.

UNIVALLATE: of a hill-fort: defended by a single bank and ditch.

UPPER PALAEOLITHIC: see Palaeolithic.

VAULT: *Barrel-vault:* see Tunnel-vault. *Cross-vault:* see Groin-vault. *Domical vault:* square or polygonal dome rising direct on a square or polygonal bay, the curved surfaces separated by groins (q.v.). *Fan-vault:* late medieval vault where all ribs springing from one springer are of the same length, the same distance from the next, and the same curvature. *Groin-vault* or *Cross-vault:* vault of two tunnel-vaults of identical shape intersecting each other at r. angles. Chiefly Norman and Renaissance. *Lierne:* tertiary rib, that is, rib which does not spring either from one of the main springers or from the central boss. Introduced in the C14, continues to the C16. *Quadripartite vault:* one wherein one bay of vaulting is divided into four parts. *Rib-vault:* vault with diagonal ribs projecting along the groins. *Ridge-rib:* rib along the longitudinal or transverse ridge of a vault. Introduced in the early C13. *Sexpartite vault:* one wherein one bay of quadripartite vaulting is divided into two parts transversely so that each bay of vaulting has six parts. *Tierceron:* secondary rib, that is, rib which issues from one of the main springers or the central boss and leads to a place on a ridge-rib. Introduced in the early C13. *Transverse arch:* arch separating one bay of a vault from the next. *Tunnel-vault* or *Barrel-vault:* vault of semicircular or pointed section. Chiefly Norman and Renaissance. (*See* Fig. 21.)

VAULTING SHAFT: vertical member leading to the springer of a vault.

VENETIAN WINDOW: window with three openings, the central one arched and wider than the outside ones. Current in England chiefly in the C17-18.

VERANDA: open gallery or balcony with a roof on light, usually metal, supports.

VESICA: oval with pointed head and foot.

VESTIBULE: anteroom or entrance hall.

VILLA: (1) according to Gwilt (1842) 'a country house for the residence of opulent persons'; (2) Romano-British country houses cum farms, to which the description given in (1)

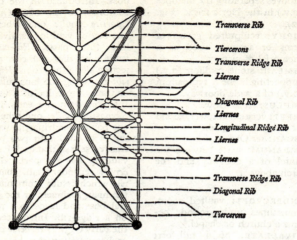

Fig. 21

more or less applies. They developed with the growth of urbanization. The basic type is the simple corridor pattern with rooms opening off a single passage; the next stage is the addition of wings. The courtyard villa fills a square plan with subsidiary buildings and an enclosure wall with a gate facing the main corridor block.

VITRIFIED: made similar to glass.

VITRUVIAN OPENING: A door or window which diminishes towards the top, as advocated by Vitruvius, bk. IV, chapter VI.

VOLUTE: spiral scroll, one of the component parts of an Ionic column (*see* Order).

VOUSSOIR: wedge-shaped stone used in arch construction.

WAGON ROOF: roof in which by closely set rafters with arched braces the appearance of the inside of a canvas tilt over a wagon is achieved. Wagon roofs can be panelled or plastered (ceiled) or left uncovered.

WAINSCOT: timber lining to walls.

WALL PLATE: *see* Roof.

WATERLEAF: leaf shape used in later C12 capitals. The waterleaf is a broad, unribbed, tapering leaf curving up towards the angle of the abacus and turned in at the top (Fig. 22).

Fig. 22

WEALDEN HOUSE: timber-framed house with the hall in the centre and wings projecting only slightly and only on the jutting upper floor. The roof, however, runs through without a break between wings and hall, and the eaves of the hall part are therefore exceptionally deep. They are supported by diagonal, usually curved, braces starting from the short inner sides of the overhanging wings and rising parallel with the front wall of the hall towards the centre of the eaves.

WEATHERBOARDING: overlapping horizontal boards, covering a timber-framed wall.

WEATHERING: sloped horizontal surface on sills, buttresses, etc., to throw off water.

WEEPERS: small figures placed in niches along the sides of some medieval tombs (also called Mourners).

WHEEL WINDOW: *see* Rose Window.

INDEX OF PLATES

ALSTONEFIELD, Church, Pulpit (*R. C. Williams*)	32
ALTON, Alton Castle, Exterior (*N.M.R., Crown Copyright*)	79
ALTON, Alton Towers, Banqueting Hall, Chimneypiece (*N.M.R., Crown Copyright*)	78
ALTON, Alton Towers, Conservatory (*N.M.R., Crown Copyright*)	75
ALTON, Alton Towers, General View (*N.M.R., Crown Copyright*)	74
ALTON, Alton Towers, Shrewsbury Memorial (*N.M.R., Crown Copyright*)	76
ARMITAGE, Church, Font (*R. C. Williams*)	7
AUDLEY, Houses and Shops by William White (*The Builder, 1855*)	90
BALTERLEY, Hall o' Wood, Exterior (*Staffordshire County Council*)	28
BARTON-UNDER-NEEDWOOD, Church, Exterior (*N.M.R., Crown Copyright*)	21
BIDDULPH, Church, Heath Monument (*James Austin*)	82
BILSTON, Church, Interior (*N.M.R., Crown Copyright*)	69
BREWOOD, Church, Chancel (*Rev. M. Ridgway*)	12
BREWOOD, Church, Giffard Monument (*G. L. Barnes*)	24
BREWOOD, Speedwell Castle, Exterior (*N.M.R., Crown Copyright*)	44
BROUGHTON, Broughton Hall, Exterior (*James Austin*)	27
BURSLEM, see STOKE-ON-TRENT	
BURTON-ON-TRENT, St Chad, Exterior (*James Austin*)	98
BUTTERTON, Butterton Grange, Exterior (*N.M.R., Crown Copyright*)	65
CAVERSWALL, Caverswall Castle, Exterior (*A. F. Kersting*)	31
CHEADLE, Hales Hall, Exterior (*N.M.R., Crown Copyright*)	41
CHEADLE, St Giles (R.C.), Exterior (*N.M.R., Crown Copyright*)	80
CHILLINGTON HALL, Saloon (*Country Life*)	64
CROXDEN, Croxden Abbey, Fragment of the West Wall (*Manchester Public Library*)	11
DENSTONE, Church, Exterior (*G. L. Barnes*)	86
DENSTONE, Church, Pulpit (*G. L. Barnes*)	87
DRAYTON BASSETT, Church, Peel Monument (*James Austin*)	81
DUDLEY, St Thomas, Exterior (*N.M.R., Crown Copyright*)	67
DUDLEY, Zoo, Entrance (*Architect and Building News*)	100
ELFORD, Church, Smythe Monument (*Rev. M. Ridgway*)	22
ENVILLE, Enville Hall, Summer House (*N.M.R., Crown Copyright*)	55

INDEX OF PLATES

ETTINGSHALL, *see* WOLVERHAMPTON, St Martin	
FORTON, Church, Exterior (*N.M.R., Crown Copyright*)	45
GNOSALL, Church, Interior (*Rev. M. Ridgway*)	8
GREAT BARR, Great Barr Hall, Exterior (*James Austin*)	56
HALES, Canal at Tyrley (*Rex Wailes*)	2
HOAR CROSS, Church, Exterior (*G. L. Barnes*)	93
HOAR CROSS, Church, Interior of Choir (*A. F. Kersting*)	94
HOPWAS, Church, Exterior (*Staffordshire County Council*)	95
ILAM, Church, Watts Monument (*A. F. Kersting*)	71
INGESTRE, Church, Interior (*N.M.R., Crown Copyright*)	36
KEELE, University, Keele Hall, Exterior (*James Austin*)	92
KEELE, University, Chapel (*R. G. Sims*)	103
KINGSWINFORD, Church, Tympanum (*N.M.R., Crown Copyright*)	6
LEEK, All Saints, Interior (*James Austin*)	96
LEIGH, Church, Exterior (*G. L. Barnes*)	85
LICHFIELD, Cathedral, Chancel, Interior (*Courtauld Institute of Art*)	17
LICHFIELD, Cathedral, Chancel, Sculpture on the Exterior (*Courtauld Institute of Art*)	19
LICHFIELD, Cathedral, Nave, Interior (*N.M.R., Crown Copyright*)	16
LICHFIELD, Cathedral, North Transept Doorway (*Courtauld Institute of Art*)	14
LICHFIELD, Cathedral, Screen at the Crossing (*James Austin*)	83
LICHFIELD, Cathedral, West Front (*N.M.R., Crown Copyright*)	15
LICHFIELD, Donegal House (Guildhall), Exterior (*Peter Burton*)	42
LICHFIELD, Johnson Monument, Relief (*Peter Leach*)	72
LICHFIELD, St John's Hospital, Exterior (*N.M.R., Crown Copyright*)	25
LITTLE ASTON, Little Aston Hall, Exterior (*James Austin*)	89
LITTLE WYRLEY HALL, Door Furniture (*Country Life*)	37
LONGNOR, Church, Exterior (*A. F. Kersting*)	46
LONGTON, *see* STOKE-ON-TRENT	
NEWCASTLE-UNDER-LYME, Holy Trinity, Exterior (*N.M.R., Crown Copyright*)	84
OAKLEY HALL, Exterior Detail (*N.M.R., Crown Copyright*)	40
OKEOVER, Church, Okeover Monument (*N.M.R., Crown Copyright*)	61
PELL WALL, Lodge (*Staffordshire County Council*)	66
ROACHES, THE (*By the courtesy of the Leek Post and Times*)	1
ROCESTER, Tutbury Mill, Exterior (*Rex Wailes*)	59
RUGELEY, Old Church, Lauder Monument (*R. C. Williams*)	35
SHUGBOROUGH, Arch of Hadrian (*A. F. Kersting*)	53
SHUGBOROUGH, Chinese House and Bridge (*A. F. Kersting*)	51

INDEX OF PLATES

SHUGBOROUGH, Dining Room, Chimneypiece (*A. F. Kersting*)	48
SHUGBOROUGH, Doric Temple (*A. F. Kersting*)	52
SHUGBOROUGH, East Front (*A. F. Kersting*)	50
SHUGBOROUGH, Red Drawing Room (*A. F. Kersting*)	49
STAFFORD, High House, Exterior (*N.M.R., Crown Copyright*)	26
STAFFORD, St Chad, Interior (*Rev. M. Ridgway*)	9
STAFFORD, St Mary, Interior (*A. F. Kersting*)	13
STAFFORD, Shire Hall, Exterior (*N.M.R., Crown Copyright*)	57
STAFFORD, Upmeads, Exterior (*Peter Leach*)	99
STOKE-ON-TRENT, Church, Wedgwood Monument (*Peter Leach*)	62
STOKE-ON-TRENT, Station, Exterior (*Peter Leach*)	88
STOKE-ON-TRENT, The Mount, Exterior (*Peter Leach*)	58
STOKE-ON-TRENT (BURSLEM), Wedgwood Memorial Institute, Exterior (*Victoria County History*)	91
STOKE-ON-TRENT (LONGTON), Boundary Works, Exterior (*N.M.R., Crown Copyright*)	60
STOKE-ON-TRENT (LONGTON), Potteries (*N.M.R., Crown Copyright*)	3
STOWE-BY-CHARTLEY, Church, Detail of Devereux Monument (*R. C. Williams*)	23
SWYNNERTON, Church, Seated Christ (*A. F. Kersting*)	18
TAMWORTH, Church, Ferrers Monument (*N.M.R., Crown Copyright*)	34
TAMWORTH, Town Hall, Exterior (*Peter Leach*)	43
TETTENHALL, *see* WOLVERHAMPTON, St Michael	
TIXALL, Tixall Hall, Gatehouse (*N.M.R., Crown Copyright*)	29
TRENTHAM PARK, Exterior, Engraving (*Country Life*)	77
TRENTHAM PARK, Mausoleum, Exterior (*Country Life*)	63
TUTBURY, Church, West Front (*A. F. Kersting*)	10
UTTOXETER, Church, Interior (*N.M.R., Crown Copyright*)	70
WALL, Remains of the Roman Bath House (*Peter Burton*)	4
WALSALL, St Matthew, Ceiling (*James Austin*)	68
WALSALL, St Paul, Exterior (*G. L. Barnes*)	97
WALSALL, West Midland Teacher Training College, Exterior (*Henk Snoek*)	104
WESTON-UNDER-LIZARD, Church, Bradford Monument (*N.M.R., Crown Copyright*)	73
WESTON-UNDER-LIZARD, Weston Park, South Front (*A. F. Kersting*)	39
WESTON-UNDER-LIZARD, Weston Park, Temple of Diana (*A. F. Kersting*)	54
WOLVERHAMPTON, Giffard House, Staircase (*N.M.R., Crown Copyright*)	38
WOLVERHAMPTON, St John, Exterior (*A. F. Kersting*)	47
WOLVERHAMPTON, St Martin, Ettingshall, Exterior (*Architect and Building News*)	101

WOLVERHAMPTON, St Michael, Tettenhall, Exterior (*James Austin*) 102

WOLVERHAMPTON, St Peter, Leveson Monument (*N.M.R., Crown Copyright*) 33

WOLVERHAMPTON, St Peter, Tower (*N.M.R., Crown Copyright*) 20

WOLVERHAMPTON, St Peter, Wolverhampton Cross (*B. T. Batsford*) 5

WOOTTON LODGE, Exterior (*N.M.R., Crown Copyright*) 30

INDEX OF ARTISTS

Abraham, Robert, 56, 58
Adam, Robert, 103n
Adams, Edward, 34, 96, 230
Adams (Thomas), Pepler & Blow, 321
Adkins, J. S., 261
Alexander & Henman, 37, 301
Allison, Thomas, 56
Angel, Joseph, 143
Archambo, Peter, 139, 257
Ardin & Brookes & Partners, 294
Armstead, H. H., 185
Armstrong, C. T., 315
Armstrong, R., 239
Artari, Giuseppe, 102
Arup (Ove) & Partners, 247
Ashbee, C. R., 327
Ashdown, J., 62
Ashworth, S. B., 255
Atkinson, William, 147
Aumonier, W., 244
Austin & Paley, 65, 67
Bacon, John, the elder, 187
Baily, E. H., 107, 261
Baker, William, 29, 104, 128, 131, 212, 218n, 267, 268, 315, 324
Bakewell, Robert, 31, 93, 103, 216, 306
Bamford, Thomas, 116
Banks, E. (of Wolverhampton), 106, 110, 320, 321
Banks, W. C., 217
Barnard, Edward, 84, 146
Barney, Joseph, 316
Barr, James & Edward, 132
Barry, Sir Charles, 38, 41, 231, 284, 285
Bateman, Hester, 55, 77
Bateman, P. & A., 190, 211
Bateman, P., A., & W., 100, 279, 296
Bateman, P. & W., 93, 211, 262, 296
Bateman, William, 201, 272
Bateman (of Birmingham), 300
Bateman & Corser, 325
Bateman & Drury, 171
Bates, Ernest, 69, 317
Batten, John D., 190
Battiscombe & Harris, 83
Bayley, Richard, 101
Beale, Richard, 174
Beardmore, J., 64, 129, 307
Beck, F. T., 144, 300, 315, 321, 322, 323, 324
Beck, Henry, 84
Beckett, J. H., 132, 260, 261, 267, 308
Bedford, Francis, 34, 209, 265
Beechey, Sir William, 268
Behnes, William, 33, 105, 262
Bell, William, 260
Bennett, Joseph B. H., 289
Bennett, William, 135
Benson, W. A. S., 311
Bernasconi, 73
Bidlake, G., 108, 269, 316, 322, 325, 326
Bidlake & Lovatt, 71, 192, 232, 308
Birch, John, 38, 154, 155, 156
Blacker, J., 122
Blackshaw, W., 244
Blanchard, M. H., 255
Blomfield, Sir Arthur, 75, 226
Blore, Edward, 158, 160
Blount, Gilbert, 40n, 95, 268, 273, 299
Bodington, John, 51, 79
Bodley, G. F., 42, 72, 87, 88, 148, 149, 150, 150n, 169n, 190, 223, 224, 279
Boeck, 149
Borgonzoli, Giuseppe, 216
Botham, J. R., 63
Boulton, Matthew, 148, 167
Boulton (of Cheltenham), 317

INDEX OF ARTISTS

Boulton & Watt, 210
Bourne, J., 199
Bower, Thomas, 69
Bradley, J. W., 317
Bradshaw, Gass & Hope, 210
Brandi, Diez, 94
Brandon, David, 163
Brealey, J., 169n
Brevitt, A. P., 282, 296
Bricknall & Donovan, 295
Bridge, John, 296, 305
Bridgeman, Robert, 192
Bridgeman & Sons, 150
Bridgewater, Shepheard & Epstein, 43, 161, 162
Bridgman (R.) & Sons, 298
Briggs, Wolstenholme & Thornely, 249
Brindley, James, 36, 101, 162, 211, 253
Brock, Thomas, 263
Brocklesby, J. S., 254, 265
Brooks, James, 37, 42, 261, 313
Brooks, William, 121
Brown, Ford Madox, 101, 200n, 276
Brown, Lancelot ('Capability'), 103, 157, 284
Brown, W., 217
Brownsword, Harold, 257
Brumby, Robert, 324
Bryans, H., 79, 106, 126, 197
Bryden, W. R., 132
Buck, John, 206
Buckler, John, 73
Burleigh, C. W., 234
Burlison & Grylls, 51, 54, 75, 149, 187, 293
Burn, William, 38, 231
Burn & McVicar Anderson, 269
Burne, C. S., 212
Burne-Jones, Sir Edward, 61, 82, 101, 135, 174, 200n, 276
Burrill, 259
Butler, A. T., 108
Butler, A. T. & G., 122
Butterfield, William, 41, 51, 223, 234, 275, 304

Cadbury-Brown, H. T., 302
Cali, Ernesto, 156
Canning, William, 90
Capey, A. G., 66
Capronnier, 261
Carline, John, 219
Caröe, W. D., 78, 125, 133
Carpenter, R. C., 115
Carpenter, R. H., 115
Carpenter & Ingelow, 37, 51, 115
Champneys, Basil, 53, 125, 126, 135, 239, 276, 299
Chance, P. F., 218
Chantrey, Sir Francis, 33, 63, 95, 110, 153, 156, 184, 185, 186, 268, 285, 286, 327
Chapman, A. G. E., 317, 320, 321, 325
Chapman, John, 119
Chatwin, J. A., 317
Chavalliaud, L. J., 150
Christian, Ewan, 70, 92, 107, 113, 116, 142, 225, 292, 306, 309, 314
Churchill, Reginald, 88
Cibber, C. G., 276
Clare, Joseph, 79
Clark, P. Lindsay, 145
Clarke, Edward F. C., 214
Clarke, G. Somers, 302
Clayton & Bell, 52, 114, 126, 151, 169n, 184, 186, 187, 200, 326
Clowes & Co., 329
Clutton, Henry, 38, 123, 124, 150
Coade, Mrs E., 237
Coker, Ebenezer, 106
Coleman, Stephen, 290
Collcutt & Hamp, 115
Collins, James, 134
Collins (of London), 146
Colombe, G. B. I., 306
Comper, Sir Ninian, 100, 199
Cooper, Matthew, 315
Cory, John, 62
Couchman, Herbert, 90
Cox, G. B., 145
Crace, J. G., 57
Cranston, James, 295

INDEX OF ARTISTS

Crouch, Butler & Savage, 299
Crump, Francis, 268
Cubitt, Thomas, 231
Culshaw, W., 201, 243
Curtis, T. F., 83
Cutts, J. E. K., 295
Cutts, J. E. K. & J. P., 296
Dall, Nicholas Thomas, 237
Darkeratt, William, 68
Darwell, John, 166
Davis, Edward, 262
Davis & Middleton, 295
Dawber, Sir E. Guy, 231
Dawkes, J. W., 303
Dawkes & Hamilton, 299
Dearle, J. H., 169
de Morgan, William, 38, 225, 311
Denman, 111
Derick, J. M., 41, 222
Diamond, Redfern & Partners, 317
Dick, Sir W. Reid, 147
Dingle, John, 219
Dix, A. J., 221
Dixon & Moxon, 84
Douglas, John, 42, 151
Downes, John, 84, 135, 289
Doyle, J. Francis, 201, 251
Drinkwater, H. D. W., 121
Drysdale, George, 109
Dudley, William, 202
Dunn, G., 294
Dunn & Hansom, 301
Earp, Thomas, 114, 169, 185, 196
Ebbles, Robert, 282, 289, 304
Eckfourd, John, 68
Edgar, Robert, 37, 100n, 170, 254
Edis, R. W., 202, 224
Egan, James, 35, 41n, 209
Eginton, Francis, 163
Elliott, William, 128
Ellis, Jonathan, 294
Emes, Rebecca, 84, 146
Engle (Bernard) & Partners, 318
Epstein, Sir Jacob, 184
Essex, Nicol & Goodman, 318
Evans, David, 262, 287
Evans, F. W., 138
Evans, W., 251, 323
Evans (of Ellaston), 184
Evans & Jolly, 88
Eykyn, Roger, 29, 315
Farmer & Brindley, 54, 83, 150, 183, 186
Farr, Thomas, 330
Farrer, Thomas, 145, 270
Fawdery, William, 235
Fehr, Henry C., 85
Feline, Magdalen, 129
Fennell, Edward, 77, 109
Ferrey, Benjamin, 275, 330
Fiddian, F. W., 204
Fitzgerald, Percy, 194
Flaxman, John, 33, 262, 323
Fleeming, T. H., 108, 199, 220, 318, 321, 326
Foley, J. H., 148
Ford, George B., 267
Forsyth, James, 122, 186, 196
Forsyth, Moira, 254
Fothergill, John, 148, 167
Foulkes, W. Tadman, 228n
Fowler, James (of Louth), 134, 190
Fradgley, Thomas, 56, 58, 60, 77, 141, 270, 290
Frampton, Reginald, 295
Francis, F. & H., 138, 170
Fraser (Ian) & Associates, 260
Freeman, John, 75
Freeth, John, 102
Fuller, Crispin, 98, 296
Fulljames & Waller, 248
Gage, Robert, 161
Gainsford, Robert, 84
Gardner, Thomas (of Derby), 281
Gardner (of St Helens), 322
Garrard (of London), 315
George, Trew, Dunn, 321
Gerente, 242
Gibbons, Grinling, 33, 276
Gibbons, J. H., 282
Gibbs, C. A., 63, 174, 305
Gibbs, James, 29, 31, 217, 218
Gibson, Dan, 258, 322, 326

INDEX OF ARTISTS

Gibson, James S., 37, 293, 294
Gibson, John (of London), 235, 278
Giles & Brookhouse, 87
Giles & Gough, 101, 325
Gill, Eric, 147
Gilpin, William, 118
Gleichen, Lady Feodora, 156
Goldie, Edward, 62, 316
Goodall, Richard, 161
Goodhart-Rendel, H. S., 150
Goodman, T. W. (of London), 133
Goodward, T. W., 246
Goodwin, Francis, 29, 34, 70, 71, 292, 301
Gough, A. D., 41, 202
Gould, John, 330
Grayson & Ould, 310
Green, Harry, 309
Green, Richard, 53, 216
Greenwood, S., 85
Griffin, W. D. (of Wolverhampton), 124, 137, 312
Griffin & Weller, 297, 299
Griffiths, Edward, 38n, 124
Griffiths, Robert, 246, 248
Grimthorpe, Lord, 86, 190n
Gulliver, Nathaniel, 116
Gurney (Richard) & Co., 95, 203, 267, 300
Gurney (Richard) & Thomas Cook, 95, 209
Habershon & Pite, 135, 270
Hadfield, Weightman & Goldie, 173
Hales, L. G., 255
Hall, Joseph, 289
Hamilton, George E., 220, 246
Hamilton & Saunders, 304
Hansom, Charles, 40, 143, 228, 263, 268, 316
Hansom, J. A., 268
Hansom, J. S., 268
Hardman, John, 57, 75, 109, 117, 186, 187, 242, 249, 306, 316
Hardman & Powell, 72
Hardman, Powell & Co., 106

Hare, Cecil, 63, 87, 149, 150, 298
Hare, E. T., 317
Hare, H. T., 37, 244
Harper, 248
Harris, Renatus, 316
Hartshorne, A., 197
Harvey, John, 30, 243
Harvey & Wicks, 122
Hay, J. W. & J., 266
Hayley & Son, 34n, 243
Hayward, Samuel, 186
Headley, W. R., 244
Heaton, Butler & Bayne, 205
Heming, Samuel, 60
Hennell, Robert, 134
Hickman, B., 289
Hickton & Farmer, 295
Hickton, Madeley & Partners, 294
Hickton, Madeley & Salt, 294, 302
Higginbotham, John, 166
Highway, Isaac, 293, 297
Hill, Oliver, 156
Hilton, William, 286
Hinchcliffe, 214
Hine & Evans, 140
Hipkiss, W., 294
Hitch, N., 143
Holiday, Henry, 39, 53, 95, 276
Holland, Henry, 269, 284
Hollemans, Garrat, 27, 133
Hollemans, Joseph, 27
Holliday, Stephen J., 301
Hollins, Peter, 33, 63, 121, 141, 186, 197, 299, 307
Hollins, William, 56
Hollins, Jones & Oldacre, 313
Holmes, Edwin, 88, 117
Holmes, William, 141
Hopper, Thomas, 56, 91
Horsley, Gerald, 42, 157, 170, 198, 258
Horton, W., 295, 296, 299
Howell, Thomas, 84, 87
Hudson, Alex, 163
Hughes, Wyndham, 320
Hulme & Upright, 313
Hulme, Upright & Partners, 254

INDEX OF ARTISTS

Hunt, F. W., 274
Hunt, H. A., 35, 262, 269
Hussey, R. C., 69
Hutchings, J., 122
Image, Selwyn, 38, 95
Ingram, W. R., 186
Ireland, Joseph, 29, 35, 144, 293, 316
Jackson, F. Hamilton, 169
Jackson, John, 72
Jeavons, H., 312
Jellicoe, G. A., 293
Jenkins, Thomas, 86
John of Colsale, 206
Johnson, Thomas (of Lichfield), 38, 41, 137, 173, 190, 212, 260–1, 279, 280, 297
Johnson (T.) & Son (of Lichfield), 70, 195, 304
Jones, Robert, 257
Jones, W. Maurice, 303
Jouvenet, Jean, 299
Joyce, Nicholas, 93, 167, 310
Joyce & Sandy, 144
Joynson, G. W. D., 299
Keatt, William, 307
Keen, William, 250
Kempe, C. E., 38, 53, 81, 95, 99, 104, 117, 148, 167, 183, 184, 185, 186, 187, 190, 200, 207, 219, 226, 228, 239, 242, 297, 299, 307, 308, 310, 311, 315, 323, 325, 326
Kempe & Tower, 99, 219, 292
Keyte, J., 29, 282
King (of Bath), 121, 148
Kinnersley, Mrs Thomas, 162
Kipling, J. L., 37, 254
Kirby, Edmund, 143, 295
Kirk, Thomas, 156
Lamerie, Paul de, 218
Latham, Jasper, 315
Lavender, H. E., 297, 327
Lavender & Twentyman, 42, 295, 322
Lavender, Twentyman & Percy, 297
Lavers & Barraud, 221

Lavers, Barraud & Westlake, 209
Lawson, F. R., 256
Leach, John, 148
Lee, Thomas, 34, 108, 208, 232
Le Sage, John, 320
Le Sueur, Hubert, 27, 315
Lethaby, W. R., 169
Lewis, Charles, 67
Lewis (G.) & Co., 92
Lewis, John (of Newcastle-under-Lyme), 158, 260
Lewis (T.) & Son, 167, 201n, 211, 256
Ley, Peter, 218
Ley, Timothy, 145
Liefrinck, 315
Livock, John, 36, 107, 195, 236
Lloyd, W. Hawky, 268
Lombard, Lambert, 184
Lough, J. G., 243n
Lovatt, Thomas, 261
Lowbridge, G. C., 122, 191, 325
Luberkin, B., 43
Lucas, Richard Cockle, 194
Lukin, William, 315
Lutyens, Sir Edwin, 270
Luxton, Samuel, 292
Lynam, Charles, 66, 69, 95, 109, 127, 136, 163, 200, 256, 261, 262, 263, 266, 268, 308
Lynam & Rickman, 207, 263
Lynam & Sons, 298
Lyons & Israel, 317
Lyons, Israel & Ellis, 71
Macdonald, Laurence, 153
McMichael, G., 137
Madin, John, 43, 301
Madin (John) Design Group, 301
Manning, Joseph, 323
Marochetti, Baron C., 331
Marsh, E., 199
Marshall, Arthur, 316, 321
Martin, W. & S. T., 89
Marton, G. Mayer, 325
Mason & Richards, 321

INDEX OF ARTISTS

Mawson, T. H., 104, 201, 255, 258, 311, 322
Meredith, Peter, 209
Meure, Peter, 257
Micklethwaite & Somers Clarke, 270
Miller, Bernard, 42, 325
Miller, Sanderson, 130
Milner, E. V., 94
Minton's, 264
Mitchell, Joseph, 84
Moorcroft, R. L., 317
Moore, John Francis, 242
Moore, J. P., 80
Moore, Temple, 42, 94
Morgan, James, 29, 315
Morgan, William de, 38, 225, 311
Morley (of Burton), 84
Morris, Rowland, 255
Morris, William, 38, 82, 101, 174, 200n, 310, 311, 326
Morris & Co., 38, 61, 82, 101, 128, 129, 135, 156, 163, 169, 170, 200, 276, 298
Morris, Marshall & Co., 100
Morris, Smith & Partners, 277
Murray, James, 263
Murray, Keith, 65
Naden, Henry, 152, 295
Nash, John, 35, 133, 154
Naylor, J. R., 55
Naylor & Sale, 87
Nelson, G., 190
Nesfield, W. A., 284
Newman & Billing, 139
Nicholls, 184
Nichols, G. B., 294
Nichols & Morgan, 294
Nicholson, A. K., 221, 322
Nicholson, Sir Charles, 80, 150, 243, 247, 268, 322
Noble, Matthew, 33, 63, 69, 107, 278, 286
Nollekens, Joseph, 63
Norman & Dawbarn, 320
Norris, E. Bower, 248n, 255
Nutting, Henry, 327
Oates, J., 34, 258

O'Connor, 106, 234
Orford, C. W., 325
Osborn & Reading, 212
Ould, Edward, 38, 310, 311
Owen, W. & S., 81
Pace, G. G., 43, 161
Paine, James, 103, 306
Paley, E. G., 323
Palmer, W., 257
Papworth, J. B., 56, 58
Parch, Samuel, 255
Parker, J. N., 161
Parker, Richard, 26
Parr, Thomas, 197
Parrott, A. T., 294, 297
Parsons, Alfred, 311
Paten, Samuel, 72
Payne, Edward J., 38, 196
Payne, Humphrey, 278
Payne, John, 235
Pearce, William, 202
Pearson, J. L., 41, 143, 228, 293
Philip, A., 301
Philip, John Birnie, 184, 186, 276
Phipps, C. J., 318
Phipps (T.) & E. Robinson, 100
Pickavance, J. A., 161, 162
Pickford, Joseph, 259
Pierce, Edward, 188
Piercy, A. R., 263
Piggott, J. R., 257
Pincher, Edward, 301
Piper, John, 324
Plant, J. W., 257
Platt, J. Edgar, 170n
Pomeroy, F. W., 86
Potter, Donald, 322
Potter, Joseph, the elder, 54, 83, 176, 187, 222
Potter, Joseph, the younger, 41, 111, 192, 194, 269
Powell's, 38, 53, 92, 170, 214, 272, 276, 302, 315
Priest, John, 300
Priest, W. & J., 276
Pritchett, J. P., 34, 98, 214
Pugin, A. W. N., 39, 56, 56n, 57, 59, 60, 70, 72, 79, 97, 109,

INDEX OF ARTISTS

110, 121, 173n, 228, 242, 268, 290
Pugin, E. W., 39, 60n, 80, 217, 249, 250, 316
Purdie, A. E., 263
Pyke, T. Hillyer, 193
Quellin, Arnold, 33, 276
Ramsey, William, 175
Read, J. Edie, 320
Reeves (of Bath), 110
Rennie, Sir John, 107
Renton (Andrew) & Partners, 139
Repton, Humphry, 133, 223
Reynolds, Edwin F., 131
Reynolds, W. H., 255
Reyntiens, Patrick, 324
Richardson, E., 127
Richmond, Sir William, 270
Roberts, James A., 303, 319
Roberts (of Trentham), 282
Robertson, Sir Howard, 160
Robinson, G. T., 37, 41n, 71, 82, 134, 254, 265, 268, 322
Robinson, John, 190, 287
Robinson, Patrick, 289
Robinson, Thomas, 136
Robinson, William, 29, 267
Rossi, J. F., 307
Rowlands, 124
Royley, Richard and Gabriel, 26
Rugg, Richard, 230
Rushworth, T. H., 144, 266
Russell & Cooper, 37, 254
Rutherford, John, 258
Ryan, P. J., 265
Rysbrack, J. Michael, 33, 105
Salviati, 276
Salvin, Anthony, 38, 53, 127, 158, 313
Sanderson, Joseph, 215
Sandy, H., 248
Sandy, T., 42, 248
Sandy & Norris, 282
Scamell, George, 88, 89, 91
Scamell & Collyer, 91
Scheemakers, Peter, 236, 238
Scheemakers, Thomas, 33, 187
Schenck, F. E. E., 244

Scott, Sir George Gilbert, 37, 40, 64, 78, 129, 138, 148, 153, 162, 176, 179, 180, 183, 184, 185, 186, 209, 216, 219, 241, 243, 251, 260, 261, 264, 275, 276, 291, 304, 305
Scott, George Gilbert, the younger, 38, 100, 101, 157n
Scott, John Oldrid, 78, 84, 148, 176, 190, 208, 219, 223, 249, 281
Scott, Lady, 192
Scott & Clarke, 108, 299
Scott & Moffatt, 37, 68, 134, 195, 249, 263, 291
Scrivener, Robert, 199, 257, 258
Scrivener (R.) & Son, 209, 217, 256, 258
Seal (A. J.) & Partners, 235
Sedding, J. D., 38, 170, 272
Shaw, John, the elder, 67, 152
Shaw, R. Norman, 42, 169, 170, 170n, 172n, 205
Shenstone, William, 130
Sheppard (Richard) & Partners, 302
Sheppard (Richard), Robson & Partners, 43, 295, 296, 302
Shrigley & Hunt, 201
Shuffrey, L. A., 311
Simpson, J. (of Leeds), 209
Sisson, Marshall, 215
Skidmore, Francis, 41, 153, 184, 186, 228
Slater, William, 115, 186
Slater & Carpenter, 37, 115
Sleath, Gabriel, 135, 190
Smirke, Sir Robert, 118
Smirke, Sydney, 176, 278
Smith, Campbell, 83
Smith, Francis (of Warwick), 30, 83, 102, 105, 272, 284
Smith, George, 309
Smith, James, 161, 229
Smith, Richard, 29, 83
Smith, Thomas, 80, 164, 166
Smith (T. T.) & G. F. Roper, 322
Smith, William, 29, 83, 303

INDEX OF ARTISTS

Smythson, John, 95
Smythson, Robert, 95, 328
Soane, Sir John, 31, 92, 102, 219
Soissons, Louis de, 191
Spence, W. (of Liverpool), 151
Spilsbury, Frank, 93
Stanger, George H., 300
Stanley, T., 206, 265
Stanton, Edward, 185, 197
Stanton, William, 72
Steell, Sir John, 156
Stephens, J., 323
Stevens, H. J. (of Derby), 107, 131, 144, 328
Stevens & Robinson, 66n, 83, 231
Stewart, W. S., 264
Stillman & Eastwick Field, 43, 160
Stokes, Joseph, 320
Storr, Paul, 248
Street, A. E., 325
Street, G. E., 42, 42n, 51, 52, 61, 72, 72n, 75, 75n, 77, 78, 84n, 106, 107, 113, 114, 125, 126n, 127, 140n, 150, 151, 163, 169, 174, 185, 186, 190, 195, 288, 289, 297, 306, 326
Stuart, James, 32, 73, 236, 237, 238
Sugden, William, 38n, 92, 151, 168, 170, 171, 172
Sugden, William Larner, 38n, 168, 172
Sugden (W.) & Son, 162, 170, 171
Sumner, Heywood, 39, 78
Sumner, William, 307
Sutton, W., 323
Tate, W., 83
Tatham, Charles Heathcote, 29, 284, 285, 286
Taylor, J., 307
Taylor, Sir Robert, 31, 65
Taylor, William, 161
Teale, J. M., 86
Tecton, 43, 122
Telford, Thomas, 79, 103, 138, 162, 271

Ternouth, John, 63
Terry (J. E.) & Co., 299
Theed, William, 326
Thomas (mason at Lichfield), 175
Thompson, William, 187
Thorneycroft, Thomas, 319
Tinworth, George, 258, 286
Traherne, Benjamin, 293
Trayes, William, 217
Trubshaw, Charles, 29n, 272
Trubshaw, James, the elder, 29n
Trubshaw, James, the younger, 29n, 34, 41, 63, 74, 82, 96, 101, 163, 258, 273
Trubshaw, Richard, 29, 29n, 73, 201, 267
Trubshaw, Thomas, 29n, 34, 41, 68–9, 78, 144, 146, 166, 206, 229, 246, 280, 297
Trubshaw & Johnson, 262, 290
Tuite, John, 153
Twentyman, Percy & Partners, 324, 325
Underwood, H. J., 34, 39, 228
Vassali, Francesco, 102, 237, 238
Veall, J. R., 293
Vertegans, R. H., 326
Vicars, Albert, 170
Viviani, B. or O., 153
Vulliamy, Lewis, 254, 319, 329
Wailes, William, 64, 70, 75, 79, 97, 101, 107, 127, 134, 166, 174, 230, 276, 330
Wakelin, Edward, 161
Wakelin, J. N., 161
Wallace, Thomas, 175
Wallis (T.) & J. A. Bowater, 262
Ward, Henry (of Stafford), 37, 61, 67, 116, 243, 244, 262
Ward (Henry) & Son (of Hanley), 82, 101, 206, 256, 258, 266, 313
Ward & Ford, 70
Ward & Hughes, 127, 140, 187, 122, 279
Warren, E. P., 264
Warrington, William, 170, 216

INDEX OF ARTISTS

Watts, G. F., 184
Weale, William, 70
Webb, Sir Aston, 247
Webb, Geoffrey, 94
Wedgwood, Josiah, 236
Wenyon, George H., 122, 282
Westmacott, Sir Richard, 84, 105, 186
Westmacott, Richard, 156
Wheat, Samuel, 330
Whipham, Thomas, 190, 203, 234, 268, 316
White, Fuller, 76, 131
White, Thomas, 53
White, William, 37, 64
White (of Vauxhall Bridge Road), 117
Whitehead (J.) & Co., 52
Whitelaw, William, 146, 268
Wilbraham, Lady, 29, 305, 306
Wilkes, James, 190
Willaume, David, 133
Willement, Thomas, 56n, 60, 124, 156, 286
William (mason at Lichfield), 175
William of Eyton, 175
Williams, David, 207
Williams, Desmond, 43, 324
Willoughby, Fletcher & Associates, 85
Wilson, Sir William, 187, 307
Wilton, Joseph, 33, 216
Winans (of London), 315
Winks, C. H., 134, 285
Winston, Charles, 320
Wint, de, 149

Wood, A. R., 37, 255, 265, 313
Wood, Edgar, 43, 250
Wood, Enoch, 254
Wood, Goldstraw & Yorath, 66, 265
Wood & Hutchings, 162, 261, 313
Wood & Kendrick, 131, 299, 302
Woodcock, P., 317
Woodhouse & Willoughby, 122
Woodland, W. A., 43, 152, 200
Woodyer, Henry, 330
Wooldridge, 92, 302
Woolf, J., 217
Wormal, 244
Worthington (Thomas) & Sons, 171
Wren, Sir Christopher, 28, 154, 155
Wright, Charles, 167, 203, 234, 268, 316
Wright, Thomas (architect), 237n
Wright, Thomas (goldsmith), 76
Wright, Thomas (sculptor), 296, 297
Wyatt, Benjamin, 31, 246, 271
Wyatt, James, 56, 94, 175, 179, 182, 196, 300
Wyatt, Samuel, 31, 231, 236, 237
Wyatt & Brandon, 282, 300
Wynne, Thomas, 257
Yates, Benjamin, 31, 216
Yorke, Rosenberg & Mardall, 227
Young, James, 126
Young, Robertson & Partners, 161

INDEX OF PLACES

Abbey Hulton, *see* Stoke-on-Trent, 21, 266
Abbots Bromley, 28, 46, 51
Acton Trussell, 52
Adbaston, 52
Aldershawe, *see* Wall, 292
Aldridge, 53
Alrewas, 25, 38, 46, 53
Alstonefield, 25, 54
Alton, 19, 24, 31, 32, 35, 36, 39, 55
Amblecote, 60
Amington, 61
Apedale, 61
Aqualate Hall, *see* Forton, 32, 35, 133
Armitage, 35, 36, 61
Ash Bank, *see* Werrington, 300
Ashcombe Park, *see* Cheddleton, 101
Ashes, The, *see* Endon, 129
Ashley, 25, 27, 33, 62
Aston, 63
Audley, 22, 23, 37, 64
Audley's Cross, *see* Hales, 138
Bagnall, 64
Bagot's Bromley, *see* Blithfield, 74
Ball Haye Hall, *see* Leek, 172
Balterley, 26, 65
Banks Farmhouse, *see* Rocester, 28, 226
Barlaston, 31, 65
Barton-under-Needwood, 22, 66
Basford, 67
Batchacre Hall, 25, 67
Beaudesert, 19, 24, 67
Bednall, 67
Belmont Hall, *see* Ipstones, 157
Bentley, *see* Walsall, 297
Beresford Dale, 68
Berth Hill *see* Maer, 201
Betley, 25, 26, 27, 45, 46, 68

Biddulph, 23, 25, 32, 33, 68
Biddulph Moor, 34, 70
Bilston, 29, 70
Bishopswood, 71
Bishton Hall, *see* Colwich, 108
Blackbrook Farmhouse, *see* Weeford, 300
Blakenall Heath, *see* Walsall, 295
Blakenhall Farmhouse, *see* Barton-under-Needwood, 67
Blithbury, 21, 71
Blithfield, 19, 23, 28, 31, 35, 72
Blore, 23, 27, 74
Bloxwich, *see* Walsall, 294
Blurton, *see* Stoke-on-Trent, 266
Blymhill, 42, 75
Bobbington, 75
Bole Hall, *see* Tamworth, 279
Bonehill House, *see* Fazeley, 131
Boothen, *see* Stoke-on-Trent, 263
Bradford Arms, *see* Blymhill, 75
Bradley, 22, 24, 27, 76
Bradley, *see* Wolverhampton, 322
Bradley-in-the-Moors, 29, 77
Bradmore, *see* Wolverhampton, 324
Bradwell Hall, *see* Wolstanton, 313
Bramshall, 77
Branston, 77
Bratch, The, *see* Wombourne, 327
Brereton, 39, 77
Brewood, 21, 27, 32, 35, 39, 42, 78
Brierley Hill, 29, 34, 40, 80
Brockmoor, *see* Brierley Hill, 80
Brocton, 31, 80
Broughton, 25, 26, 46, 81
Brown Edge, 34, 38, 82
Brownhills, 82
Bucknall, *see* Stoke-on-Trent, 266

INDEX OF PLACES

Buddleigh, see Betley, 68
Burntwood, 83
Burslem, see Stoke-on-Trent, 29, 35, 36, 37, 253
Burton-on-Trent, 21, 23, 26, 29, 36–7, 37, 40, 42, 83
Bury Bank, see Stone, 269
Bury Rings, see Bradley, 76
Bushbury, see Wolverhampton, 20, 23, 320
Butterton (nr Newcastle under Lyme), 31, 34, 91
Butterton (nr Wetton), 23, 92
Byrkley Lodge, see Rangemore, 224
Caldmore, see Walsall, 293
Caldmore Green, see Walsall, 294
Callow Hill, see Blithfield, 74
Calton, 28, 92
Calwich Abbey, see Ellastone, 21, 32, 128
Cannock, 93
Cannock Chase, 19, 94
Canwell, 21, 42, 94
Castern Hall, see Ilam, 50, 154
Cauldon, 29, 94
Caverswall, 20n, 23, 24, 26, 27, 33, 38, 45, 95
Chapel Chorlton, 96
Charnes Hall, see Broughton, 82
Chartley Holme, 24, 96
Chasetown, 34, 96
Cheadle, 30, 36, 39, 97
Chebsey, 20, 30, 99
Checkley, 20, 22, 25, 27, 99
Cheddleton, 38, 100
Chesterton, 48, 101
Chetwynd Bridge, see Alrewas, 53
Chillington Hall, 31, 32, 102
Church Eaton, 104
Church Leigh, see Leigh
Clanford Hall, see Seighford, 233
Clayton, see Newcastle-under-Lyme, 210
Cliffe Park Hall, see Rudyard, 35, 227
Clifton Campville, 22, 23, 24, 104

Cobridge, see Burslem, Stoke-on-Trent, 255, 256
Codsall, 27, 106
Colton, 23, 106
Colwich, 25, 27, 33, 107
Compton, see Wolverhampton, 326
Consall, 108
Coppenhall, 22, 108
Coseley, 108
Cotes Heath, 109
Coton-in-the-Clay, 109
Cotton, 21, 29, 39, 109
Coven, 110
Crakemarsh Hall, see Uttoxeter, 291
Cresswell, 110
Creswell, 110
Cross Heath, see Newcastle-under-Lyme, 36, 210
Croxall, 33, 110
Croxden, 21, 111
Croxton, 113
Cuttlestone Bridge, see Penkridge, 222
Dairy House, see Horton, 152
Darlaston, see Walsall, 296
Denstone, 28, 37, 42, 113
Derrington, 116
Devil's Ring and Finger, see Oakley Hall, 215
Dieulacres Abbey, see Leek, 21, 172
Dilhorne, 22, 28, 116
Dosthill, 117
Dove Cliffe, see Stretton, 270
Draycott-in-the-Moors, 27, 48, 117
Drayton Bassett, 117
Dudley, 19, 21, 24, 24–5, 25, 28, 29, 32, 34, 36, 37, 39, 43, 118
Dudley Wood, see Brierley Hill, 80
Dunstall, 38n, 123
Dunston, 124
Dunwood Hall, see Longsdon, 199

INDEX OF PLACES

Eccleshall, 20, 22, 23, 24, 27, 28, 125
Ecton, 126
Edingale, 26, 127
Elford, 23, 127
Elkstone, 29, 128
Ellastone, 32, 128
Ellenhall, 128
Endon, 38, 129
Engleton, *see* Brewood, 49, 79
Enville, 23, 27, 31, 32, 129
Essington, 131
Etruria, *see* Hanley, Stoke-on-Trent, 36, 46, 258
Ettingshall, *see* Wolverhampton, 42, 322
Fallings Park, *see* Wolverhampton, 321
Farewell, 21, 23, 29, 131
Fazeley, 131
Fenton, *see* Stoke-on-Trent, 37, 256
Flash, 132
Forsbrook, 132
Forton, 27, 29, 31, 32, 35, 132
Four Crosses Inn, *see* Hatherton, 143
Foxt, 133
Fradley, 133
Fradswell, 134
Freeford Hall, *see* Swinfen Hall, 272
Freehay, 40, 134
Fulford, 134
Gailey, 134
Gayton, 29, 134
Gentleshaw, 135
Gerards Bromley Hall, *see* Broughton, 25, 67, 81
Glascote, 135
Gnosall, 21, 135
Goat Lodge, *see* Blithfield, 74
Goldenhill, *see* Tunstall, Stoke-on-Trent, 265
Gratwich, 137
Great Barr, 35, 137
Great Haywood, *see* Haywood
Great Wyrley, 41, 137

Greenfield, *see* Tunstall, Stoke-on-Trent, 266
Green Heath, 138
Greets Green, *see* West Bromwich, 304
Grindon, 50, 138
Hales, 49, 138
Hales Hall, *see* Cheadle, 30, 98
Hall Green, *see* West Bromwich, 303
Hall o' Wood, *see* Balterley, 26, 65
Halmer End, 139
Hammerwich, 139
Hamstall Ridware, 23, 26, 139
Hanbury, 23, 27, 33, 140
Hanch Hall, *see* Longdon, 197
Hanchurch, 141
Handsacre, 141
Hanford, *see* Stoke-on-Trent, 266
Hanley, *see* Stoke-on-Trent, 29, 30, 34, 36, 37, 40, 41n, 42, 257
Harecastle Farm, *see* Talke, 274
Haregate Hall, *see* Leek, 172
Harlaston, 46, 142
Harracles Hall, *see* Horton, 152
Haselour Hall, 46, 142
Hatherton, 38, 142
Hatton, *see* Swynnerton, 273
Haughton, 143
Haunton, 143
Hawkesyard Priory, *see* Armitage, 35, 36, 62
Haywood, 35n, 144
Hazlehurst Bridge, *see* Endon, 129
Heath Hayes, 144
Heath House, *see* Tean, 32, 38, 41, 280
Heath Town, *see* Wolverhampton, 321
Hednesford, 144
Heighley Castle, 24, 145
Heywood Grange, *see* Dilhorne, 28, 116
High Offley, 145
Hilderstone, 146

INDEX OF PLACES

Hill Ridware, *see* Mavesyn Ridware, 204
Hill Top, *see* West Bromwich, 304
Hilton Park, 32, 146
Himley, 29, 147
Hints, 148
Hixon, 148
Hoar Cross, 38, 39, 42, 148
Holbeche House, *see* Kingswinford, 164
Hollington, 42, 45, 150
Hollinsclough, 151
Hopwas, 42, 151
Horton, 151
Huntington, 152
Hurst Hill, *see* Coseley, 108
Ilam, 19, 20, 22, 25, 27, 31, 33, 34, 35, 152
Ingestre, 26, 28, 32, 33, 35, 38, 154
Ipstones, 20, 28, 157
Keele, 27, 38, 43, 44, 45, 158
Kidsgrove, 162
King's Bromley, 25, 163
Kingsley, 38, 163
Kingstone, 163
Kingswinford, 20, 164
Kinver, 23, 25, 28, 48, 164
Knightley, 41, 166
Knutton, 167
Knypersley, *see* Biddulph, 69, *and* Brown Edge, 82
Lapley, 21, 167
Lawneswood House, *see* Stewpony, 252
Leaton Hall, *see* Bobbington, 75
Leek, 20, 21, 22, 23, 28, 30, 35, 36, 38n, 41n, 42, 168
Leigh, 23, 38, 41, 173
Lemansley, *see* Lichfield, 190
Levedale, 174
Lichfield, 19, 21, 21–2, 22, 23, 24, 25, 28, 30, 33, 37, 40, 41, 50, 174
Little Aston, 38, 42, 195
Littlehay Manor House, *see* Colton, 107

Little Haywood, *see* Haywood
Little Onn Hall, *see* Church Eaton, 104
Littleton Colliery, *see* Huntington, 152
Little Wyrley Hall, 28, 196
Littywood, *see* Bradley, 24, 76
Lloyd House, *see* Wombourne, 31, 327
Longdon, 20, 33, 197
Longford House, *see* Cannock, 93
Long Low, *see* Wetton, 308
Longnor, 29, 198
Longnor Hall, *see* Lapley, 168
Longport, *see* Burslem, Stoke-on-Trent, 266
Longsdon, 42, 198
Longton, *see* Stoke-on-Trent, 29, 36, 37, 40, 42, 48, 199
Lower Gornal, 199
Lower Tean, *see* Tean, 280
Loxley, 199
Loynton House, *see* Norbury, 212
Madeley, 23, 26, 38, 43, 200
Maer, 25, 26, 200
Maple Hayes, 201
Marchington, 29, 201
Marchington Woodlands, 26, 41, 202
Marston, 29, 202
Mavesyn Ridware, 203
Mayfield, 204
Meaford Hall, *see* Stone, 269
Meerbrook, 26, 42, 205
Meir, *see* Longton, Stoke-on-Trent, 261
Milford, 205
Milton, *see* Stoke-on-Trent, 267
Milwich, 23, 29, 206
Moddershall, 206
Moreton, 34, 206
Moseley Old Hall, 206
Moss Lee Hall, *see* Ipstones, 157
Mow Cop, 32, 206
Moxley, *see* Walsall, 296
Mucklestone, 26, 32, 207
Near Cotton, *see* Cotton

INDEX OF PLACES

eedwood, *see* Newchurch, 211, *and* Rangemore, 224
etherton, 208
ewborough, 208
ewcastle-under-Lyme, 19n, 21, 24, 30, 34, 35, 36, 40, 41n, 208
ewchapel, 36, 211
ewchurch, 211
ew Cross, *see* Wolverhampton, 321
ewtown, 211
orbury, 22, 23, 29, 211
orton Canes, 212
orton-in-the-Moors, *see* Stoke-on-Trent, 29, 267
akamoor, 214
akley Hall, 31, 214
cker Hill, *see* West Bromwich, 304
keover, 22, 23, 31, 32, 33, 50, 215
ld Springs Hall, *see* Hales, 138
necote, 29, 216
rgreave Hall, *see* Alrewas, 54
ulton, 40, 217
ulton Locks, *see* Norbury, 212
alfrey, *see* Walsall, 296
ark Hall Hotel, *see* Sedgley, 232
atshull, 23, 29, 31, 33, 217
attingham, 22, 25, 219
eatswood Hall, *see* Hales, 138
ell Wall, 31, 219
elsall, 220
enkhull, *see* Stoke-on-Trent, 263
enkridge, 23, 25, 27, 28, 48, 49, 220
ensnett, 40n, 41, 222
illaton, 22, 24, 222
ipe Place, *see* Wall, 292
ipe Ridware, 34, 223
otteries, The, *see* Stoke-on-Trent
restwood, 223
'ye Green, *see* Cannock Chase, 94
Quarnford, *see* Flash
Quarry Bank, *see* Brierley Hill, 80
Quixhill, 223
Rangemore, 42, 223
Ranton, 21, 224

Reaps Moor, 225
Rocester, 21, 28, 36, 38, 48, 225
Rolleston, 20, 24, 27, 226
Rudyard, 35, 227
Rugeley, 33, 34, 39, 227
Rushall, *see* Walsall, 44, 295
Rushton Spencer, 25, 46, 229
Salt, 41, 229
Sandfields, 230
Sandon, 25, 27, 32, 36, 38, 230
Sedgley, 34, 232
Seighford, 25, 27, 232
Shareshill, 29, 233
Sharpecliffe Hall, *see* Ipstones, 157
Sheen, 41, 234
Shenstone, 235
Shobnall, *see* Burton-on-Trent, 87, 90
Short Heath, *see* Walsall, 295
Shugborough, 31, 32, 36, 236
Silverdale, 239
Sinai Park, *see* Branston, 77
Slindon, 239
Smallthorne, *see* Stoke-on-Trent, 267
Smallwood Manor, *see* Marchington Woodlands, 202
Somerford, 32, 239
Springfields, *see* Stoke-on-Trent, 265
Springwood Furnace, *see* Newcastle-under-Lyme, 211
Stafford, 19, 20, 21, 22, 24, 26, 27, 29, 30, 31, 34n, 35, 37, 40, 42, 43, 45, 46, 240
Standon, 250
Stanshope Hall, *see* Alstonefield, 55
Stansmore Hall, *see* Dilhorne, 116
Stanton, 45, 251
Statfold, 251
Stewpony, 252
Stoke, *see* Stoke-on-Trent, 30, 33, 35, 37, 40, 261
Stoke-on-Trent, 19, 45, 252
Stone, 21, 29, 30, 36, 39, 40, 46, 267

INDEX OF PLACES

Stonnall, 41, 269
Stourton Castle, see Stewpony, 252
Stowe-by-Chartley, 23, 24, 269
Stramshall, 270
Stretton (nr Burton-on-Trent), 270
Stretton (nr Penkridge), 270
Swinfen Hall, 31, 271
Swynnerton, 22, 31, 38, 272
Swythamley Park, 273
Talke, 29, 273
Tamworth, 20, 21, 22, 23, 24, 26, 28, 30, 33, 38, 39, 274
Tatenhill, 279
Tean, 32, 36, 38, 41, 279
Teddesley Hay, 281
Tettenhall, see Wolverhampton, 42, 45, 324, 325, 326
Thorpe Constantine, 281
Thor's Cave, see Wetton, 50, 307
Throwley, 24, 50, 281
Tipton, 29, 282
Tittensor, 282
Tixall, 25, 31, 32, 35, 35n, 45, 282
Trentham Park, 21, 29, 32, 33, 38, 41, 283
Trent Vale, see Stoke-on-Trent, 49, 263, 265
Trysull, 23, 286
Tunstall, see Stoke-on-Trent, 30, 34, 37, 265
Tutbury, 20, 21, 24, 26, 287
Tyrley, see Hales, 49, 138
Upper Gornal, 289
Upper Penn, see Wolverhampton, 33, 323
Upper Tean, see Tean, 279, 280
Uttoxeter, 34n, 35, 39, 290
Wall, 48, 49, 50, 291
Walsall, 19, 23, 29, 30, 34, 35, 37, 41, 43, 44, 46, 292
Walsall Wood, 297
Walton Hall, see Chebsey, 99
Walton-on-the-Hill, 297
Warslow, 298
Waterfall, 23, 29, 298

Waterhouses, 298
Wedgwood Monument, Audley, 64
Wednesbury, 25, 27, 33, 43, 2
Wednesfield, 29, 300
Weeford, 300
Wergs Hall, see Codsall, 106
Werrington, 300
West Bromwich, 19, 24, 34, 3 43, 301
Weston, 22, 23, 304
Weston-under-Lizard, 28, 29, 3 31n, 32, 46, 48, 305
Westwood Hall, see Leek, 173
Wetley Rocks, 35, 307
Wetton, 50, 307
Wheaton Aston, 308
Whiston, 308
Whitehough, see Ipstones, 28, 1
Whitmore, 26, 28, 46, 308
Whittington (nr Lichfield), 30
Whittington, see Kinver, 166
Wigginton, 29, 310
Wightwick, 38, 310
Willenhall, 312
Willoughbridge, see Muckleston 26, 207
Wilnecote, 47, 312
Windy Gates, see Meerbrook, 2 205
Winshill, see Burton-on-Trent, 8
Wodehouse, The, see Wom bourne, 327
Wolseley Bridge, see Colwich, 10
Wolstanton, 27, 37, 42, 313
Wolverhampton, 19, 20, 22, 2 25, 27, 29, 30, 31, 33, 34, 3 37, 40, 40n, 41nn, 42, 43, 31
Wombourne, 31, 326
Wood Eaton Hall, see Churc Eaton, 104
Woodlane, 327
Wootton Lodge, 26, 45, 327
Wordsley, 329
Wrinehill, 329
Wrottesley Hall, 28, 329
Wychnor, 22, 330
Yoxall, 27, 330